extracted wealth, not created it, for the benefit of a privileged few. Done right, PE can play a positive role in our economy. Done wrong, its consequences are ruinous, as demonstrated in this must-read book."

—Sheila Bair, former chair of the FDIC and author of the *New York Times* bestseller *Bull by the Horns*

"*These Are the Plunderers* is a masterpiece of investigative journalism. Morgenson and Rosner expose nothing less than an organized, merciless, and astoundingly profitable attack on America's middle class. If you want to understand why Wall Street is booming, good jobs are disappearing, and venerable companies are collapsing, the story is all here. This book names the names and follows the money."

—Christopher Leonard, *New York Times* bestselling author of *Kochland* and *The Lords of Easy Money*

"A critical and urgent look behind the scenes at the characters and mechanics that increasingly dictate our systems of influence, power, and money. Morgenson and Rosner make the complex legible—and the stakes couldn't be higher."

—Mary Childs, cohost of NPR's *Planet Money* and author of *The Bond King*

"[A] definitive, inside story of how our winner-take-all economy came to be. The private equity billionaires you'll meet on these fascinating pages are the new robber barons. While the watchdogs were asleep, this investigative journalist and policy analyst show how they plundered America and, at last, hold them accountable. Ida Tarbell would sure be proud of them."

—Jill Abramson, author of *Merchants of Truth* and former executive editor of the *New York Times*

**ALSO BY GRETCHEN MORGENSON
AND JOSHUA ROSNER**

Reckless Endangerment

ALSO BY GRETCHEN MORGENSON

The New York Times Dictionary of Money and Investing

The Capitalist's Bible

THESE ARE THE
PLUNDERERS

HOW PRIVATE EQUITY RUNS—
AND WRECKS—AMERICA

Gretchen Morgenson
and Joshua Rosner

Simon & Schuster Paperbacks

NEW YORK   LONDON   TORONTO
SYDNEY   NEW DELHI

An Imprint of Simon & Schuster, LLC
1230 Avenue of the Americas
New York, NY 10020

First Simon & Schuster trade paperback edition May 2024

SIMON & SCHUSTER PAPERBACKS and colophon are
registered trademarks of Simon & Schuster, LLC

Simon & Schuster: Celebrating 100 Years of Publishing in 2024

For information about special discounts for bulk purchases, please contact
Simon & Schuster Special Sales at 1-866-506-1949
or business@simonandschuster.com.

The Simon & Schuster Speakers Bureau can bring authors to your
live event. For more information or to book an event, contact
the Simon & Schuster Speakers Bureau at 1-866-248-3049
or visit our website at www.simonspeakers.com.

Manufactured in the United States of America

1   3   5   7   9   10   8   6   4   2

Library of Congress Cataloging-in-Publication Data has been applied for.

ISBN 978-1-9821-9128-3
ISBN 978-1-9821-9129-0 (pbk)
ISBN 978-1-9821-9130-6 (ebook)

Once again, to Paul and Conor
—G.M.

To my family, friends, and clients who have
been supportive of these efforts
—J.R.

CONTENTS

CONTENTS

THESE ARE THE
PLUNDERERS

"Money-Spinning Machines"

Let the Looting Begin

In late September 1987, John Dingell, the Michigan Democrat and chairman of the House Committee on Energy and Commerce, got the important report he'd requested. A troubling takeover boom was transforming corporate America and imperiling workers, and Dingell had asked the Congressional Research Service, the non-partisan think tank housed in the Library of Congress, for an analysis of various merger and acquisition deals in the works.

Corporate buyouts were enriching investors as Oliver Stone's movie *Wall Street* riveted the nation with Gordon Gekko declaring that "greed, for lack of a better word, is good." Outside of Hollywood, deep policy questions dogged the transactions: Did buyouts increase company efficiencies and productivity by eliminating "redundancies," as their proponents claimed, or were the critics right when they said takeovers were job-destroyers that rewarded executives for short-term operational fixes rather than long-term investment and overall prosperity?

"Leveraged Buyouts and the Pot of Gold," the Congressional Research Service's report was called, and it aimed to help Congress understand and maybe even restrict the growing takeover binge fueled by a new and risky kind of debt known as junk bonds. These bonds were issued by financially weaker companies that, in earlier days, would not not have been able to raise money from investors. But now, thanks in part to these bonds, the nation's big corporations were undergoing a period of "wrenching adjustment," the study noted, following years of recession, inflation, and increased competition from companies overseas. "Suddenly businesses were up for grabs," the congressional researchers concluded, pursued by financiers whose funding came from bond investors willing to take a chance they'd lose money on the securities if it meant receiving a higher interest rate.

Were these deals good or bad for society? The report's authors dithered. On one hand, the success of the takeovers was "largely anecdotal," and on the other, the "economic dislocations were difficult to quantify." It was "open for debate" whether the plant closings and job losses that typically followed these transactions would have occurred regardless, the report said.

Everyone could agree on one thing, though. The firms doing the takeover deals were "money-spinning machines." And those machines were, for the most part, smallish partnerships formed by refugees from Wall Street who'd made enough money to go out on their own. First movers were firms like Thomas H. Lee Partners, a Boston-based investment company started by an ex-banker in the 1970s, and Kohlberg Kravis Roberts, a New York firm launched in 1976. Jerome Kohlberg, Henry Kravis, and George Roberts opened shop after successful stints at the now defunct brokerage Bear Stearns & Co., and along with Lee, recognized that many American companies currently had assets worth far more than their stock prices let on. Why not borrow money now to acquire these undervalued companies and then sell them later at a profit?

Such was the path to the pots of gold the Congressional Research Service identified. But, while the 1980s takeover surge rewarded the financiers, it coincided with the start of other shifts that would wind up punishing Main Street America over the coming decades. For example, at the same time workers began losing their jobs to corporate buyouts, their company pensions, which had long provided reliable and prosperous retirements, were starting to disappear. The 1978 Revenue Act effectively killed off the creation of new employer-funded pension plans and placed the burdens of planning for, and paying for, retirement directly on the worker. Known as 401(k)s, the program benefitted both Wall Steet and big business while exposing financial neophytes to uncertain financial futures.

During the late 1980s, Congress would hold several hearings about reining in debt-laden takeovers, highlighting the dangers of heavy borrowing and the financial machinations they required. Finally, after several years of excess, Kohlberg Kravis Roberts's gargantuan $25 billion leveraged buyout of RJR Nabisco got lawmakers' attention. So did the $75 million in fees KKR earned on that 1988 deal.

Washington tends to identify burgeoning risks but rarely acts until these threats become full-blown crises. Not surprisingly the hearings resulted in no new laws, after which legislators moved on to other issues. Buyout dealmakers had lobbied heavily against any new restrictions, the *New York Times* reported, and some in Congress worried that if they acted against leveraged buyouts, they'd cause a market crash. No one wanted a repeat of October 19, 1987, when the Dow Jones Industrial Average had fallen 508 points in a single day. At more than 22 percent, that was the biggest one-session drop in the index's history, and it still weighed on lawmakers' minds.

Some in the government played down the impact of leveraged

buyouts, predicting that "the market" would correct any excesses. This so-called free-market ideology promoted by Ronald Reagan's economic team had become the basis of a hands-off culture in Washington. Nicholas Brady, the treasury secretary under George H. W. Bush, espoused this idea, telling Congress in 1989 that he expected the troubling takeover deals would soon become "a thing of the past." Brady could not have been more wrong. In fact, the transactions were to become a *very big thing of the future*. And "Pot of Gold" didn't begin to describe the riches an elite gang of financiers would reap from them.

More than thirty years later, the effects of what began as the leveraged buyout boom in the late eighties, paired with the belief that markets and deregulation support society, are devastatingly clear. Today, there is little room for equivocation. The economic wreckage caused by the takeover titans is real and measurable. Except now they call their industry private equity—a name that conveys suave sophistication but none of its brutality. The riches amassed by the people overseeing these money-spinning machines—and most of them are white males—are simply staggering.

Armed with decades of data, we now have unsettling studies and proof of the perverse impacts these buyouts have on workers, customers, pensioners—everyone but the dealmakers. Residents of nursing homes owned by private equity firms, among the nation's most vulnerable populations, have been especially hurt: one study showed residents experienced 10 percent more deaths in facilities owned by private equity firms than in other entities, due to decreased staff, reduced compliance with standards of care, and more. Another study tied private equity ownership of nursing homes to increases in emergency room visits and hospitalizations, and higher Medicare costs.

Beyond healthcare, a major and devastating focus of the financiers, private equity buyouts across industries result in ten times as many bankruptcy filings, research shows. Waves of job losses result, wrecking families and lives and slashing tax receipts. The high costs associated with these investments deplete pensioners' benefits and add to government deficits. Even the planet bears a brunt: in recent years, as public companies have come under pressure to jettison businesses that strip-mine ecosystems or pollute the planet, private equity has rushed in to buy them, keeping alive fouling operations that might otherwise be mothballed.

Assessing the damage that this rapacious form of capitalism has wrought on our country and our citizens is overdue. In this book, we examine the how, the why, and, most significantly, the *whom* in this calamity in order to educate, inform, and maybe even end the carnage.

Those on the losing end in our economy are easy to recognize—the working poor, rank-and-file corporate employees, pensioners and savers, small businesses and the middle class. Identifying the winners and how they've ravaged our economy and exploited Main Street America is what this book is about.

Stanley Sporkin was an aggressive prosecutor, federal district judge, CIA general counsel, conservative, and the first director of enforcement for the Securities and Exchange Commission in the 1970s. He summed it up this way: "Capitalism is the greatest thing going," he said, "but unchecked, it's its own undoing."

An exhausted nurse at a Louisville, Kentucky, hospital, accused of insubordination, was sent home on the spot. It was late March 2020 and a pandemic was tightening its grip on the United States. What had the nurse done wrong? She had tried to protect herself and those around her at the Norton Women's and Children's

Hospital from being infected with COVID-19. Because the facility had failed to provide an N95 mask to wear as protection against the virus, she'd declined to treat patients who had it. She said the hospital suspended her as a result, a characterization the hospital disputed.

A few months later, in Lewiston, Idaho, nurses at the St. Joseph Regional Medical Center staged a protest rally in front of the fifty-bed facility. Amid the pandemic, the Catholic hospital had threatened to slash their fifteen-minute rest periods to ten. Wages at the facility were already 12 percent below those of other hospitals in the region. The hospital, which had previously been a nonprofit, says it is "continuing the healing ministry of Jesus."

In March 2021, after a full year of battling COVID, the Oregon Nurses Association published a damning analysis. An investigation into the sixty-bed Willamette Valley Medical Center in McMinnville, Oregon, found that 80 percent of nurses reported inadequate staffing levels there. This shortage, the report found, led to compromised patient safety or patient injury.

Across the nation, the COVID pandemic stretched hospitals and staffs to the limit. Healthcare worker exhaustion was becoming its own crisis as patient deaths soared. But these three facilities, fielding serious complaints about working conditions and compromised patient safety, had something else in common. All were associated with LifePoint Health, a nationwide hospital chain owned by Apollo Global Management, a wealthy and powerful New York investment firm. Run by a sharp-elbowed financier named Leon Black and his deal-making billionaire partners, Apollo did not directly manage the eighty-four mostly rural hospitals in the LifePoint system, but it oversaw their operations closely with one goal in mind: to raise the hospitals' profits enough so the system could be sold quickly for a gain. LifePoint employees in three different states told us similar stories about their experiences working at the company's hospitals: after Apollo bought them, they saw a sharp deterioration in care.

When hard-driving financiers like Apollo purchase hospital systems, patient care often suffers, academic research shows. Private equity–owned hospitals tend to have lower patient satisfaction and fewer employees per occupied bed, for example. And after the financiers take over, hospitals charge more for their services and report larger profits than peers that are not owned by moneymen.

LifePoint facilities may have failed their workers and patients in 2020, but the hospital system was still able to tap taxpayers for massive amounts of pandemic relief money. The company got $1.4 billion from the government, much of it in the form of loans it would never have to repay. Even as it received this funding, LifePoint slashed the amount it paid staff in salary and benefits by $166 million and reduced the charity care it provided, such as free treatments for the indigent, by 21 percent.

This taxpayer assistance helped generate an enormous profit for Apollo, Black, and his colleagues. In 2021, the Apollo partnership that held the LifePoint stake sold it, recording a $1.6 billion gain—an amount amazingly close to what the government had given it in COVID relief monies.

In autumn 2020, as COVID raged across America, the federal government instituted an eviction moratorium, aiming to keep people out of shelters and group living situations that could accelerate the virus's spread. With the pandemic shuttering businesses and workplaces and Americans losing their jobs and incomes, barring landlords from ousting tenants became a priority.

A throng of large and prosperous landlords paid little mind

to this priority, as a congressional investigation later determined. Four such landlords filed more than 15,000 eviction proceedings between March 2020 and July 2021; some even brought actions against tenants who had applied for rental assistance programs.

Besides potentially increasing COVID rates, eviction filings can wreak havoc on tenants' families, ruin their credit scores, and make it harder to find new places to live.

One of the four wealthy landlords cited by Congress was Pretium Partners, an investment firm that joined forces with private equity powerhouse Ares Management in the fall of 2020. Ares was cofounded in 1997 by Antony Ressler, an early partner at Apollo and Leon Black's brother-in-law.

Announcing the tie-up with Pretium, Joel Holsinger, partner and cohead of Ares Management's alternative credit unit, enthused: "We are excited to partner with our real estate colleagues and Pretium to benefit all of our stakeholders."

Not quite all, as eviction court records would show. Through July 31, 2021, the congressional report found, Pretium initiated 6,264 eviction actions against its tenants, some filed when residents fell as little as $500 behind on their rent.

Cristina Velez and her daughter experienced this trauma firsthand. After she lost her job, Velez reached out to her landlord, a unit of Pretium, in early September 2020; she asked if it would give her time to come up with her rent.

"I told them I was affected by COVID, but it didn't matter to them," Velez said.

Two weeks later, Velez found a set of eviction papers at her front door. She did not know about the government's moratorium and Pretium certainly had not advised her of it. "There's got to be something for people affected by COVID and being furloughed,"

Velez said she told the landlord. The answer Velez said she got: "There's nothing we can do."

Frantic to stay in her home, Velez said she had to sell her car to pay the rent. Only then did she avoid getting the boot from Pretium.

As for Pretium, a spokesman said it "complies with applicable law, including the CDC Moratorium, in enforcing rental evictions." It also said it was "committed to working with tenants, as appropriate, to try and provide assistance during these extraordinary times."

Two weeks after the World Health Organization pronounced the coronavirus a global pandemic in mid-March 2020, Ming Lin, a veteran emergency room doctor in Bellingham, Washington, was removed from his post. Days earlier he had spoken out about a lack of COVID-19 preparedness at his facility, the only emergency department serving a quarter of a million people in the area.

Dr. Lin had worked at PeaceHealth Medical Center for seventeen years. But the hospital was no longer his employer; a privately owned company called TeamHealth technically was. The hospital had hired TeamHealth, a healthcare staffing entity, to run PeaceHealth's crucial emergency department, also to handle the hiring and firing of physicians and to manage patient billing procedures.

Doctors take an oath to do no harm and put their patients' interests first, just as Lin had. TeamHealth has another priority. Its focus—and success—depends on simple math: to increase the numbers of patients moving through emergency departments and generate more revenues from them.

"Hospitals like this used to be run by nuns," Dr. Lin explained of his facility. Now they're run by financiers, "affecting our primary objectives to take care of our patients and to do no harm."

TeamHealth is owned by the Blackstone Group, a powerful investment firm headquartered in an elegant Park Avenue tower in New York. It is overseen by Stephen Schwarzman, a multibillionaire who served as a top economic advisor to President Donald Trump.

Blackstone's operations have been good for Schwarzman. That year—2021—when much of the nation was worried about where their next paycheck was coming from, Schwarzman took home $1.1 billion in compensation and dividends. Mostly based on his holdings in Blackstone, Schwarzman's net worth more than doubled that year, from $16 billion to $35 billion, according to *Forbes*.

As for Lin, he had to move on. A TeamHealth spokesman said it had not fired Lin after his public criticism but had offered to place him "in another contracted hospital anywhere in the country." It was not much of a proposition, considering Lin had made his home in the Bellingham area for so many years. He declined the offer and began working as an emergency department supervisor for the Indian Health Service, a federal entity that provides healthcare to Native American tribes.

Many Americans felt bewildered as they watched the menacing virus spread across the United States in the spring of 2020. As the disease progressed, it would expose deep divisions between Americans, becoming a political flashpoint and source of fights about freedom and rights across the nation. But the pandemic revealed something else too—in addition to killing over 1 million U.S. citizens, shuttering thousands of businesses, and throwing millions of workers onto unemployment lines, the COVID-19 pandemic unmasked astonishing frailties in the nation's financial system.

The decay had been building for decades. Stealthily, unswervingly, and with help from investors and federal and state governments, a small group of Wall Street financiers, corporatists, and money-spinners had impoverished millions while enriching themselves.

Only now was the damage becoming visible.

Many articles, books, research, and much debate focuses on the widening gulf between rich and poor in the United States, the pernicious effects our deepening income inequality has on the nation's well-being, and how our style of capitalism has failed to provide a living wage and prosperous future for so many Americans.

What has not been fully explored—something we hope to remedy with this book—is the crucial role a very small cohort of elite financiers has played in this predation over the past thirty years. While globalization and technological innovations are recognized to have left many Americans behind. The activities of a core band of privateers and their use of excessive debt and dubious practices to undermine our nation's economy have been largely overlooked. Even worse, these people have been lauded for their financial prowess.

The power and wealth these debt-fueled billionaires have accrued in recent years has rocketed. The number of multibillionaires among this group rose from three in 2005 to twenty-two in 2020, according to research by economist and Oxford University professor Ludovic Phalippou. Meanwhile, the American middle class—often espoused as the nation's backbone—has been drawn and quartered. For example, a 2019 study by the Federal Reserve Board found that fully 26 percent of American adults had no retirement savings or pension to rely on.

The titans call their industry private equity. But don't let the name fool you. Very little about their business is equitable, just, or fair.

Private equity is a catch-all phrase, but the financiers we are highlighting take over companies in transactions using high-cost borrowed money raised in the corporate bond markets from investors willing to take on greater risks. They are not entrepreneurs or traditional businesspeople, prospering while creating jobs and opportunities for others. Theirs is a distorted kind of capitalism, a setup in which they benefit while many others lose. They have perfected the art of "Asshole Capitalism," a term of art devised by Aaron James, a philosophy professor at the University of California, Irvine. It is a system where "citizens feel entitled to unlimited personal enrichment even at social cost."

Whatever you call it, the takeover of the nation's economy by these financiers has been steady, piecemeal, and hard to spot. Because they operate in secrecy, with hidden ties to the companies they control, the wreckage they leave behind is often difficult to track back to its origins. It's highly likely, in fact, that you buy products or services from these privateers each day without knowing it; their names, after all, rarely appear on the stores you patronize or on the bills you pay. One example: the surprise emergency hospital billing that incensed so many people was traced by researchers back to private equity.

Their reach extends from cradle to grave. That coffee and donut you picked up on your way to work this morning. The pre-K learning center where you dropped off your kids and the nursing home where your mom lives. The dentist's or dermatologist's office, the emergency room you visited and the ambulance that took you there. Your favorite podcast, vacation time-share, online betting platform, pet care provider, supermarket, even your rental home or apartment. All may well be owned and overseen by private equity firms that maximize for profit while slashing workers, cutting necessary costs, and harming local, state, and federal taxpayers when their companies fail.

The biggest private equity firms are Apollo, Blackstone, the Carlyle Group, and Kohlberg Kravis Roberts. They buy companies and load them with debt while bleeding them of assets and profits. A few years later, they sell these same companies off to new owners, perhaps in an initial public offering of stock, ideally at a substantial gain for themselves and their colleagues and partners. Often the companies they buy collapse in bankruptcy after the financiers have piled on the debt and extracted their profits.

These firms say they are saviors of troubled businesses, enhancing their operations to make them more efficient and better able to serve customers and keep workers employed. On paper, the practice of launching debt-fueled buyouts sounds reasonable, maybe even practical. Buy an underperforming company, shape it up, and sell it for more than you paid. It's the American Dream distilled into a business model.

Some add value to the companies they buy.

But many of these "saviors" acquire relatively healthy companies and finance the purchases with so much debt that it sickens them. To meet the interest payments on the debt, the firms typically gut the acquired company through the sale of assets or businesses, then cut costs by laying off employees and reducing worker costs like healthcare and retirement benefits. The buyout artists also use these debt financings to extract and repay themselves the often small amounts of cash they have put into the acquisitions, a practice known as dividend recapitalization. The recapitalizations can occur within a year or two of the initial takeovers, giving the privateers quick gratification while making it harder for the companies to thrive.

Many of the companies taken over by these "asshole capital-ists" wind up failing. A 2019 California Polytechnic State University study found that 20 percent of the companies taken over by these firms filed for bankruptcy—ten times higher than the failure rates in other acquisitions. Bankruptcies lead to lost jobs and health insurance, evictions, and family disruptions for these companies' former workers. But the failures do not always harm the acquirers, who legally insulate themselves from the companies taking the fall. Because the pirates typically put down a single-digit percentage of the purchase price when they buy a company, they carry very little risk if the company fails.

Between 2003 and February 2020, retailers owned by these financiers eliminated over a half million jobs across America. Among them were positions at the bankrupted Sears, Kmart, Linens 'n Things, Claire's, and Toys "R" Us. Some of these failures can be attributed to the rise of online shopping, but only some. After all, these stores had access to web shoppers, too, and could easily have built profitable presences online. A much larger culprit behind the failures was the significant amount of debt loaded onto these companies to enrich their acquirers.

Even when a worker manages to hang on to his or her job at a company owned by a private equity firm, the worker may not make enough money to pay for food. A 2020 study by the Government Accountability Office identified the top employers in nine states with the largest numbers of workers receiving food stamps. In addition to Wal-Mart and McDonald's, which headed many of the state lists, fast-food companies owned by a private equity firm were among them. They included operations in four states run by Dunkin' Donuts and Sonic, affiliated with private equity firm Roark Capital. The Safeway supermarket chain, at the time controlled by Cerberus Capital, also appeared high on the list.

In Maine, for example, 1.7 percent of the state's total food stamp recipients worked for Dunkin', while in Massachusetts, 1.5 percent receiving food stamps did. In Arkansas, 1.1 percent of the state's food stamp recipients were Sonic employees. In Washington State, 1.4 percent of food stamp recipients worked for Safeway; that figure represented the largest number of workers at one company on food stamps in the state—an estimated 1,163.

Workers are not the only ones harmed by the privateers. So are their customers. During the eviction moratorium, a report by the House Select Subcommittee on the Coronavirus Crisis found, a large landlord backed by private equity was among four companies responsible for thousands of evictions, flouting the ban. "Rather than working with cost-burdened tenants, abiding by applicable eviction moratoriums, and accepting federal rental assistance," Representative James Clyburn, a South Carolina Democrat, said, "these companies—with properties across 28 states—expedited evictions above all else."

Retirees and other beneficiaries of public pensions have also been victimized by the enormous fees these firms charge investors. In 2020, academics at Harvard University and Stanford University studied $500 billion of investments by two hundred public pensions in partnerships sponsored by the privateers. Between 1990 and 2018, the researchers found, fees in the investments depleted the pensions' returns by $45 billion. That was almost 10 percent of the dollar amount invested.

Some of these fees even require pensioners to pay "money for nothing" to the firms overseeing their funds. That's because pensions typically pay asset managers based on dollars they have *committed* to invest but have not yet invested or "put to work." CalPERS, for example, the huge California public pension, may commit $400 million to an Apollo deal, but only a portion of that amount is typically given to the firm initially, the rest in subsequent years. The fees for the entire amount are paid initially, nonetheless.

Schoolteachers in Ohio show who wins and loses in this equation. According to pension records, the State Teachers Retirement System of Ohio pays fees on committed capital—money for nothing—of as much as 2 percent of its private equity investments. That translates to an annual wealth transfer of approximately $143 million from pensioners to profiteers or $1,067 each for the roughly 134,000 retirees receiving benefits from the pension as of 2021.

In recent years, as these fees flowed to wealthy Wall Streeters, the retired Ohio teachers received no cost-of-living increases. In 2017, Ohio pension officials eliminated those retirees' increases because the fund couldn't afford them—it didn't have enough assets to cover future liabilities, they said. And yet, the $143 million in "money-for-nothing" fees to the financiers would have covered the entire cost-of-living increases they had eliminated each year.

Ohio schoolteachers are not the only losers in this arithmetic. Firefighters, emergency medical technicians, and other public workers miss out, too. So do taxpayers, who may be asked to support underfunded pensions or failing public school system budgets when they go broke.

Dr. Lin lost his job in Washington trying to protect his patients and colleagues at the hospital from the profit-hungry managers at Blackstone. Beleaguered renters faced improper evictions from billionaire-owned firms. LifePoint Health nurses confronted COVID without proper gear, risking their health and lives. At the same time, the men running Blackstone, Apollo, and other prosperous firms basked in their celebrity status and raked in hundreds of millions. For 2020 alone, Steve Schwarzman received $610 million, while Leon Black received $185 million.

Routinely lionized in the financial press for their dealmaking and lauded for their "charitable" giving, these unbridled capitalists have mounted expensive lobbying campaigns to ensure continued enrichment from favorable tax laws. Hefty donations have won them positions of power on museum boards and think tanks. They've published books on leadership extolling "the importance of humility and humanity" at the top, while eviscerating those at the bottom. Their companies arrange for them to avoid paying taxes on the billions in gains that their stockholdings generate. And, of course, they rarely mention that the companies they own are among the largest beneficiaries of government investments in highways, railroads, and primary education, reaping massive perks from subsidies and tax policies that allow them to pay substantially lower rates on their earnings.

These men are America's modern-age robber barons. But unlike many of their predecessors in the nineteenth century, who amassed stupefying riches by extracting a young nation's natural resources, today's barons mine their wealth from the poor and middle class through complex financial dealings. Their business model creates little of value for society; in fact, their job cuts, higher costs of goods and services, and exploitation of the tax code have worn the nation's social fabric thin.

Workers, customers, pensioners, and taxpayers—all sense they're being robbed. They just can't be sure by whom. So they chalk up their misery to a "system" rigged against them.

There's some truth to this view. But no "system" operates on its own. People are always at the controls.

Those manning these controls direct huge segments of our nation's economy. Almost 12 million employees, or roughly 7 percent of the U.S. labor force, work for private equity–backed businesses, according to the American Investment Council, an industry lobbying group. These companies generated about 6.5 percent of the nation's gross domestic product in 2020, the group reported.

Healthcare, which accounts for 18.3 percent of the nation's economic output, has been a special focus of the titans. Historically, the industry operated with a focus on quality and patient outcomes rather than profit margins. Efficiencies, streamlining, and cost control were secondary among the previous overseers, which were often nonprofits or affiliated with religious orders. Protecting the public interest and delivering social benefits had long been the primary goals of certain industries, including healthcare and education.

Beginning in 2005, these money-spinners began prospecting for riches in healthcare, spending over $1 trillion to buy up hospital systems, physician practices, nursing homes, medical billing services, and other companies in the field. In 2018, almost half the year's healthcare takeovers were conducted by these firms. By the time TeamHealth removed Dr. Lin from his emergency department rotation, its owner Blackstone and another private equity firm, KKR, controlled one-third of the nation's hospital emergency rooms. Higher prices and dubious practices, such as surprise medical bills that purposefully fell outside of patients' insurance coverage, resulted from these buyouts. The damage was bad enough that a deeply divided Congress came together to enact a law that curbed the practice.

Putting profits ahead of patient care is supposed to be barred in America. A century-old legal doctrine banning the "Corporate Practice of Medicine" is enshrined in most states' laws and forbids profit-seeking entities from controlling or interfering with a physician's ethical duties to put patients' interests first. As a judge opining on such a case in 1931 said about a dentist working for a profit-seeking corporation: "There are certain fields of occupation which are universally recognized as 'learned professions.' The law recognizes them as a part of the public weal, and protects them against debasement, and encourages the maintenance therein of high standards of education, of ethics, and of ideals. A corporation, as such, has neither education nor skill nor ethics."

But for decades prior to COVID-19, these laws against corporatized medicine were rarely enforced. Federal and state law enforcement—the Department of Justice and state attorneys general—stood by as investment firms bought up healthcare providers, implementing tactics that generated profits but injured patients. They often hid their ownership amid a complex web of companies that made the providers appear to be physician-owned and operated and therefore complying with laws banning corporate involvement in medicine. State medical boards, charged with policing healthcare practices within their borders, took no action to stop the problem either. In fact, by 2022, private equity had become so ubiquitous in healthcare that officials affiliated with the industry began to pop up on state medical boards, allowing them to influence important enforcement practices.

Among private equity's more common tactics when they took over healthcare services were reducing services and hospital beds, ventilators, personal protective equipment, and staff available to patients. Other tactics generated profits by booking patients for treatments they did not need, admitting them into the hospital unnecessarily or ordering more costly tests than were required. The Hippocratic Oath of doing no harm and prioritizing patients' interests was and is in grave danger.

When healthcare professionals spoke out about the patient harm resulting from the financiers' methods—as Dr. Lin did—they were met with immediate reprisals.

. . .

How have these plunderers amassed such control over the nation's economy? Over decades, with a singular drive to enrich themselves, they have quietly, almost secretly, accrued immense power. Our book will show how their stealth campaign has unfolded with little opposition; how with each triumph, no matter the victims, they became more emboldened. We will also provide solutions to the problems they pose and actions regulators and policymakers can take, right now, to stop the destruction and wrest American capitalism from their grip.

A crucial point that may not surprise you: this wrecking crew did not act alone. They had help from friends in high places, especially Washington. Initially, the assistance took the form of a deregulation push during the Reagan, Bush, and Clinton administrations. Later, Washington's assistance came dressed as incompetence or inaction, with regulators choosing to look the other way as the marauders went to work. Equally important, every time the Federal Reserve Board reduced interest rates and kept them low, as it did numerous times over the decades, it boosted the buyout barons by giving them cheaper borrowing costs.

More recently, Washington's help was more explicit: in response to the devastating COVID health crisis, for example, the United States government allocated trillions of dollars to "save" our economy. Many of the Washington patrons of these corporate welfare policies had revolved through the doors of the Reagan, Bush, or Clinton administration or were the intellectual offspring of those men. Amazingly, hundreds of billions went to prop up the very financiers, like Black and Apollo, who had weakened the economy.

The corporate bond market, where companies sell debt obligations to investors, is where private equity raises money to buy the companies it acquires. The market provides the very oxygen the titans need to assemble their fortunes. And in the spring of 2020, that market received an unprecedented $750 billion backing from the Federal Reserve Board, the nation's central bank. The Fed's program to buy billions in corporate bonds was a first; during previous times of financial stress, the central bank's securities-buying programs had been limited to less risky United States Treasuries and mortgage-backed obligations. But with the pirates on the precipice, the Fed, overseen by a former private equity executive named Jay Powell, promised hundreds of billions to keep the corporate bond market aloft, buttressing companies like Apollo and Blackstone.

Worse still, many of the financier-backed businesses that received billions in government support—such as hospitals—used COVID as an excuse to cut jobs, slash wages and benefits, or require workers to take on more hours for the same pay. The government did provide pandemic relief and support to workers and small businesses—the Paycheck Protection Program paid out almost $1 trillion in forgivable, low-interest loans. But the program was riddled with fraud, and its recipients included large, prosperous companies whose operations actually thrived during COVID.

In 2020, Apollo was one of the first firms to mount a D.C. lobbying campaign to insulate their interests from a COVID collapse. Few investment firms in America were more exposed than Apollo to the industries hammered by the pandemic—it held investments in travel, restaurants, casinos, retailing. Indeed, Apollo's stock lost 30 percent of its value early on in the pandemic as investors grew concerned that COVID would decimate the economy.

Eager to stanch the bleeding, Apollo marshaled its army. While LifePoint Health nurses toiled under duress in COVID-plagued hospitals, Apollo executives urgently worked the levers in D.C.

They argued that the burgeoning pandemic and cratering financial markets had put their operations at peril, threatening an array of companies. It was time for a government rescue.

Between 2014 and 2019, the firm had poured $7 million into congressional coffers, and it was time to call in some chits. Making sure the message resonated, Apollo spent another $4.73 million lobbying lawmakers in 2020.

It was a replay of the financial crisis of 2008, when the risky activities of big banks left them begging for taxpayer rescues. Once again, wealthy financial players were engaging in their heads-I-win, tails-you-lose version of capitalism. Having demanded that Washington stay out of their way while times were good, they were quick to turn to the taxpayer when the going got rough.

In a private talking points memo that became public in the spring of 2020, Apollo executives said that a disastrous economic downturn loomed unless policymakers delivered a bailout to avert it. The impact of the coronavirus was "significantly more grave" than even the devastating 2008 events, the memo said. And, because Apollo had had no role in creating the health crisis, it claimed, a rescue would *not* be an example of the government helping a perpetrator of a crime escape punishment, known as "moral hazard."

This was not entirely true. As noted, historically healthcare was run for patient outcomes rather than profits or efficiency, but since these firms began taking over the industry, they'd cut back on investments in ventilators, beds, excess supplies, and staff. Leading up to the crisis, some LifePoint Health hospitals' resources had been depleted under Apollo, leaving them less prepared than if they had invested in the operations. Not having N95 masks on hand for the Louisville nurse was just one example.

Nevertheless, Apollo's government rescue mission reaped big results. Not only did LifePoint Health receive $1.4 billion in federal funds, another Apollo-owned company—a trucking concern called YRC—received a $700 million bailout from the United States Treasury. The company got this money *even though* it was under investigation by the Justice Department for overcharging the government for trucking services. In March 2022, YRC paid $6.85 million to settle prosecutors' allegations that it had systematically overcharged for freight carrier services and made false statements to hide the misconduct. In reaching the settlement, the government said it had made no determination of liability.

This gravy train of government assistance was by no means the first time federal and state regulators had enabled Apollo. Between 1993 and 2018, Apollo and the companies it owns received $621 million in subsidies and contracts from federal and state governments and another $432 million in federal loans, loan guarantees, and bailouts. Most large companies receive some type of subsidies, such as tax credits, government grants, property tax abatements, and payments for bringing operations to enterprise zones. But watching such assistance go to companies that routinely exploit other stakeholders is enraging.

Apollo, Black, and his peers would emerge from the pandemic with even greater billions—an unsurprising outcome given their power. Neither was it a shock that the folks on the other side of the table—company workers, customers, and taxpayers—were the losers. The very same result had occurred over and over for almost forty years. COVID-19 just made it easier to see.

A Note to Readers

In the days when pirates roamed the seas, they boarded ships armed with cutlasses and muskets and took what they pleased. Modern privateers, known as the private equity industry, plunder without physical violence, commandeering businesses armed with spreadsheets, debt financing, and high-priced lawyers. They operate (mostly) within the letter of the law, some of which they have helped to craft. The loot these latter-day pirates carry off is infinitely richer, and the havoc their pillaging visits on their victims and on society is widespread and profound.

It's said that in Washington, the real scandal is what's actually *legal*. The same is true on Wall Street.

This is a book about modern-age plunderers, a relatively small group of financiers whose unrelenting pursuit of profits extracts wealth from the many to enrich the few. It is about a business model that is pernicious and growing, and that widens the wealth gap in this country.

Some might argue that our current state of capitalism, or much of it, is also this way—that greedy CEOs and the corporations they run wreak equal havoc on their workers, pensioners, and stockholders. To a degree, this is true. Examples of unchecked capitalism among public companies exist and generate outrage when they emerge. And even when caught with their hands in the till, white-collar criminals generally receive gentler punishments when they are penalized at all.

But the pirates we've singled out tend to be more rapacious in their dealings. Public corporations can be constrained somewhat by shareholders whose interests they must at least pretend to consider, and their public disclosures are pored over by investors, reporters, academics, and policymakers. And when these stakeholders get riled about something—say the health of the planet—some public corporations have responded with change. Not as quickly as we might like or as comprehensively, perhaps. But change does occur.

This has not been the case with private equity firms. The companies they own are private and make few, if any, regulatory disclosures. Although many of the firms' parent companies are public, their founders and top executives control so much of the stock that they have little need to listen to outside holders. If the occasional client—a public pension fund for example—tries to hold them to account, they threaten to ban them from future deals. Amazingly, weak-kneed pension overseers buckle under, viewing this "punishment" as a prospect to be avoided.

The marauders answer to almost no one. Their billions generate fawning press reports and shield them from criticism, allowing them to spend fortunes on lobbying and other tactics to manipulate outcomes and public opinion. They justify their activities based on the purportedly positive investment returns they generate. "We're helping pensioners achieve a prosperous retirement," they say. While that may have been true years ago, more recent data show private equity's returns are no better than a low-cost and transparent Standard & Poor's index fund that invests in public companies.

The model of acquiring a company, loading it with debt, cutting costs to pay that debt, extracting cash along the way, and selling it in five years is capitalism on steroids, short-termism to the max. It is greed wrapped in the American flag of efficiency, looting justified by solid investment returns.

It is also a business model shrouded in secrecy. Even regulators have difficulties penetrating these operations' labyrinthine corporate structures, their complex capital stacks and shared interests. Litigants hoping to hold these firms to account face an uphill battle.

To tell this story, we have recounted a handful of cases where companies were ransacked, workers fired, pensions devastated, and customers and taxpayers harmed. All generated enormous gains to the financiers—some of the deals were singled out as exemplary by the firms and celebrated on their websites.

Although we examine transactions involving the major firms, we focus more closely on Apollo. It has the reputation of being the most aggressive of the large firms, but we also home in on it because private equity is the direct successor of the junk bond–fueled takeovers favored by Drexel Burnham Lambert; Apollo's key founders sprang from that firm and from that era.

Obviously, not every private equity deal has all these perverse components and not every transaction enriches just the dealmakers. But many of these takeovers have done enough harm to other stakeholders that an examination of the firms' practices holds some urgency.

The American Investment Council is the main U.S. organization lobbying and advocating for the private equity industry. Its website teems with superlatives about the benefits private equity bestows on the economy and the industries in which it invests. One of its claims: Private equity is improving healthcare. Reams of unbiased academic research and a rising number of practitioners say otherwise.

We asked the Council to identify deals it believes characterize the positive impacts its industry has on all stakeholders. We hoped to learn about transactions that generated gains, not just for the dealmakers, but for everyone involved. Topping the list was Tate's Bake Shop—a tiny, specialty cookie maker purchased in 2014 by Riverside Company, a small private equity firm. Tate's had an estimated $12 million in revenues and fewer than 100 workers before it was taken over, but its private equity owners helped quadruple its sales and earnings, Riverside said. In 2018, it was sold to food conglomerate Mondelēz International, for $500 million.

Another exemplary deal, according to the Council, involved the Cosmopolitan Casino in Las Vegas. Blackstone purchased the property in 2014 and sold it for a $4.1 billion profit in 2021, the firm's single best-performing investment. In an example of how private equity spreads the wealth, the Council said, in 2022, as the casino was set to change hands, Blackstone gave each worker a $5,000 bonus.

Hilton Hotels was a third highlight deal, also involving Blackstone. The purchase, which took place in 2007, reaped Blackstone a gain of three times its investment when it sold the chain in 2018.

Finally, the Council cited Blue Yonder, a software company, bought out by Blackstone and New Mountain Capital in 2010 and sold in 2021 for an $8 billion gain. The deal involved a longer holding period than is typical and although another large company was acquired and combined with Blue Yonder, New Mountain said $5.7 billion of the $8 billion gain came from internal growth generated by the company.

Most of the transactions the Council identified generated enormous profits to the firms involved and their investors. This is the most common measure of success by which private equity judges itself and is a throwback to the now-dubious tenet of modern-day capitalism—that investor profits are all that matter, regardless of the costs to other stakeholders.

In researching and writing this book, we spoke to dozens of people, those who are knowledgeable about the ways of private equity or who have been directly affected by these firms' practices. We consulted thousands of pages of regulatory documents, government and private lawsuits, bankruptcy court proceedings, research from government agencies, public pension reports, and unbiased academic research (we excluded the work of academics that advise the industry or have close ties to it). We have also relied upon trustworthy media sources. A few of our sources requested anonymity, which we granted so that they could speak freely and without fear of reprisal.

We tried to talk to the principals of the major firms—Henry Kravis, Stephen Schwarzman, David Rubenstein, and Leon Black. Only Black gave initial consideration to our request, his spokesman said, but then he never got back to us.

To the degree we received comments or views from the firms whose deals we examined, we include them. For example, five Apollo deals are detailed in these pages. Asked for comments about them, the firm responded with information on just two. Its spokeswoman said our request "illustrates a misunderstanding of many of the facts surrounding the transactions," and noted that some are over thirty years old. "We strongly encourage you to refrain from publishing false and misleading information," she added, "regarding Apollo, funds managed by subsidiaries of Apollo Global Management, and their respective transactions."

"For those points unaddressed," the spokeswoman said, "you should not consider it a confirmation of validity. In several cases, it is either not clear what information you are requesting from us, or you are requesting information that is confidential to Apollo, funds managed by subsidiaries of Apollo Global Management, Inc. and/or their respective investors."

Our interactions with Blackstone were also notable. Perhaps the premier U.S. private equity firm, it featured in three of the four exemplary deals cited by the Council. Asking for the firm's input, we described our book's thesis involving broad harm caused by private equity practices. Its spokesman provided this statement: "The false narrative underlying your book is based on a 1980s caricature of the industry that is contradicted by the facts."

This sounded familiar and an internet search found this very same phrase—a 1980s caricature—provided by Blackstone to the *Washington Post* in 2021 for a story it reported on private equity predation.

The Blackstone statement went on to note that the firm is "proud of the positive impact we deliver for our investors, portfolio companies and communities in which we operate—including adding 200,000 net jobs at our portfolio companies over the last 15-plus years." The spokesman also said that the firm's nearly 1,000 companies have rarely failed—Blackstone's bankruptcy rate is 0.2 percent, he said.

Just as Blackstone had asked us to provide documentation underlying our questions about its operations, which we did, we asked Blackstone for the data backing its bankruptcy rate and claim of adding 200,000 net jobs. The spokesman "respectfully" declined to provide it.

Blackstone did hire a law firm, which represented the Sackler family of opioid fame, and is known for targeting investigative journalists, to send us a letter in fall 2022. In it, the lawyer expressed concern that our book would "present a false and misleading narrative about my client—specifically, to paint them, and private equity firms more broadly, in an untrue light."

KKR's spokeswoman was more succinct. "As you might expect we disagree wholeheartedly with the overarching premise of the book," she said.

American capitalism is supposed to enrich the many. And it is critical, of course, that enterprises and their investors are rewarded when they create jobs and prosperity across the United States. But privateers are not entrepreneurs. They borrow money to buy existing companies and shuffle ownership and obligations, often sucking out cash and reordering companies' capital structures to their benefit. They can, and do, destroy jobs, ravage pensions, and deplete tax bases.

There is a chance that these raiders' romp is nearing an end. But we can count on them and their enablers to work overtime, ensuring that their power and practices remain entrenched. What the future holds for these pillagers is up to Congress, the American people, and this question: Is there enough outrage over the hardships and inequities their activities produce to create change?

CHAPTER ONE

"Pizza the Hut"

Leon Black and the Art of the Fleece

Katie Watson was a brown-eyed toddler in Phoenix, Arizona, beloved by her family for her sunny, easygoing ways. In 1982, when she was not yet two, Katie had become permanently brain damaged, after a local hospital failed to treat her pneumonia properly. Her parents, Vince and Sue Watson, received a medical malpractice award in a lawsuit against the hospital and, directed by the court, invested part of it in a guaranteed insurance company contract. The investment promised to deliver a monthly stream of income to Katie to cover expenses for her care.

That court overseeing the Watsons' case steered them to buy a product issued by the Executive Life Insurance Company, then rated A+ for financial soundness—the highest grade an insurer could receive. Under the arrangement, known as a structured settlement, Executive Life, California's largest insurer, contracted to pay $9,000 a month, with a cost-of-living adjustment, for as long as Katie lived. The funds would cover round-the-clock care for Katie at home, and after a trial and settlement with the hospital, the Watsons started receiving the insurer's payments in 1986.

Four years later, Executive Life was teetering. Its investment portfolio had cratered amid a bond market meltdown, and the California insurance commissioner seized it in the spring of 1991. Then the commissioner sold the insurer's investment portfolio in a virtual giveaway to a New York financier and his partners, claiming the deal would benefit policyholders. Not exactly: Katie's "guaranteed" contract with Executive Life—and the payments it had promised—was no longer in force. Under the vastly reduced terms of the new post-takeover policy, her parents could not afford the costs of Katie's care, expenses they would now have to shoulder themselves. Unable to pay the mortgage on their home, they lost it to foreclosure. Katie, who passed away in 2017, wound up receiving millions of dollars less than Executive Life had promised to pay for her care and support.

Executive Life had over three hundred thousand policyholders, many of whom relied on it for regular payments. Like Katie, these customers took a serious hit after the company was seized and its assets sold in a deal engineered by the New York financier. A 2008 audit of the deal by the state of California tallied policyholder losses at over $3 billion, a figure that is probably low.

Which New York titan of finance won control of Executive Life's deeply discounted assets all those years ago? Leon Black, cofounder of Apollo Global Management and a billionaire many times over. Today he enjoys a sumptuous art collection, an array of palatial homes, and, until recently, a seat of power on the prestigious Museum of Modern Art board.

The multibillion-dollar bonanza known as Executive Life was the very birth of Black's fortune. In 1991, when he snared it, Black's new partnership, Apollo, had just been born. Running from the implosion of his former employer, a felonious brokerage firm known as Drexel Burnham Lambert, Black managed to wrangle the Executive Life assets on the cheap, for roughly 50 cents on the dollar.

Some called it "the deal of the century." Later, the transaction would come under federal prosecutors' scrutiny and Black would be named as a defendant in a California attorney general's conspiracy suit related to it. But that case, alleging secret arrangements that cheated the state and Executive Life policyholders, was dismissed on a technicality—the judge ruled that the AG had no standing. Black walked away with his gains.

Thirty years later, the Executive Life transaction is long forgotten. In 2021, a California court approved the state insurance department's request to destroy all documents detailing the failure, saying that the matter was closed because policyholders had finally received their last payouts. The document destruction started in early 2022.

Still, the deal is rich for reexamination. Why? Because it is Exhibit A for the kinds of financial engineering and exploitation that have led to the elevation of wealthy financiers and the degradation of other stakeholders over the last three decades. In fact, Black's takeover of Executive Life's assets is a Rosetta stone for how a small group of aggressive moneymen have extracted the wealth and treasure of the American middle class, working poor, and retirees since the late 1980s.

The Executive Life transaction stands out as a harbinger of the destruction to come in another way. In recent years, these same financiers have begun acquiring insurance companies outright, putting current policyholders at risk of losses from questionable investments, all the while generating enormous fees for themselves. Many policyholders don't even know their futures lie in the plunderers' hands or that the historically conservative assets that used to back their insurance and retirement policies have been replaced by those that carry far more risk.

But we're getting ahead of ourselves. First, consider the winners and losers in the long-ago Executive Life deal: the transaction made billions for Black and his partners, almost overnight, at the expense of retirees, pensioners, and the disabled. All were Executive Life policyholders, like Katie Watson, who'd been promised payouts or end-of-life benefits. They wound up forfeiting money as a result of the deal that Black and his partners dreamed up.

Second, even though the Black-led sale of the insurance company and its assets was overseen by a California court charged with ensuring fairness, many aspects of the deal were cloaked in secrecy and riddled with conflicts of interest unknown to policyholders. This, too, was a precursor to the present day; conflicts and secrecy—even in a judicial system that is supposed to be transparent for the public good—are key features of the private equity playbook, enabling them to put themselves and their interests ahead of workers, pensioners, and investors.

Had the Executive Life policyholders and their advocates known about the conflicts and hidden relationships, they could have agitated for a better deal. For example, if policyholders had known Black and his partners were already investors in some of the bonds they acquired in the Executive Life takeover, the policyholders could have demanded higher prices from Black for those bonds.

But the man representing the Executive Life policyholders in the deal, who was obliged to get the best possible outcome for them, was no typical seller. He was the California insurance commissioner, an ambitious politician named John Garamendi. He gave Black the Executive Life prize, claiming then and forevermore that policyholders did well in the deal. After several unsuccessful runs for California governor, in 2009 Garamendi became a congressman, a Democrat who today represents the state's eighth district, northeast of San Francisco.

Wealth transfers like the Executive Life deal, where the assets of everyday Americans wind up in the hands of cunning financiers, are often blessed by government officials. Indeed, regulatory complicity or complacency has been crucial to the successes of these elites over the decades.

More than a decade after the deal occurred, federal prosecutors contended it was infected with fraud. A foreign company, affiliated with Black's group, that purchased the insurer had unlawfully concealed its ownership stake. Although the United States Justice Department went after some of Black's associates in the transaction, and California's attorney general named him as a defendant in its conspiracy case, Black, the mastermind, was never found culpable.

Another recurring aspect of the plunder years.

Katie Watson's parents had tried to fight the sale of the insurer's assets to Black's new partnership. They'd traveled to Los Angeles to attend court hearings and argued against the sale with the insurance commissioner on the courthouse steps. None of it did any good.

Today, Vince and Sue Watson are still angry that money pledged for their daughter's care wound up in Leon Black's pocket.

"Leon Black got the deal of the century on the backs of the handicapped and the brain-damaged," Sue Watson told us. "Over the years, we tracked him and saw how he thrived with our money. Wow is all I can say. Wow."

Seeing Black pick the Executive Life carcass clean in the early 1990s was only the beginning, Sue Watson recounted. In the years that followed, she and her husband watched as he rose to dazzling wealth and status in New York City, amassing all the trappings. There was the private jet, the yacht, the real estate holdings in the Hamptons, Los Angeles, London, Westchester County horse country, and Manhattan's Upper East Side.

And the art! Black's prodigious collection included a Raphael, a famed Picasso sculpture, and the only privately held copy of *The Scream* by Edvard Munch. One of the most iconic images in all of art, Black purchased it for $120 million in 2012.

Six years later, Black ascended to the chairmanship of the Museum of Modern Art, founded by Rockefellers. He and his wife Debra gave $40 million to the museum, which named its film center for the couple. Black's fortune stood at $7 billion in 2018, according to *Forbes* magazine.

Black's climb to the pinnacle of New York City society had not been preordained. Yes, he had been raised the son of Eli Black, a former corporate CEO known for his contributions to the arts in New York City. But tragedy struck the family in February 1975, when Black, the chief executive of a conglomerate called United Brands, committed suicide just as his involvement in a significant international corporate bribery scandal was about to emerge. Weeks after the executive used his briefcase to smash a window of his forty-fourth floor Midtown office and jumped to his death, a federal investigation began. Its conclusion: Eli Black had authorized bribes to officials in Honduras to reduce his company's taxes. In addition to taking down the president of Honduras, the fraud helped produce a new law banning such payoffs—the Foreign Corrupt Practices Act of 1977.

The suicide occurred while Leon Black was finishing up at Harvard Business School. After graduating from Dartmouth with a degree in philosophy and history, he had decided to pursue a career in finance like his father. But despite obtaining his MBA from Harvard, he'd been turned down for a job at Lehman Brothers, then a prestigious investment bank at which his father had worked. Black went instead to an unglamorous accounting firm, quit after a year, and joined an obscure financial publisher called Boardroom Reports.

It was not an auspicious beginning. But soon Black secured a position at Drexel Burnham Lambert, a second-tier Wall Street firm known for being scrappy and brash. There he earned the nickname "Pizza the Hut" for his voracious appetite when toiling to meet deadlines on mergers and acquisitions deals.

Black would rise at Drexel and the firm would make him rich. But it would also emotionally scar him when it collapsed in 1990 amid a massive insider trading and market manipulation scandal. Beyond that, Black emerged from Drexel relatively unscathed, as he would in subsequent brushes with controversy.

Until, that is, the stunning details of his relationship with Jeffrey Epstein, the notorious pedophile, began to emerge in 2019.

Epstein was a Manhattan arriviste and man about town who claimed to be a financial advisor. His credentials were nonexistent—a five-year stint as a trader at Bear Stearns in the 1970s was the sum total of his Wall Street cred. Black had gotten to know him in the 1990s, their relationship involving many mutually beneficial lofty positions and rewards. Black invited Epstein in 1997 to become a director of the Black family foundation. Two years after that, an Apollo executive donated $167,000 to a foundation associated with Epstein.

In the years after Epstein pleaded guilty to procuring a child for prostitution in June 2008, the ties between the men grew stronger. In 2011, an Epstein investment unit bought a large stake in Environmental Solutions Worldwide, a small company funded by Black and where two of his sons served as directors. And when

Apollo offered shares of its own stock to the public for the first time in 2011, an Epstein entity based in the United States Virgin Islands bought $5 million worth of shares.

Next came a $10 million donation in 2015 by Black to an Epstein foundation called Gratitude America. This time, Black was careful to make his contribution through a limited-liability company he controlled that did not bear his name, the *Wall Street Journal* reported.

But after Epstein died in a Manhattan jail accused of sex trafficking in 2019, truly startling facts began to materialize about Black's decades-long association with the pedophile. In the spring of 2021, a bombshell internal Apollo investigation determined that Black had been paying Epstein millions of dollars for financial advice even after Epstein's 2008 prosecution. Over a period of five years, Black paid Epstein an astonishing $158 million; among the advice Epstein provided was how Black could lower his tax bills.

Given that Epstein was nobody's idea of a tax guru, Black's huge payments were puzzling. They also turned out to be a career-ender, because they imperiled Apollo's ability to raise money from public pension funds and other big investors. These buyers were Apollo's biggest and most profitable clients; if they turned from the firm because of the Epstein taint, its business model would collapse.

In January 2021, at the age of sixty-nine, Black finally lost his grip on Apollo, the firm he'd founded. Black said he was retiring from Apollo for health reasons, but the Epstein stigma also triggered his resignation two months later as chairman of the Museum of Modern Art. If that weren't enough, a former fashion model who had been his mistress soon came forward with tales of rape, sexual harassment, and abuse by Black, beginning in 2008. A second accuser filed suit against Black, contending he had raped her.

The titan fought back, denying both allegations and contending that the relationship with the Russian woman, more than thirty years his junior, had been "consensual." He also said she'd tried to extort money from him and that he'd paid her $9 million to keep their affair quiet. Her claim that Black had flown her to Palm Beach to try to get her to bed Epstein and Black simultaneously was fiction, Black contended. As this book went to press, both cases were ongoing.

The sordid stories, gleefully retold in New York's gossip columns, rocked Black.

But in the upside-down world of Wall Street, Black's departure from Apollo only served to increase his wealth. The firm's shares—of which he still holds millions—rose when he left. It was as if investors were relieved there'd be no more bruises for the firm with him gone.

As Black departed Apollo and the MOMA board, an aroma of disgrace filled the air. Encomiums from his peers were few upon his exit from the A-list scene. Now Black's eventual obituary would not simply recount his remarkable rise, his accumulation of vast wealth, and amazing art—it would also document his fall.

To Sue Watson, Black's woes were only fitting, a case of "what goes around comes around." Karma has everyone's address, they say.

Memories are famously short on Wall Street. But for some with longer recall, Black's ouster from Apollo over payments to Jeffrey Epstein for tax advice had a riveting parallel.

Forty-five years earlier, Black's father, Eli, had been undone by a secret scheme involving his company's taxes. A corporate takeover artist and chief executive of United Brands, a large conglomerate, the elder Black had orchestrated two bribes to reduce banana export taxes his company owed. With the scandal about to emerge, he killed himself in February 1975.

Leon Black was by no means a carbon copy of his father—hardly anybody is. But the men's business methods had striking similarities—the heavy debt used to acquire companies, the predilection for sharp tactics, the view that companies were little more than a collection of numbers. Each man has been characterized as "a pirate." Decades after his father's suicide, when Leon Black was at the pinnacle of his career, an interviewer asked him about the calamity. His response was telling. "It took me years of therapy to get over that," he said, "and to figure out where he ended, and I began."

Elihu Menasche Blachowitz was an ordained rabbi with a financial acumen. Born in Poland, he emigrated with his family to New York as a child and graduated from Yeshiva University in 1940. As a rabbi, he led a congregation in Long Island but saw opportunity on Wall Street, becoming an investment banker at Lehman Brothers and later at the now defunct American Securities.

Son Leon was born in 1951 and three years later, Eli Black became CEO of American Seal-Kap, a bottle cap manufacturer. Eli had been advising the company on financial matters while a banker at American Securities, but Seal-Kap wanted him and his expertise in-house.

As CEO, Black soon started buying other companies to bring into the American Seal-Kap fold and piling on debt to do so. His most significant purchase was the United Fruit Company, a storied and notorious banana importer founded in 1899 and based in Boston.

Once a mighty, neocolonialist enterprise founded by slave traders, United Fruit controlled massive landholdings in Central America, along with a vast fleet of ships and railroad operations. The nation's largest banana importer, United Fruit had close government connections; it played a role in the 1961 Bay of Pigs fiasco, a CIA operation that tried and failed to invade Cuba. United Fruit supplied two ships from its so-called Great White Fleet for the ill-fated invasion, according to *An American Company: The Tragedy of United Fruit*, by Thomas P. McCann, a former vice president of the company.

In 1968, United Fruit was facing higher costs of growing and exporting bananas, a major problem given that the company did nothing else. At the helm of American Seal-Kap, Black started quietly buying up United Fruit stock in the open market, with the help of an allied brokerage firm, amassing a controlling stake of 733,000 shares. In McCann's telling, the way Black cobbled together the shares may have run afoul of securities rules and led to questions from other United Fruit shareholders as well as the Federal Trade Commission.

But these questions became moot when Black proposed a takeover to the company's directors; initially dubious, all but one agreed to the deal when no other reasonable suitor materialized.

Wall Street approved and United Fruit's stock soared. Investors believed Black would breathe "new life into old United Fruit," according to *Bananas*, a critical biography of the company by journalist Peter Chapman. Black was "a thrusting 'asset manager' who would take hold of a company that for years had mismanaged its assets," Chapman wrote of investors' reaction to the takeover. A man who'd risen from poverty on the Lower East Side, Black would fix the company's problems.

American Seal-Kap was renamed United Brands in 1970. Under

Black, it took up the then current fad known as conglomeration, amassing an array of companies with disparate operations. The idea behind the conglomerate was that a collection of diverse entities all under one roof could be worth more than the sum of its parts.

By the late 1960s, most of the mergers taking place in the market were by conglomerates buying up other companies. United Brands' corporate mash-up included a banana importer, meatpacker, petrochemical maker, telecommunications concern, A&W Root Beer, and the Foster Grant sunglasses brand. For a while, this conglomeration worked.

CEO Black excelled at numbers and dealmaking, but an operating executive he was not. "Eli could not run the company and he was proving it," McCann wrote. "Increasingly, Black found himself surrounded by managers who were as incompetent as he."

Black also lacked "a moral anchor," according to McCann. His elbows were sharp and some saw him as a "pirate," a profile in the *New York Times* said. It recounted Black warning an adversary: "If you want to play tough, we can be very, very tough players."

United Brands soon struggled under its debt load taken on to fund Black's acquisition. It had to earn $40,000 each day, just to cover the debt. The company generated losses until 1973 when the operations finally began turning around, but catastrophe struck the following year when a group of Central American governments raised taxes on banana exports. United Brands had to pay $11 million in tariffs in just three months because of the increase, contributing to a $40 million company-wide loss in 1974. A devastating hurricane in Honduras and declining meat prices added to United Brands' woes.

Keen to reduce the company's crippling banana taxes, in September 1974 Black authorized a secret bribe of $1.5 million to

Abraham Bennaton Ramos, the Honduran minister of economy. Another $1 million bribe was to be paid the following year. The return on investment from the $2.5 million payoff would be significant: taxes owed by United Fruit would be slashed by $7.5 million.

But the secret bribe would not remain secret for long.

Early on the morning of February 3, 1975, Eli Black's chauffeur drove him, as usual, to his United Brands office, news reports said. It was on the forty-fourth floor of what was then called the Pan Am Building, above Grand Central Terminal.

None of Black's colleagues were at work yet, the *New York Times* profile noted. He bolted the doors to the reception area and locked his office from the inside. Then, using his oversized briefcase, he smashed a three-by-four-foot hole in one of the windows and jumped to his death. Papers from his attaché floated to the ground; on one scrap, Black had written the words: "early retirement, 55." Black was fifty-three.

Initial news accounts of the suicide noted that Black had been "under great strain because of business pressures," working eighteen-hour days. United Brands was running out of cash to meet its debt payments, some insiders said, and Black needed to sell something. Still, Black's associates and family members doubted that a "secret motive" lurked behind his death; no fraud or debilitating personal debt, for example.

At Black's funeral in Manhattan, attended by over five hundred people, he was eulogized as a patron of the arts and a man of character. Black "tried to integrate the world of scholars, the world of high morals and the world of practical affairs," one speaker said. A former teacher characterized Black as "a boy who always smiled but never laughed."

A few weeks later, the Securities and Exchange Commission, the nation's top cop on Wall Street, launched an investigation into

United Brands. A vague disclosure by the company, noting that it had resolved its banana tax problem, was a red flag to investigators in the SEC's newly formed enforcement division. It didn't take long before details about the $2.5 million bribe emerged.

The effects of the revelation were far-reaching. General Oswaldo López Arellano, the president of Honduras, was forced out in a bloodless coup, while in the U.S., a federal grand jury handed down criminal charges against United Brands. Prosecutors identified Black as a principal participant and co-conspirator in the bribe. Three years later, the company pleaded guilty to conspiracy and wire fraud and paid a $15,000 fine, the maximum under the charges.

Congress convened hearings about bribery in corporate America, where Black's Honduran bribe was discussed extensively. Raymond Garrett, the SEC's chairman at the time, called improper payments abroad "the lowest common denominator of corporate behavior."

Finally, lawmakers passed the Foreign Corrupt Practices Act in 1977, outlawing payoffs like those Black had authorized and arranged. The United Brands scandal was just one example of corporations making sketchy payments, but it played a role in the law's creation.

In his book published a year earlier, McCann recalled the quicksand in which Eli Black had stood at the end of his life. United Brands "was struggling to stay afloat in a sea of debt," he wrote. "[Black's] directors were in revolt, his management had lost respect for him, his friends had deserted him, his personal finances were at least as bad as those of the company, his ability to win people's confidence had disappeared, and he had nowhere left to turn."

Then McCann opined on Black's larger legacy. "One good way

to kill off a company is to approach it as though it has no life, no age, no spirit, no constituencies that matter," he wrote. "In other words, to approach it as Eli Black did, as though it were nothing more than numbers."

Much like the plunderers of today.

CHAPTER TWO

"Greed Is Good"

The Plunderers Come for the
American Middle Class

Leon Black was fleeing the smoldering wreckage of his high-flying brokerage firm, Drexel Burnham Lambert. It was early 1990 and as co-head of Drexel's corporate finance unit, Black had been at the heart of the firm's infamous debt-selling machine.

A years-long insider trading and market manipulation scandal had finally engulfed the firm. In September 1989, Drexel pleaded guilty to six counts of fraud and paid $650 million in fines. As clients and employees bolted, Drexel's parent company missed some of its debt payments. It filed for bankruptcy in February 1990.

Michael Milken, the head of Drexel's famed junk bond trading unit and a close colleague of Black's, followed suit in April, pleading guilty to six felonies related to his work at the firm. He paid $600 million in fines and went to jail.

(After his incarceration, Milken rehabilitated himself by making generous contributions to cancer research and other charities and starting a think tank that aimed to solve social problems using free market–based principles and financial innovations. Despite his guilty pleas, his supporters contended he'd been railroaded by ambitious prosecutors like then U.S. attorney for the Southern District of New York Rudy Giuliani. He may not have understood finance, but Giuliani did see photo gold in newspaper images of Wall Streeters in handcuffs. In 2020, Donald Trump pardoned Milken.)

Securities regulators interviewed Black when they investigated the Drexel disaster but did not charge him with any violations of laws or regulations. On the hunt for his next success, Black wouldn't take long to find it.

After joining Drexel in 1977, Black specialized in funding corporate takeovers using high-cost debt. Known as leveraged buyouts, these deals were the early phase of the manic pursuit of profits that has subsequently become known as private equity. They were the transactions Congress had expressed concerns about in the 1980s but had done nothing to rein in.

Drexel was not a top-tier firm, and it had made its money peddling debt issued by less established or riskier companies that other brokerages wouldn't touch. These companies had to pay higher rates of interest to attract investors, and their bonds were known as "junk" because of their lesser quality and the companies' significant debt loads. Drexel soon became Wall Street's juggernaut of junk.

Many of the companies in Drexel's orbit wound up borrowing more than their operations could repay. Amid a slowdown in the economy in the late 1980s, these companies' bonds started cratering, hurting mostly institutional investors, like mutual funds and banks Drexel had sold them to. Among the investors hurt most by their purchases of Drexel-issued junk were savings and loan associations; these holdings, along with questionable real estate assets, contributed to many S&L failures, exacerbating the economic woes enveloping the country in 1989. Another colossal junk investor was the Executive Life Insurance Company, California's largest insurer.

As the Drexel drama unfolded, Black moved on, trying to remake himself. In his years at the firm, he'd worked with many corporate raiders, but in the current economic downturn, takeover deals were impossible. Crucial bond investors had either gone on strike or out of business.

Working out of the Midtown office of one of those takeover titans—Bennett LeBow—Black began soliciting investors to back him in a new firm. A tantalizing possibility presented itself in March 1990 when Credit Lyonnais, a huge state-owned French bank, was looking to build a mergers and acquisitions team in the U.S. and thought Black might be interested in assembling one. Black traveled to France to talk with Jean-François Hénin, president of Altus Finance, a unit of the big bank.

Alas, the M&A scene was dead, Black told Hénin. It would rebound at some point, but for now, there were far better profit opportunities in scooping up Drexel-backed companies currently in distress. Although these companies were struggling—some were even in bankruptcy—Black recognized that many of them could be saved by restructuring their financial burdens, which, for the most part, Drexel had encouraged them to take on. He knew which companies could be resuscitated because he'd acted as financier for many, raising money for them in the junk bond market.

Sure, he'd been part of the problem, recommending they pile on the debt that ultimately sank them but earned him a fee at Drexel. No matter. Profiting from problems you've created is a long-standing tradition on Wall Street. For example, investment bankers are famous for advising corporate clients whose acquisitions don't work out to sell companies they had advised them to buy in the first place. Best of all, advisers earn fees on both deals.

Still, while Black had made a lot of money at Drexel, he didn't have the capital he required to gain control of these companies. Neither did he have an investing track record that would allow him to raise money from outside investors. He'd been a corporate finance guy at Drexel, not an investment wizard. So doing a deal with Altus would solve both of Black's problems, he thought. With money from Credit Lyonnais, the profit possibilities could be immense.

Black's meeting with Hénin went well, positioning the dealmaker for a coup. He persuaded the Frenchman that there was real money in distressed investing, not mergers and acquisitions, and that he knew how to identify companies that had fallen on hard times but that would likely recover.

Just six days after Milken's guilty pleas, a partnership agreement between Black and some of his former Drexel partners emerged. The partnership, known as Lion Advisors, would count the French bank as its main client. Black's personal enrichment machine, later renamed Apollo, began to hum.

Lion Advisors' first mission was getting its hands on the massive but troubled junk bond portfolio held by the Executive Life Insurance Company. It was a lush target the former Drexel team knew well.

There would be two groups in the partnership; one would be the French, while the other would consist of Black, his partners, friends, and outside investors. Each party would contribute an identical amount. Both funds would invest in the same debt securities of distressed companies. Many of these companies were former Drexel clients.

The partnership with the French would be enriching for Black and his crew. As advisors, they would receive management fees totaling 1.5 percent of the assets in the portfolio annually, then reap additional profits based on the assets' performance. (This type of arrangement—getting paid a percent of assets as well as income based on a fund's performance—likely originated in 1949 when a New York money manager named Alfred Winslow Jones created the first "hedged fund," a partnership that bought stocks he thought would rise while betting against those that appeared overpriced. Jones took 20 percent of the profits on his fund as compensation.)

At the end of each year of the new Apollo partnership, the agreements said, an accounting would be made of its operations and half of each year's profits, net of expenses, would go to Black and his partners. If net profits exceeded certain preset limits, Black's group would receive 60 percent of those gains. Outside investors would get 40 percent. The terms were complex, but they boiled down to this: after management fees, Apollo would earn profits based on assets of either 22.5 percent, 11.25 percent, or 5.625 percent, depending on the fund that held them. In other words, an enviable payday.

Apollo's outside investors would contribute most of the partnership's capital—88 percent—while Black and his pals funded the rest. Nevertheless, the agreement would be exceedingly lucrative for Black and his partners and presaged the terms that the private equity industry would force on their investors over the next three decades. The managers would automatically receive a sweet percentage of assets each year, then siphon off an even bigger slice of the profits.

Because Apollo was a private partnership, it did not have to identify its outside investors. One, however, was Western Union, controlled at the time by Bennett LeBow, the swashbuckling dealmaker and former Drexel client who gave Black an office to work out of after Drexel failed. Black had been LeBow's banker at Drexel, helping him acquire Western Union in 1987 with $500 million in debt raised by the firm. LeBow's investment company was called Brooke Group Ltd.; chief among Brooke's holdings was Liggett Group, a tobacco giant.

Black had further ties to Western Union. LeBow's right-hand man at the time was Richard S. Ressler, brother of Debra Ressler, who became Black's wife. Another Ressler brother, Antony, had worked with Black at Drexel and was now on the scene at Lion/Apollo. (In 1996, LeBow and Black would travel to Moscow with Donald Trump, who was interested in developing a hotel there. LeBow had properties in Moscow that he hoped to sell to Trump for the development. The deal did not go through, but the Moscow trip became part of the government's investigation into Russian involvement in the 2016 presidential election.)

The Apollo partnership drew up its terms in an April 1990 letter noting it would be executed by the end of June. The letter included this proviso: "assuming necessary authorization from the Federal Reserve will have been obtained." Because a foreign investor was involved in the partnership, it would have to pass muster with the Federal Reserve Board, the United States' central bank.

Finally, the letter outlining the partnership took up the crucial matter of secrecy. "Throughout the life of the management contract," it said, investors supplying most of the capital "will limit to the maximum extent possible the number of persons aware" of the partnership's activities.

Black, a fan of Greek mythology, named the firm Apollo, for the god of light, music, and dance. But the name had another, deeper meaning for the financier: Apollo is also the god of healing, something Black told people he'd sought after the bruising Drexel debacle.

Whatever the name, the future Apollo had at its heart two elements virtually guaranteed to generate profits for Black and his cohorts at this fractured moment in financial history. The first was Black's inside knowledge of the debt securities they were buying. Many of the junk bonds Drexel had sold were trash, but some were not. And with Black's firsthand knowledge Apollo could capitalize on the temporary market chaos caused by Drexel's implosion, picking up issues that had been unfairly battered. Sure enough, only a few months after the partnership was created, the junk bond market began to recover, indicating that profits lay ahead for those bold enough to wade back into it.

Black's insider insights into Drexel-peddled debt gave him clues other investors didn't have. Some currently distressed companies might recover if they underwent a debt restructuring, for example, in which creditors agreed to reduce their obligations. Amassing such holdings could be immensely profitable for the Apollo team.

Even though the nation's debt markets far exceed the stock market in dollar value, regulatory officials have focused much more closely on policing activities in stock trading than in bond transactions. You almost never hear of insider trading cases involving debt issues, for example.

The second key to Black's early success in the Executive Life deal was even more hidden, at least from the public. It was a web of undisclosed trades and ties that enriched Black and his partners at the expense of the insurer's policyholders who never knew about them.

Drexel had sold Executive Life a boatload of risky investments that Black had put together and that he could now pick up for pennies on the dollar. His gains would come out of Executive Life policyholders' pockets.

Like many Wall Street deals, the Executive Life transaction is labyrinthine in its complexity. But it also exemplifies the arrangements that have generated astonishing wealth for Black and his fellow financiers ever since.

In 1990, the United States was lurching through an economic downturn. Jobs were scarce, real estate values were dropping, and an oil shock had raised prices for consumers. Adding to the malaise was the aftermath of the savings and loan debacle, in which reckless lending fueled by deregulation had felled more than a thousand financial institutions.

Many companies that had gorged on debt during the eighties were experiencing the economic equivalent of a hangover—the headaches and other ill effects following a bash where everybody enjoyed too much of a good thing.

That party had been hosted by Wall Street, of course, in what would become known as the "Greed Is Good" era. Gordon Gekko, the ruthless, crooked stock trader in Oliver Stone's 1987 movie *Wall Street*, symbolized the moment. In fact, Gekko's mantra had first been uttered by Ivan Boesky, a stock trader who'd become immensely successful buying stocks on illegal tips about unannounced takeovers. "Greed is all right, by the way. I want you to know that," Boesky had told graduates in a commencement address at the University of California, Berkeley, in the spring of 1986. "I think greed is healthy. You can be greedy and still feel good about yourself."

Nowhere was the pro-greed creed valued more than at Drexel

Burnham Lambert, Leon Black's firm. The thing Boesky forgot to mention about greed, though, is that it can lead to trouble. Boesky's avarice would take down not only himself but also Drexel, the firm that had enabled him, and Milken, the junk bond genius.

As corporate takeovers fueled the go-go stock market of the 1980s, the gains they produced for investors were more or less the inverse of steep losses stock buyers had absorbed during the prior decade. Wracked by a recessionary economy, crippling energy shortages, and inflation in the 1970s, stock prices had been decimated.

During this unpleasant period, the plunderers got their start. Wall Street financiers joined together to create leveraged buyout firms, Kohlberg Kravis Roberts chief among them, that would become some of the biggest wealth-creation machines in history. With stock prices low and undervalued, the potential for gains in corporate takeovers was great. Even better, when these firms bought out companies, they always paid themselves first.

It is not a coincidence that while the 1970s served as the brilliant beginning for the buyout brigade, it also marked the end of a long period of wealth accumulation and job security for Main Street Americans. Costs of goods began to explode in a devastating inflationary spike in the seventies and interest rates soared; meanwhile, Americans' incomes were no longer growing. This double whammy made it harder for families to live within their means, and they began borrowing through revolving loans and relatively novel things called credit cards.

Financial entities were eager to accommodate the masses' need for debt, offering high-cost revolving credit arrangements. After decades of living within their means—a lesson of the Great

Depression—American consumers now embraced the "freedom" of spending money they didn't have. They began to pledge their future incomes to servicing debts taken on to support consumption of newer products often imported from countries with lower-cost manufacturing.

At the same time, the power of labor unions was in decline, reducing the leverage workers had over their employers regarding pay and benefits. Imperceptibly, the balance between employee and employer began to skew away from workers. In August 1981, this shift in the balance of power was memorialized when a pro-business President Reagan fired over eleven thousand air traffic controllers on strike for higher wages and a shorter workweek. The strikers were easily replaced, showing that labor could be cowed by management. Thus began a monumental change that would weaken workers' ability to maintain a living wage.

Finally, workers' pensions, long a force for stability and prosperity among the middle class, started being replaced by self-directed retirement accounts, known as 401(k)s. It's no surprise why corporations preferred these accounts to pensions. They require smaller contributions from a company and bigger contributions by its workers.

In 1970, for example, figures from the Social Security Administration show private employers contributed far larger amounts—almost nine to one—to their employees' pensions than the employees themselves did. By 2020, the calculus had flipped; pensions were gone and in their replacement, 401(k)s, employers typically contributed only half the amount their workers did.

Another problem: when workers had pensions, professional managers made the investing decisions that would deliver comfortable retirements for millions of workers. With 401(k)s, individuals, who knew little about investing tricks and traps, had to manage their life savings on their own. As these changes took hold, a 1978 decision by the United States Supreme Court struck another blow against consumers in favor of financiers—the court eviscerated state laws that had protected borrowers against usurious lending. The ruling allowed most banks to charge whatever interest rate was permitted in a state, and incentivized regions eager for tax revenues to welcome banks whose business models involved preying on borrowers.

That same year, the U.S. government gave a big boost to the nascent buyout firms by changing a federal rule to let corporate pension funds invest in risky private equity deals.

All these shifts favored the financiers over workers and consumers.

After years of stock market malaise, in early 1982, share prices began to stir, and the biggest bull market in history began in earnest that summer. Still, the Dow Jones Industrial Average was well below its 1973 peak of 1,052, and companies' shares remained relatively depressed. That made the issuers ripe for buyouts by corporate raiders funded by Drexel's debt machine.

These deals raised questions about potential monopolistic tendencies, but with pro-business Ronald Reagan at the helm, anti-trust regulators did not get in the way. While two units of the federal government—the Federal Trade Commission and the anti-trust division of the Justice Department—were tasked with scrutinizing mergers for anti-competitive aspects, the regulators were hopelessly outgunned, as annual reports to Congress show.

Under the Hart-Scott-Rodino Act of 1976, companies alert the government before a major planned merger or acquisition occurs so it can be reviewed for adherence to anti-trust laws. A merger cannot proceed before the review process is complete. Every year, Congress receives a report about merger deals detailing those reviewed by regulators and law enforcement. Over the decades, the government has nixed relatively few deals. In 1987, at the height of merger mania, there were 2,533 transactions according to that year's report, and the Justice Department filed complaints in just six of them. Four of the companies divested assets to secure approval on the transactions, and two of the deals were abandoned. The FTC that year sought injunctions on seven cases.

Another measure of government oversight on mergers occurs when regulators ask for additional information about deals from companies planning to make the deals. Such requests—a first step in a process that might wind up with an investigation—plummeted during the 1980s, the figures show, falling from 12.6 percent of deals in 1979, to just over 1 percent in 1989. (By 2020, the government requested additional information on 2.9 percent of mergers. But in 2021, under the Biden administration, the FTC announced a change in policy to address the surge in deals. For mergers that the commission couldn't evaluate within the prescribed time period, it warned companies it could still object after the deadline, if it determined that the deal was illegal.)

In the 1980s, securities regulators were unlikely to challenge the takeover artists either. In 1981, Reagan nominated John Shad, the former vice chairman of the Wall Street firm E.F. Hutton, to be chairman of the Securities and Exchange Commission. Shad, who had no experience in government, was "a very, very smart man," according to former SEC staffer Joel Goldberg, "but he had really drunk the Kool-Aid of the Reagan philosophy that we've got to shrink the government, the fewer rules the better."

In support of the President's Task Force on Regulatory Relief,

Shad quickly signaled a cultural change as the nation's top securities cop. The SEC would become corporate America's partner, working to reduce the hurdles to capital formation, and shift the focus away from the crucial role of policing Wall Street.

"John Shad's philosophy was that hostile takeovers were a good discipline on the market, and also very beneficial for the investors of the target company," Goldberg recalled in an oral history project sponsored by the SEC. "So we should be interfering as little as possible."

Leveraged buyouts, as they were known, had been around awhile. But they really began to take off in the 1980s alongside the new bull market. In 1984, KKR's $1.1 billion buyout of Wometco Enterprises, an old movie theater chain and media company, was the first billion-dollar deal and put the firm squarely on the map. That year also saw a hostile $2.5 billion bid for the Walt Disney Company, by Saul Steinberg, a flamboyant insurance executive and corporate raider backed by Milken and Drexel. The company wound up paying Steinberg $300 million to go away, a dubious, anti-shareholder practice that became known as "greenmail."

These debt-fueled deals worked for a key reason, at least for the buyout boys (yes, they were predominantly boys). Corporations could deduct the interest costs associated with their debts. And in 1986, a tax overhaul essentially incentivized the use of debt in takeovers by curbing or eliminating other corporate income tax shields that had been previously available. For example, the law curtailed companies' use of generous investment tax credits or allowances for depreciation—the annual reductions in an asset's value—to reduce their tax bills.

With these moves, Uncle Sam essentially promoted the debt-laden takeovers, even though they often devastated workers with lost jobs and reduced pensions. Interestingly, the same new tax law that kept debt as a tax write-off for companies eliminated deductions of interest costs for individuals. Only the home mortgage interest deduction remained for consumers as a write-off.

Crucial to the merger deals, however, was Drexel financing. As a second-rate Wall Street firm, Drexel found its edge in the aggressive world of leveraged buyouts and bruising takeovers. Now the firm's executives were sparking a speculative frenzy across corporate America and empowering Wall Street to replace banks as the leading funders of U.S. corporations. This change would drive a new obsession with short-term corporate gains over longer-term investments and growth. But it would enrich the players.

The debt-fueled buying spree resulted in almost $1.5 trillion in merger deals in the 1980s, a bonanza for Wall Street firms and their lawyers, generating over $60 billion in fees. Billions more was spent on the defenses companies needed to stave off hostile takeovers.

Even before Milken's junk bond machine was running full throttle at Drexel, he had forged a reputation of being able to control any bond financing he sought. Alongside him was Black, Drexel's aggressive investment banker, who lured the swaggering new-era raiders like Steinberg and Carl Icahn to the firm. In 1983, Black invented a novel tactic on behalf of Icahn, who was trying to take over Phillips Petroleum. It would prove to be instrumental to Drexel's lucrative but short-lived glory days.

Drexel had not yet lined up the financing necessary for Icahn's $8.1 billion bid offer Phillips. It was a massive bid, and even with Milken's growing clout, raising that much capital would be tough. So Black decided to bluff and penned a letter telling the banks he was asking to help fund the deal that Drexel was "highly confident" it could line up all the financing to complete the transaction.

This wasn't true, but on Wall Street, where a banker's word was his bond, nobody questioned the claim.

Although Icahn didn't win Phillips, the "highly confident letter" became a key tool in Drexel's takeover kit and used in many future bids. The highly confident letter was as good as money in the bank.

The buyouts propelled the financiers to immense wealth. In 1984, Milken's salary and bonus totaled $45.7 million, almost $120 million in today's dollars, but by the end of his run at Drexel, his annual compensation was $550 million. By 1989, Jerome Kohlberg, Henry Kravis, and George Roberts were worth a combined $1.1 billion, *Forbes* said. Their holdings, and those of peers like Leon Black, would only become more bounteous.

As these takeovers were enriching Drexel and other Wall Streeters, middle-class America was beginning a secular financial decline. In the 1980s, the middle class was at its peak of prosperity; what soon followed was a decay that continues to this day.

In 1985, a report presented at the University of Michigan noted, the bottom 90 percent of households in America held 35 percent of the nation's wealth. That might not seem like a lot, but it represented an enormous and hard-won gain from 1913, when this group owned only 15 percent of the wealth. Fueling the increased prosperity among the "nonrich" were rising values of workers' homes and pensions, the researchers said.

Alas, over the course of the following decades, the "nonrich" watched their wealth diminish, thanks to the evisceration of workers' pensions and heavier debt loads families took on to make ends meet, the study found. By 2016, wealth held by the bottom 90 percent of U.S. households had fallen by more than a third, to just 22 percent.

Now compare this with the wealth owned by the top 0.1 percent of the population during the period—a group of roughly 160,000 families each controlling over $20 million in assets. In 1913, this topmost group held approximately 23 percent of the nation's riches. But after the stock market crash of 1929, their holdings dissipated, hitting a low of 7 percent in 1979. Starting in the 1980s, though, the wealthy came roaring back. By 2012, they controlled almost 22 percent of wealth.

A second measure, recorded by the Federal Reserve, underscores how much financial ground the American middle class has lost since 1989. Back then, the middle 60 percent of U.S. households by income—a measure often used to define the middle class—held 36 percent of the nation's wealth, more than double the 17 percent controlled by the very wealthy 1 percent of the population. By June 2021, though, the 1 percenters had raced ahead, their wealth surging to 27 percent of the whole versus 26.6 percent of the middle class.

This significant wealth shift was far off in the future, though, as the nation watched the number of corporate takeovers soar during the 1980s. Nevertheless, some market participants, regulators, and lawmakers began to worry about their impact. Between 1985 and 1987, dozens of bills were introduced in Congress to end or rein in the junk bond–backed raiding of corporate America, but none managed to pass. As G. Chris Andersen, head of investment banking at Drexel, would later tell Bloomberg News: "There were 25 pieces of legislation entered in the Congress of the United States of America to try and outlaw the sale of junk bonds. So I took several of my guys and went to Washington for the spring and summer of 1985 and I got 25 pieces of legislation withdrawn."

The Alliance for Capital Access, a lobbying group formed by Milken and his lawyer Craig Cogut, also battled feverishly—and successfully—against heightened regulation. Cogut would soon feature prominently in the Executive Life buyout.

In early 1987, Congress convened hearings to explore the mania. Noted economist John Kenneth Galbraith, for instance, said there was "nothing economically useful" in the merger activity: "It doesn't produce goods or increased efficiency." Henry Kaufman, a respected Wall Street economist, echoed this view, telling Congress that leveraged buyouts posed "significant dangers to the economic and financial well-being of this country."

The warnings went unheeded. KKR supplied data to Congress showing that leveraged buyouts created jobs and innovations, an argument that would become ubiquitous in coming decades. Brian Ayash, a finance professor at the California State Polytechnic University, determined years later that KKR's upbeat data had been phony—the firm had omitted from its calculation the takeovers that had gone bankrupt. (KKR declined to comment on Ayash's conclusion.)

In 1988, the biggest, brashest corporate brawl of all time mesmerized Wall Street and all of America—the $25 billion battle for RJR Nabisco. Once again, KKR was at the helm, with financing from Milken and Drexel. The RJR Nabisco buyout was recounted entertainingly by investigative journalists and coauthors Bryan Burrough and John Helyar in their bestselling book *Barbarians at the Gate: The Fall of RJR Nabisco*. "Everyone in the room knew about leveraged buyouts, often called LBOs," Burrough and Helyar wrote. "Everyone knew LBOs meant deep cuts in research and every other imaginable budget, all sacrificed to pay off debt. Proponents insisted that companies forced to meet steep debt payments grew lean and mean. On one thing they all agreed: The executives who launched LBOs got filthy rich."

Corporate takeovers enriched the dealmakers as well, and often the stockholders of an acquired company, of course. But they were known to harm other stakeholders, not to mention the company itself. Charles Tate, a founder of buyout firm Hicks, Muse, Tate & Furst, noted, with clarity: "When you put too much debt on a company, it becomes dysfunctional, when a company is spending its whole time trying to meet the next interest payment, it can't concentrate on the business."

Tate's comments are borne out by data. During the 1970s, before the debt-fueled takeover mania, default rates on junk bonds were around 2 percent. By 1990, the default rate had risen to almost 9 percent.

At least one state didn't wait for Congress to act on buyouts. Eager to curtail the pernicious effects of mergers within its borders, Indiana passed a law in 1989 requiring board members of companies there to consider the impact a corporate buyout would have on *all stakeholders*, not just its investors. Under the statute, directors would have to weigh a takeover's consequences for "employees, suppliers, and customers of the corporation, and communities in which offices or other facilities of the corporation are located." It was an enlightened view of corporate America, but way ahead of its time. David Ruder, the new chairman of the SEC, ridiculed Indiana's move, calling it an example of a state's "misguided interference" in buyouts. Federal laws must be used to preempt these kinds of benighted state regulations, he said.

Congress had expressed an interest in regulating buyouts and the junk bonds that underpinned them, but it soon lost interest. After the stock market crash of 1987, lawmakers did not want to get tagged with doing anything that might slow the momentum of the equity markets. Takeovers kept stock prices buoyant, at least initially, and that made everybody happy. (Academic research subsequently showed that most takeovers wound up destroying shareholder value, but this information was not yet available to investors.)

Still, critics of the takeovers stood firm in the late eighties, with some former supporters actually changing their views. John Shad, Reagan's SEC chairman and a former true believer in hostile takeovers, had a change of heart. Midway through the decade, he sent his ruminations on takeovers to the White House, noting, "The greater the leverage, the greater the risks to the company, its shareholders, creditors, officers, employees, suppliers, customers and others. The more leveraged takeovers and buyouts today, the more bankruptcies tomorrow." He could not have been more right.

One of those bankruptcies would be that of Drexel itself in February 1990, an example to some of karma. Dennis Levine, a managing director at the firm, had been secretly testifying for years about insider trading among his clients. One of them was Boesky, the evangelist of greed; he was arrested in autumn 1986.

Two years later, the bomb dropped: a 184-page SEC civil complaint outlining an array of securities violations by Drexel; Michael Milken; his younger brother Lowell, a lawyer in Drexel's junk-bond department; and two Drexel traders. Corporate raiders and big Drexel clients Victor and Steven Posner were also named.

The complaint ran through one of the longest lists of misdeeds Wall Street had ever seen—insider trading, fraud, stock manipulation, illegal concealment of ownership, falsification of books and records, violations of margin requirements, and more. The SEC's civil charges were soon followed by criminal charges brought by the hard-charging and publicity-hungry Rudy Giuliani, the U.S. attorney for the Southern District of New York.

Drexel was done.

CHAPTER THREE

"Project Savior"

The Politician Who Gave Leon Black
His Big Start

By 1990, the recession and Drexel Burnham's spectacular collapse had the entire corporate debt market in a depression. But for investors with ready cash and an ability to analyze corporate balance sheets, this spelled opportunity, including for insider Leon Black. With his knowledge of Drexel's former customers, Black targeted First Executive Corp., a giant life insurance holding company based in Los Angeles. One of Drexel's largest buyers of junk bonds, the company's two units, Executive Life of California and Executive Life of New York, were in trouble, Black knew. The insurer held $6 billion in junk bonds that were threatening its very existence. If regulators pulled the plug on it, Black wanted to be the one carrying off the cadaver.

Insurance companies take policyholders' payments and invest them so that when it comes time to pay a claim, they will have the money they need to do so. That meant insurers typically limited their investments to staid and stable assets like high-grade bonds, mortgage securities, and government obligations. In the insurance industry, boring and predictable is good, flashy and aggressive bad. Executive Life had been flashy to the max, pushing it to the precipice in 1990. Led by an aggressive money manager named Fred Carr, the company had been a huge Drexel client, buying the risky bonds it underwrote and banking their high interest rates. Because of those lofty rates of interest, Executive Life could make richer payouts to policyholders than its competitors could.

This strategy had worked through the 1980s. Executive Life's high-paying products had lured throngs of clients—by 1990, over three hundred thousand policyholders were relying on the company, one of the nation's largest insurers, to meet its obligations. And it was rated safe—A+—by the credit ratings agencies. (Like most industries, the insurance business has grown significantly over the past thirty years. The nation's largest insurer, Northwestern Mutual, counted 6.5 million policies outstanding in 2021.)

By the time Drexel failed, junk bonds made up 60 percent of Executive Life's portfolio, compared with 24 percent on average at other large insurers. With Drexel on the skids and the market's impresario, Milken, out of the picture, Carr's high-octane strategy had gotten far too risky. Whispers about whether the insurer would be able to meet its obligations were growing louder, which caused increasing numbers of anxious policyholders to ask to cash in their contracts early.

Executive Life also had a political problem—its intimate association with Drexel. The two entities were joined at the hip, according to Bill Rider, a federal investigator scrutinizing savings and loan failures for the government. Rider worked for the Resolution Trust Corporation, a government entity set up to resolve the failed S&Ls. And in a June 1992 affidavit, he named Carr and his insurer as co-conspirators alongside Milken and Drexel in a scheme to manipulate the corporate bond market: "Executive Life assisted Drexel and Milken by making itself generally and indiscriminately available—both in initial junk bond offerings and in the secondary market—to soak up huge quantities of difficult-to-market junk bonds."

Avid junk bond buyers like Executive Life helped create the illusion that significant demand existed for those securities and that the market for them was real, Rider continued. As a result, other buyers of junk bonds had been harmed by "misrepresentations by Milken, Executive Life and their co-conspirators that a liquid market existed for junk bonds, and that junk bonds were less risky than they in fact were," Rider wrote.

In early 1990, many Executive Life assets—held to meet policyholder claims—were in distress and trading for far less than Carr had paid. Accounting rules required the insurer and its parent to record those value declines, even though the bonds still sat on the books and had not been sold. The insurer was experiencing a liquidity crisis—it needed cash.

Black knew Carr, having encountered the insurance executive often when peddling Drexel deals. But Black knew even more about the securities Carr had bought. Steeped in the underwriting of these bonds, Black understood their financial positions keenly, and recognized which companies would likely recover in an economic rebound and which would not. If he could get his hands on Executive Life's junk bond portfolio, it could be a gold mine.

By 1990, Black had already identified dozens of troubled securities in the Executive Life portfolio that could be restructured and generate massive profits in the years to come. Buying when everyone else was selling—known as vulture investing—was a time-tested route to riches, and Black had approached Carr with offers to buy some of his troubled securities. But Carr wasn't interested in selling his junk bonds to Black; the insurance executive reckoned most of the holdings would work out okay after the economy recovered. Carr was no idiot—he knew better than to sell at the bottom and to a bottom-feeder like Black.

In August 1990, the Black partnership had $400 million in place; although still awaiting Federal Reserve approval, Apollo was on its way. Black's main partners were ex-Drexelites—John Hannan was the firm's former codirector of international finance and Arthur Bilger, its former corporate finance head. Also front and center were Josh Harris, Marc Rowan, and Craig Cogut, a lawyer who had worked closely with Mike Milken and his brother Lowell in Drexel's junk bond unit.

The partners had scoured the horizon for depressed debt of over-leveraged companies, but buying piecemeal was laborious. Acquiring a large portfolio in one fell swoop would be far easier. Black had told his French investors as much, even identifying the Executive Life portfolio as ripe for the picking. Another plus: the insurer's holdings would be simpler to buy than, say, a portfolio held by a failed savings and loan taken over by the government. Those deals involved too much political interference and scrutiny.

Black knew, though, that he had a Drexel problem—his deep association with the criminal enterprise that had underwritten most of First Executive's junk. Some might find it objectionable to allow the same crew who'd saddled the insurer with ruinous securities to profit a few years later buying them on the cheap.

In other words, Black's purchase of the bonds would be a kind of inside job. The trick was to make sure it didn't look like one.

As Apollo worked toward its proposed takeover of Executive Life, the partners gave it a code name. Typical in a Wall Street deal—assigning a code name helped keep the identities of companies involved in a transaction confidential and added an element of intrigue to the process.

The insiders' name for the Executive Life deal? "Project Savior."

Meanwhile Executive Life groaned under the weight of its $6 billion junk bond portfolio. In 1990, the parent company, whose stock traded publicly, recorded an almost $800 million loss for the previous year. Its shares were collapsing.

The financial situation at its largest subsidiary, Executive Life of California, was certainly ominous. Its assets had fallen in value from $13.2 billion a year earlier to $10.2 billion, it told state regulators, while investment income had dropped from $1.2 billion to $977 million. The insurer's enormous bond portfolio, dominated by risky junk debt, was currently valued at $5.5 billion, some $2.2 billion less than what Executive Life had paid for the securities.

Carr, the gunslinging money manager who ran the insurer, knew he was on the brink. So did the California Department of Insurance, whose financial surveillance unit chief, Norris Clark, had been deployed to analyze the company and determine the necessary steps to protect policyholders. Did Carr's operation need a partner to keep it afloat or were things so bad that it required a takeover by the department, a state agency that regulated all insurers doing business in California? In the latter half of 1990, Clark was working to get the answer.

At the same time, the first-ever election of a California state insurance regulator was under way. Previously an appointee of the governor, the state's insurance commissioner would from now on be an elected official. A longtime state representative, John Garamendi, was running for the position. He'd seized on the Executive

Life mess as a campaign issue, identifying the insurer as a reckless company his predecessor commissioner had allowed to run wild.

While Garamendi was politicking, the California insurance department was trying to determine the crucial question for any insurance company's customers: whether Executive Life would be able to meet its policyholder promises. The answer was murky.

Insurance company accounting differs from that of many other corporations, which are governed by what's known as GAAP, or generally accepted accounting principles. A company's results under GAAP are reported to the Securities and Exchange Commission, and First Executive, the parent company of Executive Life, made such reports to the federal regulator.

But the company's insurer subsidiaries were subject to scrutiny from state regulators where they operated, and they had to submit far more detailed financial reports to those states under so-called statutory accounting rules. These rules focus on an insurer's ability to pay claims and whether its assets will enable it to meet its obligations.

As the California insurance department plumbed the Executive Life problem, so did a nationwide group of state insurance overseers convened by the National Association of Insurance Commissioners (NAIC). The insurance industry is not policed by any federal entities and this organization, created to help state insurance commissioners regulate the industry, published its findings on December 27, 1990. Executive Life had problems, the group said, but its California and New York insurers were not in imminent financial danger. They held $2.1 billion in cash and government securities, more than double that of their peers based on invested assets. And, on average, the bonds in the portfolio were scheduled to mature and be fully repaid in just over four years. This was good news because the company's policyholder contracts didn't come due, on average, for almost seven years. Finally, the policyholder stampede to cash in their policies—known colloquially as a run on the bank—had slowed. Fewer customers were rushing to exit.

These facts led the NAIC to conclude that a takeover of Executive Life's unit by the California and New York regulators would not be necessary to protect policyholders. "The companies are capable of meeting all current and projected obligations," the memo stated. "Unnecessary and precipitous regulatory action could have unintended results which would increase the risk of long-term financial distress."

The warning would fall on deaf ears. It didn't take into account that Garamendi, the newly elected insurance commissioner, seemed dead set on proving himself by seizing Executive Life and "rescuing" its policyholders. California's insurance market is the largest in the nation, giving its insurance overseer a position of significant power.

As the new year loomed, California's outgoing insurance commissioner, Roxani Gillespie, prepared to hand over the reins to Garamendi. He had already voiced his views on Executive Life, assailing the company and its investment strategy in stump speeches in the fall of 1990. "First Executive Life hangs onto its life with nearly 60 percent of its assets in junk bonds," he'd told a group in October, adding that he hoped it wouldn't have to file a bankruptcy that would cost hundreds of millions of dollars.

In a few months, newly elected Garamendi would take over Executive Life. His decision to sell the company and its assets to separate entities structured by Leon Black and his group would wind up costing policyholders *billions*.

· · ·

John Garamendi had been a Democratic California state senator for twelve years when he won the post of state insurance commissioner. It was a win that followed two losses for Garamendi—he'd run unsuccessfully for governor in 1982 and for state comptroller in 1986.

A graduate of UC Berkeley with a degree in business, Garamendi was also a graduate of the Harvard Business School. He and his wife Patti, whose father owned a prosperous construction company in northern California, served in the Peace Corps in Ethiopia. Upon their return, they settled down in Walnut Grove, California, in Sacramento County, to raise a family.

Becoming California's insurance commissioner meant Garamendi oversaw all insurers doing business in the state—an enormous duty. He ran as a consumer advocate; a pair of boxing gloves hung in his office in San Francisco, which he said he'd use to keep insurance companies in line.

But during his time in the state legislature, Garamendi had also shown an interest in helping wealthy investors. In 1988, he'd championed legislation that changed a state tax law to benefit the Bass brothers of Texas, a storied investor family that had bought American Savings, a troubled California savings and loan. The federal government had provided financial assistance to the Basses to facilitate the American Savings deal and the family faced state taxes on that aid. Garamendi's legislation made sure the Basses would not have to pay them.

From almost the first day he sat in the insurance commissioner's chair, Garamendi worked the Executive Life case. On January 7, 1991, he brought in a deputy insurance commissioner, Richard Baum, to help assess the insurer's standing. Baum's background was in real estate development, though, not insurance; he'd worked for Amfac, a property development company with land holdings in Hawaii and hotels and other operations in California.

Black, meanwhile, was busy drawing up plans for the Executive Life purchase. In early March 1991, Marc Rowan, a partner of Black's, wrote a letter detailing the potential deal to Jean-François Hénin, president of Altus Finance, the Credit Lyonnais affiliate that was an unnamed investor in Apollo's 1990 partnership agreements. In describing the structure of the deal, Rowan wrote that Altus and Apollo would have "significant control over the selection and pricing of the high yield bonds to be transferred" from Executive Life. Their goal was to strike a so-called private restructuring arrangement with Garamendi, behind the scenes with no competition from other bidders.

From the outset, Garamendi seemed to favor a takeover by the insurance department rather than allowing Executive Life to hobble along and raise capital through asset sales.

In his early months as commissioner, Garamendi took several meetings with First Executive's CEO Carr. At the first of those meetings, in late January 1991, Carr told Garamendi of his plan to create two companies, one to hold the insurer's bad assets and the other to hold the good. This common setup, known as a good bank/bad bank resolution, had successfully resolved many bank failures over the years. Garamendi nixed the idea.

A second meeting with Carr on February 20 seemed more promising. Carr told the commissioner and his team about possible backing from Credit Lyonnais.

Cogut, the Drexel lawyer, attended the February meeting with Garamendi. The commissioner, who had inveighed publicly against Drexel and Milken and the junk bond machine Cogut had been a crucial part of, didn't seem bothered by his presence at the meeting. Documents related to the meeting identified Cogut simply as Credit Lyonnais's "financial advisor," not as a key Drexel player.

The ex-Drexelites who'd helped create the mess at Executive Life had their foot firmly in the door.

On April 4, 1991, in a major blow to First Executive, the New York State insurance department ordered Executive Life of New York to stop writing new policies. It also had to increase by $125 million its reserves, the funds insurance companies set aside to cover future claims by customers.

The Apollo crew took this as a signal that April would be a busy month, angling for their big score as Executive Life wobbled even more under its debt burden. The stars were aligning nicely for everyone, except, that is, the Executive Life policyholders and workers.

Six days later, Carr, the architect of Executive Life's high-octane growth and now its decline, sent a sober letter to Garamendi. "It is my unpleasant duty to inform you," he wrote, "that I believe the Executive Life Insurance Company may be impaired at March 31, 1991," under the state's insurance code. The next day, Garamendi seized the company.

In a press release on April 11, Garamendi said he was taking over Executive Life because its precarious financial position made it a threat to its policyholders. Even as he was working behind the scenes with Cogut, the former Drexel lawyer, Garamendi castigated Drexel publicly and "the ethic of greed that haunts us today." Executive Life's policyholders were imperiled, he said, and the insurance department was riding to save them.

"Many got rich on leveraged buyouts financed by junk bonds," Garamendi said. "We are all familiar with the result—the savings and loan collapse, other major bankruptcies, and the conviction of Michael Milken and other architects of this financial scandal."

Garamendi had one positive piece of news for policyholders—a potential deal was in the works to acquire the insurer. "Over the past several weeks, my staff and I have had extensive discussions with a consortium of European companies and investors who have presented a definitive program to rehabilitate the company and are capable of funding such a program." The group was led by Altus Finance, he said, "a major French financial services company that is connected with Credit Lyonnais."

"We will," Garamendi added, "do everything in our power to revitalize the company and protect the people who placed their faith in it."

Garamendi made no mention of Cogut or Black, two men working Project Savior who had definitely "got rich on leveraged buyouts financed by junk bonds." Thanks to Garamendi's ill-timed takeover, they'd get rich a second time on the same securities that had felled the insurer in the first place. Even as the deal was being struck, junk bonds were rebounding—during the first half of 1991, they outperformed Treasury securities by 19 percent.

CHAPTER FOUR

"I Really Need to Understand What You Do"

One Woman Against the Machine

Four days after Garamendi seized Executive Life, Leon Black convened a meeting of Apollo, his proposed partnership, in midtown Manhattan. The team was "completely busy with the First Executive deal," the meeting minutes said. "There is a good chance of success. In that case, a huge advisory fee will be paid."

A huge advisory fee was only the beginning. Billions would gush from Project Savior, out of the pockets of the insurers' policyholders.

Well before Garamendi commandeered Executive Life, he'd been meeting with Black's group about what to do with the company. From the start, the insurance commissioner had insisted on "a total solution" to the insurer's problems, meaning that the same buyer would have to acquire both the life insurance operations and the massive investment portfolio. This demand of Garamendi's would guarantee the greatest possible profits for Black and his partners, at policyholders' expense.

Black, of course, was not interested in running an insurance company. Like his father, he was a moneyman, not an operational guy. He coveted the bond portfolio—where the real riches were—not some dreary insurer that collected nickels and dimes from the little people and then paid out when they died or retired.

One big problem was Black's financial backing. Altus Finance was a unit of the huge French bank Credit Lyonnais, and California law barred foreign companies from buying an American insurer. Federal law also forbade banks from owning more than 25 percent of a nonbanking business. Because the Federal Reserve regulated a U.S. unit of Credit Lyonnais, the board had to determine that the takeover of the insurer's bonds by Altus and Apollo didn't run afoul of those rules.

Later, it would emerge that Credit Lyonnais had hidden arrangements that let it acquire the restructured Executive Life insurance company illegally. Justice Department prosecutors would contend that concealing the French bank's majority stake had tainted the Executive Life takeover with fraud.

In the early months of 1991, as Garamendi sought his total solution to Executive Life's woes, Black met numerous times with Jean-François Hénin, the Frenchman who headed Altus Finance, about Executive Life.

Still, there were concerns. The Federal Reserve was dragging its feet in approving the Apollo partnership set up roughly a year earlier. By the time Garamendi took over the insurer in mid-April 1991, that approval had still not come. The sticking point seemed to be French involvement in the deal, but the result was a partnership in limbo.

Minutes recorded at Black's partnership meeting on April 15, 1991, show talk of the Fed holdup. Lawyers representing the part-

THESE ARE THE PLUNDERERS

nership were doing what they could to get it approved and had visited William Taylor, the Fed's top banking regulator, to discuss the matter. Working the case for Apollo was none other than H. Rodgin Cohen, "Mr. Fed," according to Black. The foremost U.S. lawyer to financial institutions, Cohen was a magician when it came time to make regulatory problems disappear. His demeanor and size—Cohen was a gnome-like figure—belied his power. Years later, when the U.S. financial system was imperiled by the mortgage meltdown, Cohen would advocate on behalf of the big banks that had created the crisis, successfully shielding them from significant federal liability.

"So far he has not heard anything prohibiting the setup of our operation," the minutes noted, referring to Cohen. But as the talks dragged on, Black suggested adding another year to the contract with the French, to be safe.

Cohen was certainly the man to handle the Fed for Black. But even Mr. Fed couldn't solve a bigger problem Black and his cohort faced: whispers were circulating that somehow Mike Milken might be involved in the Executive Life takeover, in the shadows, of course. This was disastrous—any involvement by Milken, an admitted felon, would poison the deal. Scotching the Milken rumor was imperative if Black's partnership was to cart off the insurer's treasure.

The Milken chatter had the ring of truth for several reasons. For one, a behind-the-scenes involvement by Milken would be precisely his MO. At Drexel, he'd excelled at using others to achieve desired outcomes, like convincing Fred Carr and an array of savings and loan executives to buy billions in junk bonds to make the market seem substantive and real, as investigator Rider had noted.

"Drexel worked through proxies," noted Bill Black, the government's top investigator in the savings and loan debacle and author of *The Best Way to Rob a Bank Is to Own One*. "This was a network processing scam in which the whole thing was to have people who didn't appear to be involved, involved."

Another reason the Milken rumors seemed believable was because of Leon Black's involvement in the buyout. He was a close Milken ally and a codefendant in many Drexel lawsuits. Aware that his association with Milken would be a problem, Black had been careful not to attend meetings with Garamendi in the early months of 1991.

As it turns out, Black needn't have worried. The insurance department's due diligence on the dealmaker was a joke. It consisted of a database search on LexisNexis, which turned up a cache of newspaper articles on Black, a Garamendi deputy told an investigator later.

Did those articles reach Garamendi? the deputy was asked. "I don't know," he replied. "There was no reason not to proceed with the Altus transaction simply because Leon Black was the head of the advisors that they had," the deputy said.

Black had dispatched Cogut as his proxy to work with Garamendi so as not to set off alarm bells with the commissioner and bring unwanted attention to the buyers' deep Drexel ties. But Cogut had his own vast and publicly disclosed ties to Drexel and Milken and had been cited in news coverage of the scandal. So if Garamendi ordered any due diligence on Cogut's ties to Drexel, it too raised no alarms.

In addition to being Lowell and Mike Milken's lawyer, Cogut had set up the Alliance for Capital Access, the Milken-backed lobbying group created to thwart congressional actions that might harm the junk bond market. In 1988, Cogut testified before Congress extoling the virtues of junk bonds on behalf of the alliance.

"There is no evidence that the use of high yield bonds in takeovers and LBOs [leveraged buyouts] has any harmful effect on the economy," he'd said. "In fact, there is evidence that high yield bonds have financed hundreds of productive acquisitions, and saved and created jobs over the years."

Cogut wasn't telling the whole story, of course. That year, the United Savings Association of Texas, a savings and loan, failed at a cost to taxpayers of $1.6 billion, just one of many S&L collapses. United Savings had been a big purchaser of Drexel's junk bonds and held $1.8 billion worth when it failed. The institution was run by a favored Drexel client, Charles Hurwitz.

But one of Cogut's most significant jobs with the Milkens and Drexel involved setting up the secret and lucrative partnerships that benefited the firm's executives and favored clients. Cogut had personally participated in some of these partnerships, which were unearthed by government investigators in their criminal case against Drexel. News stories about the behind-the-scenes partnerships began appearing in 1990. Like Black, Cogut was not prosecuted for his Drexel activities. (Later he would testify that key information about the illegal nature of the partnerships had been withheld from him by Lowell Milken.)

As the investigators found, lucky participants in the partnerships would receive warrants, a stock-like security that had been issued alongside the junk bonds by Drexel's corporate clients. The warrants were supposed to be attached to the bonds when they were sold to mutual funds, insurance companies, and other buyers, giving them an extra shot at a profit. If the companies that issued the debt did well, the warrants would rise in value; they were an inducement to buy the riskier bonds, known on Wall Street as a sweetener.

But instead of going to the purchasers of the junk bonds, many of the warrants went instead to Drexel executives, including

Milken and Cogut. Black was a general partner of several of these partnerships, according to a government lawsuit. The transfer of the warrants proved to be extremely valuable, worth hundreds of millions of dollars, investigators would later conclude. Because the warrants let their holders buy common stock in the company that issued them, the securities gave those investors a bigger stake and even greater control if the issuing company had to go through a restructuring.

For example, Milken and his brother Lowell together realized a gain of about $172 million from just one of the partnerships, the government said. Executive Life held many of the bonds issued with warrants. So to the degree that Milken or Black held warrants in those particular companies, they also held undisclosed interests in those companies' futures. And as Black's partnership took over control of those companies after acquiring the Executive Life portfolio, that meant any warrant holders would have had an interest in the outcome of the Executive Life buyout.

(We asked a Milken spokesman in an email if his boss was an early investor in Leon Black's partnership or held warrants in companies whose debt was owned by Executive Life. He did not respond.)

In any case, with gossip circulating of a possible Milken involvement in the Executive Life deal, Cogut got busy. On April 16, 1991, from Apollo's Los Angeles headquarters, he sent an urgent fax to Hénin at Altus Capital in France. "In light of certain bizarre rumors that are floating around," the cover sheet stated, "a letter to the Commissioner [Garamendi] along the lines of the attached is in order. We will call you to discuss."

Behind the cover sheet were two pages ghostwritten by Black's team for Hénin to sign and send to Garamendi. It was not the first letter the deal-hungry ex-Drexelites had ginned up for the French-man to send to the insurance commissioner.

"I understand your concerns about the rumors which we both have heard in the financial community that Michael Milken has some type of undisclosed role or interest in Altus Finance, Credit Lyonnais, or our proposed transaction," the letter began. "These rumors are totally without merit and are ludicrous."

They "may be due to the fact that principals of one of our financial advisors, Lion Advisors, LP, were at one time associated with Drexel Burnham Lambert Inc.," the letter's authors conceded. Without naming Black, the letter contended that there was nothing unusual in this—Drexel refugees had landed at many Wall Street firms following the firm's failure. (This was not exactly an apples-to-apples comparison; other firms might have had ex-Drexelites here and there, but the partnership that would become Apollo was Drexel through and through.)

Cutting to the chase, the correspondence continued: "I can further inform you that it is my understanding that not only is there no business relationship between these people and Mr. Milken, but the personal relationship between Mr. Milken and these people is at best distant, and in many cases strained or even acrimonious." Perhaps, the ex-Drexel folks wrote ominously, a conspiracy was involved. "I cannot say what are the motives of the people who spread such false rumors. I can surmise, however, that they are spread by those who would wish to see the expeditious transaction that you have proposed stopped," the fax stated.

Happily for the Apollo crew, the Cogut letter seemed to have the desired effect. Rumors of a Milken involvement in the Executive Life takeover began fading away.

Soon, the chatter was overtaken by more dire news in the case. A day after the fax went out, the New York insurance regulator took control of Executive Life's unit there. Weeks later, First Executive, the insurers' corporate parent, filed for bankruptcy.

Maureen Marr was worried. It looked to her as if the Executive Life debacle was going to drive a lot of trusting policyholders into a ditch.

Marr, forty, wasn't a lawyer, but she knew her way around a financial failure. An activist who'd worked as a media consultant for several California ballot initiatives and director on two California propositions—one to raise a cigarette tax and another on campaign finance reform—Marr could get to the heart of an issue and frame it cogently. She was also empathetic, good at listening to people's problems and connecting them with reporters to publicize them.

A year or so earlier, she'd organized and advocated for investors harmed in a massive savings and loan failure in Arizona. Lincoln Savings and Loan, the forty-second-largest thrift in America, had collapsed in 1989, a fraud that also involved Drexel and junk bonds. It was starting to look like the situation at Executive Life might be a repeat, Marr thought. Lincoln had been overseen by Charles Keating, a high-flying financier who'd taken over the previously conservative financial institution in 1984 with help from Drexel and Milken. After Drexel sold Lincoln $600 million in risky junk bonds, the institution collapsed; the federal government seized Lincoln, absorbing almost $3 billion in losses. Like Milken, Keating went to prison for fraud.

In the Lincoln mess, Marr had organized a support group for the company's bondholders, working with their lawyers and publishing a newsletter to keep investors up on case developments.

She'd also arranged for media interviews with bondholders who'd lost money with Lincoln, getting the word out about their plights.

Marr had finished working the Lincoln failure when she started reading about Executive Life and its imperiled policyholders. The insurer was headquartered in Los Angeles, right in her backyard. Like Lincoln, it was a big investor in Drexel-peddled junk.

When an insurance company fails, regulators are supposed to make policyholders the top priority in a rescue. Unlike large bank failures, whose bailouts involve federal authorities, insurance companies are overseen by state regulators who step in, as Garamendi had, when things go bad. State resources are much more constrained than federal monies are when dealing with these types of problems, and state insurance commissioners have less experience handling failures than federal regulators.

After reading about the debacle and connecting with a policyholder, Marr reached out to Garamendi's press unit and asked if the commissioner would attend a meeting with Executive Life customers. They needed detailed information about the conservatorship process, she reasoned.

A few days after the company was seized, the first of these events took place at the insurer's Los Angeles headquarters. Garamendi couldn't make it (his office was in San Francisco), but Marr spoke, offering a phone number policyholders could use for information updates.

The response was epic. "I burned out two answering machines in short order as hundreds of policyholders left their addresses to be on a mailing list," Marr told us. "I hadn't realized what a big deal the conservation of an insurance company was."

So began the Action Network of Victims of Executive Life (ANVEL). Within a month, Marr had contacted two thousand policyholders across the country; the group ultimately grew to twice that number.

About a month later, another meeting for policyholders took place downtown at the Los Angeles County Board of Supervisors Hall. Hundreds attended; one was Vince Watson, who'd driven in from Arizona to make sure his daughter Katie would continue to receive the money necessary for her care.

Garamendi attended the meeting, at which two policyholders spoke. When the commissioner got up to address the crowd, Marr briefly introduced him. As she commended the Executive Life policyholders for banding together to make sure they'd receive fair treatment, Garamendi bristled, Marr noticed. That momentary flash of anger was her first inkling that the commissioner might not be supportive of the group.

"Anxious policyholders lined up to ask him questions," Marr recalled years later, a scene captured by a *Los Angeles Times* photographer and published on the paper's front page the next day. One asked Garamendi how best to choose a safe insurance company. "He replied, 'Look at the ratings,'" Marr recalled. The audience groaned—Executive Life's product ratings had been A+ until the end.

It was not an auspicious beginning.

On the back of his heels before the crowd, Garamendi once again tied the insurer to Milken's "greed is good" ethos, describing its investment portfolio as containing the "worst of the worst" junk bonds. Then he said he was talking with a group interested in saving the insurance company and its policyholders. "He didn't mention Leon Black," Marr said, a name she would only learn later.

After seeing Garamendi's first presentation to policyholders, Marr remembered feeling uneasy that he hadn't been better prepared. "I didn't know Commissioner Garamendi, but I knew it was imperative that he be extremely competent in managing what he had wrought," Marr told us.

In touch with thousands of Executive Life policyholders, Marr soon learned about the vast array of policies the company had sold across the country and how much it had promised to pay on them. She became policyholders' advocate and spokesperson, as well as their eyes and ears throughout what would be a protracted courtroom conservation process. She attended every hearing, often accompanied by a policyholder, and her regular ANVEL newsletter kept policyholders apprised on the case. Marr also connected frantic customers with reporters.

"Those stories were always about their shock that this could happen to them," Marr said of the policyholders. "They were conservative investors in seemingly conservative investments who believed they had planned responsibly for themselves and their families' futures."

Marr worked pro bono out of a borrowed apartment; occasionally a policyholder would send her a small check to cover some of her expenses. She welcomed the assignment—it was a way to ensure the Executive Life policyholders had a voice throughout the bailout process. Her work also served as a distraction from a very real personal threat she was under. Her ex-husband, an abusive and controlling man who'd once held a gun to her head during an argument, was continuing to menace her, even after their divorce. The Executive Life advocacy effort took her mind off him.

Still, the activist knew she couldn't do much if Garamendi wasn't on her side, also fighting hard for policyholders. After all, the commissioner's office was the only entity that could bring lawsuits on their behalf. Policyholders were barred from bringing their own private legal actions against Executive Life, which forced them to rely on Garamendi for restitution. That prohibition would cost them mightily, it turned out.

From her earliest interactions with Garamendi, Marr had doubts about him. He seemed to have a temper and to resent her role leading the policyholders.

In mid-July, another meeting for policyholders took place in San Francisco. The room teemed with people. PBS's *MacNeil/Lehrer NewsHour* was there recording.

"When Commissioner Garamendi arrived, I spoke to him personally for the first time," Marr said. After his opening remarks, Garamendi took questions. He soon became tense and cut the session short in anger, Marr remembered.

"I don't remember what specifically disturbed him about the questions," she said. "I do know that I've always regretted that I didn't call him out at the time and at least tell him, in front of the policyholders, that we would like him to respond to all who came here to put their concerns and questions to him."

Maureen Marr was sitting alone in a conference room at the elegant offices of a Los Angeles law firm. Garamendi had told the Apollo people they needed to work with Marr, to secure her support and that of her policyholder group for the transaction they'd planned. So she'd been summoned to the law firm's offices in the late fall of 1991 for an audience with Apollo.

Marr had asked Wallace Albertson, a local policyholder, to accompany her. She wanted to convey to the Apollo folks that real human beings were being hurt by the failure and should be the first consideration in any deal. But Albertson had bailed at the last minute, so Marr waited in the glassed-in room by herself, certain she was being watched.

Finally, four men strode in, led by Craig Cogut, the Milken lawyer. Leon Black was not among the four.

"They wanted to know who I was," Marr recalled. "They wanted to know how I had dealt with Charlie Keating and Lincoln Savings. They were kind of joking around. It was really offensive."

Keating, whom Drexel had financed, was in the news at the time because he was on trial for securities fraud in Los Angeles, accused of selling his company's risky junk bonds to investors and claiming that they were federally insured. The state trial had become a spectacle with many elderly bondholders who had lost money in the scheme in attendance. They would yell at Keating as he came and went each day; on one occasion, an older woman got close enough to pummel him with her fists. A photo of this incident ran on the front page of newspapers around the nation. Keating was sentenced to ten years in jail and wound up serving just over four.

Cogut and the Apollo team wanted to ensure that the Executive Life hearings wouldn't turn into a circus like Keating's. Marr and her angry policyholders could not be allowed to mess up their lucrative deal.

Cogut was in charge and meant to size her up, Marr could tell. "What is it that you do?" he asked her. "I really need to understand what you do." But he didn't have a lot of time now, he explained.

As the meeting drew to a close, Marr learned that Apollo had directed an outside lawyer to work with her—John F. Hartigan, a partner with the big New York law firm Morgan, Lewis & Bockius. Hartigan laughingly told Marr he'd been asked to manage or babysit her.

Marr didn't know it at the time, but Hartigan had intriguing connections to Black. The lawyer had spent eight and a half years in the enforcement division of the Securities and Exchange Commission, starting there as a staff attorney in January 1975. He was a member of the SEC's enforcement staff when it took up the Eli Black bribery scandal.

Rising to become assistant director of enforcement at the SEC in May 1981, Hartigan had departed at the end of 1984, a period that coincides with the agency's scrutiny of Drexel Burnham Lambert. In a classic revolving door move, Drexel tapped Hartigan for help in 1989 when it was in trouble with the SEC and federal prosecutors. Hartigan was asked to conduct a deep review of Drexel's compliance procedures, such as they were, and to devise a new compliance manual for the firm. Alas, Drexel filed for bankruptcy before Hartigan could finish the job.

In the meeting with Marr, Hartigan offered to help ANVEL. Escorting her to the elevator, he made a passing reference that baffled Marr. He said something about warrants—those inducements or sweeteners that were supposed to have gone to junk bond buyers in every Drexel deal. The Executive Life portfolio should have contained a bunch of warrants, Hartigan told Marr, because the insurer was such a huge junk bond buyer. But they were nowhere to be found.

Back then, Marr didn't know what a warrant was. She would later learn that some missing Executive Life warrants had wound up with Apollo.

CHAPTER FIVE

"The Fire Sale Approach"

How One of the Greatest Giveaways
Came About

As the spring of 1991 moved into summer, the junk bond market gave signs of rebounding. True, many of the Executive Life bonds continued to struggle, but others were on the rise. Surely this recovery would benefit policyholders in the still-unfolding bailout of the company.

Garamendi outlined this goal in a memo detailing the objectives of the Executive Life takeover, saying the deal would be structured so that policyholders would be "treated equitably in the event ELIC assets turn out to be more valuable than currently anticipated."

It was another promise Garamendi would not fulfill.

In fact, *every penny* of improvement the insurer's bonds generated, post-takeover, went into the pockets of the lucky buyer— Black and his partners. Policyholders got none of those gains.

Naturally, in a deal of Executive Life's magnitude and complexity, the valuation of its many assets would be key to securing the best outcome for policyholders. The insurer held more than seven hundred different corporate bonds, for example, as well as direct investments in the Checker Cab company, thousands of apartments in New York City, a Malibu ranch, and other real estate.

The bonds were by far the insurer's biggest asset group, however, and early on, Garamendi said his office had commissioned "an immediate and thorough evaluation of the current market value of the company's junk bond investment portfolio."

Any seller who's interested in getting the best possible price for what he or she is peddling must first know that item's value. Even first-timers on eBay know this is Rule Number One.

But an asset's market value is not necessarily the same as its inherent value, especially when the market for an asset is in disarray as junk bonds were in early 1991. And, distressingly, Garamendi's insurance department never performed one of the most basic steps in a sale process—independently assessing the bonds' worth over the longer haul, by analyzing the cash flows the companies would be likely to generate and the valuations investors would typically pay for those cash flows once the market upheaval ended. Instead, Garamendi's team seemed to believe that putting the entire portfolio up for auction would produce the best price for policyholders, even though they had not assessed its total value or worth. It was not clear how the commissioner arrived at this wrongheaded notion.

"We did not price the portfolio when it was sold," said George Bull, one of Garamendi's lieutenants. "We held an auction for the portfolio. So we did not put prices on the portfolio, on every item, and say this is the value of this, you will pay this."

Neither did Garamendi conduct a restructuring analysis to determine which of the troubled bonds in the portfolio would likely generate recoveries above current market prices if the companies reorganized and eliminated some of their debt. The potential for restructurings represented an upside to any buyers of the bonds, as Black well knew.

Years later, Norris Clark, the insurance department's financial surveillance chief, would tell an investigator how little the regulators had understood about Executive Life's bond holdings. "We just didn't know how good they were," Clark said. "See, the problem was, everybody thought they were debt. Man, they were equity." Had the insurance department recognized the equity value in the bonds, Clark continued, the better route would have been to rehabiliate Executive Life and let policyholders capitalize on the subsequent rise in asset values.

Everybody in the insurance department may have thought the insurer's junk bonds were debt. But the eager Apollo partners knew otherwise. And a 1994 cover article about the deal in *Forbes* magazine summed up the knowledge gap between Leon Black and John Garamendi succinctly: "Smart Buyer, Dumb Seller" the headline blared. Over a decade later, the story still rankled Garamendi, according to his testimony in a 2005 deposition on the Executive Life matter.

Another regulatory blunder, costing some policyholders almost $3 billion, was Garamendi's decision to set the valuation date of the bond portfolio on the day he seized the insurer—April 11, 1991. Instead, as two academics later concluded, the commissioner should have set the valuation date when the deal was finalized in mid-1992 and the value of the assets to benefit policyholders was certain. This error essentially shifted $2.6 billion in profits to the new insurance company that should have gone to policyholders. In an article in 1999, Howell E. Jackson, a Harvard Law School professor, and Edward L. Symons, Jr., a professor at the University of Pittsburgh School of Law, analyzed Garamendi's valuation date decision. They argued that the commissioner had not only erred in pinpointing April 11 as the day, but had possibly violated California's insurance code as well. The valuation date should have been set on July 31, 1992, the academics argued, when the Executive Life rehabilitation plan was finally approved by the judge overseeing the matter. If an insurer's assets increase in value before it is liquidated, "valuing the estate as of the conservation date will not yield the total net value of the estate available for distribution to claimants," the professors wrote.

Recall that Garamendi had promised any recovery in the junk bond market would go to policyholders. And from their standpoint, setting the later valuation date made total sense. The seizure date of April 11 was near the nadir in junk bond prices, and by July of the following year, many of the insurer's holdings had rebounded. Indeed, from April 1991 to July 1992, the professors estimated, Executive Life's assets increased in value by $2.6 billion. Had Garamendi set the valuation date in July 1992, policyholders would have been the ones to record those gains, not the new insurer created by Wall Street sharpies.

Also dubious, the professors opined, was Garamendi's claim that he had discretion to choose the April date because he was in charge of rehabilitating Executive Life. "We conclude that the valuation date selected cannot be supported," Jackson and Symons wrote.

When he seized the insurer, Garamendi had, of course, made much of the toxic waste in the Executive Life portfolio. It helped justify the takeover, after all.

But an in-depth analysis of the portfolio produced a few months later showed about half of Executive Life's holdings were doing fine. Once again, this crucial fact was never disclosed to policyholders.

In November 1991, Salomon Brothers, then the premier bond

house on Wall Street, generated a security-by-security analysis of Executive Life's roughly $8 billion investment portfolio. Among its findings: 57 percent of the insurer's bonds were performing on their obligations and paying bondholder interest. Roughly 55 percent of the bonds were in healthy industries, it said, while 45 percent were in fourteen depressed sectors.

Around $3.8 billion of the insurer's holdings—almost half its investment portfolio—carried minimal risks, Salomon determined. The companies that had issued these securities were money-good, in Wall Street parlance, and would not need to be restructured. They were healthy.

The other $4.2 billion were troubled, Salomon Brothers concluded. But echoing the December 1990 assessment by the National Association of Insurance Commissioners, the firm noted that 80 percent of Executive Life's bonds would not mature until between 1996 and 2000. That meant the companies backing the debt had between five and ten years to bolster their shaky financial positions before they had to repay bondholders in full.

A conservative estimate for the value of the entire portfolio, Salomon concluded, was $5.2 to $5.5 billion.

The Salomon report suggested that all was not bleak at Executive Life. But it was never shared with policyholders. The report also indicated something even more significant that Garamendi either declined to see or did not understand: The makeup of the Executive Life portfolio was extremely varied, with plenty of good bonds and bad. Therefore, selling it to one entity, in the "total solution" Garamendi was insisting on, would not be the best way to generate top dollar in a sale of this diverse group of assets.

A better idea would be to separate the bonds into tranches based on their quality and risk level—a move that would likely attract more bidders. And the more bidders competing for an asset, the higher the overall deal price would likely be for policyholders.

If maximizing the proceeds to policyholders was the goal, insisting on one buyer for the whole shebang was the wrong way to achieve it. But that was the deal Garamendi demanded from the start. As one person involved in analyzing the Executive Life portfolio told us decades later: "The way to assure *minimizing* proceeds is to throw the whole thing in the public market, asking participants to bid all or none."

Garamendi explained his approach by saying he didn't want a buyer to be able to cherry-pick the best bonds out of the portfolio and leave the toxic waste behind. But what he did not seem to realize was that the genuinely sketchy bonds would have been of interest to a certain type of distressed buyer at the right price.

By insisting on selling the bond portfolio to one party and in setting the portfolio's valuation on April 11, 1991, Garamendi ensured that the Black group got one of the greatest deals of the twentieth century.

To be sure, Garamendi had no experience running an investment portfolio and could not be expected to know the intricacies of the junk bond market. But he had hired multiple Wall Street advisors to provide sophisticated guidance to his office on how to get the best deal for policyholders. He just wasn't interested in what they had to say, one of them told us.

"It became pretty obvious within weeks that Altus had the inside track and it was likely a deal had already been done," said a person who worked on the Executive Life portfolio during the summer of 1991. The fact that Cogut and other Drexelites were at the Executive Life offices daily, closely monitoring the activities, supported this thesis. "This was a setup—whatever we recommended would carry very little weight and the portfolio would get sold to Altus even if we mildly disagreed with it," the person added.

Another sign that attracting more bidders did not seem to be a priority for Garamendi came in May, when the insurance department asked other companies to submit bids for Executive Life. But the wording of Garamendi's request was telling: first, the insurance department highlighted that it had had extensive talks with Altus Finance. Then it said if those talks did not progress, Garamendi would consider other bidders.

Assigning this priority status to Altus seemed a strange way to encourage other financial entities to bid more for the company. But it was in keeping with the approach Garamendi had taken from day one on the deal: the Black group held a favored position with the insurance department for reasons unknown and was likely to win the deal.

In any case, the advantage given to Black's partners by Garamendi led to a terrible outcome for Executive Life's policyholders. He'd allow assets needed to fulfill Executive Life's promises to be sold off for far less than they were really worth. What's more, whether the insurer needed to be taken over at all was questioned in a 1994 article published in the *Journal of Financial Economics*, which concluded that, thanks to the rebounding junk bond market, Executive Life would have been solvent again within a year of its takeover.

Garamendi had sold at the bottom of the market. That was pretty much exactly where the ex-Drexelites had hoped to buy, propelling Apollo to its start.

By July 1991, the Fed had still not blessed the Black partnership arrangement. This delay was worrisome enough, but a new hitch had arisen—the Federal Deposit Insurance Corporation, or FDIC. It was one of the government entities suing Milken, Black, and others for their roles in destabilizing the nation's banks by selling them piles of junk bonds.

"FDIC must be a major brake in our venture approval process," fretted Black, according to minutes of a partnership meeting in New York.

The minutes do not specify what might concern the FDIC or even what basis Black had for his surmise. But this much *is* known: the FDIC was suing Black in the big Milken case involving fifty-five failed S&Ls. And, not surprisingly, the Executive Life junk bond portfolio held stakes in three of the very S&Ls central to the suit: $42.3 million in Crossland Savings, $14.4 million in Great American First Savings, and $1.3 million worth of Guardian S&L.

Black's deal to buy failed S&L bonds out of the Executive Life portfolio even as he was being sued for his role in those failures was yet another red flag in a transaction rife with them. And for these $58 million of bonds, Black's group would pay just $65,000.

Despite a possible FDIC snag, the Executive Life proposal was breezing forward with the California insurance commissioner. Threats to the deal from competing buyers were not a problem. "A handshake should occur this week; the announcement will be made at the end of the month," the minutes said.

That handshake occurred in August, and in classic Wall Street style, the team celebrated the Executive Life takeover by Altus and Apollo at a so-called deal dinner on August 6, 1991. The festivities took place at Chasen's, then a Hollywood haunt favored by movie stars, politicians, and other luminaries. Hénin and Cogut were there for Altus (once again, Black was nowhere to be seen); Garamendi signed a menu commemorating the transaction.

"Jean-Francois, may our deal be good for all involved," the commissioner wrote.

The next day, Garamendi's office announced the transaction with the French. The headline figure everyone was waiting for: Executive Life's policyholders would get at least 81 cents on the dollar for their policies. Garamendi characterized it as a great payout, considering the dire condition Executive Life had been in. Policyholders should be pleased, he said.

It was the first of many grandiose and erroneous claims Garamendi would make about policyholder recoveries in the case.

Under the terms of the deal, Executive Life's assets would be transferred to three entities. First was a company created by Altus to serve existing policyholders and continue its insurance operations. It would be called Aurora National Life Assurance Company, named for the Roman goddess of the dawn, and Altus would invest $300 million in it.

A second entity would hold the massive junk bond portfolio and a third would be a trust set up to liquidate roughly $700 million in real estate and other long-term assets owned by Executive Life. The proceeds from these sales were to be distributed to policyholders.

A little-known fact about the Altus/Apollo bid is that it contained a clause stating that the buyers could walk away from the deal if the overall liquidation value of the bonds exceeded an amount equaling 55 cents for every dollar of face value. This was a steep discount—others involved in the case had testified that the bond portfolio's value should have been as high as 75 cents on the dollar. Nevertheless, miraculously and magically, 55 cents on the dollar was where the final liquidation value came in.

A September 26, 1991, memo written by Karl Rubinstein, the

lawyer for the insurance department, outlined how that liquidation value would be determined. Those in charge of the assessment "will assume the bonds must all be liquidated within a 6-month period," he wrote. It was a ridiculously short period for the sale of more than seven hundred different issues. But there was more. "Once they provide me with their estimate of fair market value based upon this 'fire sale' approach," the memo continued, the department could set a price.

Fire sale approach. Even a dullard knows a fire sale is precisely the wrong way to get the highest price for something you want to sell. And yet a fire sale was the method Garamendi's team ordered.

It makes you wonder: Whose side were these guys on?

As the junk bond market recovered, some in the financial world began to criticize Garamendi's Executive Life deal as a giveaway. And finally, Apollo got a little competition.

In September, the National Organization of Life and Health Insurance Guaranty Associations, known as NOLHGA, announced its own proposal to take over the insurer. This is a group that represents the guaranty funds set up in every state to ensure policyholders are protected and paid in an insurance company failure. Recall that the insurance industry has only state regulators, not a federal overseer.

NOLHGA was keenly interested in the outcome of the takeover because state guaranty funds are required to make up policyholders' losses when insurers collapse. And in a flop as enormous as the Executive Life case, some state funds could face big policyholder payouts to make up the difference between what customers received in the liquidation and what they were owed under their contracts. Every state has different rules and limits governing what its guaranty fund will pay policyholders in a failure. Making policyholders whole in a failure was by no means assured.

In announcing its deal for Executive Life, NOLHGA said policyholders' costs would be far less than those to be levied in the Altus arrangement. This made it an attractive option.

Even more compelling competition for Apollo and Altus emerged the following month, when Garamendi received a letter from Eli Broad, a respected insurance executive in Los Angeles who ran a company called Sun Life America. Broad, who knew his way around the financial markets, criticized the Altus deal, suggesting that Garamendi reopen the bids for Executive Life to secure a better deal for policyholders.

"Since May, there has been the greatest bond market rally in recent history, dramatically increasing both the demand for and value of the junk bond portfolio," Broad wrote of the Executive Life holdings. Advising Garamendi that this rebound gave him more options than he had had earlier in the year, Broad went on to say that he'd discussed the portfolio with various Wall Street firms and all had concluded that the bonds could be sold for 10 percent more than Altus had agreed to pay. Garamendi should allow three or four proposals "to be aired in public and in considerable depth."

Finally, Broad condemned the Altus deal, alluding to the ex-Drexelites' involvement in it. The bid "embodies the type of 1980s gamesmanship that caused Executive Life to default on its obligations in the first place," he wrote.

What impact this letter had on Garamendi is unclear. But a day later, on October 24, 1991, Garamendi shocked the Apollo crew by announcing that Executive Life would now be sold to the group of state guaranty funds, NOLHGA. Its bid offered the highest return to policyholders, Garamendi said—a 90 percent recovery versus Altus's 81 percent.

But before the deal could be finalized, NOLHGA had to meet nine conditions set by Garamendi to prove it had the financial means to implement the bid.

Before announcing this shift, Garamendi phoned Marr to let her know. "Do the French know that you've chosen NOLHGA?" she recalled asking him. "No," he chuckled, "but they soon will."

Seconds after Marr hung up, another call came through. It was Hartigan, the Apollo lawyer. Angrily, he told Marr he'd heard Garamendi was choosing NOLHGA and wanted confirmation. "It was so obvious he had listened in on Garamendi's short call," Marr said years later. "My phone had to be bugged."

Distraught by the switch, Cogut and the Apollo group sprang into action, upping their promised recovery to match the 90 percent offered by NOLHGA. Then Apollo began negotiating directly with NOLHGA; a November 9 memo written by a group monitoring the deal shows the Apollo group promised NOLHGA an interest in the new insurer, Aurora, and future profits springing from it. In addition, the Aurora rehabilitation plan gave NOLHGA recoveries from the real estate trust that had been set up to liquidate assets and deliver the proceeds to policyholders. The ultimate rehabilitation plan also agreed to pay NOLHGA's expenses related to the Executive Life deal.

To Marr, these giveaways seemed designed to neutralize NOLHGA as a competitive bidder or as an entity that might carp about the Aurora deal later. In any case, the money that went to NOLHGA could have gone into policyholders' pockets instead. It was yet another hit they took.

Happily for Black and his partners, though, Garamendi soon flip-flopped again, announcing that he was supporting the Altus/Apollo bid after all. Black was back on track.

"I am happy to announce we have avoided debilitating losses," Garamendi said, adding that "most policyholders will get back 100 percent of their funds."

Both were mischaracterizations. But policyholders wouldn't find that out until years later, by which time Garamendi would have moved on to even more powerful positions. Nevertheless, the commissioner crowed to the *Los Angeles Times* that policyholders "should be elated."

The Apollo partners were the elated ones. Under the terms of the sale, Altus would ultimately receive almost $6 billion worth of bonds for around $3 billion.

Under the Apollo/Altus deal, partnership documents show, the juicy Executive Life bond portfolio would be divvied up into three different groups based on quality—A, B, and C.

The "A" bonds—for which the partnership paid $818 million—were lower quality, "larger positions, strategic positions and restructuring opportunities which have the potential for producing satisfactory investment returns over time," an Apollo memo stated.

The "B" bonds—some $1.67 billion—were higher quality and would be held to maturity because they were money-good. These would all stay with the French partners.

Finally, there were the "C" bonds, the memo noted, stakes with "little or no strategic potential." For this pool the group paid $420 million.

In the transaction, Apollo would receive fat management fees for overseeing the entire portfolio. But it also took for itself roughly half the "A" bonds, paying $400 million, and another $100 million, or a quarter, of the "C" bonds.

An intriguing fact that went unnoted at the time: among the "A" bonds that Apollo received were three issued by Western Union, the Bennett LeBow company that was an Apollo investor. Neither was it publicized that the "A" bonds included stakes in three companies Black's partnership already held interests in: CNC Holding Corp., Farley Inc., and Memorex Telex Corp. Receiving additional bonds from the Executive Life deal gave the partnership added leverage to control those companies' futures.

As for the "C" bonds, the Apollo memo's characterization of them as holding little or no strategic potential was false in some cases. "C" bonds included debt issued by Gillett Holdings, for example, a company that owned the swanky Vail ski resort and whose restructuring would pay off handsomely for Apollo a decade later. The cluster also contained debt issued by Telemundo Group, the Spanish-language television station company owned today by Comcast, reaching viewers in 90 percent of U.S. Hispanic households. Revco Drug Stores was another; it sold out to CVS five years later for $2.8 billion.

The "C" group contained other gems, including a $19 million stake in Salant Corp., for which the Black partners paid $950,000, or 5 cents on the dollar. A manufacturer of men's and women's apparel and a former Drexel client, Salant was currently distressed because it had taken on too much debt. Salant had filed for bankruptcy in mid-1990. Still, over the next eight years, Apollo would restructure Salant and control the company as it returned to profitability. During those years, Apollo profited from its Salant stockholdings acquired in the reorganization, milked Salant for fees, and laid off workers. All were pages from the playbook the plunderers would use continually over the next three decades.

Even though the Executive Life deal was now signed and sealed, delivery of the insurer's junk bond trove to the Black partnership was still on hold. Garamendi's "total solution" had meant selling both the insurance operations and the bond portfolio in one transaction. Transferring seven hundred securities issued by four hundred companies would be relatively easy compared with shifting more than three hundred thousand policyholders' records to a new insurance company. Getting Aurora, the new insurer, off the ground would take time.

Apollo worried. Until the partners got their hands on the bonds, the deal could be unwound by the court overseeing the process. Time was their enemy, as was the rising junk bond market. Every dollar of price appreciation it registered raised the risk that people would discover the gift that this bond portfolio was for Black. Overturning the deal was a real possibility.

Once again, Garamendi came to the rescue. In late December, he asked Kurt Lewin, the California superior court judge overseeing the Executive Life rehabilitation, to speed up the process. Lewin should approve the transfer of Executive Life's junk bonds now, before the onerous work setting up Aurora was completed. Suddenly, Garamendi was splitting his treasured all-in-one deal into two.

Garamendi argued in court that policyholders would be hurt if his office held on to the bonds while the policies were transferred to Aurora. This was ridiculous on its face—junk bond prices were rising and takeover deals were rebounding. Nevertheless, the insurance department recommended that the judge sever the junk bond sale from the insurance handover, delivering the bonds to the Black partnership.

It was an aggressive ask. Garamendi was seeking approval to sell the bonds to Apollo/Altus even though his own department *had not yet concluded* its regulatory review of the full transaction. Nevertheless, Judge Lewin agreed, following a pattern of rarely overruling Garamendi throughout the process. The Black partnership would receive the bonds *before* the necessary regulatory certificates were signed, he ruled.

Phil Warden was a lawyer representing a group of banks to recover on Executive Life insurance contracts they had bought. In court and on behalf of his clients, he fought the sale of the junk bonds to Apollo/Altus. "I objected to that stupid sale, it was unfair on the low side," Warden told us years later. "Our economist came up with a reasonable analysis that showed the price being paid was grossly unfair."

Responding to Warden's objection, Judge Lewin came up with a compromise. He directed the insurance department to try one last time to solicit a higher bid for the bonds. The department should post a public notice asking for fresh bids, the judge said, and if nobody wanted to write a check for the entire portfolio, the judge would allow the sale to go through under the existing terms.

This may have seemed fair in theory, but in reality, a new bidder would be highly unlikely to appear under Lewin's terms. The judge not only gave new bidders just a few short weeks to do their due diligence on the massive portfolio, he also required a buyer to swallow the whole thing. Through his ruling, the judge was basically ensuring that the Altus/Apollo deal would go through.

"Nobody in the world, except maybe Goldman Sachs, could have pulled it off," Warden said. "What we said was if you would have broken the portfolio down into chewable buckets, somebody could have purchased it at a higher price."

Other advisors had told Garamendi the same thing. But it was not to be. In February 1992, Judge Lewin approved the sale of the junk bonds. The $3.2 billion transaction occurred on March 3.

Asked decades later about this lucrative deal and how it had enriched Apollo while hammering policyholders, Apollo's spokeswoman had this to say: "Since Apollo did not purchase ELIC's insurance policies, it also did not guarantee them and was not involved in any changes to the policies that may have happened." As for how the deal unfolded, she said: "The sale processes of the high-yield bonds and other assets were active, competitive and transparent. Ultimately, Apollo was the highest bidder for the entire high yield bond portfolio after a long process. Apollo, just like any bidder, was required to bid on the entire portfolio; a bidder was not permitted to pick and choose based on quality."

It wasn't until later that it became apparent how disastrous the deal would be for policyholders. Courts in at least two states—Illinois and Pennsylvania—later concluded that the buyout arrangement driven by Garamendi had been unlawful. As a result, guaranty funds in those two states had to make up their Executive Life policyholders' losses.

Most everyone else did not get made whole on their losses. In 2001, a forensic auditing firm concluded that policyholders' damages were $3.9 billion.

Even just a year after the transfer, people began to question the hurried junk bond sale. "What's most remarkable about the Executive Life saga, and what has largely avoided notice," a *Bloomberg News* story stated in 1993, "is the fact that Black and his management firm, Lion Advisors, have been able to insinuate themselves into the rescue process so intimately that at times they almost seem more agile in dealing with the unfolding events than Garamendi."

Through Black's adroit maneuvering, the story went on, he and his partners had bagged a billion-dollar bonanza. In just two years, Executive Life's $3.2 billion junk portfolio was worth $5.2 billion, Bloomberg said.

In Garamendi's mispriced deal, Apollo's gains were policy-holders' losses.

CHAPTER SIX

"No Boy Scout"

Plunder's Many Rewards

It didn't take long for Leon Black and his partners to start banking their winnings from their Executive Life coup. But Project Savior would generate many more bonanzas for Apollo.

At Drexel, Black had been expert at extracting fees from clients, which he continued at Apollo when it took control of companies whose bonds were held in the Executive Life portfolio. Vail Resorts, a unit of Gillett Holdings, for example, paid management fees to an Apollo company each year. In 2004, for example, these fees totaled $500,000.

With Apollo in control at a company, Black and his partners would also generate additional income for themselves by joining its board of directors. In 1994, *Forbes* magazine estimated that Black and his partners held at least sixty corporate directorships, mostly a result of the Executive Life takeover. These positions generated well over $1 million a year for the partners, the magazine reported. Black's partner and brother-in-law, Antony Ressler, then thirty-two, was one beneficiary. He sat on at least six boards of various Apollo companies during the firm's early years, earning at least $120,000 annually, *Forbes* said. And from 1993 to 1997,

Cogut, the Apollo partner and former Milken lawyer, sat on the board of Salant, the clothing manufacturer Apollo controlled and milked after the Executive Life purchase.

But the real gold mine Black secured in his deal with Garamendi was a brilliant investment record, something he hadn't had before and desperately needed. At Drexel, Black had been a banker, helping companies raise junk debt to fund acquisitions. Never mind that many of his client companies had been crushed under the weight of this debt when their fortunes soured. Now, on the strength of the Executive Life transaction and its hefty annual returns, Black had spectacular investment results to brag about. Apollo's 40 percent annual returns from the bond portfolio—bought at fire sale prices ahead of a market rebound—became a magnet the firm could use to draw in new investors. And every one of those clients would pay lush fees—2 percent of assets and 20 percent of profits—for the privilege of being in an Apollo fund.

In this way, Project Savior would be foundational for Apollo. The money coined in the Executive Life buyout would be a lot like one of the insurer's annuities, throwing off income to Apollo for years.

These gains didn't emerge out of thin air, though. They came from the pockets of Executive Life policyholders. From 1991 through 2004, for example, Katie Watson wound up receiving $2.3 million *less* than she had been promised under her original insurance contract, Aurora documents show.

Profiting at the expense of others would become part of Apollo's business model. In this way, the insurance transaction was a sign of things to come at the firm and at its swashbuckling peers. Each time it acquired an entity, no matter the industry, Apollo would extract money and assets from other stakeholders just as it had from the Executive Life bond portfolio. Sometimes the firm would levy substantial "management" fees on the companies it bought, diminishing their earnings; at other times, Apollo would cut worker pay or benefits.

Black and his partners wasted no time capitalizing on the Executive Life score. Soon after securing the junk bond portfolio, they were out raising money for a new vehicle—Apollo Investment Fund III. (Apollo's first two funds had been dominated by Executive Life holdings.) By 1995, the third fund had collected $1.5 billion from investors eager to do business with Apollo.

One of those early investors was the California Public Employees Retirement System, or CalPERS. The nation's largest public workers' pension fund, CalPERS was a bellwether whose investment decisions were closely tracked—and mimicked—by its peers. Whatever investments CalPERS favored, other pensions would quickly buy as well. CalPERS had traditionally invested in stocks, high-quality bonds, and real estate, but in 1990, the giant fund signaled its growing interest in "alternative" investments like Black's fund by allocating $1 billion to the strategy. Other pensions soon followed CalPERS's lead.

For Black and his fellow Drexel refugees, a CalPERS investment would give their firm much-needed legitimacy. After all, in 1995, the Drexel taint remained a menacing reality for Apollo. Sure, its returns were tantalizing, but what about Black's immersion in Drexel's sharp dealings? What about the savings and loan failures, the corporate bankruptcies, and Milken's jail time?

Scrubbing this stain from their backgrounds was vital if the ex-Drexelites were going to attract money from other institutional investors. Public pensions were where the big fees would come from.

As CalPERS considered Apollo's investment pitch, a former board member recalled an unusual occurrence. Ahead of a meeting, the board would typically receive information from CalPERS's chief investment officer about topics to be discussed. In this particular package, board members found photocopied sections from *Den of Thieves*, James B. Stewart's virtuoso account of Drexel's collapse and Mike Milken's misdeeds. The excerpts focused on Black and his exploits, including some Executive Life details, the board member said.

The message from the chief investment officer was clear. If they were going to invest with Apollo, they needed to recognize that its founder was no Boy Scout.

In the end, the prospect of generating superlative gains from the Apollo fund outweighed the potential reputational damage CalPERS might suffer investing with Black. Apollo got the pension's money. It was the first step in what would be a long and sometimes bumpy road together.

As it turned out, the new Apollo fund was just an average performer among its peers.

After Garamendi persuaded the conservation court to sell the bonds separately, the handover of the Executive Life insurance operation dragged. By the middle of 1993, over a year later, the purchase by Aurora National Life Assurance, the French company affiliated with Credit Lyonnais, had yet to take place. Executive Life policyholders were on hold.

Throughout this period, Apollo had been busy working the Executive Life junk bond portfolio. A key strategy for the partners: pushing for the restructuring of a troubled company whose bonds it held, so it could swap those bonds for a big stake in the company's shares. Such restructurings gave a company a fresh start by jettisoning its heavy debt load; then, once the company rebounded, Apollo could sell its equity stake in an initial public offering of stock, banking enviable profits.

Salant Corp., the maker of Perry Ellis shirts and other clothing, was a case in point. Out of the Executive Life portfolio, Apollo had acquired $19 million worth of Salant bonds for which it had paid just $950,000. Apollo added to this stake and by 1994 controlled 41 percent of the company, according to *Forbes*. In the process, the value of its investment quadrupled. Some of Apollo's profits came out of policyholders' pockets.

At the same time, Apollo was also calling the shots at Aurora, the new insurance company that had taken over Executive Life policies. In June 1993, as the Aurora buyout inched toward the finish line, Apollo informed the French there would be a change in ownership of the insurer. Suddenly, a new investor was acquiring a one-third stake in the old Executive Life operation, according to 2007 testimony from Hénin, the head of Altus.

The new investor was Sun Life America, the insurance company run by Eli Broad in Los Angeles. Broad was the executive who had warned Garamendi in late 1991 that he was selling the junk bond portfolio to Altus/Apollo for too little. Broad had also tried to bid on the bond portfolio but had lost out to Altus/Apollo. And according to a report in *Bloomberg*, Broad had informed Garamendi in early June 1993 that he planned to make a bid to buy the insurance company.

Such a bid posed a direct threat to Apollo's profit plans. The best way to neutralize Broad was to let him join the Aurora investors with a significant stake.

To this end, Hénin recalled an early June 1993 phone call he'd received from an Apollo partner. The conversation shows not only the backroom nature of Apollo's dealings with Garamendi's insurance department on Executive Life but also the degree to which Apollo controlled all aspects of Project Savior.

By Hénin's recollection, the Apollo partner explained "that Sun Life was a major contributor to Mr. Garamendi's election campaign and that it might be a smart move or even politically favorable to approve or promote Sun Life's presence with the other investors" in Aurora. Hénin had had no discussions with Sun Life about taking a stake in Aurora, he said. In fact, he didn't know anything about it before this phone call. It was Apollo's idea and it was a fait accompli.

"The negotiations took place directly between SunAmerica, Apollo and I believe the Commissioner's office and the conclusion of such negotiations were imposed upon us," Hénin testified. "We never gave any instruction of any sort to Apollo. Apollo discussed things directly with the Commissioner's office and his advisors. And when they were that way inclined, in other words in a good mood, they would inform us of the result."

What negotiations had resulted in Broad getting such a big piece of the insurance deal are unclear. Broad, a multibillionaire, died in 2021 at the age of eighty-seven. But the deal to let Broad in as an Aurora investor would have inoculated Apollo against another threat the executive might have posed—to overturn the March 1992 junk bond sale. Broad had already advised Garamendi he'd sold too cheaply. Now, over a year later, as the market for junk debt continued its recovery, calls to rescind the deal were rising.

Well aware that the bonds sold in 1992 were now worth far more, Maureen Marr's ANVEL group and other policyholders began talking among themselves about asking the court to unwind the deal. Apollo had to beat back this peril. The solution, Cogut would later testify, was for the Apollo partners to work closely with Garamendi "to get him to oppose those motions." Apollo's efforts succeeded, and Garamendi refused to discuss any recission of the bond sale. Judge Lewin ruled alongside him.

Meanwhile, Apollo's junk bond portfolio wasn't the only part of Executive Life that was surging in value. So, too, was the insurance operation. Aurora registered such impressive gains, so early in the deal, that they posed a very real problem to the buyers. Explaining the situation years later, Cogut recalled that Aurora was "profitable, very profitable from the beginning," a clear sign that Garamendi had sold the company too cheaply. But even as Aurora recorded these gains, Executive Life's policyholders were receiving significantly reduced benefits under the deal. The "haircuts" they were required to take under the deal wound up generating more profits to Aurora than were anticipated.

If policyholders had learned that Aurora was getting rich on their losses, there'd have been hell to pay, Cogut testified. He said he'd suggested to Aurora that it return some of its profits in a special dividend to policyholders, but this didn't occur.

This damning secret about Aurora's immediate profitability did not emerge for years, like so much else about Project Savior. By then policyholders knew they'd been had. But because California barred policyholders from bringing their own lawsuits when an insurer failed, their hands were tied. The insurance department, the very entity that had come up with the dubious deal, was the only entity that could sue on behalf of policyholders.

Executive Life's policyholders didn't know about Aurora's big gains or Apollo's many ties to companies whose debt was in the insurer's portfolio. One hidden connection involved Western Union, the venerable telegraph and money transfer entity run by

Black's friend Bennett LeBow. Western Union was in trouble because it had taken on too much debt, some of which was held by Executive Life. But this set up a conflict for Apollo: because Western Union was also a financial backer of Apollo, its primary duty would be to benefit Western Union, whenever possible. In a bankruptcy case, advisors like Apollo must disclose all potential conflicts of interest so that participants understand where others' interests lie. For example, Western Union's investment in Apollo could have disqualified Apollo from buying the company's bonds as part of the Executive Life purchase, if it had occurred in a bankruptcy. But even outside of a bankruptcy, this type of conflict should be disclosed so that a deal can be adjusted to ensure fairness. Had policyholders known about the Western Union investment in Apollo, for example, they might have demanded the Western Union bonds held by Executive Life be sold to another buyer without ties to the company. Or they could have demanded Apollo pay a better price.

Certainly, the person selling the Executive Life portfolio, Garamendi, should have known about and aired this conflict with policyholders and resolved it to their benefit. But again, he and his insurance department did not tell policyholders.

The Western Union holding in the Executive Life deal generated a windfall for Black. In 1992, Apollo paid policyholders just $12.4 million for $50 million worth of Western Union debt. The company was now called New Valley Corp. And in late 1993, New Valley and LeBow, its chairman and a former Drexel client, announced a reorganization plan. The company's principal equity investor was none other than Apollo. In restructuring New Valley, the Apollo partnership received $1.95 for every $1 of securities it held. That translates to an almost 100 percent gain on the bonds, which went directly and only to Apollo. The dollar amount of the profit could not be determined because the partnership was private.

After its reorganization, New Valley thrived, transforming itself into a financial services and commercial real estate powerhouse. It is now a part of Vector Group, chaired by LeBow, which owns the storied New York City real estate firm Douglas Elliman. LeBow and Black remained friendly; over two decades later, in 2016, New York gossip columns reported the two men were part of a group of finance high rollers who'd convened for a steak dinner together every six weeks for the past twenty years. At the 2016 confab, also attended by Mike Milken, the group cleaned out the steakhouse's supply of caviar, the gossip rags dished.

Such were the outcomes of Garamendi's "fire sale approach."

The Executive Life deal had other hidden aspects as well. Even before Black got his hands on the insurer's junk bonds, he'd begun buying up depressed corporate debt that he reckoned would rebound. Many of these obligations were issued by companies whose bonds were also in the insurer's portfolio, and acquiring them to add to his existing stakes would allow Apollo to increase control over those companies' futures in a restructuring. This control—having the upper hand over a troubled company's other debtholders and creditors—was crucial to reaping the gains Apollo sought.

Companies that require restructuring help usually have an outsized amount of debt weighing on them—like a homeowner whose mortgage costs exceed what he or she can pay. When a company tries to renegotiate its debt—as when a homeowner asks his or her bank for a loan workout—that company is asking its creditors to reduce the amount they are owed. Companies typically have many different types of creditors, and each creditor's likelihood of being repaid is based on the terms of his or her debt contracts and where they stand versus other creditors.

In complex corporate reorganizations where companies negotiate with lenders to reduce their debt obligations, there's a hierarchy among creditors that determines who gets paid first and most generously. Fights between a company's creditors are common in restructurings as holders of different types of debt battle to recover all they can.

At the top of a company's capital structure pecking order—those with seniority—are holders of bank debt and obligations secured by the company's assets. They typically receive more in a restructuring than investors holding junior issues or unsecured debt. Equity holders sit at the bottom of the heap.

Because such restructurings are essentially battles between holders of varying types of corporate debt, the more securities Apollo owned throughout a company's capital structure, the greater the firm's control would be over that company's rehabilitation. And the more control Apollo had, the more likely it could enrich itself at the expense of other creditors. Adding Executive Life's holdings to Apollo's existing stakes increased the firm's sway over that vital process.

One existing stake Apollo held was Gillett Holdings, the company with interests in meatpacking, television stations, and the Vail ski resort. In 1990, knowing that Executive Life needed cash, Black had gone to Fred Carr, the head of the insurer at the time, with a list of its bonds he was keen to buy. Carr agreed to sell just two of them. One was a portion of the insurer's holdings in Gillett. Executive Life recorded a $40 million loss on this transaction.

Overseen by George Gillett, an entrepreneur and former Drexel client, Gillett Holdings was struggling under its Drexel-issued debt. In August 1990, it defaulted on $170 million in loans; Gillett officially lost control of his empire the following June when it filed for bankruptcy. The company's creditors began bickering about how to restructure the company.

As they argued, Black's partnership quietly amassed big stakes in the company's debt, adding to the Executive Life bonds it had bought directly from Carr. Black knew the Gillett situation well—he'd sat on the board of a Gillett-owned television station that he'd persuaded Gillett to buy.

What Black paid for the Gillett holdings debt he amassed on the open market is unclear because those transactions were private. But we do know what he paid for the Gillett bonds that Executive Life still held when Garamendi sold it to Apollo: $9.8 million for Gillett debt with a face value of $35 million. That translates to 28 cents on the dollar.

The trade would turn into a monster home run for Apollo. Holding an array of Gillett stakes, Apollo became a major creditor of the company and took control of its restructuring. By January 1992, its plan was to slash Gillett's debt and divest the company of its meatpacker and TV stations. Later, Black's group would contribute $40 million in cash and receive approximately 60 percent ownership in the new company.

The plan was revised slightly, but Apollo Ski Partners became the new majority owner of Vail, with Black and Cogut on the board of directors. In 2003, Apollo entities held six million class A shares; that stake alone was worth $110 million when Apollo distributed this holding to limited partners in 2004.

Time and again, Garamendi's "fire sale approach" would have the same result: enriching Apollo at the expense of Executive Life's policyholders. Two other companies, whose debt Black bought ahead of the insurance takeover, were the retailer Cole National and Memorex Telex, a computer tapes and peripherals maker. Holding these existing stakes while negotiating to buy the Executive Life bonds, Apollo would probably have been willing to pay more for the Cole and Memorex bonds in the portfolio, since they stood to enhance the firm's position in a potential restructuring. But rather than push for higher prices on certain holdings, Garamendi held his fire sale.

The junk bond sale had other defects, including that Apollo's position as creditor in a company's capital structure sometimes placed it higher than the position held by the insurer.

Cases where Black's stakes ranked above the insurer's place in a company's debt hierarchy gave Black the power to force Executive Life to take smaller payouts in a restructuring. In Wall Street vernacular, this is known as a "cram-down"; for policyholders, it was just another conflict that translated to losses.

Finally, in at least one case, involving Farley Inc., the Executive Life portfolio included holdings in a restructuring that was expected to involve litigation. Black had been a director of the company, owned by Drexel client William Farley, and Garamendi's office expected a legal fight over its reorganization. That put the insurance commissioner in the position of litigating against the same man with whom he was negotiating to buy the insurer's holdings.

As the sorry Executive Life saga unfolded, all of these conflicts were hidden from view.

Keeping policyholders in the dark on the Executive Life deal was a regular practice at the California insurance department, as a 2008 report by California's Bureau of State Audits declared.

"Overall, inconsistent reporting and auditing have contributed to a lack of information available to former ELIC policyholders and other parties who have an interest in the ELIC estate," the report said, referring to the acronym for Executive Life Insurance of California. An example: audited financial statements of the California insurance unit were "unavailable" during the critical Executive Life years of 1991 through 1993.

Among other secrets: What happened to the warrants Executive Life should have received as part of its junk bond purchases during Drexel's heyday? Did those securities that Hartigan had flagged to Marr as mysteriously missing somehow wind up with Apollo, giving it additional control in potentially valuable corporate restructurings? Were former Drexel partners who owned the warrant holding partnerships, like Milken, investors in Apollo?

Neither is there a detailed record of how, where, and to whom Executive Life's valuable real estate and other assets were sold. There's no trace of transactions involving assets valued at $728 million when the insurer was seized, including properties in New York City, Florida, and even a Malibu ranch. Under the terms of the Executive Life conservatorship, these assets were to be liquidated and supervised by three court-approved trustees, with the proceeds distributed to policyholders. Garamendi was one of the trustees of the Executive Life Real Estate Trust, created in February 1994. After selling all the assets, the trust was closed in December 1996.

Marr recalled being in court one day when a Garamendi factotum petitioned Judge Lewin for permission to destroy the records from the real estate trust. Today, the insurance department website dedicated to the Executive Life rehabilitation has no record of the transactions.

During each year the trust operated, policyholders received a brief report of dollar amounts generated by the real estate sales.

But details were scant—there was no inventory of properties or valuations, just proceeds net of costs and indebtedness. There was no way to tell if the sales were fair.

After the trust closed out in December 1996, a report to policyholders said it had distributed $424 million to policyholders over its life, net of mortgage debt. That totaled 58 percent of the value carried on Executive Life's books, net of indebtedness. But a different document from Aurora puts a lower number on what was generated on these asset sales. A March 2006 letter to a policyholder says that from 1995 to 2000, distributions from these Executive Life assets totaled only $284 million.

Either way, the proceeds were oddly small, given that real estate, like junk bonds, had recovered nicely during the early to mid-1990s. If $284 million is the number, that's less than half the valuation assigned to the assets when the insurer was seized, a period of deep depression in the real estate market.

In the early 2000s, Fred Carr, the former Executive Life chief, was asked what had happened to the company's real estate. "I wish I knew," he said. "There were hundreds and hundreds and hundreds of apartments in New York. I can't even imagine what they would be valued at today."

CHAPTER SEVEN

"The Real Players"

Skating from the Crime Scene

By the summer of 1993, Marr had been working on the Executive Life deal for more than a year at ANVEL. She'd been attending every court session to keep policyholders up on the developments, often recruiting them to accompany her. ANVEL had sponsored five meetings for policyholders to learn more about the Aurora deal from the principals—Garamendi, his associates, or Hartigan, the Apollo lawyer. "I passed information gathered on the ground to policyholders through our ANVEL newsletter and our hotline," she explained.

Throughout the process, Marr made sure to have no back-channel communications with Garamendi—she said she knew that would be inappropriate in her role as an advocate. "I only heard in real time what the policyholders heard from him and his aides and attorneys," she recalled. "I read his official mailings about hopeful projections, attended the lengthy court proceedings, and was on the legal service list for some years, so I read the hundreds of briefs submitted during most of the out-of-control litigation."

ANVEL's advocacy had a big impact. "Policyholders wrote let-ters, requested hidden information about funds and their distribution, and thankfully requested that the California state auditor perform an audit of the whole mess," Marr said. Those requests resulted in the 2008 audit that was critical of the insurance department. Unfortunately, by the time the audit appeared, policyholders could do nothing about it.

Initially, Marr said, Garamendi had feigned an interest in working with ANVEL. But the moment the judge approved the bond transfer to Apollo and Altus, he gave up all pretense of getting along with her. Instead, he would side with the buyers of Executive Life rather than policyholders. For example, when ANVEL requested the identities of investors in Aurora and their percentage stakes in the company for vetting purposes, both Garamendi and Aurora said no.

In March, Marr received a call from Hartigan, the lawyer hired by Apollo to "mind" her, summoning her to a meeting at his law firm. When she arrived, he invited her into his office and shut the door.

"I was completely on guard," Marr recalled years later. "He was nervous, he almost hovered over me and, in a stage-whisper, asked me to consider joining the Aurora board" as the policyholders' representative.

It would be a paid position, of course, and Marr, newly divorced and under attack by her abusive ex, could have used the money. But she declined, recognizing the invitation as an attempt to neutralize her and gain her support for the deal. Later, as the harsh terms of the Aurora purchase became clearer, Marr realized that had she joined the board, she'd have been stuck with the task of communicating to policyholders about the losses they'd absorb.

Months later, Marr asked for a meeting with Garamendi. She wanted to ask the court's permission to retain an actuary to analyze the Aurora deal on behalf of policyholders and have the Executive Life estate pay for the analysis. That estate, overseen by Garamendi's office, was paying millions in insurance department expenses during the conservation. Marr wanted Garamendi to support her request to the judge. "We were getting close to his rush to get Aurora approved in court and we knew so little about the deal," Marr said.

When Garamendi said he'd think about it, Marr pushed. If he didn't approve, she told him she'd issue a press release about his decision.

Garamendi erupted, Marr recalled, "charging me with his big briefcase held like a battering ram. His staff had to restrain him."

Marr got her way on the actuary, but it would be too late to make a difference.

As the hearing for court approval of the Aurora deal neared, Marr was still against it. ANVEL had seen no accounting of how the purchase would affect policyholders "in real dollars and cents," she said. Until that information was produced, policyholders would stand against the deal.

Days before the final Aurora hearing, Apollo lawyers told Marr that if ANVEL didn't withdraw its objection, all three hundred thousand plus policyholders would forfeit a bonus of 1.4 cents per dollar of their policies' value. Aurora was offering this sweetener as a way to get policyholder support for the deal.

Marr had contact information for thousands of policyholders but not all. She had no way of getting directions from the entire group, within a few days, on how to proceed. Marr felt ANVEL had no choice but to drop its objections to the Aurora plan.

Black would often use this kind of hardball tactic with adversaries in the years to come. Marr is convinced the move also had Garamendi's blessing. As she recalled, "One of the other attorneys in the courtroom that day told me he overheard Karl Rubinstein [Garamendi's lawyer] say 'this is the day to get rid of ANVEL.'"

On September 3, 1993, Judge Lewin's gavel came down. Aurora's purchase of Executive Life was official.

Looking back years later, Marr said she was simply outgunned in her many efforts to help the insurer's policyholders. "We held meetings, sent newsletters, watched from the courtroom gallery, testified in Congress, talked to reporters throughout the country, wrote letters, demanded accountability," she said. "We seemed to be respected and heard, but we were bit players."

Who were the Executive Life policyholders up against? "The political power, the canny financial power, the insurance industry itself under the guise of an 'association,' the misleading lawyers and actuaries, the lobbyists, the judge who let it all happen in his chambers instead of in public, the clueless judges of last resort upon appeal—they were the real players," Marr said.

Judge Lewin's approval of the Aurora deal was by no means the end of the Executive Life saga.

Five years later, a whistleblower would come forward with explosive details of how the French company's purchase of the insurer and a subsequent related transaction had been fraudulent. The insider told of hidden ownership maneuverings by Credit Lyonnais to secure the deal, violating U.S. bank rules—paralleling the issues raised in the early Apollo partnership meetings. The whistleblower's details would spur a flurry of investigations and lawsuits into the Executive Life transaction; one from the United

States Department of Justice, another by the attorney general for California, Bill Lockyer. The state's insurance department—now under Garamendi's successor, Chuck Quackenbush—would also file a lawsuit against the French in 1999.

Black and the other Apollo partners were not named as defendants in any of the suits, but their deep involvement in the transaction made many wonder whether they'd be added to the list of defendants in one or all of them.

By this time, Garamendi had moved on from the insurance department. If he'd hoped his "rescue" of Executive Life would propel him to political heights in California, he would be disappointed. In 1994, he ran unsuccessfully for governor of California for a second time (a previous attempt in 1982 had also failed), with the fallout from the Executive Life deal a major liability. *Bloomberg News* reported that because of the insurance deal, Garamendi "ended up with his reputation tarnished and his dream of running for governor in 1994 clouded."

In August 1995, Garamendi was sworn in as deputy secretary at President Clinton's Department of the Interior in Washington, D.C. Less than three years later, in early 1998, he became a partner at the Yucaipa Companies, a Los Angeles–based investment firm owned by Ron Burkle, a takeover artist, a close friend of Bill Clinton's, and a former Milken client. When Garamendi ran for governor in 1994, Burkle and his wife gave his campaign almost $100,000, half of which was a loan, according to the *Los Angeles Times*. Burkle hired Garamendi to open Yucaipa's Washington, D.C., office.

Yucaipa had close ties to Apollo. In 1995, the two firms had invested together in Dominick's, a California supermarket chain. Six months after Garamendi joined Yucaipa, Dominick's was taken over by Safeway, a much larger company. Apollo and affiliated entities run by Black and other former Drexel principals owned 28 percent of Dominick's at the time. At $49 a share, the takeover generated huge gains for Apollo, whose cost basis was less than $7 each, according to reporting by *Crain's*. "He's real smart and he's real hungry," Black said about Burkle.

While Garamendi was at Yucaipa, various investigations into the Executive Life deal began to bear fruit. The California insurance commissioner's case, for example, was gaining traction, as was the attorney general's.

Then, in December 2001, a bombshell: the *Wall Street Journal* reported that Black and his Apollo team would testify against the French—their former partners—in the California insurance department's lawsuit. They said they'd had no idea that the French stake in Altus when they put the deal together had run afoul of federal banking laws. The French had hidden this disqualifying ownership from them, the Apollo partners contended. In exchange for their testimony, the Department of Insurance under Quackenbush freed Black and the other Apollo partners from future liabilities involving the case.

An Apollo spokesman told the *Journal*: "The California commissioner of insurance, after an extensive investigation, agreed to a conditional release of Apollo, having determined that he had no credible evidence that Apollo" knew of the secret ownership structure before the whistleblower came forward to highlight it. As a result, Apollo had agreed to "provide truthful and accurate testimony as well as any other relevant evidence," the spokesman said.

But Black and his Apollo partners were not fully off the hook. Lockyer, the California attorney general, was still snooping around. And some Executive Life policyholders, outraged that the insurance department had released Black and his partners from future liabilities arising from the deal, were asking the attorney general to right this wrong. In January 2002, Wallace Albertson, a vocal Executive Life policyholder who had suffered losses in the deal, wrote Lockyer asking that he add Leon Black, Craig Cogut, and others as defendants in his complaint. Cogut had left Apollo in 1995 to start his insurance advisory firm, Pegasus.

The insurance department's "agreement/release of Black et al perpetuates the falsehood of their innocence and causes us to look to you to overturn this wrongful, probably illegal, agreement," Albertson wrote to Lockyer. "Recently uncovered documents will paint the Department of Insurance with the same brush of untruthfulness as they do to Black."

Lockyer obliged a few months later, adding Black, Cogut, his firm Pegasus, and other Apollo folks to the defendants he was suing on behalf of Executive Life policyholders. His case asked for $6 billion in damages, but he ran into heated opposition, as he told Marr in a meeting in his Sacramento office. "He said, off the cuff and not responsive to any question, that he was getting a lot of pressure," Marr recalled. "He said he'd had a call from 'big political lawyer' to make the case for Apollo and Garamendi."

Lockyer did not respond to an email seeking an interview.

Lockyer's attempt to pursue Black and the other ex-Drexelites would fail. Three years later, his suit was dismissed when a judge ruled that Lockyer did not have proper legal standing to sue on behalf of Executive Life policyholders. Only the insurance department did, the court said, the very entity that had struck the disastrous deal and later freed Black and his partners from future liabilities in the matter.

The court also ruled that the California False Claims Act did not apply to assets transferred to the insurance commissioner in connection with an insurer's insolvency. This meant no cases could be brought against the Department of Insurance regarding its handling of assets in the Executive Life case.

Black and his cohort were now fully in the clear.

In 2003, more than a decade after the Executive Life deal, Credit Lyonnais and a throng of French defendants pleaded guilty to making false statements to federal banking regulators when they acquired the insurer. Hénin was among the defendants agreeing to pay $770 million to settle the case without admitting the allegations. Some $100 million would go to the California Department of Insurance to distribute to policyholders.

Over the years that followed, other questionable aspects of the Executive Life deal would trickle out. That 2008 audit by the state of California that put policyholder losses at over $3 billion, for example, also noted that the insurance department failed to monitor $225 million in distributions made by Aurora from 1998 through 2006. Neither could the department assure policyholders "that the distributions Aurora made during this period were distributed in accordance with the [Executive Life] agreements."

The audit also criticized a settlement agreement the insurance department had struck with Aurora in 2005. Under that agreement, Aurora paid $78.5 million to the department, which then released the company from any liability for conduct prior to February 2005. While the audit noted that such releases are common in settlement agreements, it added: "In agreeing to this release, the commissioner may have further limited his ability to monitor Aurora's past compliance with the [Executive Life] agreements." By this time, Aurora had been sold to another insurance company.

Who was the commissioner who had limited his ability to monitor past activities at Aurora? None other than Garamendi. Oddly, he had departed his job at Yucaipa to run for a second time as insurance department commissioner, an election he won in 2002.

During that campaign, Garamendi was dogged by his years-earlier handling of the Executive Life case. His opponent, Gary Mendoza, a former deputy mayor of Los Angeles, criticized the outcome of the case. "The sale of the assets was at best negligent," the *Los Angeles Times* quoted Mendoza as saying. "People called it a fire sale. He calls it the best he can do. Shame on him."

The Executive Life takeover was a losing deal for policyholders, but it was a money machine for the California insurance department's lawyers and consultants. Early on in the case, the *Los Angeles Times* reported the insurance department was paying financial advisors about $500,000 a month. One of those advisors, George Bull, received $110,000 a month to assess the insurer's junk bond portfolio, even though he had no experience with these types of securities. He had been hired at the suggestion of Rick Baum, a Garamendi deputy who'd met Bull at a swim meet where their children were on the same team.

Needless to say, these advisory payments added up over the decades, diminishing the amounts left over for policyholders. From 1991 through 2020, records show, the department spent an astounding $580 million administering the insurer's estate. More than half a billion dollars.

Whenever Garamendi was asked about his handling of the Executive Life seizure, he'd stick to his story—he'd done a great job and policyholders had won big. His frequent claim was that 92 percent of policyholders were made whole.

An impressive assertion, but impossible to verify. Policyholders in states whose guaranty funds limited the amount of money they'd receive in a failure were sometimes left with recoveries around half of what they'd been promised. Documents provided to the Watsons, for instance, show they incurred a 46.6 percent loss on their Executive Life contract, while John Bennett, a North Carolina policyholder, recovered 62.3 percent. Even worse, some policyholders who had continued to receive payments from their accounts during the early years of the Executive Life conservation were forced to pay that money back because it was later deemed to have been a loan.

Policyholders in two states—Illinois and Pennsylvania—*were* made whole by their state guaranty associations but only because the courts forced the associations to pay them. (Guaranty associations fund their operations by collecting money from insurance companies doing business in their states.) The Pennsylvania court was especially harsh in its criticism of Garamendi's deal. In 1999, it concluded that the notice to policyholders outlining the terms of the takeover "substantially misinformed Pennsylvania policyholders" and that "because the notice provided materially false information, we cannot conclude that it was reasonably calculated under any circumstances to apprise ELIC policyholders in Pennsylvania of their respective rights in ELIC's insolvency."

After the court battles, policyholders in both states received the difference between what they got in the Executive Life conservation and what they'd been originally owed.

The Pennsylvania court ruling echoed Marr's experience. Before the deal closed, she had asked Apollo how much value policyholders would get for their accounts if they decided to go with the new insurer, Aurora. "Not only did they refuse to give ANVEL the aggregate Aurora account values of each type of policy going forward," Marr said, "they also refused to disclose the terms of those policies."

As a result, some clients who went with Aurora were hurt badly under the deal. Marr recalled one example of an elderly man with a $500,000 policy that had a $250,000 cash value at the time of the seizure. Under the Executive Life arrangement, his cash value could have funded a loan to pay a premium due in 1994, but Aurora had changed the terms of the policy without advising him, Marr said, and he missed a payment. Two months later, citing the missed payment, Aurora modified the policy to non-renewable term insurance expiring in two years. The client's wife poured $53,000 more into the account, but when the client died shortly after the policy expired, his beneficiaries got nothing.

With the myriad inquiries into the Executive Life deal, some policyholders called for Garamendi himself to be investigated. Dru Ann Jacobson was one. An Executive Life contract was supposed to have provided for her mother and sister following a devastating automobile crash, but they, like so many others, had received far less in Garamendi's deal than they were owed.

Testifying before a congressional hearing on the Executive Life debacle in October 2002, Jacobson did not mince words. Unfortunately, Garamendi was not there to respond. He had declined the committee's invitation to speak, saying his testimony might help the French buyers of Executive Life in their litigation with the Justice Department. "We regret that the Justice Department has not investigated former Insurance Commissioner John Garamendi's role," Jacobson told the committee. "To begin with, why did Mr. Garamendi charge the policyholders millions of dollars for consulting fees of top investment bankers to set a value on Executive Life's junk bonds when he never disclosed any of their findings? This enabled him to tell the court that he hadn't known the value of the bonds and to sell them to Credit Lyonnais and Leon Black at fire sale prices. Whatever happened to a report that his own staff completed that set a value to the bonds but was never made public? Mr. Garamendi's actions beg for a thorough examination."

That examination would never come.

In 2020, the California insurance department disbursed its final payment to Executive Life policyholders. After almost thirty years, the case was now officially closed. The money left in the estate was insufficient to pay the remaining $7.5 billion in "allowed contract holder liabilities," the court filing noted. Such is the timeline for a complex insurance company workout. This fact alone should concern regulators and policyholders who rely on an insurer's ability to pay claims. These customers include the thousands of retirees whose pension obligations have been purchased by Athene, an insurance company Apollo started in 2012 in Executive Life's image.

After the final payments went out to Executive Life customers, the California insurance department asked a state judge overseeing the case for permission to destroy all documents related to the matter. Lawyers for the insurance department said they were making the application "in the best interests of the Executive Life estate and its contract holders and beneficiaries." Given "significant storage expenses involved" and the fact that three decades had passed since Executive Life was seized, destruction of the case documents should proceed, the lawyers said.

The judge agreed. After a delay owing to COVID, the shredding of the Executive Life documents was allowed to commence in January 2022.

With so many unanswered questions still swirling around the deal, in the fall of 2021, we asked the judge in a letter to the court to reverse her order allowing the document destruction, arguing that the Executive Life matter continued to be of interest to the public. We did not receive a response. A lawyer for the insurance department declined our request to intervene and preserve the documents.

THESE ARE THE PLUNDERERS

Former California insurance commissioner Roxani Gillespie was perplexed by the document destruction request from the department she had overseen just prior to Garamendi.

"It was not protocol to destroy documents when I was insurance commissioner," Gillespie told us in an interview. "These were litigated cases. You wouldn't destroy the documents."

Thirty years on, Marr, now eighty-one, finds it grueling to summon up the Executive Life calamity. She has boxes of Executive Life documents, materials she hoped would someday expose the deal's inequities and maybe even make policyholders whole. She talks to policyholders on occasion. Sue Watson, Katie's mom, is one. Dru Ann Jacobson another.

She says she feels remorse about not having done more for her constituents but acknowledges she didn't have a chance at winning. A non-lawyer and grassroots organizer up against Leon Black?

"Maureen fought for us as best as anyone could," Sue Watson said. Garamendi, not Marr, is the one who should feel guilty, she added. He sold the bond portfolio "way too fast when people were pleading with him not to," Watson observed. "He wanted to be some kind of a hero."

Katie Watson died in 2017 at age thirty-seven. Despite receiving less than half their promised payments from the Executive Life contract, her parents had continued to care for her at a smaller home in Arizona until her death. Because her costs of care were so great, Sue and Vince fell behind on their mortgage and lost their original home to foreclosure. "We downsized," Watson said. "We all tried to adjust down to where we had been taken." She went back to work and Katie's siblings took jobs to help out.

Others involved in the deal did better. John Hartigan, the lawyer hired by Apollo to ensure the luscious junk bond deal went through, became the secretary of the Aurora board of directors. He continued to work for Apollo. In 2021, Hartigan's signature was on securities filings issued by Apollo-owned companies including OneMain Financial, a high-cost consumer lender. Hartigan did not respond to our request for an interview about Executive Life.

After a second stint as insurance commissioner in California, Garamendi won a congressional seat in 2009, representing the tenth district in northern California. Today, with redistricting, he represents the third district, in the same region, and sits on the House Armed Services and Transportation and Infrastructure Committees.

After receiving no response from multiple emails requesting an interview, we reached Garamendi's spokesman by phone. He said he would forward our request to the congressman. We did not hear back from him.

In a 2010 congressional hearing, Garamendi was still casting Wall Street greed as the culprit in the Executive Life morass. "It comes back to certain values," he intoned. "Wall Street's value was 'greed is good.' That's not an American value. That's a unique Wall Street value. Greed is not good. Greed leads to some real serious problems."

True. Just ask the Watsons.

As for Marr, she understands that greed is not just about money. "There's greed for power, specifically greed in political power," she said.

"I'm old now," she continued. "I think with love of that frightened older woman who left messages on the low-tech ANVEL hotline each week to express her gratitude for our work. She never left her name, but she always expressed her gratitude that she had this one way to keep some hope she was not going to lose everything."

What about Leon Black and the Apollo partners who got rich

on the backs of Executive Life policyholders? "There are monsters who prey on unsuspecting people," Marr said. "To dig into every crevice where wealth can be extracted from them, who delight in destroying them."

Marr says she believes the Executive Life debacle may be the biggest public-private fraud in U.S. history. "There were more than four hundred companies in the Executive Life portfolio, whose millions of workers were quietly played like a huge deck of cards," she said. "Leon Black took control of their lives, their families' lives, their pensions. Huge job losses, towns and cities impoverished when factories closed, many relocated abroad."

Sue Watson echoed this view. As she watched the Apollo partners become billionaires in the Executive Life deal, her take was simple. "They were thieves in the night," she said. "The bloodsuckers came in and the number one bloodsucker is Leon Black."

Neither Watson nor Marr could have known it at the time, but their involvement in the Executive Life mess gave them front row seats to a business scheme that would replay time and again, with different casts, over the next thirty years. Regulators, judges, lobbyists, and lawmakers all would assist as a growing group of privateers pillaged Main Street America for their own enrichment.

Executive Life was not just a one-off disaster. It was a portent of things to come.

CHAPTER EIGHT

"Strong Enough to Stand On"

Savaging an American Powerhouse Called
Samsonite

Jesse Schwayder was the very embodiment of the American Dream, building a wildly successful business in the early 1900s that would dominate its industry for decades. He employed thousands at his company, a luggage manufacturer called Samsonite, and under his family's tutelage, it became one of the biggest, best-known brands in the world.

In the 1990s, however, Schwayder's marvel was a mess. A few years earlier, Samsonite had become a pawn in the plunderers' game, and in just a few years, they'd sucked it dry, banked their profits, and moved on. Samsonite bonds were part of the Executive Life portfolio, and soon the company fell into Apollo's extraction machine.

The story of Samsonite is just one of a hundred like it in recent years, unfolding quietly at companies across the nation. A highly performing operation is taken over and crippled with heavy debt taken on to pay for its acquisition or to allow the financiers to cash out. Real estate and other assets are stripped and sold, paying off those in control. Pensions are slashed and employees fired or their jobs moved offshore. Decimated, the company flails and the financiers head to their next triumph.

Sometimes these tales get attention, though they largely happen under the radar. Local reporters will pick up on these tragedies, interviewing fired workers and detailing the hell these deals unleash on communities. But soon these reporters are on to the next story, pushed by their editors to chase news in the name of keeping readers up to date.

Academic research can be better at showing the devastation that occurs over long periods at these companies. For example, that 2019 study by academics at the California State Polytechnic University found that roughly 20 percent of private equity buyouts had filed for bankruptcy after ten years versus 2 percent among other companies. And a 2019 study published by the government's own National Bureau of Economic Research concluded that among ten thousand company buyouts between 1980 and 2013, employment fell by 13 percent when a private equity firm took over a public company. Employment declined by even more—16 percent—when private equity acquired part of a company, say a unit or division.

Mark Cannon worked as a sales representative at Samsonite and watched his company get savaged. Years later, Cannon said, "It's sad to see all these companies get thrown on the bonfire after the financial people liquidated all the assets they could get out of them."

At first, the downfall of Drexel Burnham Lambert, the epicenter of 1980s greed, seemed like something of a reckoning. Aggressive teamwork to pursue both Drexel's crimes and the predation at U.S. savings and loan associations resulted in eleven hundred cases referred to prosecutors by special government task forces. In addition to Milken, more than eight hundred bank officials went to jail in the aftermath of the disaster, including chief executives like Keating of Lincoln Savings and Loan and David Paul of CenTrust Bank in Florida.

It felt like a teaching moment, proof that a single-minded pursuit of unbridled profits, at others' expense, would be met with rebuke and consequences.

Alas, that moment quickly passed. As the nineties progressed and the century turned, prosecutions of financial fraudsters fell precipitously. With a couple of high-profile exceptions—like the pursuit of executives at Enron and WorldCom—the accountability stance of the late 1980s became an anomaly. Unfortunately, the government's failure to pursue financial and corporate misdeeds sent a clear signal to future miscreants that crime can pay. And the bigger and more powerful the institution caught in a dubious or illegal scheme, the less likely it or its executives would be held to account. This phenomenon has a name—too-big-to-fail—and it generated immense anger during the aftermath of the mortgage crisis in 2008. Even with all the political hand-wringing and promises of accountability that followed the massive government bailouts of banks and bankers, TBTF continues to this day.

"An exceptional criminogenic environment" was how Bill Black, the federal government's director of litigation during the savings and loan crisis, characterized the mortgage mess. "There were no criminal referrals from the regulators. No fraud working groups. No national task force. No effective punishment of the elites here," he said.

Justice Department data compiled by Syracuse University's Transactional Records Access Clearinghouse (TRAC) backs him up. In 1995, bank regulators referred 1,837 cases for prosecution to the Justice Department; by 2006, that number had fallen to 75.

And in each of the four subsequent years, a period encompassing the worst of the mortgage crisis, bank regulators referred an average of only 72 cases for criminal prosecution.

One reason for the decline: after the Al-Qaeda attacks of 9/11, counter-terrorism became the FBI's top priority, reducing resources available for other crimes, including the financial variety. But another factor was the view increasingly taken by prosecutors and policymakers that large financial firms were too integral to our economy and too interconnected to be taken out and shot when they behaved badly.

As financial prosecutions declined, so did overall white-collar crime prosecutions. The TRAC database shows that by 2021, white-collar crime prosecutions stood at an annualized rate of 4,727, or roughly half the level of twenty years earlier. Of those cases, only about 10 percent were against financial institutions; more cases involved identity theft and fraud in federal programs and healthcare.

While financial regulators were referring fewer cases for prosecution, they were also easing up on existing rules designed to rein in risk among these institutions. A key goal of the Clinton administration, which took over in 1992, was removing constraints on banks established after the Great Depression of the 1930s. Robert Rubin, a former Goldman Sachs partner who was Clinton's treasury secretary, led the charge in early 1995 to abolish Glass-Steagall, the legislation that had protected the financial system from excess risk for sixty years. It took until 1999 for Rubin to finish the job, but after he did, he went on to earn tens of millions at Citigroup, an institution that benefitted from his activities and had to be bailed out three times by taxpayers in 2008.

The problem with letting up on financial predators is that they flourish as a result. And that is precisely what happened from the mid-1990s on. This is when lenders started to target small businesses with usurious loans and when the takeover artists' extraction business took hold. It's when the deck really gets stacked against Main Street America for the benefit of influential financial players.

You see it in the government actions that wound up benefitting investment partnerships, corporations, and their executives during the 1990s. In 1996, for example, Congress passed the National Securities Markets Improvement Act, opening to more clients private investment partnerships like those set up by Apollo. Previously the number of investors allowed in one of these deals had been limited to ninety-nine; now five hundred investors could pile in. It was the first step toward allowing individual investors—often unsophisticated about firms' financial tactics—to buy into the partnerships, a change that finally came about in 2020 under President Trump.

Another change in the 1996 law reduced investor protections by barring state securities regulators from being able to scrutinize these partnerships. The act made it easier for entities to raise money from out-of-state investors but also increased the likelihood that fraud in these partnerships could spread unchecked because traditionally aggressive state cops were off their financial beats. G. Philip Rutledge, of the Pennsylvania Securities Commission, said the new law, largely the result of deregulatory fervor among the Republican-controlled House and Senate, represented "the most comprehensive reallocation of authority among state and federal government for regulation of financial services in the United States" since the 1930s.

Investors flocked to the privateering partnerships. In 1996, buyout firms raised $20 billion in fresh money, $6 billion of that going to KKR, crafters of the monster RJR Nabisco deal and others. By the following year, there were roughly 120 leveraged buyout firms in operation, twenty with more than $1 billion under management. At decade's end, private equity firms would collect $60 billion from investors in one year.

Congress eased other rules for wealthy investors and investment funds. The Taxpayer Relief Act of 1997 cut capital gains taxes from 28 percent to 20 percent and raised the amounts exempted from estate tax levies. The administration also made it easier for foreign private investment funds to invest in the U.S. without subjecting their profits to U.S. taxes.

Private investment fund managers continued to enjoy exceedingly favorable tax treatment on their earnings from these partnerships, known as carried interest. Because these earnings are considered long-term capital gains, they are taxed at a much lower rate than salaries.

This advantageous tax treatment is an enormous driver of the wealth gap in the United States and could raise billions in revenues to the government if it were eliminated. It had been accepted practice for years, but in 1993 the Internal Revenue Service codified it in a general administrative rule. Since then, the benefit has enabled private equity kingpins to amass billions while paying lower taxes than a schoolteacher or nurse might. Every time legislators try to attack carried interest, private equity lobbyists swarm and the bills go nowhere. The latest example of this occurred in August 2022 when Congress passed a law targeting climate change and prescription drug costs. Initially, the legislation curtailed the carried interest benefit, generating revenue to the government. But this element disappeared after then-Democratic senator Kyrsten Sinema of Arizona refused to support the bill unless the private equity benefit was restored. Without providing details, she characterized her actions as good for the people of Arizona.

Outsized executive pay is another force widening the wealth

gap. But when Congress moved to curb it in 1992, it only wound up ushering in excesses in executive compensation practices that continue to this day. Congress's barring of tax deductions on corporate salaries over $1 million actually encouraged corporations to supplement CEO salaries with enormous grants of stock options and other share-based compensation. These moves ballooned their total compensation while that of rank-and-file workers stagnated: in 1989, the average chief executive made 69 times the average worker's pay; by 2021, that CEO was making 324 times that average.

While these benefits were accruing to the financial and corporate elites, American workers continued to struggle. The 1997 Taxpayer Relief Act did throw some bones to Main Street, including the child tax credit and a college savings plan that let families set aside money and grow it, tax-free. But other factors undercut these gains.

Not surprisingly, consumers had to take on more debt to make ends meet. As wages languished, consumers' median credit card debt rose 57 percent from $818 in 1983 to $1,900 in 1998. The student debt mountain also began to build during this period as college costs rose. In 1989, one year's tuition at a private college averaged $25,000, inflation-adjusted. Now it's around $50,000. In 1992, the median amount borrowed to fund a four-year degree from a public university was $6,300. By the end of the decade, it had risen to $15,000; it now approaches $30,000.

Pensions that had been so crucial to workers' financial well-being and prosperity in retirement were disappearing as well, taken over by insurance companies like Apollo's Athene or replaced by inferior 401(k) accounts employees had to direct themselves. Retirement savers were now at the mercy of Wall Street. And in 2020, private equity finally got the green light from the Department of

Labor to peddle their high-cost investment strategies to unsophisticated 401(k) holders, who'd previously been off-limits.

Small businesses also became targets. Often referred to as the backbone of the U.S. economy for all the workers they employ, smaller merchants found themselves abandoned by the big banks that had previously loaned to them. Those institutions chose instead to focus on large corporations for more profitable lending. Unregulated lenders stepped into the breach and began preying on small businesses with loans carrying annualized interest rates in the triple digits.

Finally, the 1990s witnessed the startup of Wall Street's loan securitization machine, allowing unregulated and predatory mortgage lending to metastasize, which almost brought down the economy a decade later.

The government's favors to powerful financiers and the companies they back are reminiscent of another time in America, some financial historians say: the post–Civil War era when the railroads and the men who financed them were the pirates.

In their 2014 book, *The Citizen's Share: Reducing Inequality in the 21st Century*, Professors Joseph R. Blasi, Richard D. Freeman, and Douglas L. Kruse recount how, following the Civil War, a "new superclass of bankers emerged, flush from profits on their war bonds." These bankers deployed much of their cash to fund the railroads, building out the nation's first coast-to-coast transportation system. The railroads received enormous land grants from federal and state governments, and local and regional oversight of the roads was displaced to Washington. Corruption ruled, the authors say, with railroad executives often holding secret ownership in construction companies that did most of the building.

Similar to the outcomes experienced among companies backed by private equity, many of these railroads would go bankrupt.

When these downfalls occurred, a railroad's shareholders and workers were left holding the bag, but its executives kept the wealth that had been generated by the related construction companies. Another commonality with today, many of the railroad companies' profits came from mergers, not from ongoing operations.

This system was known as industrial feudalism. Now it's private equity feudalism. Author Blasi, a professor at Rutgers, says he believes the problems associated with today's feudalism may soon be irreversible.

The beginnings of Samsonite go back to the turn of the twentieth century when Jesse Schwayder, born in 1882 to Polish immigrant parents in Denver, struck out on his own. His father, a former Jewish rabbi like Leon Black's father, opened a furniture store in Denver, but as a young man Jesse headed to New York City, where he prospered selling luggage on commission.

Returning home to Denver in 1910, Schwayder used his savings to start the Schwayder Trunk Manufacturing Company. Hoping to differentiate his company from other luggage makers, Schwayder characterized his goods as extra-durable. The company scored a marketing coup in 1916, when Jesse, his father, and four brothers were photographed standing on a plank balanced atop one of their suitcases. "Strong enough to stand on," the photo caption read in company advertisements. Sales took off.

To convey how tough his products were, Schwayder called his bags "Samsons," after the biblical strongman. Among his workers, Jesse also promoted the Golden Rule to do unto others as you would have them do unto you. Each employee received a marble with the rule engraved on it.

"We have found for practical as well as moral reasons, the

Golden Rule is the finest program we could adopt," Jesse wrote to employees. "The Golden Rule has more power than the atomic bomb. With its help, men can still work wonders."

Jesse remained president until 1961, when his son King David Schwayder took over. The company was renamed Samsonite and employed four thousand people at its headquarters in Denver, where it also made furniture. It was by far the biggest manufacturer of travel bags in the world.

Samsonite was a classic American success story. But by the 1980s, the company was under siege to a throng of Drexel-fueled financiers that had come along to strip-mine it; in the 1990s, Apollo joined in. Against this group, even the mighty Samson would have been powerless.

The Schwayder family was still running Samsonite in the 1970s; Jesse's son King had expanded its operations to Japan and Europe. He believed in integrating his workforce well before other companies did; in charge of the company's Detroit operations, for example, King backed the appointment of a Black foreman over the objections of white workers, a company history said.

But in 1973, Beatrice Foods, a giant maker of foods, chemicals, and other products, came knocking with a takeover deal. Beatrice, a believer in the conglomeration craze that Leon Black's father had pursued, owned a constellation of brands and wanted Samsonite in the mix. The Schwayder family sold out, and thus began a series of Byzantine transactions in which Samsonite would be shuffled from owner to owner, each extracting from the company whatever it could, whenever it could.

After the conglomeration craze gave way to the leveraged buyout mania of the eighties, even giant acquirers like Beatrice became targets of corporate raiders. In 1985, leveraged buyout kingpin KKR swallowed Beatrice for $6.2 billion; Drexel peddled junk bonds and warrants to finance the deal, with the warrants winding up in Milken partnerships.

Two years later, KKR spun off Samsonite and some other Beatrice units in an initial public offering. The company took the lackluster name E-II Holdings and was soon acquired by two more suitors in even more head-spinning transactions.

By 1990, loaded with Drexel debt, E-II was in distress. Vultures began circling for a restructuring score; among them were Black and Apollo, who began buying E-II bonds. They had some competition—corporate raider Carl Icahn was also a creditor and interested in gaining control of E-II.

By 1991, though, Black had an advantage, the Executive Life portfolio. The insurer held two issues of E-II junk bonds with a face value of $233 million; best of all, the larger of the two stakes was a senior debt obligation that would give Apollo an upper hand for control of the company.

Apollo and its partners paid just $106 million for the positions when they secured the Executive Life portfolio. Alongside Apollo as an investor in E-II was Francois Pinault, the French billionaire investor whose company, Artemis, would be found guilty by a jury years later of conspiracy to acquire assets fraudulently in the Executive Life buyout.

In the Executive Life deal, Apollo had classified E-II's bonds in the "A" group: "restructuring opportunities which have the potential for producing satisfactory investments over time." In July 1992, a few months after Apollo received the bonds, E-II collapsed into bankruptcy, flattened by $1.5 billion in junk debt. Most of the companies in the E-II hodgepodge were hobbled and in need of restructuring. Not Samsonite; it was healthy, posting earnings gains throughout the tumultuous period. Less than a year later, E-II emerged from bankruptcy with a new name—Astrum International, from a Latin word meaning "star." Apollo had won control and Black became a director of Samsonite.

In 1993, Astrum bought Samsonite's primary competitor, American Tourister. Two years later, Astrum spun off the other E-II companies and brought back the Samsonite name, focusing the company once again on the manufacture of luggage and furniture. It issued shares to the public in 1996.

To keep track of all the spin-offs, share offerings, and restructurings that Samsonite endured was dizzying. What's important to remember is that with each spin of the revolving door, the deal-makers generated fees and paydays for themselves. And those fees diminished Samsonite.

In 1994, before it issued public shares, Samsonite had earned almost $900 million. But the effects of the pillagers were starting to emerge. In the following year, Samsonite began reporting losses that would continue throughout Apollo's ownership. Then came the inevitable job cuts, with the company eliminating 450 of 1,400 U.S. positions in 1996 for a $3.3 million savings. Most of those laid off had worked at American Tourister, the newly acquired competitor, in Rhode Island and Florida.

Samsonite's stock was still trading near its high when Apollo's rival Icahn exited the company in early 1997, selling his shares to the public. That year, Samsonite began offering its shares to employees in a stock purchase plan and added the company stock as an investment option in its 401(k) plan. The timing could not have been worse: in 1998, the company's shares traded around $40, but by the following year they had plummeted to $5.

As Samsonite flagged, Apollo looked for the exits. In 1998, the firm announced talks to sell half its Samsonite stock to unnamed investors and use the proceeds to pay a $30-a-share dividend to stockholders. Never mind that paying this dividend would impair the company—it would massively enrich Apollo, Samsonite's largest shareholder. Rewarding themselves with dividends from stock or bond offerings would become a key play for the marauders in coming years.

This time, though, the plan backfired. Investors balked and the plan to sell the stake fell through, forcing Samsonite to reconfigure the deal. Now the company offered to repurchase half of its shares at a 30 percent premium to prevailing market prices. Again, the deal would enrich Apollo at Samsonite's expense—the $700 million necessary to fund the buyback came from selling Samsonite bonds and borrowing from its banks. As it would often do, Apollo was leveraging Samsonite's future to generate current gains for itself.

Investors didn't like this deal either and they pummeled Samsonite's stock. "It became increasingly clear that the transaction had effectively transferred about $200 million in wealth from non-tendering [outside shareholders] to tendering shareholders" or insiders, the *Harvard Business Review* reported. Apollo was the biggest tendering shareholder.

More bad news arrived in a shareholder lawsuit accusing Samsonite of accounting fraud. Ahead of the $700 million buyback deal that benefitted Apollo, shareholders said Samsonite had improperly juiced its earnings by selling more merchandise to its retailer customers than they would normally buy, a tactic known as channel-stuffing. One suit alleged the scheme had been devised to inflate Samsonite's stock price and allow Apollo to sell its company shares at an artificially high level. Samsonite settled this and other suits in 2000, agreeing to adopt a "wide ranging, comprehensive corporate governance program designed to prevent a reoccurrence of the harm." It paid $24 million to shareholders who had claimed losses of $56 million.

Samsonite was in a downward spiral. Moody's Investors Service cut the company's credit rating in 1999, citing its heavy debt including the amounts taken on to complete the payoff to Apollo a year earlier. The ratings agency dropped the company deep into junk status, which meant Samsonite's borrowing costs would rise substantially. Once again, the company was paying a hefty price for the money Apollo had taken for itself in the $700 million stock repurchase transaction.

In early 2001, Samsonite announced it was moving its Denver manufacturing operation to Mexico. Another 340 jobs vanished.

Bob Knapp was one of those laid off in the move. He'd spent forty years at Samsonite and was sixty when Leon Black's pink slip arrived. He figured he was too old to learn new skills, so he and his wife cut back on their expenses and made do until his Social Security checks started coming in. "I didn't figure I was marketable," he said.

Other Samsonite workers had difficulties transitioning after the axe fell. Diane Ziebarth had worked at Samsonite for thirty-two years, assembling and packing luggage. After she was fired, she went back to school at the Community College of Denver working toward an associate's degree. She made honor society and hoped to fashion a new career path. When that didn't work out, she did people's taxes, until she passed away in 2017.

Although Samsonite's sales had risen in 1999, the company generated nonstop losses in each of the following four years. By January 2003, the company's net worth was in negative territory; Apollo had loaded it with liabilities of $630 million against $494 million in assets.

But Apollo was out of the company by then. In December 2002, the firm had dumped its last Samsonite shares.

Samsonite was in a liquidity crisis and facing the possibility of bankruptcy in early 2003. Debts were coming due that the company said it could not repay, and its shares had fallen to around $1. The Nasdaq stock exchange, where Samsonite traded, delisted its shares. Any Samsonite employee who had bought the company's shares was facing losses.

It had taken a decade for Apollo to gut this once-thriving and iconic American luggage maker. Asked to discuss Apollo's impact on Samsonite, the firm's spokeswoman declined.

Still, the deal was such a source of pride to Apollo that in 2022, the firm singled out Samsonite as one of its most memorable transactions on its website. Under the headline "American Value" superimposed on a photo of an American flag, the firm described its stewardship of Samsonite. "The first of many successes," was how Apollo characterized its degradation of the venerable company, the extraction of cash, the layoffs and losses, the lawsuits and the brush with bankruptcy, the cratered stock.

To Apollo, its management of Samsonite had established the firm's "reputation for acquiring, rebuilding and growing domestic businesses."

The plunderers' worldview, in a nutshell.

As Black and Apollo were extracting money from Samsonite, they were profiting from other Executive Life stakes the firm had gotten on the cheap. One was Telemundo, the big Spanish-speaking broadcast network that had groaned under a heavy debt load. Telemundo filed for bankruptcy in July 1993 but emerged in 1995;

Apollo had a controlling stake in the broadcaster, and Black became chairman.

Executive Life's portfolio had contained $83.5 million worth of Telemundo notes, for which Apollo and its partners paid $28.7 million. These sat in the bucket of "C" bonds, the junkiest of the junk. Along with another $40 million in Telemundo bonds purchased elsewhere, Apollo was able to gain control of the company.

By 1997, Apollo and another investment firm held a 50.1 percent stake in Telemundo, and new investors Sony Pictures and Liberty Media put in $539 million for the rest. That transaction valued Telemundo at over $1 billion and gave Apollo a gain of $70 million on its investment. Black personally earned more than $9 million on the sale.

In 2000, Apollo exited Telemundo with a further gain: $88 million.

Another Executive Life stake that Apollo said had "little or no strategic potential," in the "C" bucket, was Zales, a twelve-hundred-store chain of jewelers, the nation's largest. It had filed for bankruptcy in 1992, but Zales would provide an enviable gain for Apollo and its partners.

In the Executive Life deal, Apollo picked up $45 million worth of Zales debt for $9.7 million, paying 21 cents on the dollar.

As Apollo did with its other Executive Life stakes, it used the Zales positions to bolster debt the firm had previously purchased in the retailer. In the company's bankruptcy, Apollo was able to exchange those holdings for equity. By 1996, the *Times* of London reported that Black was planning to sell Apollo's Zales stake for $100 million. The firm would score a 40 percent profit, *annualized*, the paper said.

· · ·

As a new millennium approached, Apollo and its founder were flourishing. Mergers were coming back to life and Apollo had new funds devoted to investing in real estate. The firm was branching out beyond its focus on distressed debt.

In 1998, the firm raised $3.6 billion from investors in a new private equity vehicle, Investment Fund IV. The offering's performance record included the phenomenal returns from the Executive Life deal.

Firms like Apollo raise money for a fund before they have identified prospective companies they might buy. After they attract money from investors, they scout around for acquisitions, typically buying up to a dozen companies in each fund. Each fund has its own manager.

With Investment Fund IV, the firm began a foray into healthcare, orchestrating the merger of two nursing home companies, Living Centers of America Inc., in Houston, Texas, and GranCare Inc., of Atlanta. The $1.8 billion merger created the second-largest long-term care provider in the country. After the dust settled, Apollo owned 39 percent of the combined companies.

Siphoning off profits from healthcare companies would soon become one of the titans' biggest plays, generating huge gains for them and their investors while putting patients at risk. Those gains had another cost—a lack of preparedness for a major health crisis, like a pandemic.

In 1998, a pay-to-play scandal involving a Connecticut state pension plan was unfolding. It involved Paul Silvester, the state treasurer, who had been appointed to the position in 1997 by Governor John Rowland. An Apollo executive was also in the mix.

A former investment banker, Silvester made the investment decisions for a $19 billion state employees' pension fund. He invested heavily in risky and illiquid private equity deals.

An investigation ensued, and in 1999 Silvester admitted he'd steered the pension into certain investment funds in return for kickbacks. At his trial, he testified that he'd handed out state funds to help friends get jobs or to receive big finders' fees. He also parlayed state money to help his brother win a state judgeship. Silvester was sentenced to fifty-one months in prison for racketeering and money laundering.

A fund offered by Apollo Real Estate Advisors, an entity founded in 1993, was one of five state pension investments related to Silvester's crimes, prosecutors said. During the trial it came out that William Mack, cofounder of the Apollo real estate unit, had agreed to hold a fundraiser for Governor Rowland at his Manhattan apartment in 1998 if the state invested with Apollo. That event occurred, generating $50,000 in donations to Rowland. Less than two weeks later, Apollo Real Estate Advisors received a $75 million state pension fund investment authorized by Silvester, prosecutors found.

Apollo wasn't prosecuted as part of the scheme.

Flipping companies among themselves for fun and profit is another ploy of the pirates, as Samsonite shows. For example, in early 2003, Samsonite received a capital infusion from new investors. Among them was a familiar face—Antony Ressler, ex-Drexelite, Black's brother-in-law, and former Apollo partner. Ressler had left Apollo in 1997, creating his own private equity firm, Ares Capital, named for the Greek god of courage and war. Then, in 2007, another spin of the revolving door took place when Ares and Bain Capital sold Samsonite to CVC Capital, a global private equity firm. CVC tried to list Samsonite shares on the London stock exchange but failed.

Samsonite International shares eventually found a home on the Hong Kong stock market in 2011. Still the world's largest maker of branded luggage, the company was carrying a massive debt of roughly three times its revenue. This gave the company "a limited cushion to absorb any potential performance declines," Standard & Poor's said in a report.

Then, COVID slammed Samsonite's sales, as worldwide travel shut down. In December 2021, the company reported a big increase in sales but barely eked out a profit for the year. It had net debt of $1.7 billion.

Cannon, the former Samsonite employee who was there during the eighties, said he had watched in shock as his company was mauled by one buyer after another. When we talked, he said it had been years since he'd thought about Samsonite. Even so, Cannon had strong views about what happened during his time there.

"It was well run, very prestigious," he said of Samsonite in those days. "I never quite understood the cannibalism that happened. It seemed like all of a sudden the financial people found out they could make great deals of money there."

Still, Cannon considers himself lucky because he was young enough to find another job when the company went down. "I had the ability to go out and earn money," he told us. "But some people were in their late fifties and sixties when this happened, and they didn't have the capacity to do so. It's pretty disappointing to see all of that happening for no good reason, outside of 'I can do this and make some money.' "

CHAPTER NINE

"We Have 2,500 Families That Depend on Us Getting It Right"

Bleeding New Madrid, Missouri, Dry

New Madrid, Missouri, is a town of three thousand hugging the Mississippi River in the southeastern "Bootheel" region of the state. It is neither a tourist destination nor wealthy. In fact, New Madrid, founded in 1788, sits in one of the poorest parts of Missouri, with a poverty rate approaching 20 percent. The national average is 11.4 percent.

Still, locals take pride in its Mississippi Observation Deck, where you can watch the mighty river roll by. And the New Madrid Historical Museum has exhibits on the Great Earthquakes of 1811 and 1812 and the pre-Columbian people, known as the New Mississippians, who once lived in the region.

A source of even greater esteem, though, is the vast aluminum smelter on the river's edge outside town. It produces 263,000 metric tons of primary aluminum annually, roughly 15 percent of all the metal's U.S. output, and for years had offered nine hundred well-paying jobs to local residents. Having been in operation for over forty years, the smelter had some workers who were second- and third-generation there and earned $50,000 a year, with benefits.

Apollo bought the smelter, Noranda Aluminum, in May 2007. The company was not only the biggest employer in the region, it also generated almost one-quarter of the taxes paid in all of New Madrid County and accounted for about one-third of its school district's revenues. Noranda, obviously, was a sustaining element of the community.

To secure its Noranda deal, which also included operations in Arkansas, North Carolina, and Tennessee, Apollo paid $1.2 billion. As usual, only a small portion of that—$214 million—was Apollo's money. The remaining $1 billion necessary to fund the transaction came from debt raised by Noranda.

Kip Smith, Noranda's chief executive working for Apollo, was upbeat about the deal. "We want a company that not only achieves financial success in the short-term but will also be here in 100 years—to provide high-quality manufacturing jobs for several generations to come," Smith told a local media outlet. "We have 2,500 families that depend on us getting it right."

But getting it right for those families would take a back seat to getting it right for Apollo. In less than a decade, Noranda would be bankrupt and the people of New Madrid bereft. The county's school district would suffer, as teachers and students were forced to make up for millions in lost tax revenues from the failure. Even residents of other Missouri towns felt the pain as they had to pay higher utility bills as a result of the plant's operation under Apollo.

For Apollo, though, the deal was a triumph. Bleeding the company through a series of debt and equity offerings, Apollo generated almost three times its money on the Noranda investment. In other words, Noranda was a pirate's idea of perfection.

Like Samsonite, the deal was also a terrifying example of the harm private equity has wreaked on industrial America, companies that had previously supported a community's tax base and provided solid jobs and pension benefits for the working class. Losses in these manufacturing arenas have typically been attributed to globalization and technological advances; it's high time policymakers began to acknowledge the privateers' central role.

By the time it homed in on Noranda, Apollo was thriving along with the rest of the leveraged buyout brigade. But just a few years earlier, when the new century turned, the financial markets were in turmoil. The dot-com stock mania that had captured investors' imaginations through the late 1990s topped out in March 2000 and soon began an epic cratering. By 2002, the Nasdaq index—dominated by so-called "new economy" stocks with no earnings—had lost 80 percent of its value. Massive accounting frauds at companies like Enron, WorldCom, and Tyco International pointed to an epidemic of white-collar crime, while hedge fund failures and other financial scandals made periodic headlines. The devastation of 9/11 only added to the misery.

As stock investors tallied their losses in the tech wreck, the Federal Reserve Board slashed interest rates to avert an economic decline. Unfortunately, the Fed kept rates too low for too long, allowing another mania to build with the dollars it added to the economy. This time the bubble was in real estate and it entailed vast multiples of the money that had flowed into internet stocks. Rising home prices driven with the Fed's easy money supported speculative investments on expectations of further increases. When *that* bubble burst in 2008, it would imperil the entire U.S. economy.

The Fed's decision to drop rates during the early 2000s had another, more hidden effect: it fueled Apollo and its peers who relied on debt to make their buyout schemes work. Lower interest rates meant more modest debt costs and eased the way for private equity's takeovers of companies across a broad swath of industries. A second buyout boom, like the one in the 1980s, commenced.

Finally, though, institutional investors were starting to scrutinize the large and powerful buyout firms. Of particular interest was how closely these so-called competitors worked together on their deals. Such collaborations could be illegal and harm investors if they wound up receiving lower prices for their shares in the takeovers.

To outsiders, the buyout firms appeared to be fierce rivals, competing assiduously to beat each other out for the companies they hoped to acquire. In reality, the firms were cozy collaborators, members of a club that meant richer profits for them and fewer for everyday investors.

Those were the stunning allegations in a 2007 lawsuit that rocked Wall Street to its core. Filed by participants in the Detroit Police and Fire Pension, the suit contended that some of the nation's top private equity firms had conspired to keep prices of the companies they took over in twenty-seven deals unnaturally low. The pension's lawyers cited transactions that had occurred between 2003 and 2007, including those involving Toys "R" Us, Freescale Semiconductor, Neiman Marcus, AMC, and Harrah's. Among the big-name firms named as defendants in the suit were Bain & Company, Blackstone, Carlyle, KKR, and TPG.

The Detroit pension had owned shares in all of the companies acquired in those deals. And in every case, the suit stated, the privateers buying the companies had colluded to keep the takeover prices down, secretly agreeing that they would not compete so that their "rivals" could acquire the firms at a cheaper price. While that benefitted the acquirers, it meant the Detroit firefighters and police had received artificially lower prices than they would have gotten for the shares they tendered in the deals if there had been more competition. It was reminiscent of the Executive Life deal, in which Apollo had been, for all practical purposes, the only bidder.

Buttressing the allegations were explosive emails between private equity chiefs demonstrating their clubby ties. The only thing missing was a smoke-filled room and cigars.

Listen, for example, to Tony James, a top Blackstone executive, writing to George Roberts, cofounder of rival KKR: "We would much rather work with you guys than against you. Together we can be unstoppable but in opposition we can cost each other a lot of money." And in a takeover of HCA, the giant hospital company, an executive at Carlyle, the politically connected private equity shop in Washington, D.C., said the firm would not horn in on the deal because "the likely outcome is forcing KKR and Bain to pay $1 billion more and souring two relationships."

The collusion lawsuit stunned Wall Street with its details. The emails exposed the supposed rivals for what they were—a friendly group working together to get richer at the expense of investors. Even worse, the case attracted the interest of the Justice Department, which began asking the firms to provide information on the deals. For the first time in years, the pillagers were in the crosshairs.

Initially, the case had been sealed, but as it inched through the legal process, more facts emerged. Finally, in 2014 with the trial drawing near, the firms agreed to pay $590 million to settle the suit. In doing so, they neither admitted nor denied the allegations, as is typical.

Also typical: none of the firms' executives paid any part of the settlements out of their own pockets. As a matter of fact, covering litigation costs associated with these troubling actions was rarely the financiers' responsibility; under their contracts with clients, paying those costs usually fell to their investors.

The settlement was enormous, moneywise. Alas, it was also the end of the investigation. Federal inquiries into the firms' collusive behavior that the case had brought to light died quietly in the Obama administration's Justice Department. No anti-trust charges came.

Once again, the plunderers were allowed to skate from the scene.

That three of the takeovers cited in the Detroit pension litigation involved retailers—Michaels Stores, Neiman Marcus, and Toys "R" Us—was no surprise. During Takeover Boom 2.0, starting in the early 2000s, retailing had become a favored plunder zone.

There were several reasons for this. Retail operations generated good cash flows, of course, but many of the largest chains had something even more valuable: real estate holdings under the stores that could be sold off, or "monetized" in Wall Street parlance. (The same lust for real estate assets made nursing homes and hospitals highly attractive to these wrecking crews.) In addition, retailers had hundreds of thousands of workers on the payroll, presenting profit opportunities for new owners set on "streamlining" the operations by slashing jobs and benefits.

Swarming the industry, the marauders would spend almost $120 billion to buy up more than one hundred retailers, including Sears, KMart, Toys "R" Us, PetSmart, and Dollar General. Some were successful buyouts, but many went bankrupt, as servicing the heavy debt loads associated with the deals proved too onerous. The new owners also failed to invest in store improvements and upgrades; shoppers fled. Private equity "tends to drop retailers off a cliff," one industry expert said.

Beginning in 2002, a subsequent analysis of these retail buyouts shows, some 15 percent wound up filing Chapter 11. Of those retailers that soldiered on, many did so in distress.

That certainly was the case among supermarket chains, another focus of the pirates since the mid-nineties when Apollo had teamed up with Ron Burkle's Yucaipa to buy those California grocery chains. Seven major grocery chains backed by private equity filed for bankruptcy between 2015 and 2018, while no publicly traded chains did, according to two experts on private equity: Eileen Appelbaum, senior economist at the Center for Economic and Policy Research, and Rosemary Batt, a professor at Cornell University.

Employees suffered as these stores shut their doors. A 2019 analysis by the Private Equity Stakeholder Project, an advocacy group that monitors the industry's damage, found that over the previous decade almost 600,000 people lost their jobs as retailers collapsed after being bought by private equity.

Local taxing authorities were also hurt by the failures. When companies file for bankruptcy, tax revenues disappear in towns and cities where they're located. This means less money for schools, parks, firefighters, and other municipal services.

Wayne, New Jersey, where the giant retailer Toys "R" Us had been headquartered, is an example. The town was among the many losers when the KKR- and Bain-backed company filed for bankruptcy in 2017. Toys "R" Us paid $2.7 million in taxes to the New Jersey township that year, 2.5 percent of its operating revenue. Those inflows subsequently vanished.

Since its earliest years as a partnership, Apollo had showed a keen interest in retailers. In the Executive Life giveaway, it had snared bonds in Zales Corp., the national jeweler chain. In the 1990s, Apollo had also bought supermarket chains Ralph's and Dominick's, a deal Apollo did with Yucaipa, the firm where Garamendi landed after his stint at the Interior Department. Both holdings were sold to competitors at fat gains. Another winner for the firm was its 2003 purchase of the General Nutrition Centers chain, a seller of vitamins and food supplements. After Apollo couldn't cash out quickly by selling shares to the public, the firm wound up flipping GNC in 2007. The buyers: the Ontario Teachers' Pension Plan and Ares Capital, run by Antony Ressler, Black's brother-in-law and former Apollo partner. Ares had bought Samsonite in 2003 after Apollo exited.

The GNC trade generated more than 100 percent profit to Apollo. Then the retailer issued shares to the public in 2011, allowing Ares to exit. GNC's operations declined and it filed for bankruptcy in 2020.

Just before the GNC score, in 2006, Apollo led the buyout group acquiring Linens 'n Things, a housewares retailer with almost six hundred stores. Two years later, it was bankrupt. Apollo bought Claire's in 2007, a fashion jeweler with mall locations; it, too, filed for bankruptcy in 2018.

Still capitalizing on its Executive Life profits, Apollo was swimming in investor money. In April 2001, it launched its fifth investment fund with $3.7 billion in investor commitments. GNC and Linens 'n Things were among that fund's investments. Apollo also developed two new affiliates during this period; one was Apollo Distressed Investment Fund Management in 2003, which bought up troubled companies' securities. The other was Apollo Investment Corp., a publicly traded business development company that loaned money to small businesses at high rates of interest. It changed its name to MidCap Financial Investment Corp. in 2022.

The firm was growing, with new Apollo offices springing up in Singapore and London. Except for the occasional inquiry from prosecutors continuing to nose around on the Executive Life deal, life was good.

Boom times ended with a hard stop in 2008, when the real estate mania collapsed and investors began to understand how pernicious the banks' mortgage misdeeds had been. After peaking in October 2007, the stock market was trending down.

Apollo had received a massive boost in June 2007 when CalPERS, the giant California pension, made a $600 million investment directly in the firm. This capital infusion was separate from the $920 million the pension had already committed to Apollo's private equity partnerships. All in, CalPERS invested $3.6 billion in Apollo funds between 1998 and 2019.

But by 2009, CalPERS's $600 million bet on Apollo was not doing well. In the private market, where other institutional investors could buy and sell Apollo's shares, they had fallen to $6 each from $24.

By the time the giant pension exited the investment three years later, CalPERS had broken even. Better than a loss, but disappointing still.

Other bad tidings arrived in the spring of 2008, when Apollo failed to launch an initial public offering of its stock. Its rival Blackstone had already sold shares to the public, and KKR was on the same path. But Apollo's timing was off. A few weeks before its deal was expected, the Federal Reserve Bank of New York was forced to broker a bailout of Bear Stearns, an investment bank crippled by its exposure to toxic mortgages. Investors were uneasy. In April 2008, Apollo filed to sell almost 30 million shares to the public. Apollo tried to attract investors with boasts about its investing prowess. In its regulatory filing, the firm cited Vail Resorts and Telemundo as two successes, but as the offering made the rounds among investors, news reports chattered that bankruptcy was near for Apollo's investment in retailer Linens 'n Things. The Apollo public offering fizzled. Black and his partners would have to wait until 2011 to sell.

In the meantime, they launched a new company that would take Apollo back to its beginnings. Athene was a life insurer that would borrow several pages from the Fred Carr Executive Life playbook. Athene would use aggressive reinsurance deals, as Executive Life had; sell annuities; and take over corporate pension obligations, just as Carr had done, imperiling retirees. And, while Executive Life had served as a dumping ground for Drexel's risky bonds, Athene was a great place to dispose of Apollo investments the firm might have trouble selling elsewhere.

At the time of Athene's creation in 2009, nobody much remembered Executive Life. Insurance is boring, after all. And memories on Wall Street are short.

Back in the Show-Me State of Missouri, demand for aluminum was strong in 2007, rising 5 percent a year since 2000, double the annual rate of growth the commodity had seen for decades. Not surprisingly, several buyouts of aluminum producers generated headlines that year. One was Apollo's $1.15 billion bid for Noranda in May. Purchased from Xtrata PLC, an Anglo-Swiss company, the deal made Noranda a stand-alone producer for the first time.

Noranda's New Madrid smelter on the banks of the Mississippi had prospered over the years for many reasons. One was its

250-acre location in Missouri—a plus, from a cost standpoint. Most of its customers were nearby, so the smelter could guarantee a one-day delivery for 75 percent of its buyers in the U.S. The facility was also the closest smelter to the Gulf Coast, the entry point for the vast majority of alumina shipped into the U.S. Ample electricity was also available—Noranda's long-term power supply contract with Ameren, the Missouri utility, provided a low and stable cost structure. Apollo cited the electricity contract as a reason Noranda made such a good profit prospect.

But an even bigger draw for Apollo was that global aluminum supply was not keeping up with demand and Noranda could capitalize on that imbalance. In addition to the smelter, the company had three aluminum rolling mills in the region.

"It's really all about making Noranda the company we always wanted to work for," said Smith, its Apollo-appointed chief executive.

In fact, it was really all about making Noranda the company Apollo could extract cash from. And *just three weeks* after the deal closed, that extraction process began. On June 7, Noranda issued $220 million in new debt, adding to the $1 billion raised in the takeover. But instead of this money being put toward new equipment for the company or operating assets, it disappeared into Apollo's pockets.

This kind of financial engineering has a name. It's called a dividend recapitalization, and it meant that Apollo had recovered, in three weeks' time, *its entire $214 million investment in Noranda*. It had done so by heaving more debt on the already leveraged company. So what? Less than a month in, every dime Apollo would make on Noranda from then on was gravy, even as the company itself would struggle to survive under the weight of such debt. This was instant gratification on a monumental scale.

Extracting cash through debt-fueled dividends is common among the money-spinners. During 2007, the year Apollo recouped its investment in Noranda, the firms raised some $20 billion in debt to pay themselves dividends. By 2021, that figure had more than tripled, to $70 billion.

Apollo was especially aggressive at this game. From 2009 through 2017, a report from Moody's Investors Service found, Apollo reaped dividends from almost two-thirds of its acquisitions *before one year had passed*. Apollo was not the top firm in this regard; on a percentage basis, it was just behind Thomas H. Lee Partners, a Boston-based private equity shop, Moody's said. But Apollo did win first prize based on the number of deals: within one year, it bled dividends from seven of eleven companies it had taken over during the eight-year period Moody's studied.

As for Noranda? Well, thanks to its new owner, it now shouldered immense debt. Before the transaction, the company had $160 million in long-term obligations; afterward, $1.15 billion. Noranda also had to pay costs to Apollo that the firm incurred when it acquired the manufacturer, another common practice among the buyout brigade.

Apollo's ownership had an immediate effect on the company. Before Noranda had made money; for 2007, it recorded a loss. The costs of servicing its debt load made the difference.

The financial crisis of 2008 brought another ill wind to Noranda—a slowdown in aluminum demand. Still, that didn't stop Apollo from sucking an additional $101 million from the company in June 2008. Earnings for the year ending December 31, 2008, were not enough to cover Noranda's fixed charges—routine expenses of running the business—which included debt, leases, salaries, and utilities; the company posted a $74 million loss.

Worries about the company's viability were growing in the region. "Noranda is the crown jewel of our manufacturing community in the Bootheel," said state senator Robert Mayer at a meeting of the Missouri Public Service Commission in August 2008. "It is very important that they continue to operate here in Southeast Missouri and remain profitable for years to come."

Apollo wanted Noranda to be profitable, of course, so it could continue to milk the company. But its heavy debt load made that difficult. So Noranda began quietly laying off more than one hundred employees.

Then, the company began agitating to reduce its electricity costs at the New Madrid smelter. This required approval by the state utility commission, and because Noranda was Ameren's only large industrial customer in the area, any reduction in Noranda's rates would have to be picked up by other ratepayers in Missouri, mostly residential customers.

Yet again, Apollo worked to ensure that others paid a price for its enrichment. With Executive Life, it had been retirees and the disabled. With Noranda, it would be local electricity customers and New Madrid schoolchildren.

As Noranda struggled in Missouri, so did Apollo's IPO back in New York City. After the firm submitted its initial offering statement to the SEC in spring 2008, officials sent back a twenty-six-page letter asking for additional information and clarification of claims Apollo had made in the filing. Apollo responded in August, but soon the financial markets were reeling from the Lehman Brothers failure and the collapse of insurance behemoth AIG. Buying new shares in a private equity firm was the last thing investors were interested in.

Meanwhile, the debt Noranda had issued to finance Apollo's immediate-gratification dividend was in distress. In April 2009, the Standard & Poor's ratings agency cut to "D" its grade on those obligations, the level assigned to companies that had breached a promise to creditors, defaulted on their debt, or filed for bankruptcy.

Paying down its debt was becoming urgent, so in mid-May 2010, Noranda offered shares to the public. Apollo had originally hoped to raise $230 million, but investors balked. The company took what it could get—$80 million.

Noranda continued to plead with public utility regulators for a new, lower electricity rate, warning that it would close the smelter if it didn't receive the cuts it sought. Reduced electricity charges were the only way Noranda could remain competitive with other aluminum smelters in the U.S., it argued. Unmentioned, of course, was the key reason for the company's competitive disadvantage— the heavy debt piled onto it by Apollo, so the firm could bleed it of cash.

The public service commission turned down Noranda's rate cut request. Again, Apollo squeezed Noranda, sucking out $54 million in cash in February 2012, after the company issued $550 million in fresh debt. A month later, the company sold some of Apollo's Noranda shares to the public; Apollo, not Noranda, reaped $108 million more.

Over five years, Apollo had siphoned off more than $400 million from Noranda in dividends and $13 million in fees. Adding in the value of Apollo's Noranda stockholdings, its gain on the aluminum producer was more than 300 percent.

As Christmas 2013 approached, more layoffs began. Noranda was cutting 190 jobs; conceding that issuing the pink slips was "difficult," CEO Smith said they were "a necessary part of our commitment to continue to enhance our cost structure and create shareholder value." The company estimated it would save $225 million over two years from the job cuts.

Even as it continued to drain the company, Apollo kept pushing for a $25 million reduction in Noranda's electricity rate. Because other ratepayers in the state would have to cover the costs if Noranda won its cut, the Missouri public service commission invited the public to comment on the case. It got an earful.

"Why should Noranda get special privileges?" David Aten of St. Louis asked. "Sounds like corporate greed par excellence to me. How can Leon Black of Apollo justify $331 million private payout, then ask Missouri ratepayers to support him? Yes, Missouri needs jobs, but we don't need to be taken advantage of."

Another St. Louis resident, David DeWeese, chimed in. "Please oppose the Noranda bailout!" he implored. "We should not allow what essentially is a bailout to Noranda (Apollo Global Management) to be subsidized on the backs of Missouri's electric customers."

One savvy attendee at a public hearing said: "Imagine what Noranda's liquidity would be if even half of these dividends had been left in the company. Imagine what it would be if Apollo had earned only 170 percent return instead of 340 percent return."

As the commission weighed Noranda's rate request, the company made $250,000 in contributions to state officials in 2014, local reports noted. Then, in September 2014, to make sure it got the desired outcome, Noranda went nuclear: it was slashing two hundred jobs, terminating a $30 million expansion project, and maybe even taking its plans to build a new mill in Missouri to a neighboring state instead. It didn't have to be this way, Noranda said. If it got the $25 million electricity reduction it wanted, Noranda might be persuaded to stick around, keep its workers employed, and keep the local expansion plans on track.

The following April, the Missouri public service commission buckled. Under direct pressure from Governor Jay Nixon, a Democrat, and Lieutenant Governor Peter Kinder, a Republican, the supposedly independent public service commission gave Noranda its rate reduction. Some 1.2 million other customers of the utility would have to pay the difference, amounting to an extra $1 per month per household by one estimate. "It's a direct transfer of wealth from our customers' pockets to Noranda's equity and bondholders," an Ameren executive said.

Under the terms of the deal, Noranda agreed to keep at least 850 workers at the New Madrid plant and make $35 million in capital investments within a year. Another noteworthy stipulation: the company could pay no more special dividends to investors— Apollo.

But these concessions didn't end up mattering. In May 2015, just weeks after winning its rate cut and burdening Missouri rate-payers with the difference, Apollo dumped its remaining stake in Noranda—some 22.8 million shares. Noranda itself reaped no money from the sale, and the four board members affiliated with Apollo resigned. The stock skidded on the news, and by June the shares were trading below $1 each.

Bankruptcy followed in February 2016, when Noranda said it was idling its operations at the New Madrid smelter. The company's $50 million payroll vanished from the town's economy, as did the taxes Noranda had been paying. Midway through its budget year, the New Madrid County School District learned that Noranda wouldn't be making the $3.1 million payment it owed, accounting for roughly 17 percent of the district's revenue. "Plans had already been made and expenditures had already been acted upon with the assumption we would get that money," Ryan Eddy, president of the New Madrid Board of Education, told the *St. Louis Post-Dispatch*. Because of the shortfall, the district froze salaries, offered retirement incentives, and asked its staff to start paying 20 percent of their health insurance premiums.

Many Noranda employees, with nowhere to work, prepared to leave town. "Yeah, that's about the best paying job around," Tina Lowe, a local resident, told the *Post-Dispatch*. Everyone knows someone who works at the plant, she said. "It's always been there."

After the Noranda smelter closed, the average household income in the county dropped by $6,000, a news report said, a steep decline given the area's $38,000 median income. Even before this drop, almost one in five county residents was living in poverty. Don Rone, a Republican state representative in the area, spoke with emotion about the situation on the House floor that May. "I serve some of the finest people you ever want to be with," he said. "But they are all so poor."

When Noranda went bankrupt, its five pension plans also collapsed. The Pension Benefit Guaranty Corporation, backed by U.S. taxpayers, had to take them over. Noranda's pensions, with 4,260 participants, were underfunded by $219 million and accounted for the sixth largest PBGC bailout that year. The nation's taxpayers were on the hook—another example of making the wrong people pay for actions that made Leon Black and his partners wealthier.

Apollo's spokeswoman declined to comment on the Noranda debacle.

During the summer of 2016, the bankruptcy court approved the purchase of Noranda's assets. Gränges, a Swedish company, paid $324.2 million for the bulk of them—less than the amount of dividends Apollo had extracted from the company during its ownership. The New Madrid smelter went to Swiss-based ARG International for $13.7 million.

Dallas Snider had headed the local steelworkers union in New

Madrid. He told the *Post-Dispatch* he'd been worried for a while what might happen to Noranda after the New York sharpies arrived. "When Apollo robbed all our money and took off, I had an idea [the smelter would close] if the price of metal didn't stay up," Snider said.

CHAPTER TEN

"Capitalism on Steroids"

No Lusher Target Than Healthcare

Pillaging individual companies could be profitable, as Apollo discovered with Noranda. But looting an entire industry? That would offer far more possibilities. And with $2.16 trillion in expenditures in 2006, healthcare was ripe for the picking. It accounted for a stunning 16.5 percent of the nation's gross domestic product.

The healthcare industry hadn't always dominated economic activity in the U.S. In 1970, for example, healthcare spending generated only 7 percent of GDP, compared with much larger contributions from manufacturing. But as the largest bracket of the population aged and the government involved itself in more of the industry's payments—federal healthcare spending exceeded $2 trillion in 2006—the money spigot was too rich to resist. Fragmented healthcare markets, such as physician practices in lucrative specialties, also posed opportunities for the buyout barons, as did advancements in biotechnology.

While the impact of private equity on industries tends to be negative, in healthcare it can be deadly. It is not hard to imagine how the need to generate quick profits from an investment through cost-cutting or price-gouging could put patients at risk.

Soon after private equity started savaging healthcare, cases of patient abuse were being documented by whistleblowers and academic researchers.

The industry's business model "puts pressure on doctors to increase volumes of patients seen per day," Appelbaum and Batt found in their stellar research on private equity, "to overprescribe diagnostic tests or perform unnecessary procedures, or to save on costs by using shoddier but less costly supplies and devices."

In the early days, private equity firms bought hospitals and nursing homes, amassing them into large chains—Apollo's 1998 merger of GranCare and Living Centers of America is an example. Later, the titans would target hospital emergency departments, typically the most profitable unit of a hospital, and acquire doctors' groups, especially in lucrative specialties such as dermatology, radiology, and anesthesiology. These troubling buyouts continue today, encountering few objections from anti-trust authorities.

Privateers can strip-mine healthcare operations in several ways. Some of the tactics were summarized in a 2021 report to Congress by the Medicare Payment Advisory Commission. MedPAC, as it is known, is an independent congressional agency established to advise Congress on issues affecting the Medicare program.

First, hospitals owned by private equity firms tend to increase charges to patients after being acquired, MedPAC found. And when a private equity firm owns an array of hospitals, it can cut costs by slashing staff and replacing higher cost physicians with less costly clinicians, such as physician assistants.

The plunderers also arrange to have the entities they buy do business with other companies they own, guaranteeing several streams of income from their investments. For example, a hospital may be required to buy administrative or debt collection services, not from the best or even lowest cost supplier, but from a company affiliated with the same private equity firm. These arrangements are known as "related party transactions."

Strategies to reduce costs focus on staffing and labor practices. Privateer-owned nursing homes slash staffing levels, for example, and their hospitals bring in less expensive clinicians as substitutes for more expensive doctors, MedPAC said.

Finally, these firms often require their healthcare entities to pay them monitoring or management fees for overseeing and managing the operations. A nursing home owner can extract up to 6 percent of its gross revenues in management fees, one private equity investor told MedPAC.

An even greater source of riches in healthcare is the real estate under the hospitals and nursing homes. Exactly like retailers with their array of stores, hospitals and nursing homes can hold vast numbers of properties nationwide. The pirates have wasted no time monetizing these assets in healthcare. By 2021, some 11 percent of the nation's nursing homes were owned by private equity.

As owners of these facilities, with their especially weak populations, private equity firms structure their operations to make sure they are insulated from any potential legal liabilities that may arise, said Laura Olson, distinguished professor of political science at Lehigh University who specializes in elder care. "If you want to take them to court, you can only take them one by one," Olson noted. "You can't take the whole chain to court, only the individual nursing home, and it has no money in it anyway. They set it up so it's almost impossible to make the owner liable. Then of course, you have the additional complication that the owner is a private equity firm and not accountable."

Even as they limit their legal liabilities, the plunderers have found nursing homes to be a source of significant profits. In 2011, for example, the Government Accountability Office found that profit margins were higher in private equity–backed nursing facilities, and total nurse staffing ratios were lower than in other facilities, including those run by for-profit entities not backed by privateers.

A 2017 academic study by Aline Bos of Utrecht University and Charlene Harrington at the University of California, San Francisco, tracked nursing homes bought by private equity firms. Examining transactions from 2000 through 2012, they found that total deficiencies rose by 18 percent after such purchases while overall staffing per patient per day dropped significantly after a buyout. The research also determined that these buyers typically established new companies to contract for services with the purchased nursing homes, creating additional revenue streams for themselves and potentially forcing the facilities to pay higher prices for those services.

Tony Chicotel, staff attorney at California Advocates for Nursing Home Reform, has worked on behalf of nursing home residents in the state since 2003. While many for-profit operators try to maximize profits over care, he said in his experience private equity owners go further.

"Private equity is capitalism on steroids," he said. "It games the nursing home system, exploits the loopholes, and ruthlessly looks at profit as opposed to outcomes."

One 2007 deal epitomizes these tactics. The Carlyle Group acquired HCR ManorCare, a Toledo, Ohio–based operator of over five hundred nursing, rehabilitation, and assisted living centers. The acquisition of the nation's second-largest nursing home chain turned out to be a good one for Carlyle—within four years, it had recovered more than its original investment. But the transaction was woeful for patients and taxpayers. In 2015, a trio of company insiders would detail allegations of a massive Medicare fraud at

ManorCare; later, an investigation by the *Washington Post* recounted a shocking rise in healthcare violations after Carlyle bought the company. More on this later.

Hobbled by the wealth extraction of its private equity masters, HCR ManorCare went bankrupt in 2018. A year before, in a radio interview, David Rubenstein, a billionaire Carlyle founder and industry giant, explained the role of private equity: "While we're not perhaps guardian angels, we are providing a social service, and that social service is making companies more efficient."

Unlike other private equity behemoths that headquarter in New York City, the Carlyle Group prefers a Washington, D.C., home base. This is no accident; since its founding in 1987, the firm has been a way station for many high-profile politicians after their stints in public service. Among the luminaries that have done time at Carlyle are President George Herbert Walker Bush, who was a senior counsel; James A. Baker, a former treasury secretary; Frank Carlucci, former defense chief under President Reagan; Arthur Levitt, former SEC chairman under Bill Clinton; and Richard Darman, a former director of the Office of Management and Budget under President George H. W. Bush.

Jay Powell is another example. Appointed chairman of the Federal Reserve Board in 2017 by Donald Trump, Powell had worked at Carlyle from 1997 to 2005 and is credited with creating a unit that invested in industrial companies. Private equity people don't typically ascend to these levels of government, but Powell was a member of the firm's powerful investment committee and participated in all the firm's U.S. buyout activities. His affinity for the private equity world would become clear in 2020 when under his tutelage, the Federal Reserve would announce an unprecedented program to buy $750 billion of corporate bonds, shoring up the market that is crucial for the privateers.

Carlyle has also been tarred by involvement in a high-profile pension scandal. In 2003, the firm paid a placement agent to help it win investments from the New York State Common Retirement Fund, the state's biggest public pension. The placement agent, a Democratic operative named Hank Morris, was close to the official overseeing the enormous pension—New York State comptroller Alan Hevesi. Carlyle's $13 million in payments to Morris ensnared the firm in the fiasco. It broke open in 2009, in an investigation launched by Andrew Cuomo, then the New York attorney general. Hevesi admitted taking $1 million in gifts, trips, and campaign contributions in exchange for approving $250 million in pension fund investments with a private equity firm called Markstone Capital Partners.

Until it hired Morris, the investigation found, Carlyle had "experienced limited success in obtaining investments" from the New York State fund. After the hiring, Carlyle received more than $730 million in New York State pension fund commitments. Carlyle employees also donated $78,000 to Hevesi's campaign in 2005 and 2006, some of which was solicited by Morris, according to the investigation.

Both Morris and Hevesi served jail time in the case. Carlyle said it didn't know Morris was a crook, but the firm paid $20 million to "resolve its role" in the ongoing investigation. Not even close to a cost of doing business. The firm also agreed to a new code of conduct prohibiting the use of agents.

Before the pay-to-play scandal emerged but just as the subprime mortgage crisis was developing, Carlyle's $6.3 billion ManorCare coup took place. The July 2007 purchase appealed to Carlyle because almost three-quarters of ManorCare's revenues came from higher-paying Medicare and private-pay patients, versus as little as 53 percent at peer companies, analysts said.

But ManorCare's biggest lure centered on its five hundred nursing home properties—well maintained and in good locations. These facilities were owned, not leased, and carried little mortgage debt. They were also valued on ManorCare's books at less than cost because the company had previously written off amounts owing to wear and tear of the buildings. That "undervaluation" made the properties exceptionally attractive to a strip-miner who could sell them for a lush profit.

Carlyle's takeover of ManorCare was not without its critics. The Service Employees International Union, some of whose members work in nursing homes, expressed concerns that Carlyle would do the usual plundering at ManorCare and cut back on care and employee benefits. In response, Carlyle sent a "patients first" pledge to state regulators across the country promising to provide quality service to patients and proper training to staff. Carlyle also said it would make the necessary investments to ensure ManorCare's facilities would be kept up and not allowed to deteriorate.

The firm failed on both counts.

In 2008, as the financial crisis ravaged world markets and the U.S. economy, some of Carlyle's investments took significant hits. In fact, three of the firm's portfolio companies filed for bankruptcy that year—Hawaiian Telecom, a company created by Carlyle; Edscha, a German auto parts maker; and SemGroup, an energy concern. Carlyle Capital Corp., a debt fund, also disintegrated in 2008, as did an in-house hedge fund called Blue Wave.

Carlyle was in desperate need of a home run. And in April

2011, a very fat pitch sailed over home plate. In a deal generating $6.1 billion to the firm, ManorCare sold 338 of its facilities to a real estate investment trust—a typical private equity maneuver to suck out the value of key corporate assets. ManorCare would continue to run the homes, but the transaction allowed Carlyle and its investors to recover *all* the $1.3 billion they'd invested in ManorCare in 2007. The rest of the proceeds were used to pay down some of ManorCare's enormous debt. Anything that Carlyle earned on ManorCare from now on would be profit, while they continued to bill the company for management fees.

For ManorCare, the sale was disastrous. Now the company had to pay high rents on the properties it had previously owned—some $40 million in lease payments were going out the door every month to the new property owners. But Carlyle was happy because it had reaped the gains from selling the properties. From the moment Carlyle cashed out and until the company's bankruptcy, ManorCare's annual revenues failed to cover its rent costs.

In a vise of Carlyle's design, ManorCare had to look elsewhere to generate the revenues it needed to survive. One of its earliest decisions was to lay off hundreds of employees.

But pink slips wouldn't be enough to stop the hemorrhaging. Increasing profits would be required. And it soon became evident, to workers, patients, and some federal investigators, exactly what that meant.

Helping residents at the three ManorCare nursing facilities in northern Virginia was more of a calling than a job, in Christine Ribik's view. A licensed occupational therapist, Ribik helped her patients overcome physical limitations, and take care of themselves to the degree they could. She gave elderly people a better life experience, which in turn gave her a sense of pride.

Ribik didn't like it when management told her how to help her patients. And soon she started noticing an alarming trend: her superiors were trying to force her and her peers to provide inappropriate therapy sessions to ManorCare patients. Even if a patient didn't need the therapy or shouldn't have it, employees were pushed to give it. Sometimes medically unstable patients, even those who were unresponsive or near death, were pressed into therapy at ManorCare. The company billed for treatment time, Ribik said, even when patients were "asleep, walking to treatment, toileting, or because of dementia, were actively resisting care."

It was disturbing, it was wrong, and it wasn't very hard to spot, Ribik said. "It was so easy to figure out the fraud, it wasn't rocket science," she told us.

Under federal Medicare rules, nursing facilities receive a daily reimbursement rate for rehabilitation therapy services offered to qualifying patients. The rate varies based on the level of care and number of therapy sessions provided. Medicare's most lucrative rate, known as "Ultra High," is only allowed among patients who require at least two types of therapies and receive at least twelve hours of rehab each week. Fewer than half of a typical nursing home's population would qualify for "Ultra High" reimbursements.

ManorCare's abusive therapy sessions seemed designed to generate higher Medicare reimbursements, so Ribik began documenting them. After she criticized the practice internally, ManorCare pushed her out. In 2009, Ribik filed a whistleblower claim with the government alleging Medicare fraud. Her lawyer, Jeffrey T. Downey, also sued Carlyle.

Carlyle, remember, had pledged to improve the care it provided to ManorCare residents when it bought out the company. Instead, it was ramping up billings for unneeded therapy treatments, company records later showed. This wasn't because ManorCare's patients had changed, rather it was a conscious management decision to juice revenues "without regard to its patients' actual conditions or needs," prosecutors would contend. "Consider each patient Ultra High and work down, not up as needed," one internal ManorCare communication noted.

The shift in billing numbers was damning. In October 2006, before Carlyle bought ManorCare, the company sought Medicare reimbursement at the "Ultra High" level during 39 percent of the days in which it billed for rehabilitation therapy. By February 2010, the company was billing more than 81 percent of its rehabilitation days at the "Ultra High" level, over twice the pre-Carlyle percentage.

At some facilities, the jumps were gigantic. Pre-Carlyle, a ManorCare facility in Muskegon, Michigan, billed only 8.4 percent of its rehabilitation days at "Ultra High"; by October 2009, that facility was over 93.3 percent. A Sunnyvale, California, property billed 53 percent of its rehab days as "Ultra High" in 2006, before the Carlyle takeover; by February 2010 its percentage was 91. At a Virginia facility, ManorCare increased its "Ultra High" billings from 24 percent in October 2006 to 89 percent in March 2010.

Ribik was not alone in her concerns; other ManorCare therapists in Michigan and Pennsylvania were detailing similar patient abuse and company misconduct designed to increase Medicare reimbursements. They, too, had been let go by the company after speaking out about the problems. A total of three whistleblowers would file cases on behalf of the American taxpayers footing the bill for Medicare. These courageous employees provided government investigators with damning emails, detailed patient cases, and performance evaluations ManorCare used to identify workers who were refusing to go along with its manipulative practices.

In January 2010, for example, ManorCare executives identified a problem at its Stratford, Virginia, facility. The rehab director there wasn't "demonstrating an effective system to ensure full Medicare Entitlement related to service delivery," the company said. To fix the issue, ManorCare targeted the director, making him send an email every day to his boss listing the names of patients *not* receiving "Ultra High" therapy. To make sure the director understood the consequences of *not* advancing the company's therapy goals, he had to sign a document saying: "Failure to meet the agreed upon outcomes in the time line established, will lead to disciplinary actions up to and including termination."

The allegations from Ribik and two other insiders were made public on April 21, 2015, in a Justice Department press release. Along with the phony "Ultra High" billing, prosecutors said, ManorCare administrators frequently kept patients in their facilities despite recommendations from treating therapists that the patients should be discharged. Pressure to meet Medicare billing and length-of-stay targets at ManorCare was undermining therapists' clinical judgment at the expense of its patients' well-being, the Justice Department said, citing numerous complaints from inside and outside the company. But ManorCare had "made no changes in response to these complaints."

Specific cases of residents coerced into unneeded therapy sessions were excruciating to read. At a ManorCare facility in Illinois, an eighty-four-year-old man was receiving physical therapy, occupational therapy, and speech-language pathology services, but after a month, his condition began to decline, the government found. The patient "hurt all over," felt tired all the time, and was not progressing in his therapy, prosecutors said. Still, he was forced to endure "excessive" therapy treatment and qualify for "Ultra High" Medicare billing. One day, the resident had difficulty breathing and was verbally nonresponsive; his physician had ordered only palliative care and comfort treatment for him, but ManorCare insisted on putting him into group therapy. Less than a week later, ManorCare again tried to force therapy sessions on the patient; he died that day.

A Bataan-like death march of therapy sessions at ManorCare was not the only change patients experienced after the Carlyle buyout. The 2018 investigation in the *Washington Post* found a 26 percent rise in health code violations at the company's facilities between 2013 and 2017. Citations rose for medication errors and problems preventing or treating bed sores at these facilities, failure to provide special services for people involving injections, colostomies, and prostheses, and not assisting patients with eating and personal hygiene.

"The rise in health-code violations at the chain began after Carlyle and investors completed a 2011 financial deal that extracted $1.3 billion from the company for investors but also saddled the chain with what proved to be untenable financial obligations," the *Washington Post* concluded. For its part, Carlyle officials attributed the company's financial woes to the U.S. government, specifically the Medicare program, which in October 2011 reduced the amounts it covered for nursing home services. Responding to the *Post* investigation, Carlyle said their nursing homes "offered excellent service based on the ratings issued by Medicare."

. . .

By the time the DOJ took up the three whistleblowers' allegations and sued ManorCare in 2015, it had already deployed enormous resources to the case. The federal government had relied on help from no fewer than eight U.S. attorneys' offices in five states and six state attorneys general. Inspectors general from the Defense Department and Health and Human Services assisted, as did the FBI, the National Association of Medicaid Fraud Control Units, and the Defense Health Agency, a federal combat support unit. It was "all hands on deck" for a civil case estimated to involve between $500 and $700 million in taxpayer damages.

The Justice Department's sixty-two-page complaint contained pages of Medicare claims data from ManorCare properties, emails and internal communications exhorting employees to do their part in the Ultra High campaign. It was a dispiriting but powerful recitation of facts.

Benjamin C. Mizer, principal deputy assistant attorney general of DOJ's civil division, said the civil suit against ManorCare was an example of holding healthcare providers to account when they pushed medically unnecessary services to lift Medicare profits. "We will not relent in our efforts to stop these false billing schemes and recover funds for federal healthcare programs," Mizer said when announcing the case.

But relent the DOJ did, just two years later and on the eve of trial. It dropped the case entirely, abandoning Ribik and the other whistleblowers in a November 8, 2017, court filing. To be sure, the government had faced an inhospitable judge and had made an embarrassing legal mistake with a key witness. But ManorCare had admitted to a 100 percent increase in "Ultra High" billing and had produced documents showing how their administrators had improperly tried to influence billing levels of therapists. Junking the half-billion-dollar case seemed bizarre, if not suspicious.

Also troubling: because the government sought a dismissal in the case rather than a settlement, the decision would not be subject to a court review based on the "fair, adequate and reasonable standard" that normally applies to such deals. The case would simply sink from sight.

With DOJ ditching the matter, the ManorCare insiders who had come forward with their stories faced other consequences. As in all whistleblower cases taken up by the Justice Department, Ribik's name had become public in the matter. Her role, especially after the government dropped the case, took an immense toll on her. She contemplated suicide for the first time in her life, Ribik told us; she thought she had blown her entire career. Sure enough, she said she has had difficulty finding work in subsequent years.

After all that she had done to try to hold a powerful corporation accountable, Ribik could not believe the government's decision to forsake the case. "I thought the government would do their job—I did," Ribik said years later. "But they were incompetent; it was almost like they wanted it to fail. At the end they were such cowards—when they bailed on the case, they filed the paperwork at night."

Carlyle, of course, was exultant. "Today, we are vindicated," said Steve Cavanaugh, ManorCare's chief executive. "With no payment of any kind by HCR ManorCare, the lawsuit is over."

But ManorCare's woes were not behind it. Four months later, in March 2018, the company filed for bankruptcy with $7.1 billion in debt. It was purchased by ProMedica Senior Care, a not-for-profit healthcare company, in a $1.4 billion deal. Cavanaugh went with the company to ProMedica and was later quoted saying that Carlyle had starved ManorCare of capital, leaving it unable to reinvest in the business as it had promised to do. With a new owner, ManorCare planned to plow as much as $75 million back into the business, according to Cavanaugh. One specific step would be to fund major renovations at forty to fifty facilities the following year.

Carlyle's impact on the ManorCare residents was not a one-off. In fact, what ManorCare was accused of doing to its patients seems almost benign when compared with the findings in the stunning 2021 nursing home study published by the National Bureau of Economic Research. That study showed nursing homes owned by private equity firms experienced *10 percent more resident deaths* than occurred in facilities not owned by private equity. Some twenty thousand additional lives were lost at private equity–backed nursing homes during the years studied of 2005 to 2017, the researchers reported. Declines in nursing staff and reduced compliance with standards of care explained the dire results, academics at New York University, the University of Chicago, and the University of Pennsylvania concluded.

The study was shattering and bulletproof. For once, the pirates made no claims that the results were biased or inaccurate.

Sabrina Howell, assistant professor of finance at New York University's Stern School of Business, was one of the report's authors. She told us she was surprised by the findings, as she considers private equity to be a productive player in some industries. But when the companies are providing a public good paid for by taxpayers— such as nursing homes generating revenues from Medicare—profit incentives can have troubling outcomes, she said.

"It's in these sectors that we want to worry about really high-powered incentives to maximize profits," Howell observed, "because they are misaligned with the implicit contracts that are the basis for economic activity in these sectors. What my work has suggested in education and healthcare is that private equity tends to breach those implicit contracts because there is a way to create short-term value by doing so."

CHAPTER ELEVEN

Call to Action Went Unheeded

Standing By While Corporations Practice Medicine

The pillagers launched a full-throttle assault on the healthcare industry in the early 2000s, of which Carlyle's takeover of ManorCare was just one example. Only during COVID, almost two decades later, would it become clear how these buyouts had enriched the titans while hobbling the nation's ability to provide crucial healthcare services during a deadly pandemic.

The healthcare gold rush began in 2005, and during the following year, the raiders took over a record $80 billion worth of companies in the industry. That frenzied activity was unmatched again until 2018, when eight hundred deals, worth $100 billion, were completed.

As the buyout mania spread, important research on the nation's healthcare industry was underway in Washington. In late 2005, the Congressional Budget Office (CBO), a nonpartisan government agency that provides economic information to lawmakers, was tasked with answering this question: Is the United States healthcare system adequately prepared for an influenza pandemic? Requesting the analysis was Bill Frist, then the Senate majority leader from Tennessee and one of the few physicians in Congress; he also asked CBO to research the economic havoc that a pandemic might wreak on the nation.

Landing in May 2006, the twenty-two-page report was written in the bloodless prose common to economists everywhere, but its message could not have been more dire. "Were an influenza pandemic to occur," the report concluded, "local health care systems would not have a sufficient number of beds or enough staff or supplies to meet the demand (and observe routine standards of care)." The report also noted that FluSurge, a simulation tool crafted by the Centers for Disease Control, had produced estimates that "a severe pandemic in an urban area would increase the overall demand for hospital beds and staff three times beyond the current capacity and the demand for intensive care beds seven times beyond the current capacity."

Eerily prescient, the CBO said the nation's hospitals would have to undergo increased decontamination and waste management in a pandemic and would face severe shortages of protective equipment, such as surgical masks, gloves, and gowns. The report spelled out precisely what emergency department physicians like Ming Lin would later face in hospitals across the country.

There was more. "Ventilators would be of particular importance," the report said, noting that the United States had approximately 100,000 ventilators available at the time, with three-quarters of them in use on a typical day. Yet, "a severe influenza pandemic like the one in 1918 would require 750,000 ventilators to treat victims."

To prepare for such a disaster, CBO advised, hospitals nationwide should spend about $5 billion developing plans and training and stockpiling protective equipment and supplies. This translated to a roughly $1 million investment by the average hospital in

America; investing in antiviral drugs or high-cost equipment such as ventilators would cost even more.

Finally, the report estimated that a pandemic could result in a 4.5 percent drop in the nation's economic activity. (The estimate wasn't far off—in 2020, amid COVID-19, economic output fell by 3.5 percent from the year earlier.) "Paying the full costs for complete preparation today may not be a sound investment, but paying some of the costs is prudent," CBO concluded.

CBO's crystal ball would be freakishly accurate about the events that began unfolding in March 2020. And yet, this urgent call to action went unheeded.

What CBO had not foreseen in its analysis was how much of the nation's healthcare industry would be appropriated by people looking to strip these companies of assets and drain them of cash, rather than invest more in them under a preparedness campaign. Even CBO's wise forecasters could not see what these privateers had determined: prudence is a bore next to the compelling profits to be bled from the industry. Healthcare operations abounded with costs to be cut and government programs, like Medicare, to be milked. Plus, implementing a more aggressive approach to collecting unpaid hospital bills and managing healthcare data could likely generate sky-high returns.

There were simply too many rich veins in the healthcare industry to be mined to spend time worrying about a possible pandemic.

As a result, between 2005 and 2020, private equity giants including Apollo, Blackstone, the Carlyle Group, and KKR took over wide swaths of this crucial sector, completing $500 billion in healthcare deals. They exploited assets in nursing homes and rural hospitals, and rolled up physician practices in lucrative fields like emergency medicine, dermatology, anesthesiology, and radiology.

In 2006, just a few months after CBO's warning, an investor

group, led by three private equity giants—Bain Capital, KKR, and a Merrill Lynch unit—purchased the nation's largest hospital chain, Hospital Corporation of America, for $33 billion. HCA was the largest-ever debt-backed buyout at the time, having edged out the 1988 RJR Nabisco deal for that prize. Along for the ride as a major investor was the same Senator Bill Frist who'd asked the CBO to study the nation's influenza preparedness.

In 2010, just four years later, HCA's privateer investors got most of their money back when the company paid them a $4.3 billion "dividend." The next year, HCA sold shares to the public, generating even more profits for the private equity firms that had kept a small stake in the company. According to an analysis by *Fortune* magazine, after the IPO, Bain Capital reaped $1.2 billion from its initial $64 million equity investment in HCA.

But HCA would be dogged by accusations of worker mistreatment.

In August 2020, COVID-weary HCA nurses accused their employer of willfully violating workplace safety standards by forcing them to share break rooms, computers, desks, phones, and nursing stations in seventeen hospitals. Even worse, the nurses said, HCA failed to notify workers when they had been exposed to COVID-19.

Jamelle Brown was an emergency department technician at HCA-owned Research Medical Hospital in Kansas City when he contracted COVID on the job. Charged with sanitizing and sterilizing twenty-eight rooms in the department, he made $13.77 an hour. His local union, Service Employees International, had been trying to get him and his peers to $15 an hour along with back pay and an extra day off for bereavement. HCA countered by offering a raise of 13 cents an hour.

Brown lived with his sister because he did not earn enough to pay for his own apartment. This made it difficult to spend one-on-one time with his thirteen-year-old son. If he made $15 an hour, he said, just over $1 an hour more, he'd have enough to "make a living for me and my son."

Happily, Brown's COVID case was not severe, and after quarantining, he went back to work in the fall of 2020. When he returned, his unit named him Employee of the Month, and gave him a gift card. The amount on the card: $6 to be used in the hospital cafeteria.

"That stung me to the bone," said Brown, who had worked at the hospital for almost four years. "It made me sit back and say, 'this place doesn't care for me.'"

Meanwhile, HCA had been immensely profitable, reporting earnings of $3.75 billion in the pandemic year of 2020, up from $3.5 billion the year earlier. Its shares have risen more than 700 percent since it went public again in 2011. As HCA offered Brown a raise of 13 cents an hour, HCA's chief executive Samuel Hazen received a pay increase of 13 percent in 2020, to $30.4 million. Compared with what the median HCA worker made that year, Hazen's pay was a staggering 556 times as much. Many of those employees, like Brown, had risked their lives as front-line workers in the pandemic.

Hazen's pay amounted to roughly 1,000 times Brown's. How did that sit with Brown?

"It feels like my hard work and everyone else's hard work is making everyone richer but us," he said, "those who are actually doing the job."

"We value our colleagues and the work they do to care for their communities," HCA's spokesman said in a statement, "and we are committed to offering competitive compensation and benefits packages, as well as opportunities for professional development and career advancement."

The private equity takeover of healthcare has had countless negative consequences. But nowhere has it been more damaging than in the field of emergency medicine. In this crucial arena, where people seeking urgent treatment are least able to fight back or ask questions about who is caring for them, the predators have run amok.

By the time COVID arrived in 2020, two of the wealthiest firms—Blackstone and KKR—had won contracts to run more than one-third of the nation's emergency rooms. Other private equity firms' interests brought the industry's control of ERs to over 40 percent.

KKR's staffing company, Envision HealthCare, was the largest emergency medicine group in 2022, providing physicians and other employees at 540 healthcare facilities in 45 states. Its main competitor, TeamHealth, was a Blackstone company; Team-Health oversaw PeaceHealth Hospital's emergency department in Bellingham, Washington, where Dr. Ming Lin was removed after speaking out.

Still, delving so deeply into healthcare posed risks to the plunderers. The profits in the industry were indeed immense, but many of the takeovers could run afoul of laws in roughly thirty states barring corporations from practicing medicine. On the books for decades, these statutes had obvious aims—to make sure physicians put their patients' interests first and were not compromised by profit-hungry owners or managers. State laws also ban entities from splitting fees with physicians in these operations, meant to prevent greed from poisoning patient care.

California, Minnesota, Ohio, Pennsylvania, and Texas are among the states with laws preventing non-physicians from influencing clinical decisions in medical operations. They require healthcare to be provided only through a professional corporation owned by licensed practitioners in that state.

Clever private equity firms, however, have devised ways to conceal their ownership of physician practices. They instead operate under professional associations that appear to be owned or run by medical doctors but are in fact overseen and controlled by a corporation. The firms set up structures under which they purport solely to provide administrative or other support services to medical practices, which would not run afoul of corporate practice laws. In reality, however, the firms are also making crucial decisions about care being provided by doctors, such as how many patients are seen and what treatments are prescribed.

Both Envision and TeamHealth use such arrangements to run emergency departments at hospitals. They hire physicians to be the owner "on paper" of the practice, but that owner is completely controlled by either Envision or TeamHealth. The doctors employed as figureheads have titles such as president, secretary, or chief executive of each entity. They receive a salary for the use of their licenses. They have no oversight of the operation and can be terminated by the corporation anytime, having signed codes of conduct in which they promise to advance the interests of the corporation.

Some of the doctors who agree to these arrangements "own" hundreds of practices in an array of states. Gregory J. Byrne, an emergency physician in Houston, Texas, has "owned" as many as three hundred practices for Envision across the country during any given year. There's no way Byrne can possibly oversee the goings-on at all these practices. Byrne says the companies he "owns" don't manage medical care. "That is a physician responsibility," he told us, declining to comment further.

But another story emerges when the true relationships between these doctors and the corporations they serve come under scrutiny. For example, corporate records for Byrne's operations in California, Florida, Massachusetts, New York, and elsewhere trace back to Envision's headquarters address in Tennessee. Envision forwards "operational documents for Byrne to sign," a court filing stated, and the profits from these operations flow to Envision, not Byrne. Though Envision "is careful to maintain corporate formalities between itself and its various subsidiaries," the court filing said, "the subsidiaries are managed and operated by persons who are agents of the subsidiaries but who are also directly connected to the parent corporation."

In other words, the doctors who lend their names to these practices preside in name only. They are not involved in the day-to-day operations, and instead executives from TeamHealth or Envision run the show.

The companies were aware of the risks posed by their practice of medicine and use of contracts allowing them to split fees with doctors. In a 2009 securities filing issued before it was bought out by Blackstone, TeamHealth warned that the legality of its business model could be questioned.

"The laws and regulations relating to our operations in 46 states vary from state to state," the filing said, "and many states prohibit general business corporations, as we are, from practicing medicine, controlling physicians' medical decisions or engaging in some practices such as splitting professional fees with physicians. We believe that we are in substantial compliance with state laws prohibiting the corporate practice of medicine and fee-splitting."

However, the filing continued, "Other parties may assert that, despite the way we are structured, TeamHealth could be engaged in the corporate practice of medicine or unlawful fee-splitting. Were such allegations to be asserted successfully before the appropriate judicial or administrative forums, we could be subject to adverse judicial or administrative penalties, certain contracts could be determined to be unenforceable and we may be required to restructure our contractual arrangements."

Blackstone, TeamHealth's owner, downplayed the risks the company's business model poses as described in its former SEC filings. "TeamHealth's organizational structure is fully compliant with long-established laws and precedents," its spokesman said in a statement to us. "TeamHealth has prevailed in every instance when facing judicial scrutiny of its organizational structure due to lawsuits filed by the same small group of vocal activists." That group of vocal activists, by the way, are emergency department physicians concerned about how the corporate practice of medicine imperils patients across the nation.

Few patients seeking urgent medical care in an emergency department are aware of the potential for harm from these relationships. But behind-the-scenes details emerge periodically in lawsuits, showing how the firms achieve their end runs around laws barring the corporatization of medicine. They also show instances where the takeovers of hospital emergency departments by these exploitative groups threaten patient care and doctors' livelihoods.

A most disturbing example came in a 2017 wrongful dismissal lawsuit filed by a former army doctor in Kansas City named Ray Brovont. A native of San Francisco, Brovont had become medical director of the emergency department at Overland Park Medical Center in Kansas City, Kansas, in 2012. Overland Park is owned by HCA, which often contracts with Envision and TeamHealth to run its emergency departments. When Brovont began running the hospital's emergency department, HCA had contracted with EmCare, a hospital staffing company, to manage it. EmCare was owned by private equity firm Clayton, Dubilier & Rice at the time but was sold to KKR under the name of Envision in 2018.

Brovont's hands were full when he began helming Overland; as a Level II trauma center, the facility was required to provide twenty-four-hour immediate coverage by general surgeons, as well as by specialists in orthopedic surgery, neurosurgery, anesthesiology, emergency medicine, radiology, and critical care. Brovont was ready and up to the task—he'd seen combat in Iraq and earned the prestigious honor of Fellow of the American College of Emergency Physicians. His seven years in the army taught him to tackle problems quickly after they arose, Brovont said. "I brought that paradigm with me to the civilian side of practicing medicine," he told us. "The goal was to identify an issue before there was a bad outcome."

One possibility for a very bad outcome at Overland Park, Brovont said, had to do with its policy regarding "code blues," the distress calls for help when a patient was no longer breathing or did not have a pulse. The policy was outdated and dangerous—it had been instituted in 1993 and required an emergency department doctor to be available to attend to code blue calls elsewhere in the hospital even if it meant leaving the emergency department without a physician to handle code blues there. For many hours each day, the emergency department was staffed with only one MD. If the doctor had to leave for a code blue elsewhere in the hospital, the ER would not have a physician on hand to treat anyone needing urgent help.

Overland Park's code blue policy became an especially urgent peril to patients, Brovont concluded, after the hospital doubled its size in 2014, adding a new and separate pediatric emergency room.

Now the hospital's lone emergency physician might need to be in three places at once to respond to code blues. Not only would this be impossible, the policy also violated guidelines set out by the American College of Surgeons requiring Level II trauma centers to have a physician in the emergency department 24/7. What's more, Overland Park's policy did not comply with the Emergency Medical Treatment and Labor Act, a federal law requiring an emergency room physician to be available immediately for anyone arriving in the department with urgent needs.

Brovont and every one of his physician colleagues were deeply concerned about the code blues. Starting in 2015, Brovont began expressing the unit's grave concerns about the policy to his superior, Patrick McHugh, an executive at private equity–backed EmCare. McHugh told Brovont additional money was unavailable to hire another physician to keep the emergency department fully covered even during code blues elsewhere in the facility. But Brovont kept pushing.

At one point, McHugh asked Brovont if he would like to take a position at another hospital nearby, seemingly a promotion. But Brovont said he'd rather stay at Overland Park and complete the work he'd started in building the department and changing the code blue policy.

In July 2016, Brovont convened a meeting with McHugh and all the physicians in the emergency department. He spoke of the violation of federal law that the code blue policy represented and the anxiety it was causing among the doctors. McHugh was not amused.

A short time later, McHugh emailed Brovont and his colleagues. His message was blunt. "HCA is a for-profit company traded on the New York Stock Exchange," McHugh wrote. "Many of their staffing decisions are financially motivated. EmCare is no different. Profits are in everyone's best interest."

Obviously, the situation was not being resolved, despite Brovont's efforts. So in late September 2016, he composed a letter outlining the patient safety threats created by the continued use of the policy. Brovont shared the letter with his eighteen physician colleagues, making sure they agreed with its message, then sent it to McHugh and another EmCare executive on the group's behalf.

Silence. Until, that is, Brovont ran into McHugh in a hallway. "Did you get my letter?" Brovont asked. McHugh snarled his response. "Why would you ever put that in writing?"

On January 17, 2017, McHugh asked Brovont to meet him at a bar after work. There, he told Brovont he was unfit to remain as medical director at Overland Park and was being removed. The physician was "more oppositional than supportive," McHugh explained, and kept "fighting against things." Finally, McHugh said: "You know you cash the check every month to be a corporate representative, and there is a responsibility as the corporate representative to support the corporation's objectives."

Brovont was stunned. But there was more. Enraged by the incident, McHugh made sure Brovont could not get a job at any other emergency department serviced by EmCare in nearby Kansas or Missouri hospitals.

After Brovont's dismissal, the same emergency room physicians who'd agreed to send the letter but who stayed at Overland Park became frightened for their jobs. Their work environment was a "weird cult of coercion" where you'd be fired if you didn't do what you were told. Younger doctors, shouldering significant amounts of student loan debt, reported being especially fearful of losing their positions if they complained. So they went quiet on the code blue policy, which the hospital did not change until years later.

Brovont was unemployed for about three months; then he secured a job as acting medical director at a facility not under contract with EmCare. In 2017, he sued EmCare for "wrongful discharge in violation of public policy." As the case inched through the courts, it brought out details about how EmCare had employed Dr. Gregory Byrne as the owner "on paper" of the physician association running the emergency department at Overland Park. Byrne testified that he had not been involved in the department's operation or the firing of Brovont, proving that EmCare was indeed a corporate practicing medicine at the hospital. Brovont was shocked to learn that Byrne was supposedly his boss; he testified that he'd never met or heard of the man.

In 2020, a jury awarded Brovont $29 million, including $20 million in punitive damages. On appeal, the award was cut to $26 million, but the finding of wrongful dismissal stood.

McHugh no longer works for Envision. He did not respond to a request for comment.

A spokeswoman for Envision, EmCare's parent, said in a statement that the company complies "with state laws and operates with high ethical standards that put patients' health and safety first. Envision clinicians, like all clinicians, exercise their independent judgment to provide quality, compassionate, clinically appropriate care based on their patients' unique needs. The concern raised by Dr. Brovont was related to a hospital policy, not an Envision policy, and predates Envision's current leadership team."

Brovont now works at a small emergency department and in private practice in Prairie Village, Kansas, near the Overland Park facility where he fought his battle for patient safety. In his practice, he helps veterans and other patients overcome mental health challenges such as depression and post-traumatic stress disorder.

"The crisis of corporatization has really reached a peak in emergency medicine," said Robert McNamara, MD, a professor and the chair of emergency medicine at Temple University Medical School. "During the pandemic, we had doctors getting pay cuts from these corporate entities and denying physicians due process, which is their right, when they spoke about patient safety. Your typical emergency physician is afraid to speak up for fear of termination."

McNamara has made it something of a crusade to educate the public about the ills associated with corporations practicing emergency medicine. He has filed numerous complaints with state medical boards and state attorneys general over the years with no success. A group he is affiliated with sued Envision in California court in December 2021, contending that the company had violated state laws when it took over staffing of the emergency department at Placentia-Linda Hospital in Placentia, California, earlier that year. Envision's control over the physicians in the practices it acquires is "profound and pervasive," the suit alleged. A medical director of the physician entity is appointed by Envision.

The company also determines how many physicians are hired, their compensation, and their work schedules, and sets other terms of employment, staffing levels, and numbers of patient encounters. Envision controls how to code and bill patients and insurers for services without telling physicians what has been billed. "Decisions are not made by the medical directors," the suit says.

Envision also establishes its own internal standards for treating patients, a form of clinical oversight barred under California law, the lawsuit contends. Envision scores physician performance against those standards, interfering with the doctors' independent medical judgment.

"In the drive for profits, you have the patients seen by less experienced, less qualified providers, or they are pressuring doctors to see too many patients too fast," McNamara told us. "Another cost to patients of private equity is trying to make as much money as possible with high bills and collection policies, and the doctor has no clue as to what's going on. They have no information about what's being billed and paid in their name."

The lawsuit against Envision is ongoing; in summer 2022, a judge rejected the company's request to dismiss the case.

Inappropriate and costly admissions to hospitals from emergency departments are another result of the push for profits by these firms. Medicare pays at least three times more for inpatient admissions than it does for care billed as observation or emergency room visits. Taxpayers are on the hook for these improprieties.

Medicare abuse in circumstances like these was the basis for a 2017 Justice Department case against EmCare, the entity that fired Brovont. Several physicians came forward with allegations of Medicare fraud, stating that EmCare had admitted Medicare patients unnecessarily to hospitals from emergency departments it oversaw. The company had received remuneration from the hospital chain for doing so, prosecutors said.

Without admitting the allegations, a deplorably common outcome in Justice Department cases, EmCare agreed to pay $29.8 million in December 2017 to settle the case. (The hospital chain settled with prosecutors later, paying $260 million, also without admitting the accusations.) When EmCare settled, Envision, its parent company, entered into a corporate integrity agreement with the Department of Health and Human Services. As is typical under such a deal, the HHS inspector general agreed not to seek to exclude Envision from participating in Medicare or other federal healthcare programs, but only if it changed its practices.

Envision committed to "full compliance with all Federal health care program requirements" and created a compliance program with training on anti-kickback measures. Its corporate integrity agreement was set to expire in December 2022—five years' time being typical under these arrangements.

As the plunderers have swarmed healthcare, flouting state laws that bar the corporate practice of medicine, few state attorneys general have moved to shut them down. On the rare occasion when a prosecutor does enforce the law, the settlements struck with the private equity–backed companies have been a slap on the wrist, not a real rebuke.

In 2015, for example, later disgraced New York attorney general Eric Schneiderman filed suit against Aspen Dental Management, a company that provides administrative services to dental offices nationwide. Aspen is backed by three private equity firms, one of which is Ares Capital, which is run by Antony Ressler, the former Apollo partner and brother-in-law to Leon Black.

Aspen Dental claimed it was simply providing back office administrative support for dentists, not actually doing dentistry. But Schneiderman's investigation found this claim to be false. Aspen Dental routinely incentivized or pressured staff to increase sales of dental services and products in their offices, Schneiderman determined; dental hygienists, for example, were pushed to sell more products to patients. Aspen Dental also shared in dentists' profits, a direct violation of the law.

Included in Schneiderman's settlement with Aspen Dental was internal correspondence demonstrating the company's improprieties involving hygienists. "I am reviewing Hygiene results and am discouraged to see that we fell further behind budget for the year! (-4.3%)," one memo from June 2011 said. "My real frustration comes from knowing that if we deliver good comprehensive care—we will close this gap!" The gap the memo writer was talking about amounted to $52 in income per day.

"Did you offer each patient whitening?" the memo went on. "Did you make sure every patient was scheduled for recall? Did you offer MI paste as a solution to patients with sensitivity? Fifty-two dollars per day . . . I know we can do this . . . who is with me??"

In bringing the case, the New York AG boasted how his actions had protected New Yorkers. "By enforcing New York's laws banning the corporate practice of medicine and fee-splitting between medical practitioners and non-licensed individuals and entities," Schneiderman crowed, "today's agreement ensures that New Yorkers receive quality dental care."

But the settlement Schneiderman struck with Aspen Dental was a joke. The company generated $645 million in annual revenues at the time, but under the AG's deal, Aspen had only to pay $450,000 to make the case disappear. Neither did Aspen admit the allegations. And while the company agreed to reform its practices, consumer complaints and employee lawsuits continued to be lodged against Aspen Dental years after the settlement, suggesting that the reforms were ineffective.

State medical boards have also been unusually passive about enforcing rules against doctors enabling the corporate practice of medicine. Complaints sent to medical boards in Pennsylvania, Minnesota, and Texas outlining breaches of their laws and requesting sanctions against the doctors participating in the schemes have resulted in no reprimands or actions by the boards in recent years. Those lodging the complaints and providing evidence of physicians allowing corporations to practice medicine improperly in their names have been advised by the boards that there's nothing to see here. Move along.

Given the increasing sway private equity has in the healthcare field, this inaction may not be all that surprising. Potential conflicts of interest exist as well. For example, Sherif Z. Zaafran, MD, the president of the Texas Medical Board, is a board-certified anesthesiologist affiliated with U.S. Anesthesia Partners, a private equity–backed company. U.S. Anesthesia Partners provides anesthesia services in seven states and the District of Columbia and is owned by private equity firms Welsh, Carson, Anderson & Stowe; Berkshire Partners; and GIC.

A spokesman for the Texas Medical Board said decisions about whether to pursue complaints were made by all board members, not just the president.

As Brovont battled EmCare in the Missouri courts, the company was making big headlines back east. In 2017, researchers at Yale University published a blistering study showing that patients treated at emergency rooms run by EmCare were more likely to receive unexpected and significantly higher bills for service than patients at non-EmCare hospitals. The ploy, soon vilified as "surprise medical bills," arose when the treatments received by patients were billed as "out of network" and therefore not reimbursable by a patient's insurance company. Stunned patients were forced to pay the difference and hounded by debt collectors if they could not.

The Yale researchers examined 2.2 million emergency room visits nationwide. They found that when EmCare took over the management of an emergency department, it immediately dumped the existing insurance network arrangements. Then, it proceeded to *almost double the charges to patients* that had been levied by prior physicians at the facility. The "average" surprise bill was $622.55, the researchers calculated, but since that was an average, it meant that others amounted to thousands of dollars.

Given that the typical U.S. family does not have an extra $400 on hand to cover an unexpected expense, this price gouging was meaningful. It was also an outrageous example of preying on unsuspecting consumers in a time of need.

There was more. The researchers determined that for-profit hospitals, like HCA, were significantly more likely to contract with EmCare physicians to run their emergency departments than nonprofit facilities were. Money was why: EmCare physicians increased patient charges for other services, like CT scans, as a way to compensate hospitals for letting them conduct their out-of-network scheme. "After EmCare physicians took over ERs at the hospitals in our data, facility payments rose by 11 percent, which were driven, in part, by increases in the rates for patients who received imaging studies ordered by EmCare," the study said.

Additionally, when EmCare was running the emergency department, patients were 23 percent more likely to be admitted to a hospital, not discharged. This, too, translated to higher profits for the hospital. It was the basis for the 2017 Justice Department's investigation into EmCare that had found the company improperly admitted patients from the ER to gain higher Medicare payments.

"The practice of out-of-network billing from inside in-network hospitals undercuts the functioning of health care labor markets, exposes patients to significant financial risk, and reduces social welfare," the study concluded drily.

Outrage over the findings was immediate. The lead researcher traveled to Washington a dozen times to explain the findings to lawmakers and their staffs and made a presentation at the White House. Disgust over the practice was bipartisan, and Congress began working on a response to rein in the pernicious activity. Even President Trump, who counted Steve Schwarzman, the CEO of Blackstone, as a top economic advisor, said he was against surprise billing.

But the money-spinners were unrepentant. They quietly created a phony grassroots entity to fight back against legislation targeting surprise billing. Called Doctor Patient Unity, it launched a blizzard of dark and ominous attack ads; one said legislation against surprise billing "would only serve insurance companies who are already making record profits, and hurt those who really matter . . . patients . . . us."

The ads' content and the entity's name—Doctor Patient Unity—made it seem like it was working on behalf of patients. Still, the organization was shadowy—no one knew who was funding it, and emails and phone calls to its headquarters went unanswered, a report in the *New York Times* said. Its corporate filing in Virginia listed only one agent, whose name was on more than 150 other political action groups, and its filings to the Federal Communications Commission regarding ad buys identified a sole employee who also worked for an array of Republican political groups.

While people in Washington, D.C., tried to guess who was behind Doctor Patient Unity, it became clear that whoever it was had money to burn. The *Times* calculated the group spent $28 million on ads in just a few weeks, plus hundreds of thousands of dollars on Facebook and Google and in direct mailings.

Then, in July 2019, facing questions from the media, the entity pulled back the curtain on its main backers: KKR-backed Envision, which had bought EmCare in 2018, and TeamHealth, the Blackstone staffing company. They were behind the scary advertising that aimed to keep surprise medical bills in place and profitable.

Anger over the surprise medical bills was powerful and pervasive. It would bring about a January 2022 law reducing, but not entirely eliminating, the likelihood that patients would be victimized by the practice. The legislation wasn't perfect—special interest groups, including private equity titans, had succeeded in protecting some of their arenas from impact. These included urgent care centers, hospice facilities, addiction treatment centers, and nursing homes. But the response to private equity's profit grab in surprise medical billing was the first genuine chink in the armor of the healthcare strip-miners. For once, they had gone too far for Washington to avert its eyes, their monumental greed too visible, easily understandable, and reprehensible.

Blackstone's spokesman contended to us that TeamHealth "has a longstanding policy" against surprise billing and that it supported the legislation to end the practice "through independent arbitration" as the final law stipulated. The behind-the-curtain role it took in Doctor Patient Unity was no secret, the Blackstone spokesman said, but "in a politically charged environment, the coalition did not want its critical message overshadowed by Doctor Patient Unity being characterized solely as a 'private equity' group. That would be a distraction and counter to its goal of stopping this harmful legislation and protecting patients."

As for Envision, investors quickly understood that a ban on surprise billing would hurt the company's profits and its ability to pay down its heavy debt. Envision bonds hurtled into distress territory and in early 2022 the company conducted two debt restructurings in 100 days. In the deals, Envision shifted valuable assets away from existing bondholders in what S&P Global Ratings called an "aggressive, out-of-court restructuring." Such asset shifts are alarming to bond investors, S&P said, because "they can materially erode the credit quality of existing lenders."

Increased scrutiny soon turned to other problems related to private equity's rising role in medicine. As the *Harvard Business Review* reported, the firms had also been buying and growing other specialties that generated a disproportionate share of surprise bills, such as anesthesiologists and radiologists. Freestanding emergency rooms owned by the privateers were becoming another target of patient outrage; treatments at these facilities "can be 22 times more expensive" than at a doctor's office, the report said.

Finally, the privateers' active role in hobbling the nation's already fragile healthcare system was getting some attention. It had taken more than a decade and a global pandemic, but it was a step in the right direction.

Leon Black quickly rose to lead mergers and acquisitions at Drexel Burnham Lambert and was a key figure at the firm when it failed. Black had worked on many of the Drexel bond issues that found their way into the Executive Life portfolio, giving him a crucial understanding of the value in the insurer's holdings. *George Lange*

John Garamendi, pictured here with President Bill Clinton in 2008, was the California insurance commissioner whose sale of the Executive Life bond portfolio gave Leon Black's Apollo Global Management its first big payday. *Zuma Press*

Maureen Marr, creator of the Action Network of Victims of Executive Life, a grassroots organization that fought on behalf of policyholders. Apollo dispatched a lawyer to monitor her. *Gretchen Morgenson*

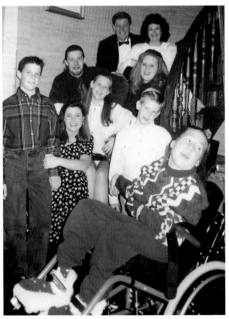

Vince and Sue Watson with their family in 1994. Upon receiving a malpractice award for brain damage suffered by their toddler Katie, her parents bought an Executive Life product to finance her care. Katie wound up receiving millions less than she'd been promised, while Leon Black and his partners generated billions. *The Watson Family*

The Schwayder Family of The Schwayder Trunk Manufacturing Company, later Samsonite, advertising how strong—like Samson—the company's products were. But even the mighty Samson would have been powerless against Drexel-fueled financiers. *Courtesy Beck Archives of Rocky Mountain Jewish History, University of Denver Libraries*

44-Story Plunge Kills
Head of United Brands

By PETER KIHSS

Eli M. Black, chairman of the billion-dollar United Brands Company, which has vast interests in bananas and meat-packing and other enterprises, plunged to his death at 8 A. M. yesterday from the 44th floor of the Pan Am Building.

A sealed quarter-inch tempered plate glass window had been smashed open, and Detective John P. Duffy of the Third Homicide Zone said it had apparently been broken with Mr. Black's heavy attaché case. "It will be classified a suicide," Mr. Duffy said.

The 53-year-old executive, who had built up a company producing milk-bottle caps until it took over the nation's fourth largest meat packer and then the United Fruit Company, was described by associates as having been "under great strain because of business pressures."

The company had incurred heavy losses in Central American banana plantations from last September's Hurricane Fifi, had undergone new burdens with export taxes on bananas imposed by Central American republics and had sustained

Rafael Macia/Forbes magazine
Eli M. Black

losses in its John Morrell & Co. meat-packing division as a result of increased costs of feeding cattle.

But Edward Gelsthorpe, who became executive vice president last November, declared that under Mr. Black's leadership Continued on Page 10, Column 1

Eli Black, CEO of United Brands and Leon Black's father, leaped from his office in the Pan Am building in 1975 just before his involvement in a bribery scandal emerged. Black had directed secret payments to a Honduran official to reduce his company's taxes. *Rafael Macia, Forbes Magazine*

"American Value": Apollo Global Management trumpets its success with Samsonite. *Apollo*

In 1996, Donald Trump traveled to Russia to look at real estate development opportunities. Accompanying him were Howard Lorber, Bennett LeBow, and Leon Black.

Stephen Schwarzman, cofounder of the Blackstone Group. When the Obama administration talked of raising taxes on private equity titans, Schwarzman likened it to Hitler invading Poland. *MediaPunch Inc / Alamy Stock Photo*

Henry Kravis, cofounder in 1976 of Kohlberg Kravis Roberts, best known of the leveraged buyout kings. Their takeover of RJR Nabisco in 1988 created anxiety in Congress about job losses in buyouts, but nothing was done to stop them. *Reuters / Alamy Stock Photo*

David Rubenstein of the Carlyle Group with Donald Trump at Mar a Lago in 2016. Explaining the role of private equity, he said: "While we're not perhaps guardian angels, we are providing a social service, and that social service is making companies more efficient." *AP Images / Evan Vucci*

Dr. Ming Lin, emergency department physician who was removed from his position at PeaceHealth St. Joseph Medical Center in Bellingham, Washington, after protesting the lack of protective equipment for hospital workers during the COVID-19 pandemic. TeamHealth, owned by the Blackstone Group, staffed the department. Financiers are "affecting our primary objectives to take care of our patients and to do no harm," Ling said. *Courtesy of Ming Lin*

Dr. Raymond Brovont, emergency department physician who served as an Army doctor in Iraq in 2005, was fired for raising patient safety concerns to his private equity–owned staffing company. He was told he had a responsibility to "support the corporation's objectives." *Courtesy of Raymond Brovont*

Eddie Martinez and his mother, Maria, who died from COVID in a private equity–owned nursing home in Capitola, California. The home's administrator barred him from visiting his mother after he voiced concerns about her care. *Vanessa Martinez*

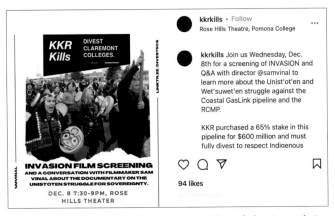

In late 2021, as a result of KKR's ownership of the Coastal Gas Link and its impact on Wet'suwet'en native lands in Canada, students at Claremont College demanded the school divest its KKR holdings and remove trustees Henry Kravis and George Roberts.

At a Melanoma Research Alliance (MRA) Scientific Retreat, Mike Milken discussed accelerating cancer research with Jonathan Simons (left), president and CEO of the Prostate Cancer Foundation, and Leon Black (right), cofounder of the Alliance. *Michael Milken*

CHAPTER TWELVE

"Like When Hitler Invaded Poland in 1939"

A Special Tax Treatment That Mints Billionaires

For buyout giant KKR and its billionaire founders, the firm's 2004 stake in Jazz Pharmaceuticals, a struggling biotech company, was a dim star in a vast and glimmering firmament. Jazz had some drugs in development but no actual product sales; it generated an $85 million loss in 2005, the year KKR first backed it.

Against the $15 billion KKR counted in assets under management, the $130 million it put into Jazz was less than 1 percent—a rounding error. Still, as is typical in the private equity world, KKR installed executives on Jazz's board of directors to watch over its investment. These board seats gave the firm a deep inside knowledge of company operations as well as a check on decisions management made. One KKR director sat on the company's audit committee, charged with ensuring the company's financial reporting was sound. By 2007, KKR had three board seats; the directors were paid approximately $36,000 a year and almost three thousand shares in the company, worth more than $50,000, for their service; the directors chose to defer the stock compensation, documents show.

With KKR's commitment of $130 million and another $120 million from additional private equity firms, Jazz had a crucial war chest it could use to buy other drugs and drugmakers. And in April 2005, before KKR finalized the deal, Jazz announced its acquisition of Orphan Medical, a Minnetonka, Minnesota–based company specializing in drugs to treat relatively rare illnesses affecting small numbers of patients. "Orphan" drugs, as they are known, treat illnesses experienced by fewer than two hundred thousand patients a year. Small though these drugs might be, the Orphan acquisition would build Jazz's "commercial organization," the company said. The purchase immediately jacked Jazz's results, bringing in $12 million in revenues over six months.

Orphan's main product was Xyrem, which treated cataplexy, a rare type of muscle paralysis experienced by narcolepsy patients. The Food and Drug Administration had approved Xyrem as a treatment for cataplexy in 2002. The number of patients with cataplexy in the U.S. was minuscule, but Xyrem had an outsized history. Also known as sodium oxybate or gamma-hydroxybutyrate, it's a Schedule III Controlled Substance and for years had been used illicitly as a date-rape drug. Popular on the nightlife scene in New York City in the 1990s, the drug's overuse and abuse had led to seizure, respiratory depression, coma, and death. It was so powerful, using only a minuscule amount more than prescribed could kill.

That dark history was well known, and the drug's potency meant it couldn't be sold or distributed to anyone other than for its prescribed use, the FDA said. But Xyrem's marketers wanted to widen the market and had applied to the FDA to expand its potential patient population. For example, the company maintained the drug also helped narcolepsy patients experiencing excessive daytime sleepiness.

In November 2005, with KKR as a major investor, the FDA agreed to allow Jazz to offer this new indication for Xyrem. Still, the FDA required a so-called black box warning on the drug, advising physicians and patients that side effects associated with its use could be deadly. And the FDA said Xyrem should only be dispensed through one central pharmacy for the entire country, so it could be tracked closely.

When the FDA approves a drug for use, it limits usage only to patients with diseases against which the drug has proven effective. These parameters are known as label indications, and they aim to restrict the numbers of patients to whom a drug can be prescribed. Doctors who prescribe drugs to patients with ailments outside of those indicated are said to be prescribing "off-label."

As soon as the FDA ruled, Jazz expanded its Xyrem sales force to fifty-five employees from thirty-six. The sales reps received a salary and incentive pay that went up as they peddled more of the drug. One sales representative later said he'd been directed to sell 520 bottles of Xyrem a year, a legal impossibility based on the small patient market.

Beginning in 2003, before KKR appeared on the scene, Orphan's sales representatives had been pushing doctors to promote Xyrem off-label, government records show, and the scheme continued when Jazz acquired the company two years later. Jazz oversaw a speaking program, for example, where physicians were paid to promote a throng of off-label Xyrem indications to other doctors. (Paying doctors to speak on behalf of pharma products at such dinners was common, of course, but it took on a fresh and powerful taint when used by Purdue Pharma to promote opioids, a practice detailed in *Dopesick*, the award-winning television miniseries and bestselling book by journalist Beth Macy.)

Dr. Peter Gleason, a psychiatrist on Long Island, had been a passionate speaker for Orphan and now began pitching for Jazz. In numerous presentations, Gleason downplayed Xyrem's date-rape drug history and lauded other unapproved uses for it, saying it was safe to give to children and the elderly. Jazz paid Gleason well for his evangelism: he received $450 for each Xyrem presentation made to an individual physician, $750 for each luncheon speech, and $1,500 for a dinner program. In 2005, Gleason earned $285,000 from Jazz for this work.

Unfortunately for Gleason, a whistleblower had reported these dubious activities to the federal government. In the spring of 2005, as KKR was pouring money into Jazz, the FBI, the Department of Health and Human Services, and other agencies were investigating the doctor and his ties to the company. A year later, in April 2006, Jazz received subpoenas from the Justice Department for documents related to Xyrem sales; at the same time, Gleason was indicted for working with company officials to promote Xyrem for off-label uses. "Indistinguishable from a carnival snake-oil salesman" was how the FBI described the doctor.

As Jazz fielded prosecutors' inquiries, the company was also preparing to issue stock to the public for the first time. It was still showing losses, but revenues had risen smartly; for 2006, Jazz reported $45 million in sales, more than double the previous year's results.

In its stock offering document, Jazz had to disclose that it was under investigation by federal prosecutors in the Gleason matter. Nevertheless, on June 1, 2007, shares in Jazz Pharmaceuticals began trading at $18 each, raising a total of $108 million from investors. Jazz and KKR had hoped for far more, but at the last moment, the company had had to slash the stock price after an article in the *New York Times* cited Xyrem's date-rape drug history and called it "as dangerous as heroin or LSD." Investors were spooked, and the stock closed its first trading day below the offering price, never a good sign.

Six weeks later, more bad news arrived. Jazz pleaded guilty in federal court in Brooklyn to felony charges of promoting Xyrem for unapproved uses alongside Gleason. Jazz agreed to pay $20 million in fines and restitution and said it would cooperate with the government's ongoing criminal investigation into the matter. Investors were stunned, even though they'd been warned in Jazz's offering statement that this outcome was a possibility. The company's stock tanked.

Government scrutiny on the company took a toll on Jazz's business. By 2008, its sales growth was slowing, losses were rising, and its shares had skidded to under $1 each. It laid off 24 percent of its workers and paused its drug development program so that it could service its KKR-induced debt load. Jazz also warned investors there were "substantial doubts" about the company's ability to "continue as a going concern."

Prospects looked dire for Jazz. But as the sole manufacturer of Xyrem and with no generic drugs on the market to compete with it, Jazz's executives had an ace up their sleeves. They could raise the drug's price, and patients, with no other options, would simply have to pay. (A lawsuit in 2021 would allege that Jazz blocked generic competition and colluded with manufacturers to keep Xyrem prices high.)

In other words, Jazz was an early adaptor of a price-gouging tactic that would soon become popular among other drug companies. Valeant Pharmaceuticals, run by a former McKinsey consultant, took up the practice especially aggressively. But the most notorious price-gouger was Turing Pharmaceuticals, run by a former hedge fund manager named Martin Shkreli, which in one day raised the price of Daraprim, an anti-parasitic medicine, from $13.50 a pill to $750. Shkreli went to jail in 2018 for securities fraud in an unrelated case.

By 2010, Xyrem patients were paying four times what they'd paid just four years earlier for the drug, with a year of Xyrem treatment costing $35,000. Jazz's executives were, well, jazzed. On a conference call with Wall Street analysts that year, Bob Myers, the company's president, said, "There is a price ceiling that we want to stay below to not raise the scrutiny of [Medicare] payors or [insurance] plans. But quite frankly we're nowhere near that ceiling right now. We could more than double that current price and still be below that ceiling."

Soon Jazz was reporting record sales, and in 2011 the company booked an astounding $125 million profit. The stock was back above $40 that September when the company merged with Azur Pharma Ltd., a Dublin-based entity. Under the controversial deal, known as an inversion, Jazz left the U.S. and became an Irish company, so it could slash its corporate tax rate to 15 percent from the 35 percent rate stateside. Because of their obvious benefits, inversions were becoming popular with all kinds of companies; the tech sector and pharma companies were among the biggest devotees.

Throughout this upswing, KKR had been selling its Jazz shares periodically, and in 2014, it exited completely. It had been dicey for a while, but ultimately KKR had excelled. Jazz was among KKR's top three performers in its private equity portfolios during 2011, the firm reported to shareholders. In 2013, when KKR held just over 6 percent of the company's shares, that stake alone was worth $334 million, versus its initial $130 million investment.

Patients who paid for Xyrem, and the taxpayers who covered its enormous costs through Medicare reimbursements, didn't do as well, though. By August 2021, the FDA had logged 27,000 "serious adverse events," such as hospitalization, life-threatening experiences, and disability, and 753 deaths with this drug, according to the *New York Times*.

As for Gleason, the doctor who had promoted Xyrem off-label for Jazz? In 2010, he pleaded to a federal misdemeanor and received a $25 fine and one-year probation. Financially destitute, he faced state medical board disciplinary proceedings. In 2011, one month after the end of his probation period, Gleason killed himself.

KKR's spokeswoman told us the 2005 investigation in Orphan "addressed behavior that took place before Jazz's (and by extension, KKR's) ownership, although it potentially may have continued for a short period under our ownership," adding that "it would be misleading to characterize KKR's ownership as the reason or cause for bad behavior." She also stressed Jazz's other products that addressed narcolepsy, epilepsy, cataplexy, and acute lymphoblastic leukemia, among others. When KKR initially invested, Jazz "had little to no portfolio, and by the time we had fully exited, it had significantly grown its product offering. I am confident a close look at the filings and earnings calls would show this growth and diversification as key contributors to the company's profitability."

Still, Xyrem remained responsible for a vast majority of Jazz's net sales from 2014 through 2017, its SEC filings show. And the KKR spokeswoman did not address the Xyrem price hikes that were so costly to patients. In August 2021, the civil anti-trust suit against Xyrem and a group of generic drug makers was allowed to proceed in the southern district of New York. "Since 2007, Jazz has raised the price of Xyrem from approximately $2.04 per milliliter to approximately $29.69, an increase of over 1,350%," the suit noted. "For a patient taking a dosage in the middle of the effective range, the monthly cost of Xyrem exceeds $13,000. One study showed that Jazz raised price more than any other pharmaceutical company for price increases on a single drug."

The mortgage crisis of 2008 hit the U.S. like a freight train, revealing an almost inconceivable array of corrupt practices by major financial institutions. The entire nation was rocked by tales of mortgage lenders making loans to borrowers they knew could not repay them, prestigious investment banks selling securities that had been designed to fail, and bankers foreclosing on homeowners without the legal proof of ownership.

As the debacle unfolded, another disturbing element emerged: financial regulators, charged with keeping the system safe, had in fact looked the other way as misdeeds in the home loan frenzy had metastasized. Even worse, some of the overseers had encouraged the behavior.

It was a colossal, 360-degree failure. Greed might be expected from bankers, but incompetence and complicity by regulators and the courts? It was shocking.

And yet, while borrowers' belongings piled up on curbs in front of foreclosed homes, banks received billions in taxpayer bailouts. The Wall Street elites—bankers, financiers, regulators—got a pass in the debacle. No top executive of a significant financial institution went to jail in the aftermath, unlike the almost eight hundred officials who'd received prison time following the S&L crisis of the late 1980s. Main Street, meanwhile, got the shaft—drowning borrowers receiving little in the way of a government lifeline throughout the crisis. The paradox was disturbing: borrowers who'd already been harmed by the banks' dubious activities were hurt yet again. The perpetrators, meanwhile, were rewarded with bailouts.

No surprise, then, that murmurings grew louder accusing the American system of being rigged in favor of the elites. On the left, a protest movement called "Occupy Wall Street" set up an encampment in Zuccotti Park in New York's financial district and called out economic inequality. The occupiers coined a new term for the everyday people oppressed by corporate greed and the Wall Street financiers—the 99 percent.

Among those travelling to Zuccotti Park to show their support were workers at Momentive Performance Materials, a maker of adhesives, silicones, and sealants headquartered near Albany, New York. Momentive had recently been acquired by Apollo, which quickly slashed four hundred unionized workers' pay by half, violating their contract. The company would file for bankruptcy in 2014.

On the political right, the rigged-game views also gained in volume and sway, setting the stage for a carnival barker, serial bankrupter of companies, and self-avowed anti-elite named Donald Trump to win the presidency in 2016.

With the nation's economy and stock market in a tailspin and bank malfeasance the focus, few paid heed to the private equity titans. Blackstone's Schwarzman drew scorn for holding an obscenely lavish sixtieth birthday party for himself in February 2007, just as the mortgage storm was gathering. Spending $3 million on the event, Schwarzman had Rod Stewart and Patti LaBelle perform for his 350 guests inside the Park Avenue Armory in a truly fin de siècle moment.

The growing economic storm didn't stop Blackstone from issuing public shares for the first time later that year, raising $4 billion in investor money. Its top executives were now firmly in billionaire territory; Blackstone's filings showed Schwarzman had received $400 million in cash distributions the previous year.

Apollo had tried to go public, but pulled its 2008 offering amid the mortgage mess. Still, *Forbes* pegged Leon Black's fortune at an estimated $4 billion. The following year, Jeffrey Epstein would be prosecuted for soliciting sex with a minor in Florida; he'd have to register as a convicted sex offender, but Black continued their relationship.

Despite Apollo not going public and Blackstone's shares taking a beating in the 2008 mayhem, as most financial stocks did, the private equity industry actually wound up getting a boost from the disaster. Researchers studying the titans' returns concluded that their investment funds had not fallen as far as the broad market indices had. Then, in the subsequent upswing, they had recovered far more swiftly. This relative outperformance allowed the titans to lure even more institutional investor money into their coffers.

As the pirates of finance amassed their billions, the debt burdens of the average American family also swelled to record levels. In the first decade of the 2000s, according to Federal Reserve data, household debt grew to 1.22 times that of personal income, up from 0.84 times in 2000. By late 2007, debt service payments by households peaked at 13.2 percent of disposable income, up from 10.4 percent in 1993.

Meanwhile, 2005 legislation passed by Congress claiming to reform the consumer bankruptcy process actually harmed small borrowers. The law made it tougher for consumers to file for a type of personal bankruptcy called "Chapter 7," under which most of their debts are forgiven. The law also limited the so-called homestead exemption, which allowed borrowers to protect their homes from the reach of creditors.

After the bankruptcy law passed, consumers tapped their credit cards to cover bills. Credit card debt soared, hitting a peak of $1.3 trillion in July 2008. The average credit card debt per household was $8,640, having more than doubled from 2001. The biggest contributors were unexpected medical bills—many generated by private equity.

The wealth gap in the U.S. was widening by the year. In 2007, the richest 10 percent of the population controlled 72 percent of the nation's wealth, up from 67 percent in 1995. Meanwhile, the bottom 90 percent of the populace held 25 percent of the wealth in 2007, down from 34 percent in 1983. The gulf between the two would only deepen, accelerated by the housing crisis, government bailouts to the banks, and private equity operating in the shadows.

As the nation inched back to normalcy after the 2008 cataclysm, the financiers were amassing greater power and titanic wealth. In 2010, President Barack Obama threatened to raise taxes on Leon Black, Steve Schwarzman, and other private equity titans by eliminating the loophole that lets them pay 15 percent on their income versus the far higher rates levied on working-class and wage-earning taxpayers. Eliminating this rich man's giveaway had broad support—it would have been fair. "It's a huge windfall to some of the best-off people in society," observed Len Burman, a fellow at the Brookings Institution, a Washington think tank.

Moreover, closing the loophole would generate tens of billions for the U.S. government, according to estimates. The driving force behind all attempts, unsuccessful though they have been, to end this egregious billionaire benefit is Victor Fleischer, a professor of tax law at the University of San Diego law school. He has testified before Congress that the tax treatment was "designed with small business in mind, not billion-dollar investment funds" and correctly notes that it widens the income inequality gap in the U.S.

But fairness isn't a priority for this crowd. And each time the loophole comes under assault, they and their firms spend millions lobbying against changes to the law that so enriches them. In 2010, for example, when Obama surfaced the idea of eliminating the tax treatment, its chief beneficiaries sprang to action. The Private Equity Growth Capital Council, at the time the industry's largest lobbying group, urged its members to wage a "grassroots" campaign against the change. And Schwarzman of Blackstone chimed in with a stunning comment. "It's a war," he declared at a private board meeting of a nonprofit organization. "It's like when Hitler invaded Poland in 1939."

It was outlandish, of course, to equate an increased tax on billionaires with the takeover of a sovereign nation that began the extermination of millions of people. But Schwarzman had shown his true colors. The tone-deaf executive had revealed two characteristics that ran deep among the marauders and were central to their activities—narcissism and grandiosity. Never mind that when this crowd got their way, everyone else was the loser.

After the absurd comment became public, Schwarzman apologized. What he had really meant, he said, was that the government needed to "work productively with business for the benefit of the overall economy." Schwarzman backtracked, but he couldn't erase the image he had created—private equity barons, with their multimillion-dollar birthday parties, sumptuous homes, and magnificent art collections, would become the equivalent of Adolf Hitler's victims if they had to pay higher taxes.

· · ·

After beating back the proposed tax increase, which the industry would do again and again, private equity was on a roll. In 2010, after a series of fits and starts, KKR finally brought its shares to the U.S. public market on the New York Stock Exchange, revealing that cofounders Henry Kravis and George Roberts had each earned $70.5 million in the previous year.

Apollo finally got its stock offering done in 2011. But the $348 million sale was not a resounding success—the price range of the Apollo offering was reduced shortly before it launched. And when the stock started trading, it fell rather than rose, not an auspicious beginning.

Jeffrey Epstein was a big buyer of Apollo's initial public offering. Financial Trust Company, an Epstein entity based in the U.S. Virgin Islands, purchased $5 million worth of the shares. It seems to have been a believer, as the entity still held the stock in 2019 when Epstein died in his lower Manhattan jail cell.

But other investors had given Apollo's offering a big thumbs-down. The offering documents had been confusing, some investors said, and had not specified how the company planned to use the money beyond "for general corporate purposes and to fund growth initiatives." Furthermore, unlike KKR and Blackstone, Apollo had experienced difficulties reselling some of the companies it had purchased on the public market. Among investors, this raised questions "about the overall quality of Apollo's leveraged buyout portfolio and their investment management decisions," one commentator said.

In 2010, for example, Apollo was forced to withdraw a public offering of shares in gambling giant Harrah's, because investors rejected the share price assigned to the deal. While Apollo and its fellow Harrah's owner TPG had wanted to issue stock at a price between $15 and $17 a share, investors said the appropriate number was $10, tops.

In the years after the Apollo offering, the company's shares never quite traded at the same valuations as its peers, Blackstone and KKR. Apollo's shares generally traded at a discount to its competitors. The "Leon discount," some called it.

In September 2010, the SEC created a new rule in response to the pay-to-play pension scandal that rocked the New York State Common Retirement Fund. It prohibited registered investment advisers, like Apollo and KKR, from providing their investment advisory services to a government entity (a pension, say) for two years after they had donated to any of its officials. The goal was to ensure that investment advisors were chosen based on their merits rather than their campaign contributions.

Under the rule, advisors had to keep records of their donations. And it barred investment advisors from paying third parties—such as the placement agents involved in the New York scandal—to solicit advisory business from a government entity unless those agents were already subject to pay-to-play regulations. Advisors had a year to comply.

The SEC started out tough on violators of the new rule, going after everyone from hedge funds and investment advisors to venture capital funds and private equity funds. Its first case came in 2014, when it charged TL Ventures, a Philadelphia-based private equity fund. The fund had made $4,500 in donations to public officials even as it was paid to provide investment advisory services to state and city pension funds. TL Ventures paid $300,000 to settle the case without admitting or denying the allegations.

"As we have done with broker-dealers, we will hold investment advisers strictly liable for pay-to-play violations," warned Andrew Ceresney, director of the SEC's enforcement division.

Three years later, the SEC brought actions against ten firms who agreed to pay an aggregate $660,000 in penalties. In these cases, the SEC had gone after firms whose executives had contributed as little as $400 to a public official. And three more cases in 2018 brought in penalties of over $700,000; an A-lister in the group of violators was Pershing Square Capital Management, the hedge fund overseen by the self-promoter William A. Ackman.

But even as the SEC enforcement division pursued these cases, a counter effort was going on behind the scenes in another unit of the agency. Starting in 2013, staff in the division of investment management, charged with overseeing money managers, began to give rule violators a pass. Using a little-known administrative process known as delegated authority, investment management staff began granting waivers to big, well-known firms that had violated the rule. From 2013 through the first half of 2018, the SEC granted twelve waivers to major firms and banks, agreeing not to pursue them for their rule violations. Recipients of the waivers included T. Rowe Price and Fidelity, the enormous mutual fund managers, and Brookfield Asset Management, the huge Canadian real estate and private equity firm.

Apollo also got a pass. In April 2016, an Apollo executive had written a $1,000 check to the presidential campaign of John Kasich, the Republican governor of Ohio. As governor, Kasich appointed one member of the Ohio state pension board, which oversees pensions Apollo was running money for. In other words, it was precisely the type of case the rule was designed to address.

The contributor was Stephanie Drescher, Apollo's global head of business development and investor relations management, regulatory documents show. Drescher "made the contribution because of her interest in the Presidential election and not because of any desire to influence the client's selection of an investment adviser," Apollo assured the SEC. She had forgotten to pre-clear the donation with the firm because "she was focused on the Presidential election and not the Adviser's preclearance requirement," Apollo explained.

There was no evidence, the firm went on, that Drescher "intended to, or actually did, interfere" with the pension fund clients' process for the selection or retention of advisory services based on merit. But most important, Apollo said, enforcing the rule would cause the firm to serve the Ohio pension funds "without compensation for a two-year period." This would result "in a financial loss of approximately $9 million, or 9,000 times the amount of the contribution."

Asking for forgiveness is easier than asking for approval, of course. But to any law-abiding citizen, Apollo's argument would seem to be a nonstarter—the firm should be excused from having to follow a rule because it would cost it significant money to do so? It would be like a polluter contending that it shouldn't be prosecuted for violating an environmental law because following it would be too expensive.

In early 2019, the SEC let Apollo off the hook. In a delegated authority ruling that went unnoticed, the commission said its move "was necessary and appropriate in the public interest and consistent with the protection of investors."

Few in the money management business had welcomed the SEC rule when it was implemented. And in recent years, some firms have urged the SEC to water it down or eliminate it altogether. In 2019, for example, the Investment Adviser Association wrote a comment letter to the SEC claiming the pay-to-play rule's costs and compliance burdens "are substantial." The association added ominously that the rule "may be negatively affecting participation in the political process."

Still, the exemptions granted by the SEC to big firms have continued. Makes you wonder: Why write rules if you're not going to enforce them?

That isn't the only "free pass" from securities laws Apollo has received from the SEC in recent years. Beginning in 2010, Apollo and its lawyers started working the SEC to relax a law created in 1940 governing transactions among related financial companies. The law was aimed at investment advisors to prevent self-dealing, where related entities conduct deals that benefit money managers at the expense of their investors. The specific practice governed a practice called co-investing among various units of a money management firm. It fell under the Investment Company Act of 1940, which came about after Congress determined the securities regulations created in the 1930s had not covered advisors adequately. As a result, investors remained at risk of abuse, Congress believed.

"In the exhaustive study of the industry which preceded passage of the Act, it was found that, in many instances, investment companies had been operated in the interests of their managers rather than in the interests of their shareholders," the SEC concluded in a 1966 report.

Making sure that managers don't put their interests ahead of their investors' is a problem that can arise when financial firms have an array of units making investments on behalf of their investors. For example, Apollo Investment Corp. is a business development company, making loans to small businesses at exceedingly high interest rates. As a publicly traded company, its fiduciary duties are to its shareholders. Meanwhile, another Apollo entity requesting the exemption from the 1940 Act was a closed-end Apollo fund that invests in bonds and other obligations of corporations, whose duty is to its fundholders.

The law Apollo was seeking to relax required that any investments under consideration for one entity—say its business development company—must also be offered to other Apollo entities at the same terms. This ensured that one unit's investors would not be rewarded with sweet deals that another one never got a chance to invest in.

When firms like Apollo ask for relief from the rules, they almost always characterize them as too burdensome and costly. This case was no different: lawyers for Apollo said the rules required "onerous amounts of information to be shared between affiliates and a substantial compliance framework to manage all of the regulatory obligations." Without the SEC's okay, "in many circumstances the regulated funds would be limited in their ability to participate in attractive and appropriate investment opportunities." In addition, investors would not be at risk, it said, because Apollo had protections in place to ensure that its practices would not "involve overreaching by any person concerned, including the advisers."

Finally, in March 2016, the SEC gave in, granting Apollo an exemption on its self-dealing rule, "after years of negotiation," as the firm's lawyers wrote in a 2018 commentary. No longer would the board of a firm like Apollo have to present investment opportunities to all of a firm's entities. Now Apollo's board could limit the range of transactions that had to be presented to a particular fund.

The Apollo spokeswoman said the firm "didn't push the SEC to change any rules. Apollo, along with numerous other entities, participates in the Coalition for Business Development, which had conversations about modernizing rules and regulations that were passed as long ago as 1940." The rules needed modernizing, she said.

Since the SEC began relaxing the 1940 Act rules against self-dealing among investment advisors, there's been no evidence that investors have been harmed by the actions. Time will tell, of course, if misdeeds emerge. But this much is clear: Apollo's success launched a tidal wave of activities among investment firms, its lawyers boasted. And in a 2021 application to renew the SEC's approval, Apollo pointed to more than one hundred other cases in which the regulator had granted exemptions to financial firms seeking to escape the self-dealing rule. Many of those rulings involved private equity funds. Once again, Apollo, the most aggressive of the private equity pack, had been ahead of the curve.

CHAPTER THIRTEEN

"Money for Nothing"

Investigators Home In on Fleecers' Fees and Practices

You may not have heard of Taminco Global Chemical Corp., but you've almost certainly used the company's products. Taminco makes something called alkylamines, which go into shampoos, dish liquids, and surface cleaners as well as water treatment, animal nutrition, and herbicides. Alkylamines are organic compounds produced through the reaction of an alcohol with ammonia, and Taminco, based in Allentown, Pennsylvania, and Ghent, Belgium, is the world's biggest producer of them. Owned since 2014 by the Eastman Chemical Company, Taminco has operations in Brazil, the Philippines, and Germany.

Twice in recent years, Taminco has been flipped by private equity firms. Its story illustrates how the plunderers make money behind the scenes at the companies they buy.

Taminco is illuminating in another way as well. Under one of its private equity masters—CVC Capital—the company violated federal narcotics rules by lax practices that ended up supplying Mexican drug cartels with enough of a chemical called monomethylamine, or MMA, to create $3.2 billion worth of the street drug methamphetamine.

CVC Capital is a big private equity firm that bought Taminco in 2007 for approximately $1.1 billion. (The firm did not respond to an email seeking comment on this incident.) Immediately after the purchase, a report in *Bloomberg News* says, Taminco began a push to boost chemical sales, increasing them by 14 percent from 2007 through 2010. The goal was the usual sale or public stock offering, allowing CVC to exit at a profit, Bloomberg said.

But Taminco was neglecting its regulatory obligations, prosecutors would conclude, and its products were winding up in the hands of Mexican drug dealers. By the time prosecutors made their case in 2015, though, CVC was long gone from the company. Taminco was then owned by Apollo, which was in the process of trying to flip the company again after purchasing it in December 2011 for $1.4 billion. Taminco had become the proverbial hot potato.

Taminco had 820 employees, maintained seven plants, and operated in nineteen countries. Almost one-third of its sales were in agriculture and another 25 percent in animal nutrition and personal care. Some of its products dominated their markets, holding 50 percent or 75 percent shares.

Like many chemical companies, Taminco was registered with the Drug Enforcement Administration, because some of its products, while legal, could also be used to manufacture controlled substances or street drugs. As such, by law Taminco had to confirm the identity and legitimacy of its customers receiving products from the U.S. and immediately report to the DEA any unusual loss or disappearance of a product.

As prosecutors later learned, the company failed on both counts. But no executive would be punished for the lapses.

In August 2011, a few months before Apollo took over Taminco, DEA officials discovered that some of the company's MMA shipments had gone missing. In December 2011, as Apollo was buying the company, Customs and Border Protection officers found five of the missing barrels when they intercepted a trucker trying to transport the Taminco MMA across the Mexico-U.S. border at Nogales, Arizona. It is unclear whether Apollo had any idea these investigations were underway, but the following April, DEA agents found and seized six additional Taminco drums of MMA at a self-storage unit in Nogales. The drums seized by the DEA were traced back to March 2010 shipments Taminco had made to a Mexican customer it had not put through the required vetting process.

While these events were unfolding at the Mexico-Arizona border, Apollo was taking over Taminco's operations. The firm installed five directors on the company's eleven-person board and quickly extracted a $243 million dividend from the company as it had done with Noranda a few years earlier.

Under Apollo, Taminco swung from a profit to a loss and its sales essentially flatlined from when CVC owned it. But Apollo made out well. In addition to the dividend, the firm reaped another $150 million when Taminco issued shares to the public in late 2013. That offering was not as lucrative as Apollo had hoped—investor appetite was lackluster and the price per share had to be cut from $18 to $15, down from the $22 high the stock had traded at during that quarter. After selling 10 million shares in the offering, Apollo was left with a 53 percent stake in Taminco.

In the meantime, Apollo was extracting fees from Taminco for management consulting, legal, and acquisition costs. Every year Apollo owned Taminco, for example, it charged the company $3.9 million for consulting services plus "out-of-pocket costs and expenses in connection therewith." Taminco also paid $14.6 million to Apollo Global Securities, in connection with the acquisition and, a regulatory filing shows, Apollo received an additional $44 million in legal and general advisory fees from the company as of September 30, 2012.

Most egregious of all, though, was Taminco's separate $35 million payment to Apollo in 2013, to cover years of future monitoring and oversight by Apollo. Because Apollo sold Taminco in 2014, the fees the company was paying went for services Apollo *would never have to render*. In other words, Taminco's $35 million payment to Apollo was the equivalent of paying money for nothing.

Money-for-nothing payments are a clever plunderer ploy and one of the hidden fees these financiers can reap when they buy and sell companies. Here's how they work: Monitoring fees are typically paid annually by a portfolio company to their private equity overseers for management guidance and advice. But these fees are generally struck in long-term contracts, extending at least ten years. So, even if a private equity firm sells the portfolio company before the ten-year contract is up, that company must still pay all the monitoring fees remaining under the contract.

Getting paid for work they never perform is free money for the financiers. But it comes at a cost to those on the other side of the equation: workers, customers, pensioners, and Apollo's fund investors. Even as the fees plump the raiders' profits, the hundreds of millions of dollars paid by these companies for no-show advisory services leave them with less money for workers, pensioners, and investors, and to invest in their operations.

Consider the monitoring fees racked up by Apollo in just one year, 2013. That year, Apollo stood to collect up to $126 million in such fees from six companies *it had already sold*. Apollo was being paid for forty-three years of advice it would never have to provide.

The $35 million Taminco agreed to pay Apollo was a part of

that $126 million. And the payments *exceeded* Taminco's net income for all of 2011. Paying the $35 million certainly hobbled Taminco, but it enriched Black and his partners.

In September 2014, Apollo flipped its majority interest in Taminco to Eastman Chemical for $2.8 billion. A federal grand jury in eastern Pennsylvania had quietly issued a subpoena to Taminco in July 2014 requesting information related to the narcos investigation, a request that was not public. On August 7, 2014, Taminco disclosed the existence of the investigation to the public, stating that it had received a subpoena from the Justice Department "requesting documents and information concerning export shipments of monomethylamines to a former customer in Mexico, a portion of which was diverted and subsequently seized by the US Drug Enforcement Agency in 2011." The filing also noted that Taminco had been cooperating with the government.

The investigation emerged just as Eastman was doing due diligence on the purchase, *Bloomberg News* reported. After Eastman concluded that the crimes were no longer occurring, the acquisition went through.

When the Justice Department filed its criminal complaint against Taminco in October 2015, CVC was long gone and Apollo was halfway out the door. Eastman wound up on the hook for the sins of Taminco's previous overseer; it pleaded guilty to receiving approximately $210,000 from the illegal sale of twenty-two thousand gallons of MMA made while Taminco was owned by CVC, and paid $860,000 in criminal penalties and a civil fine of $475,000. As mentioned previously, no executive went to jail as a result of the investigation.

. . .

In 2015, the SEC launched a broad investigation into private equity practices and revealed a staggering assessment: half of the fees charged by the firms were either improper or in violation of disclosure laws.

Among the fees under the SEC's microscope were the money-for-nothing monitoring fees levied by the industry. In the crosshairs because of its monitoring fee practices, Blackstone paid $39 million to settle a related case. And Apollo had to pay $53 million to settle an SEC case against it in 2016. After the SEC brought the cases, Blackstone stopped charging monitoring fees to its new investment vehicles, its spokesman said.

Of all the cases filed by the SEC on this activity, Apollo's fine was the largest. The case involved three Apollo funds, V, VI, and VII, formed between 2000 and 2007. The SEC said Apollo had not told its own investors that it was dunning portfolio companies for years of monitoring fees the firm would never earn. The lump sum payments received by the Apollo advisors essentially reduced the portfolio companies' value prior to their sale or IPO and reduced amounts available for distribution to fund investors.

Apollo agreed to cease and desist from further violations without admitting or denying the findings, the SEC reported. It said it would distribute the $37.5 million in disgorgement and $2.7 million in interest to its fund investors. Apollo agreed to distribute the amounts to affected fund investors.

Asked about the investigation, Apollo's spokeswoman said that since its conclusion, Apollo "has increased its assets under management from $188.6 billion to $514.8 billion, which we believe provides a strong indication of investors' ongoing trust in Apollo."

GRETCHEN MORGENSON AND JOSHUA ROSNER

As usual, the SEC's fines were not even a cost of doing business for the players. And no individuals had to pay any of these fines out of their own pockets.

The SEC's new interest in private equity's business practices disturbed the takeover barons. But the scrutiny provided a business opportunity for at least one participant—in 2021, Igor Rozenblit, a lead investigator on these cases at the SEC, announced he was leaving the commission. His destination? A new consulting firm he set up to help private equity firms prepare for regulatory investigations and design compliance programs. A classic case of the revolving door.

As the results of the private equity investigations sank in, some wondered if public pensions would continue to invest with the firms. After being ripped off by these powerful and wealthy firms, shouldn't they fire them? Apparently not.

The Pennsylvania Public School Employees' Retirement System was one investor Apollo had not advised about its monitoring fee extractions. Under its agreement with the SEC, Apollo paid $30,000 to the pension, essentially admitting that it had improperly taken $30,000 from the pockets of public school workers across the state. And yet, the following year, the Pennsylvania pension agreed to invest a fresh $100 million with Apollo. Was it because Apollo had done so well for the pension? Not according to an analysis by *Philadelphia Inquirer* columnist Joseph DiStefano, who concluded that Apollo's returns for the pension had been less than 3 percent annually over nineteen years. Far below, in other words, what stock market returns had been.

The Pennsylvania pension's decision to keep investing with Apollo mirrored similar actions taken by public funds across the country. They throw their beneficiaries' money into high-cost investments rewarding the very same plunderers who fire lower- and

238

middle-class workers and diminish government revenues through tax loopholes. As such, these pensions are among the chief contributors to the widening wealth gap in the U.S., a gulf that harms the very people the pensions are supposed to benefit.

This anomaly is even more puzzling when viewed against the findings in a 2020 pension study by academics at Harvard University and Stanford University. Analyzing $500 billion of investments in private equity funds by two hundred public pensions between 1990 and 2018, the researchers found that excessive fees levied by the predators depleted some pensions' returns by $45 billion, or *almost 10 percent* of the pie.

Who are the losers in this arithmetic? Firefighters, teachers, sanitation workers, librarians, bus drivers. Taxpayers also land in this category, when they are called upon to shore up public pensions that cannot meet their obligations because their assets have been depleted.

As for the winners—well, we know who they are: Leon Black, Henry Kravis, and Steve Schwarzman, of course. But lesser employees in Plunderland benefit, too, as a 2020 compensation study found.

Over most of the prior decade, the study concluded, the vampire capitalist industry had enjoyed steadily rising pay. In fact, employees earning between $150,000 and $1 million in private equity accounted for 68 percent of respondents in 2020, up 7 percent from the previous year. In the history of the survey, there had never been a higher percentage of employees reporting annual earnings greater than $150,000.

Remember that this all-time high was set during the pandemic. A year when many were losing their jobs, being evicted from their homes, facing crippling medical bills, and watching family members die. A year when the federal government backstopped the financial markets so that the privateers could continue spinning their schemes.

Another data point from 2020 shows how corporate business models made unsustainable by heavy debt loads are a rising problem for U.S. companies. Companies experiencing this difficulty are known as corporate zombies, and their numbers are increasing, thanks in large part to private equity's Dr. Frankensteins.

In the late 1980s, only 4 percent of public companies across fourteen different economies qualified as zombies, according to a 2020 analysis by the Bank for International Settlements. By 2017, however, that percentage had almost quadrupled, to 15 percent.

Shareholders of these companies aren't the only ones imperiled by the near-dead entities. Also under siege are employees, pensioners, suppliers, and local communities whose schools, police, and fire departments rely on corporate tax receipts.

It is difficult to watch the toil of the many fattening the pockets of a rapacious few. And yet, on it goes.

CHAPTER FOURTEEN

"Oppressing Indigenous People"

Bulldozing Through Our Wetlands

The rage was palpable from the people of Bayonne, New Jersey, an industrial and immigrant city of seventy-two thousand on New York Bay south of the Statue of Liberty. It was 2022, and ten years earlier, Bayonne's mayor had agreed to sell the city's municipal water and sewage operation to a private investor group, pledging flat rates or modest increases and a modernized system. But after the deal was signed, water rates rocketed and residents' bank accounts began hemorrhaging.

"My water bill is $900!!!!" exclaimed Paola Hernandez on a website created in 2021 to try to rescind the arrangement. "It's hard enough to make ends meet and now rent will go even higher because of this!" a resident named Laura Kobelski complained. Dino Stanisic chimed in: "My water bill has doubled—just received a bill for $1,030. Only rich people can afford the charges."

With a median household income of $70,000 in Bayonne, $1,000 water bills every three months were not just a burden. They meant meaningfully less money for rent, food, and other living expenses.

To be sure, Bayonne had mismanaged its finances for years and, at the time of the 2012 deal, was at risk of being taken over by the state. It had not put through a water-rate increase in over a decade and had long underinvested in necessary upkeep, upgrades, or repairs to the water system.

But the deal to sell the water and sewer operation came at a high cost to Bayonne's populace. And their struggles to pay for water wound up enriching one of the most storied wealth extraction firms of all time—KKR. The private equity colossus that helped advance leveraged buyouts in the 1980s, KKR was the driving financial force behind Bayonne's disastrous water privatization deal in 2012. It was the same firm whose leaders Henry Kravis and George Roberts had each received $70.5 million two years earlier, the folks who'd made all that money in Jazz Pharmaceuticals, the price-gouging company whose main drug was associated with date-rape.

KKR is proud of its involvement in the Bayonne water plan. Like Apollo, which cited its looting of Samsonite as an exemplary deal, KKR trumpeted the Bayonne transaction as an example of the firm's commitment to socially responsible investing. It was a case study in corporate citizenship, KKR said on its website in 2014, "a new model to address water infrastructure needs." The investment in the municipal water system of Bayonne "is a prime example of a public private partnership that is working well."

Working well for KKR, yes. The deal guaranteed 11 percent annual returns to the firm and its partner—a staggering level in the prevailing low-interest-rate environment where the ten-year U.S. Treasury bond yield was well under 3 percent. Then, six years later, KKR flipped its stake in the Bayonne system to another private equity investor, reaping 2.8 times what it had paid.

Still, KKR didn't leave the scene entirely; the firm acts as moneylender—for a fee—to Bayonne if its water revenues don't meet a certain threshold and the city must borrow to cover the shortfall. It has had to do this often.

KKR's spokeswoman says that Bayonne was better off under the deal, improving the city's financial position by providing a $150 million initial payment and helping it eliminate existing debt. She also says KKR invested in upgrades and repairs to the water system as well as increasing workforce safety requirements.

Still, the structure of the water deal bled the people of Bayonne while it rewarded KKR. Ratepayers had to make up the difference if the utility failed to generate enough money to pay the promised 11 percent return to KKR. It was reminiscent of the Apollo-Noranda fight over electricity bills.

Not surprisingly, between 2012 and 2021, Bayonne's water bills rose almost 50 percent. And when residents fall behind on their bills, the city can place liens on their homes; if left unpaid long enough, liens can result in foreclosures.

"Bayonne Municipal Utilities Authority maintained control of rates charged to users, which are determined by a formula in the agreement," the KKR spokeswoman explained. But the actual rate increases were much higher than those specified in the agreement and the formula governing the rate increases is only one of the costs to residents. They must also shoulder the cost of system repairs.

The unhappy outcome in Bayonne following the water deal is not an anomaly. Similar events have unfolded in other municipalities where public water systems went private. A 2021 report by the Association of Environmental Authorities, a public utility nonprofit, said the average annual bill for privately owned water systems in the U.S. was 60 percent higher than that of publicly owned systems: $501 versus $315. And in privatized arrangements, low-income households spent 1.55 percent more of their income on water than they did if they were in a public utility's area.

Agreements like Bayonne's are "forms of privatization that can put investor interests ahead of those of ratepayers," the association's report said in an understatement. Thankfully, such arrangements are also unusual because they often encounter political opposition or local authorities decline to give up control of essential infrastructure.

As public outcry over Bayonne's water debacle soared, Jodi Casais, a Bayonne Board of Education trustee, asked the New Jersey Board of Public Utilities to investigate. She accused the former mayor who struck the deal with KKR of conducting the transaction "in some backroom."

That former mayor is Mark Smith, a policeman-turned-politician who lost a runoff election for mayor in 2014. Now director of Homeland Security for the Hudson County Sheriff's Office, Smith defended the water deal in an open letter to critics in 2022, saying the water transaction was no backroom pact. "It relied upon careful, thoughtful and continuing oversight by municipal government to ensure each of the parties was holding up their end of the agreement," he contended. In addition, he noted, it had been praised as innovative by the Clinton Global Initiative, the Bill Clinton organization that "convenes global and emerging leaders to create and implement solutions to the world's most pressing challenges."

Still, Smith allowed, the water deal was "not a perfect solution" when executed.

Former mayor Smith certainly shoulders some blame for locking his city into the ruinous forty-year contract. To get out of it, Bayonne would have to pay $300 million today. And yet, does anyone believe a small city mayor and former patrolman was on an equal footing when negotiating with a Wall Street sophisticate like KKR?

Smith has moved on, but Bayonne's residents cannot. They are experiencing firsthand the transfer of wealth from their pockets to the financiers' purse.

"Please break this contract," an anonymous online commenter pleaded. "It was a terrible thing to do to the hard-working and retired people of this beautiful town."

The Bayonne water fiasco is not the only investment KKR touts on its website as an example of good citizenship. Another highlight, believe it or not, is the firm's stake in Toys "R" Us, the giant and now defunct retailer. KKR took Toys private in 2005 with Bain & Company and Vornado, a real estate investor, buying it for $6.6 billion and piling $5 billion in debt onto the company. By 2017, Toys was bankrupt.

And yet, in 2012, KKR rated the Toys investment a triumph because it had helped veterans and active-duty military personnel build their careers. "The company is proud to support members of the U.S. armed forces," the case study trilled. "In 2012, the company bolstered its initiatives to get troops back to work by actively recruiting through military job boards, at career fairs, and on military bases." KKR lauded Toys "R" Us for hiring twelve hundred veterans for full-time and seasonal positions in its stores, corporate headquarters, and distribution facilities.

Five years later, Toys "R" Us was in bankruptcy, its stores shuttered, and those veterans, if they were still with the company, were among the thirty-three thousand workers who'd lost their jobs and health benefits. KKR, Bain, and Vornado had extracted $470 million in management fees driving Toys "R" Us into the ditch, but they claimed to have lost money in the failure overall.

Only after the firms were shamed by a handful of pension fund clients did they agree to create a $20 million severance fund for Toys workers—a pittance considering they had lost everything.

Asked about its role in the failure, KKR told Congress: "Toys R Us's troubles were caused by market forces—specifically the growth of e-commerce retailers—and the decision to liquidate was made by the company's creditors, not KKR."

It may seem odd that KKR can claim good corporate citizenship in calamities like the Toys "R" Us buyout or the Bayonne water deal. But to these operators, spin is central to the business model. Back in the eighties, don't forget, KKR supplied incomplete and misleading numbers to a Congress that was concerned about job losses at the companies it had taken over. Brian Ayash, the finance professor at California Polytechnic State University, found that KKR had excluded from its job loss calculus the firm's takeovers that had gone belly-up. That made their numbers look better than they actually were.

Notice, too, according to their narrative that Toys "R" Us's troubles had nothing to do with the massive debt KKR, Bain, and Vornado heaved onto the retailer. Among the plunderers, failure is always someone else's fault.

"Responsible investment is a way of doing business that we believe makes us smarter, stronger investors," KKR proclaims on its website. It cites an array of awards won by the companies it owns for their exemplary environmental, social, and governance practices. The firm says it is focused on "aligning returns for our investors with the interests and needs of the people and places affected by our investments."

As socially responsible investing has gained traction in recent years, it is not surprising that a thickening fog about these practices has emanated from the privateers' public relations machinery. Fact-checking their claims, especially as they relate to how their operations are harming the environment, could not be more important. The First Nations people of the Wet'suwet'en territories in Canada's northwest know this firsthand.

In 2019, when KKR took a controlling interest in a massive Canadian pipeline project known as Coastal Gaslink, it was already mired in controversy. For over a year, First Nations people in the Canadian province of British Columbia had been protesting the four-hundred-mile pipeline, saying its plan to carry fracked gas to a liquid natural gas terminal on the BC coast threatened the environment and their way of life. Opposing the pipeline, they said it violated their land rights, imperiled their waters, and would generate enormous polluting emissions.

KKR invested in the $6 billion project in partnership with the National Pension Service of Korea. KKR claimed the pipeline benefitted the environment because natural gas transported through it would displace coal and diesel fuel generation in Asia, cutting global greenhouse gas emissions.

But some among the Wet'suwet'en say they have never given their permission to construct the pipeline. Unlike Native American tribes in the U.S., Canadian First Nations people have not signed treaties surrendering title to their land, according to Sleydo', a land defender and matriarch of the Gidimt'en clan of the Wet'suwet'en Nation. "By violating our ability to be a self-determining people," Sleydo' told us, "they are not respecting that and not dealing with the proper title holders."

As the Coastal Gaslink construction has continued, behind

schedule and over budget, disturbing skirmishes have flared between the Royal Canadian Mounted Police, residents, and protesters. Sleydo' said she has been arrested and transported to a jail four and a half hours away, for example; Coastal Gaslink workers destroyed a Wet'suwet'en encampment where Sleydo' and her family have a cabin.

It feels like a war zone, Sleydo' said. "The helicopters, the sniper rifles pointed at you on many, many, many days. They've been literally bulldozing through all of our wetlands with no mitigation."

The Canadian courts are of little help because they don't recognize Indigenous law, Sleydo' said. The result has been a lopsided series of court rulings, mostly against First Nations people asking for injunctions to stop activities on their land.

A report by the Yellowhead Institute, a First Nations–led research center at Ryerson University in Toronto, Ontario, found that in one hundred recent cases, Canadian courts denied 81 percent of the injunctions filed by First Nations people trying to stop corporations from operating on their land. Corporations get different treatment—the courts granted 76 percent of their injunctions filed against First Nations people.

In late 2021, the Coastal Gaslink conflict centered on a work site near the Morice River, known to the Wet'suwet'en as Wedzin Kwa. Coastal Gaslink was preparing to bury its pipeline under the river at the headwaters of the Wet'suwet'en's main water supply, Sleydo' said, which could cause problems to the spawning salmon habitat and create work site sediment in drinking water.

Sediment pollution is a significant environmental hazard, according to the Environmental Protection Agency, and it has dogged the Coastal Gaslink pipeline, regulatory filings show. In the fall of 2020, the project failed to comply on 16 of 17 items inspected, according to the Environmental Assessment Office, an agency of British Columbia. Coastal Gaslink's practices in the field "did not align with site-specific erosion and sediment control plans," the report said.

As a result, Coastal Gaslink was forced to hire an independent auditor to monitor and report on its work to prevent site runoff that can pollute streams and harm fish. Coastal Gaslink was fined $72,500 for the infractions.

This followed two diesel spills of 130 gallons each in May 2020, reported at separate locations in the Morice area. Two further spills, in August 2021, occurred when 13 gallons of diesel fuel and 250 gallons of diesel exhaust fluid were released into the environment.

"They don't have a good track record," Sleydo' noted. "They kind of just do whatever they want." And why not? That is, after all, the way of the titans.

KKR's investment in Coastal Gaslink is one of many energy assets it holds on behalf of its clients—endowments, public pensions, and other institutional investors. Even as the firm claims to be an environmentally aware investor, as of 2021 it had poured far more money into fossil fuels and other conventional energy assets than it had into renewables.

KKR is not alone in this approach—many of its private equity brethren do the same. Between 2010 and 2020, private equity firms committed almost $2 trillion to energy investments, according to Preqin, a private equity database. About $1.2 trillion has gone into conventional energy investments, such as refineries, pipelines, and fossil fuel plants, compared with $732 billion in renewables like solar and wind power, Preqin tracked. That's a 60-40 split.

As of October 2021, ten of the top private equity firms held 80 percent of their energy investments in fossil fuel assets, according to the Private Equity Stakeholder Project, a nonprofit that's critical of the industry's impact on communities.

During the ten-year period prior, KKR invested $13.4 billion in conventional energy assets versus $4.9 billion in renewables, reported Alyssa Giachino of the Project. In other words, three-quarters of its investments went toward conventional energy. KKR did not dispute the figures.

Because private equity firms are so secretive, their investors often don't know what they own or the risks associated with those holdings, Giachino explained. "Pension funds end up with more fossil fuel exposure than maybe they realize and there's not a full accounting of the risks." They include heavy impacts on communities of color, risks of litigation and environmental penalties, and longer-term climate impact, she added.

The Coastal Gaslink project has generated unwelcome publicity for KKR, which says it is undergoing "a sustainable energy transition." While KKR likes to focus attention on its environmentally conscious investments, students at Claremont McKenna College in California, where KKR founders Henry Kravis and George Roberts are trustees, are having none of it. Along with students at the four other Claremont Colleges, they started a protest project in 2021 called "KKR Kills" to bring scrutiny on the firm's investments in fossil fuels and other assets that imperil the lands of Indigenous peoples.

Malcolm McCann, a student at Pitzer, one of the five Claremont Colleges, organized "KKR Kills" and in a February 2022 interview with the college newspaper said he wants KKR to exit its investments in "companies that infringe on Indigenous rights" and "commit these types of evil colonial violence." The firm has declined his request.

Indigenous people are known to be better stewards of the land than interlopers like Coastal Gaslink. So said a 2019 report published by the Intergovernmental Science-Policy Platform on Biodiversity and Ecosystem Services, an independent intergovernmental body. It found that Indigenous people maintain more biodiversity in their lands because they "often manage the land and coastal areas based on culturally specific world views, applying principles and indicators such as the health of the land, caring for the country and reciprocal responsibility."

Reciprocal responsibility? That's a foreign concept to the privateers.

KKR's spokeswoman said the firm is "committed to investing in a stable energy transition, one that supports a shift to a clean energy future while recognizing the ongoing importance of supplying the conventional energy needed for well-being and economic growth around the world today." KKR recently added a team focused on energy transition investments in North America.

Peter Dien, a Claremont College student, class of 2025, who has been working with "KKR Kills," said the firm's solar investments or its commitment to an energy transition don't undo their damaging activities. "If you're still oppressing Indigenous people," he told the student newspaper, "you can't balance it out with doing something good."

As for the Coastal Gaslink project, KKR's spokeswoman said: "The project is supported by elected leaders of all 20 First Nations groups and has cross-party government support. More specifically, the elected chiefs of all 20 First Nations whose lands are crossed by the pipeline (including the Wet'suwet'en) signed on. Within the West'suwet'en, in addition to the elected leaders, there are 13 hereditary chiefs who are unelected but are unofficial leaders within the community. Of those 13 hereditary chiefs, five are opposed."

It's important to note that the elected First Nations leaders KKR identifies as supporting the deal are not the hereditary leaders or leaders recognized by the First Nations; rather they are part of a governance system imposed on the First Nations, by Canada, in 1876.

"While we recognize that the Office of the Wet'suwet'en and some of the Hereditary Chiefs are not supportive of the project," an official for Coastal Gaslink said, "we continue to engage to understand and mitigate concerns that are raised, while also working with the many Wet'suwet'en members and elected representatives who support the project."

The KKR spokeswoman added that "the overwhelming majority of First Nation community members not only support the project, but are also exploring ways to invest in it (sixteen First Nations bands recently signed an equity option agreement to purchase a 10 percent equity stake)."

Nevertheless, the fight against Coastal Gaslink goes on. "According to Wet'suwet'en law we have to do everything to protect our territory for future generations," Sleydo' said. KKR "walked into this knowing there was a huge conflict here. That's very challenging for us, but also very telling about what the actual principles of the company are."

What's especially interesting about KKR's energy strategy is how unproductive it has been for investors as well. Three of KKR's big energy deals have gone bankrupt, and KKR's energy-focused funds have been poor performers, regulatory filings show. Its 2021 annual report said two of its twenty-five funds with more than two years of performance had negative returns. Both were invested in energy deals: the 2010 Natural Resources Fund was down 29.2 percent, while the 2013 Energy Income and Growth Fund was down 9.3 percent.

Must have been someone else's fault.

* * *

For those who believe that saving the planet is a matter of some urgency, watching certain public companies move to dump their fossil fuel investments has been encouraging. Unfortunately, the plunderers often stand ready to buy those assets, prolonging their life spans because they will serve these firms' immediate-gratification business models. Expecting to extract what they can from the investments over only a few years, the pirates don't care about the long-term impact these operations will have. By the time of any reckoning, they plan to have taken their profits and left the scene.

Not all private equity firms are pillagers, said Clark Williams-Derry, an energy finance analyst at the research firm Institute for Energy Economics and Financial Analysis. But, he adds, some definitely are. "The real trouble happens when a private equity firm comes in and is just trying to strip-mine the company and the workers for whatever they're worth and get as much cash out of these companies that they possible can," Williams-Derry noted. Even worse, "some private equity firms buy companies and then run them into the ground, leaving behind messes for someone else to clean up."

In 2016, for instance, the private equity firm ArcLight Capital Partners of Boston bought into Limetree Bay, an oil refinery and storage facility in St. Croix, U.S. Virgin Islands. After a spate of toxic spills, the operation went bankrupt, but it reopened in February 2021. Just three months later, however, Limetree Bay closed again after unleashing petroleum rain on nearby neighborhoods, sickening many residents. In July 2021, the Justice Department filed a complaint alleging that the refinery "presents an imminent and substantial danger to public health and the environment." That month, the refinery filed for bankruptcy again.

In many cases, private equity titans keep planet-unfriendly operations alive—like dirty coal-fired power plants—that might otherwise be mothballed. "Private equity thinks it can squeeze a couple more years out of them," said Tyson Slocum, director of the energy program at Public Citizen, a nonprofit consumer advocacy group. "And they are often immune from investor pressures."

The soot from coal-fired power plants contributed to an estimated fifteen thousand premature deaths in the U.S. as of 2014. This is just one illustration of many operations kept on life support by private investors. In 2015, for example, KKR and three other investors bought out of bankruptcy Longview Power, a coal-fired power generator in Maidsville, West Virginia. Seven years later, it would file for bankruptcy a second time, even though President Donald Trump had promised to revive the coal industry and bring back its glory days.

When it went bankrupt the first time, the Longview generator had been operating for only about a year and a half; plagued by construction problems, the facility operated at 68 percent capacity because of outages. "The plant liked to advertise itself as the cleanest coal-fired power plant, but it still was a very significant source of greenhouse gas emissions, truck traffic, and noise in the local community," said Jim Kotcon, an associate professor at West Virginia University. At first, the plant was supposed to operate as a "mine-mouth coal facility," meaning the coal would go directly from the mine to the power plant. But then the adjacent mine closed and Longview needed to transport the coal from a different mine and up a steep mountain road.

"They tore the road to bits—it's been a serious impact to local residents," Kotcon said. "The plant was in a relatively poor location to begin with and KKR's investment back in 2015 gave it a lifeline to keep operating. It would not be operating today but for those investments." Mothballing the plant would eliminate 150 jobs, creating economic hardship in the area. Still, is the potential to save 150 jobs worth the plant's potential to pollute the planet?

In August 2022, Moody's Investors Service, the ratings agency, upgraded Longview's debt rating but noted, "Longview is highly exposed to environmental risks, including exposure to carbon transition risks, and faces highly negative demographic and social trends relating to coal fired power generation."

KKR went so deep into fossil fuels over the years that in 2013, its former head of energy investments called the firm "a mini oil and gas company." KKR kicked off an immense undertaking in shale oil and fracking with a 2009 investment in a Pennsylvania oil and gas exploration company called East Resources. The company's founder, Terrence Pegula, had amassed some 650,000 acres in the Marcellus Shale formation in Appalachia, but KKR's $330 million in cash financed a push by the company to increase the number of horizontal wells being drilled. Just a year later, KKR and Pegula sold East Resources to Royal Dutch Shell for $4.7 billion, generating over $1 billion for KKR, or a 371 percent return in under a year.

In June 2010, KKR put $400 million into Hilcorp Resources, a driller in the Eagle Ford Shale formation in South Texas. With KKR's money, Hilcorp added four more horizontal rigs, and a year later Marathon Oil bought the company for $3.5 billion. KKR received $1.13 billion on that trade.

KKR's profits in shale made it all seem easy. But things were about to become trickier, and in subsequent years, three of KKR's energy investments would file for bankruptcy. Their investors' returns would get slammed.

The biggest debacle for the firm was its participation in the $48 billion deal known as Energy Future Holdings. It involved the 2007 acquisition of Texas Utilities, the largest supplier of retail electricity in the state, with 2.1 million customers. The transaction was massive, even bigger than RJR Nabisco, the deal that had put KKR on the map twenty years earlier. KKR, TPG, and a Goldman Sachs unit together invested $8 billion in cash and financed the rest with a $40 billion mountain of debt.

Seven years later, Energy Future Holdings collapsed into bankruptcy, crippled by the decline in natural gas prices and the massive debt taken on to do the transaction. KKR had extracted fees along the way, but wound up losing its entire investment, as did TPG and Goldman.

KKR's third energy bankruptcy came a year later, in 2015, when Samson Resources, an oil and natural gas company, caved in. KKR and a consortium of investors had paid $7.2 billion to buy the family-owned company in the largest leveraged buyout of an oil and gas producer. The investor group paid cash for roughly half of the purchase price, and Samson borrowed to cover the rest. Before the buyout, Samson had had the necessary cash on hand to pay off nearly all its debts, but the new obligations required payment of hundreds of millions of dollars in annual interest costs.

Shortly after the transaction closed, natural gas prices fell to their lowest level in a decade. This blow, combined with the heavy debt Samson now carried on its books, dragged the company under. Between Energy Future Holdings and Samson Resources, KKR and its investors lost at least $4 billion.

KKR's investors are not the only ones who've been hurt by its energy operations. Samson Resources has been subject to fines by the EPA, a study by the Private Equity Stakeholder Project found. In 2013 Samson paid $75,000, and two years later it paid $12,100 for a toxic water spill from a pipeline on the Southern Ute Indian Tribe reservation.

Another KKR-owned entity—Spur Energy—operates oil and

gas assets in the Permian Basin in New Mexico. Purchased in May 2019, Spur Energy has locations in New Mexico's Eddy and Lea Counties, home to large Latino communities. In 2020, the company spilled more than twenty-one hundred barrels of oil and toxic water in Eddy and Lea Counties, and during just the first two months of 2021, the company generated almost twenty spill incidents. One-third were deemed "major" by the New Mexico Oil Conservation Division, their report said.

Despite this dismal record, KKR continues to win investments from CalPERs and other large public pension funds who claim to care about the environment and social issues. The plunderers depend on their hypocrisy.

CHAPTER FIFTEEN

"Hiding in the Background, Rarely Held to Account"

Mining for Medicare Gold

The buyout barons' pernicious impact on the nation's well-being became obvious in 2020, amid the healthcare crisis created by the coronavirus. And no patient group took a graver hit than those living in nursing homes. According to the Centers for Medicare and Medicaid Services, this population had suffered 158,000 COVID deaths as of mid-September 2022, or 15 percent of total U.S. deaths from the disease.

During a pandemic, nursing home residents would be a likely group to suffer greatly. But some of the carnage could have been avoided if the private equity owners of these facilities hadn't been so hell-bent on squeezing every dime out of them in the years leading up to the crisis. Cutting back on staff was a common approach given that payroll is these operations' biggest expense, but upkeep and building maintenance posed other costs the financiers would rather not pay.

Some 70 percent of the nation's nursing homes are for-profit entities, according to the Centers for Disease Control and Prevention. An estimated 11 percent of these facilities are owned by private equity firms, according to academics who have studied the field, but opaque ownership data means the figure could be higher, they say.

Tony Chicotel, staff attorney at California Advocates for Nursing Home Reform, said: "Nursing home owners are exploiting the system that has been set up, and private equity is more surgical and professional about exploiting it. There's all sorts of gaming that goes on in providing care that maximizes profits rather than outcomes."

All that gaming meant these operations were decidedly ill-equipped to handle the impacts of the pandemic on their residents. In some cases, family members told us, financial decisions made early in the crisis seemed to put residents at even greater peril.

As soon as COVID struck, Deb Timms became concerned about her elderly aunt, a resident at the Gilroy Healthcare and Rehabilitation Center in Gilroy, California. But when she learned that Gilroy was taking in patients from nearby hospitals, she scrambled to remove her aunt from the facility, fearful she would contract COVID from the newcomers.

"That's outside money for them," Timms told us. "It felt like this was all about financial gain, not about safety."

Unfortunately, Timms couldn't move her aunt in time—good nursing homes are hard to find, even more so when there's a pandemic. Her aunt soon tested positive for COVID and passed away in September 2020 at the age of ninety-four.

"I felt like I was watching my aunt sitting in a car that's rolling to the edge of a cliff and I couldn't do anything to stop it," Timms said.

Gilroy is part of Covenant Care, a nursing home company owned by Centre Partners, a private equity firm in New York and

Los Angeles. Since Centre was founded in 1986, it has invested $2 billion in eighty companies, its website says; thirty of its nursing facilities are in California and Nevada.

The death rate at the 134-bed Gilroy facility where Timms's aunt lived was better than many, government records show. By late July 2021, it had reported nine COVID deaths, roughly 8 percent of its confirmed cases, a government measure. That compared favorably with the 20 percent death rate on confirmed cases reported by nursing homes nationwide at that time.

Still, Timms's concerns about care at Gilroy being driven by the bottom line were not an idle fear. Government data shows a surge in September 2020 in the facility's admission of patients who had been previously hospitalized and treated for COVID. Those admissions went from 10 residents to 29 through the month. Timms's aunt died that month.

As of March 2022, Gilroy held a 3-star rating out of 5 from the federal government's nursing home comparison website, a rating Medicare considered "average." Gilroy's staffing ratio was also average, but its record on health inspections was below average, Medicare said. (By October 2022, Gilroy's rating had risen to 4 stars and its record on health inspections had increased to average.)

During the spring of 2021, when Wanda Malik moved her mother to the Vintage Faire nursing home in Modesto, California, she was optimistic. She'd heard good things about the facility and her mom needed physical therapy after suffering a massive stroke. Vintage Faire is a Covenant Care facility.

Problems emerged immediately, Malik observed. Her mother's requests for water often went unanswered, and other needs were ignored. "They'd say, 'I'm sorry, we're so short-staffed right now,'" Malik recalled.

Three days after she was admitted, Malik's mother fell out of her bed and crashed to the floor.

"We thought we would trust Vintage Faire with my mother," Malik told us. "It's very obvious they look at patients as dollar signs only."

Malik's experience at Vintage Faire is common at for-profit nursing homes, according to Chicotel. "Staffing is their biggest cost," he noted. "And the best way to make a profit is to cut staff or have residents who don't have much in the way of needs and you can ignore them." They approach residents and family members who request more attentive care as threatening the balance between tending to patients and generating profits, Chicotel added.

In 2021, COVID deaths totaled 19.6 percent of confirmed cases at Vintage Faire, government data shows. The following year, its Medicare rating was below average—two stars—and the Medicare site comparing nursing homes warned that the facility had been cited for resident abuse. Health inspection reports were below average, the site said, and staffing was only average.

A Covenant Care spokesman did not respond to our request for comment on these cases.

Chicotel's view on for-profit nursing facilities is supported by research from academia, think tanks, and the U.S. government. The 2021 study showing that there were 10 percent more deaths in private equity–owned homes was the most devastating, of course. But there's additional research, too. Ten years earlier, for example, the Government Accountability Office found that for-profit homes, including those acquired by top private equity firms, had more total deficiencies than nonprofit facilities. Profit margins were higher in private equity–backed homes, GAO concluded, and total nurse staffing ratios were lower than other facilities, including those operating for profit.

Another study, in 2017, tracked what happened at nursing homes that had been acquired by private equity firms. Academics Aline Bos and Charlene Harrington examined transactions from 2000 through 2012 and found total staffing, per patient per day, dropped significantly after a buyout.

Increased emergency room visits, hospitalizations, and higher Medicare costs are outcomes at nursing homes acquired by private equity firms, a *Journal of the American Medical Association Health Forum* study found in 2021. Examining the period 2013–2017, residents of titan-owned nursing homes were 11.1 percent more likely to have an acute coronary syndrome emergency department visit and 8.7 percent more likely to have a related hospitalization, compared to for-profit nursing homes not owned by private equity. What's more, total Medicare costs were almost 4 percent higher than at their peers, the study found.

A 2020 analysis of New Jersey nursing homes by Americans for Financial Reform Education Fund found that the sixty-one private equity–owned and backed facilities in the state had higher resident infection and death rates and a larger share of coronavirus cases and deaths versus for-profit, nonprofit, and public facilities. Nearly three-fifths of residents in these homes contracted coronavirus; this infection rate was almost 25 percent higher than the statewide nursing home average and 57 percent higher than at public facilities. COVID-related deaths based on number of residents were also 33 percent higher in these private equity–run homes.

The Long Term Care Community Coalition is a nonprofit that advocates for improved nursing home care. In a 2020 report, it noted that while problems with care at these facilities had been a long-standing issue, poor care *more recently* was the result of "fundamental problems in the management, ownership, or financing arrangements under which an increasing number of nursing homes are operating. The growing sophistication of the nursing home industry has enabled some owners to leverage and direct assets in a manner that maximizes profits without meaningful accountability for nursing home quality."

Sound familiar?

One problem Chicotel sees often in his work is a practice known as "dumping," in which a nursing home acts to keep its Medicare revenues high by evicting residents who are about to lose full-pay Medicare benefits. Over 1.4 million Medicare beneficiaries lived in nursing homes in 2022, according to the inspector general of the Department of Health and Human Services.

Medicare only reimburses nursing homes in full for a patient's stay until his or her twentieth day in a facility. After that, a copay requirement kicks in that many residents can't afford or don't pay immediately. By evicting these residents, the facility can keep the Medicare money flowing by replacing copay patients with full-pay Medicare recipients. Then the process begins again.

"We see a lot of rushed, inappropriate discharges," Chicotel explained, "awful discharges like sending people to homeless shelters or hotels. If they keep the resident there and don't replace them with a new Medicare resident, they're forgoing up to $1,000 a day."

Improper evictions also occur when operators of nursing homes want to kick out residents because they are difficult or their families are demanding, Chicotel said.

Eddie Martinez found this out firsthand with his mother, Maria, a resident of Pacific Coast Manor in Capitola, California, also part of Covenant Care. Only after Chicotel helped him with his case was Martinez able to keep his mother in the facility and continue to see her there after he had spoken out about her care. During the five years that Maria Martinez lived in Pacific Coast

Manor, Eddie visited her almost daily. She'd been immobilized by a stroke in 2016 and he was vigilant about her care. When he saw deficiencies, he'd notify the home's administrator or nursing staff.

"I'm not a complainer," Martinez told us. "But when it came to my mom, I was on top of it to make sure she got proper treatment."

Over the years, these requests about his mother's care grated on the facility's management, Martinez said. One staffer told him that if he didn't like the treatment she was getting, he should take his mother elsewhere. "I thought by going and addressing the concerns that they would handle it," he stated. "Instead, it was met with a battle."

In 2019, Pacific Coast tried to evict Maria and bar Martinez from seeing her because of "complaints of intimidation, aggression, inappropriate actions toward staff," a memo from the home's administrator shows. Only after Chicotel interceded on his behalf was Martinez able to keep visiting his mom.

Two former workers at Pacific Coast Manor told us they never saw Martinez being difficult or hostile with staff. Both confirmed that the owners of the facility seemed more interested in cutting costs than in caring for patients.

Helene Luna is one. She worked as a certified nursing assistant at Pacific Coast Manor in 2015 but only lasted there a year and a half. "They didn't care about residents or workers," she said. "They were always short-staffed, the turnover was so high. No one wanted to stay."

Another former worker at the facility reported that management repeatedly put off repairs to keep costs low, including failing to repair a roof leak properly for five years. "A lot of times we'd have to close the dining room because we were afraid the Sheetrock would fall on somebody," he said. "For a couple of years, it had a tarp over that section. It seemed like if you're going run that type of business, you have to have a dry place for your residents."

Seven heaters were supposed to service the building, the former employee said, but three were out of service for years. "A lot of sections would be too hot and other sections too cold, so nobody was happy," he said. "They were just totally cheap, penny wise and dollar foolish."

After COVID struck, Martinez became alarmed when he saw large groups of people coming in and out of the facility. They were nursing students, he said the home's administrator told him; he grew concerned they might bring the virus into the facility.

In September 2019, after Eddie's mother was hospitalized with breathing difficulties, Pacific Coast Manor's administrator barred her from returning to the home. The only way she could come back, the administrator said, was if Eddie agreed to stay away from the facility and stop serving as the family member responsible for his mother, according to a memo from the administrator that we reviewed.

"It's a horrific thing to ask the family member to do," Chicotel said. But restraining orders are common in nursing homes, especially when family members point out deficiencies in care, he added. "When visitors are concerned about care their loved one is getting, staff or management will see the resident is targeted as challenging," Chicotel said. " 'You call every day? You force us to provide care in a way we don't want to.' "

After Chicotel's organization got involved, Maria was allowed back at the facility without any restrictions.

One day in November 2020, Eddie Martinez was visiting his mother through the window of her room at Pacific Coast Manor.

Family members were not allowed inside the facility because of COVID, and this was the only way he could see Maria. After a few minutes, a police officer approached Martinez. He'd been called by officials at Pacific Coast Manor to remove Eddie from the premises. When Martinez told the officer he was visiting his ailing mother, the officer let him stay, he said. Disgusted, the cop criticized the home's management for calling in the police. "The officer told them, 'Don't call me again to bother a family member,'" Martinez recalled.

Maria Martinez died of COVID in December 2020 at age eighty-four. Her death at Pacific Coast Manor was one of fourteen total COVID-related fatalities reported by the facility as of late July 2021, federal documents state. When she died, the facility's death rate from confirmed COVID cases was 23 percent, government statistics show. As of late July 2021, Pacific Coast Manor's total death rate had declined to 18 percent of confirmed cases.

The only communication Martinez received from Pacific Coast Manor after it informed him of his mother's death was a message left on his cell phone. It asked when he would be coming to retrieve her belongings.

Just as the Congressional Budget Office had predicted in its 2006 report, U.S. hospitals were disastrously unprepared for the pandemic in 2020. Patients took the brunt of this outcome, but healthcare workers were devastated, too. Stories soon unspooled of doctors, nurses, and technicians who were mistreated, overworked, and subject to pay cuts or removal if they spoke out, as emergency department doctor Ming Lin had done in Bellingham, Washington.

The U.S. has six thousand hospitals currently, the American Hospital Association says, about half of which are not-for-profit. Roughly twelve hundred are investor-owned and for-profit, while the rest are owned by federal, state, or local governments. Historically, most hospitals were owned by public and nonprofit entities.

When COVID-19 hit, hospitals owned by private equity firms were among the first to cut their workers' pay and benefits because their operations could no longer generate profits on elective surgical procedures delayed due to the pandemic. Alteon Health, a private equity–backed healthcare staffing company, cut its doctors' benefits in response to the coronavirus pandemic, "even as many of those same doctors work to treat patients infected with the virus," according to an April 1, 2020, report in *Stat*, a health-oriented website owned by the *Boston Globe*.

Alteon, based in Maryland, employed about seventeen hundred emergency medicine doctors and other physicians at hospital emergency rooms across the country, *Stat* said. In response to the pandemic, the company suspended paid time off, stopped matching contributions to employees' 401(k) retirement accounts, and halted discretionary bonuses. The company also said it was reducing some clinicians' hours "to the minimum required to maintain health insurance coverage," *Stat* reported. Administrative workers' pay was also cut by 20 percent and executives' pay was slashed by 25 percent.

Two years after the pandemic began, Alteon was sold by the private equity firms that had owned it, New Mountain Capital and Frazier Healthcare Partners. The buyer? US Acute Care Solutions, a health system financed by Apollo. Financial terms were not disclosed.

"Private equity–backed health care has been a disaster for patients and for doctors," said Mark Reiter, residency program director of emergency medicine at the University of Tennessee. "Many decisions are made for what's going to maximize profits for the private equity company, rather than what is best for the patient, what is best for the community."

Consider what occurred on April 2, 2020, at a community hospital in rural northeastern Massachusetts. COVID was metastasizing, but Steward Health Care, owned by private equity giant Cerberus Capital, suddenly suspended intensive care unit admissions at its Nashoba Valley Medical Center. The seventy-three-bed community hospital in Ayer, Massachusetts, quietly deployed its equipment and staff elsewhere to meet COVID demand, according to a memo from the president of the facility, leaving the community without an intensive care unit just as a spike in COVID cases was occurring in the region. It "completely took out an entire level of service," said Audra Sprague, a longtime registered nurse at the facility. "Anybody that needed ICU care, we didn't have one, we couldn't keep you."

Before a hospital can discontinue a service or close a unit, Massachusetts regulations require it to notify the state's Department of Public Health about its intentions at least ninety days prior and to convene a public hearing at least sixty days before the planned closure. But Steward, which bought the hospital in 2011, did neither of those things, suspending the unit anyway, at the start of a global pandemic. The move drew outrage from the staff and the public.

During Sprague's many years at Nashoba Valley, the hospital has been owned by a for-profit company as well as a private equity firm. Private equity is worse, she said. "Even when you say something is unsafe there's little change that comes out of it," Sprague said of her privateer managers. "If there's a profit in it, then they'll do it. They're not going to do a single thing that doesn't benefit them, first and foremost."

Darren Grubb, a spokesman for Steward, said that the suspension had "not impacted patient care" at the Nashoba Valley facility and called Sprague's view a "baseless, selective, hypergeneralized claim."

But Sprague is right about these firms' laser focus on profits, which means less money to plow back into a hospital's physical plant and equipment. Their fast-buck tactics contributed to shortages of ventilators, masks, and other equipment needed to combat COVID-19.

Even as hospitals owned by private equity firms cut staff pay and slashed investments in plant and equipment, patients paid higher costs at these facilities, research shows. A 2021 study by Tong Liu at the University of Pennsylvania's Wharton School found that private equity buyouts led to an 11 percent increase in total healthcare spending for those who had private insurance. These cost hikes were driven mostly by higher prices demanded by the privateers for hospital services, Liu found.

Liu had a suggestion. A ban on private equity buyouts of hospitals would "increase patient surplus by an amount equal to 10.7 percent of health expenses. If antitrust regulators who conduct merger reviews ignore PE-backed acquirers' unique features, they risk greatly underestimating the impact of hospital mergers."

As COVID raged in 2020 and 2021, so too did the dealmakers, with healthcare buyouts surging to $300 billion, up from $225 billion in 2018 and 2019, according to PitchBook. Once the privateers recognized that the Federal Reserve Board stood ready to bail them out of bad trades, they returned to the trough. With a vengeance.

And no one stopped them. Anti-trust regulators had been notably silent in recent decades as the plunderers acquired healthcare companies worth hundreds of billions of dollars. Despite clear evidence that industry concentrations and monopolistic tendencies translate to higher costs for consumers, the nation's anti-trust artillery had taken no aim at the private equity barons. They could have stopped deals, broken up highly concentrated firms, or taken actions on any number of anti-competitive practices. They did not.

The result has been an unremitting and detrimental concentration in the mammoth healthcare industry. Academics at the University of California, Hastings College of Law studied healthcare concentration in major metropolitan areas across the U.S. in 2018. They found the vast majority of those areas had highly concentrated hospital and specialist physician markets. The result of all this high concentration? Greater costs to patients and lesser care. "As unrelenting consolidation in healthcare provider and insurer markets continues, policymakers need additional options to protect the public from escalating healthcare prices and low-quality care," the researchers said.

Simply stated, because they are relatively small in dollar amount, the vast majority of the privateers' healthcare deals have flown under the radar of anti-trust regulators. Under federal rules, companies making acquisitions need only alert anti-trust regulators to their deals if each one's value exceeds $101 million (this figure is adjusted annually and began at $50 million in the late seventies). In the healthcare arenas subject to the greatest number of recent buyouts, such as dermatology and emergency physician practices, many acquisitions do not meet this bar, especially when the acquirers set up separate entities to obscure their ownership and get around corporate practice of medicine rules. Neither does each small takeover increase industry concentration, technically speaking. The deals, therefore, are exempt from the requirement to notify anti-trust regulators; the consolidation goes on, in stealth mode.

Consider the ongoing transformation in hospice care, another vulnerable patient group. From 2011 to 2019, private equity ownership of hospices tripled; by 2019, more than 300 were providing care to over 112,000 Medicare recipients. While this is less than 8 percent of the 1.46 million Medicare hospice patients in 2019, it still represents a more than 300 percent increase in plunderer involvement in end-of-life care. Once again, there's a reason hospice has attracted these buyers—it is a rich profit center. Medicare is a system the financiers know well how to tap. Indeed, between 2013 and 2020, according to a study by Eileen O'Grady at the Private Equity Stakeholder Project, twenty-five healthcare companies backed by private equity have paid settlements totaling over $570 million for allegedly defrauding government programs.

Medicare generally pays hospice providers the same rate per daily patient visit, regardless of that person's medical needs. About 51 percent of all Medicare recipients who died in 2019 were enrolled in hospice at the time of their deaths, according to the Medicare Payment Advisory Commission, up from 48 percent in 2017. Demographics are also at work here. With the bulk of the baby boomer population at or near the period of their lives when they're likely to require hospice services, the potential for profits in this arena will grow and grow.

Melissa Aldridge, vice-chair of research at the Icahn School of Medicine at Mount Sinai in New York, summed up private equity's hospice forays in a 2021 research piece: "It is difficult to identify a health care sector more detrimentally affected by the mismatch between profit maximization incentives and quality of care than hospice."

Too bad no one was listening.

If you have any residual doubts about the potential for riches in healthcare, let the "patient mining" program at Apria Health-care Group, a provider of home healthcare equipment, lay them to rest.

Acquired by the Blackstone Group in 2008, Apria handles the needs of patients on home respiratory therapy, including oxygen and non-invasive ventilators. The company, then based in Lake Forest, California, delivers and sets up ventilator equipment and supplies and instructs patients and their caregivers on how to use them. Apria also processes patients' medical claims for reimbursement to insurers, Medicare, and other payors.

After acquiring publicly traded Apria for $1.7 billion, Blackstone immediately began sucking out management fees and installing directors on the company's board. By 2021, three Blackstone executives served on Apria's board. The fees Apria paid to Blackstone were many and munificent, depleting Apria's resources.

Here are some particulars of the Blackstone extraction process. First was an $18.7 million transaction fee when the deal was struck. Then came the management fees; even though Blackstone owned Apria for only three months in 2008, the company paid its acquirer a $1.23 million management fee that year. Going forward, Apria had to pay Blackstone annual management fees of either $7 million or 2 percent of the company's operating income, whichever was greater. While this policy diminished Apria's results, it benefitted the buyout kings, a clear indication of their priorities.

In 2007, prior to its acquisition by Blackstone, Apria had generated $86 million in net income under generally accepted accounting principles, and for the full year of 2009, it turned in a $4 million loss. That performance continued, rising to a $750 million loss under GAAP in 2011 and a $260 million loss in 2012. During the first nine months of 2013, Apria lost another $54 million.

Apria's losses under Blackstone are germane, because beginning in 2014, the Justice Department would later say, Apria executives saw a way "to quickly improve" the company's "revenue, profit, and cash position." Soon the company began fraudulently billing Medicare for reimbursements it should not have received, the government said. In the Apria complaint, federal investigators noted that the company did not have enough employees to visit patients and determine their need and use of the equipment as required for Medicare payments. Through a "series of cost-cutting measures" between 2015 and 2017, prosecutors said, Apria had "repeatedly reduced" the number of workers whose job it was to verify that the Medicare billings were proper.

These missed visits were "widely recognized within Apria," the government said in its complaint. For example, it cited an internal company analysis showing that in December 2016, the Apria workers "failed to complete more than half of the visits" within all three of Apria's operational zones to patients as mandated by the company's clinical procedures.

The Justice Department's allegations against Apria read like a how-to guide for healthcare heists. Consider the company's approach to the federal reimbursement rules governing ventilator equipment. Before companies like Apria can receive Medicare reimbursements for supplying patients with non-invasive ventilators, they must determine that those using their equipment are required by their doctors to have it. One reason for this: patients using non-invasive ventilators, a relatively new technology and more complex, generate much higher reimbursement rates—$1,000 per month or more—versus $100 to $300 for other devices. In addition, reimbursement allowances for non-invasive ventilators can extend far longer than on other equipment—Medicare can pay for five years on such equipment versus thirteen months on others. This policy makes non-invasive ventilators far more profitable to providers than other types.

You can probably see where this is going.

In April 2014, after years under Blackstone's ownership, Apria's executives took up an internal strategic review, government investigators said. They started discussing whether the new non-invasive rental business should be a high priority for the company. A crucial element of those meetings was Medicare's high reimbursement rates on non-invasive equipment.

Eureka! Peddling non-invasive rentals could jump-start the company's revenues, profits, and cash, the executives recognized. And so, in August of that year, senior executives at Apria made the expansion of this business a top priority for the company, the investigators said. The executives established a goal for Apria to increase its rental revenue from this equipment from $5 million in 2014 to $30 million in 2015—an enormous jump.

Apria's top executives also directed its company managers to institute targets for its sales force to increase non-invasive ventilator orders and find new patients for the equipment. Salespeople who generated large numbers of new users received annual bonuses worth "tens of thousands of dollars," federal investigators found, while those who failed to meet the sales targets "were at risk for termination."

It gets better. To maximize the number of non-invasive ventilator rentals, Apria initiated a "patient mining" program, a nice Orwellian-sounding name. Mining for patients, Apria's sales and clinical staff would comb through medical records looking for customers using cheaper equipment; then the salespeople would try to place the patients on the costlier non-invasive ventilators.

As for meeting the government's requirement that it ensure patient use of non-invasive ventilators was "medically necessary," Apria didn't bother. Its personnel didn't conduct regular visits to patients to make those determinations. Not only that, Apria provided the non-invasive ventilators to patients—and billed Medicare for them—even though cheaper gear would have met their needs, investigators found.

Apria submitted thousands of false claims to federal health programs and obtained millions of dollars in improper payments. Taxpayers, of course, were on the hook in these rip-offs.

In December 2020, amid the pandemic, Apria settled the government's case. It agreed to pay $40.5 million and admitted it had sought reimbursement even *after* it had information indicating its customers had stopped using their ventilators. Still, Apria did not admit that any of its conduct was illegal or otherwise improper.

Nevertheless, Apria entered into a corporate integrity agreement with Health and Human Services as part of its settlement, just as the Envision unit did when it was caught improperly admitting patients into hospitals to reap higher Medicare reimbursements. The agreement, lasting five years, required the company to implement board oversight, undergo a Medicare claims review process by an independent monitor, and take "other compliance steps designed to foster adherence to federal health care program requirements."

The Apria matter was the second time prosecutors have pursued a Blackstone-owned healthcare entity. In 2015, a unit of Vanguard Health Systems, a Blackstone company from 2004 to 2013, settled an investigation alleging it had submitted false claims to Medicare, in part when owned by the firm. Among the allegations: billing federal healthcare programs for services not properly supervised by a physician or performed by medical "fellows" but billed as if seen by a physician. Another allegation: amounts owed by patients were inflated because they were billed using codes that did not accurately reflect the work done by the physicians.

Vanguard paid $2.9 million under the agreement, which the government said was "neither an admission of liability by Vanguard nor a concession by the United States that the allegations are not well founded." Blackstone sold Vanguard in 2013 for more than double its purchase price.

Neither government complaint named Blackstone, and the firm's spokesman said, "No government body has ever claimed that Blackstone was aware of, participated in, acquiesced, or improperly failed to stop any alleged improper conduct."

Laura Olson, the Lehigh professor, finds it frustrating that the financiers backing these companies are rarely identified when fraud is alleged, especially given their constant push for profits at the entities they own. The money-spinners' ties are often concealed by complex ownership structures designed to shield the firms from liabilities and what Wall Street calls "headline risk" or negative publicity about their activities and actions, Olson said.

"Private equity can do terrible, terrible things, and the portfolio company itself is responsible, not the private equity firm," Olson said. "If the private equity owners were liable, then it goes without saying that they would have to be more cautious about how they raid these companies and strip them of the ability to provide decent care."

In February 2021, a few months after Apria's settlement with prosecutors, the company conducted an initial public offering of its shares, raising approximately $150 million. By November of that year, Blackstone had reaped over $500 million by selling some of its Apria stock to the public. It still held almost 40 percent of the company's shares, worth around $500 million.

Let's do the math: In 2013, Blackstone sold Apria's home infusion business for $2.1 billion. Then, from 2018 through 2020, Blackstone extracted $450 million in dividends from Apria. The Blackstone fees we know about—and there are some we can't see in its filings—totaled at least $63 million and its stock sales generated $500 million.

That's not all: Blackstone benefitted from its Apria ownership through the purchases of goods and services by other entities the firm owned. Between 2017 and 2021, regulatory filings show Apria paid $46 million to nine Blackstone-owned companies, for bill collection services, supply chain management software, office space, and other services. Blackstone's spokesman said these were "regular-way business transactions" that benefitted both the companies involved and those who invest with Blackstone.

In January 2022, Apria announced that it was being acquired

by Owens & Minor, a healthcare logistics company, for $1.45 billion. In spite of the fraud allegations and the corporate integrity agreement, Blackstone made three times its investment on Apria, according to its spokesman. "It was a highly successful investment," he said.

CHAPTER SIXTEEN

"Special and Symbiotic"

Apollo Goes Back to Its Roots

By 2021, thirty years had passed since the devastating failure of the Executive Life Insurance Company. Almost nobody recalled the losses its policyholders had been forced to absorb or the billions in gains the disaster had produced for Leon Black and his new partnership. Scooping up the gems in the Executive Life portfolio that should have gone to its policyholders showed the financiers what they could get away with. And spinning the deal as benefitting the insurance company's customers, even as they were being skinned, was a PR tactic that would be used repeatedly as the dealmakers marauded through corporate America. Even now, for example, private equity lobbyists say they are improving healthcare and "saving lives." That's their story and they're sticking to it.

A few people would never forget the Executive Life outcome, of course. Sue and Vince Watson, Maureen Marr, Dru Ann Jacobson, were examples. But the story of the company's collapse and takeover—including its crucial lessons about the risks insurance companies' investments can pose to policyholders—had been forgotten for the most part.

As it happened, this memory lapse would benefit both Black and Apollo.

Starting in 2009, Apollo had set out to create an insurance company of its own amid the deadly aftermath of the mortgage crisis. Insurers were failing, so Black saw an opportunity to make a profit "rescuing" them, his tried-and-true trade. In keeping with their grandiose Greek god construct, they had called their new insurer Athene. (Not to be confused with Aurora, the insurer that arose out of the Executive Life takeover.) Just as Executive Life had done, Athene would specialize in selling annuities to risk-averse investors looking for a steady stream of income in retirement. The insurer would also buy up billions of dollars of pension obligations from corporations like Lockheed and Bristol Myers, mimicking a big Executive Life practice that put more than a hundred thousand retirees at risk. In creating Athene, Apollo was returning to its beginnings, or as Maureen Marr would say, to its original sin.

Starting an insurance company was an ingenious move for Apollo in several ways. For starters, as always with Apollo, Athene charged fees. Athene generated hundreds of millions of dollars in fees to Apollo each year for its "asset management services." These fees would only grow as Athene did, because they were based on the dollar amount of assets the insurer collected from policyholders. In 2019, for example, the investment management fees Athene paid to Apollo accounted for 27 percent of Apollo's total in such fees. During the three years ending in 2020, Athene paid Apollo $1 billion in management fees.

But this fee spigot was just the start of Apollo's enrichment scheme. Perhaps even more beneficial in the Athene arrangement was how it allowed Apollo to use the insurer as a receptacle for assets it might have difficulty selling elsewhere. The firm would also use Athene as a tool to invest ahead of or alongside investors in its private equity funds when it felt this could reap profits.

An insurance company has one job—to generate enough money to pay policyholders' claims. To do that, it needs income-producing investments. Apollo has many of these to sell; and what could be better than a captive insurance company ready to buy what Apollo was peddling?

But, as the Executive Life disaster had shown, insurers must also weigh the risks in the investments they buy. The greater the risks, the greater the chance that policyholders could lose big in a market dislocation or, worse, an insurance company failure.

With Athene under Apollo's roof, the insurer could buy risky securities issued by the companies Apollo had taken over, for example, or mortgages originated by an Apollo lender. If Apollo had difficulties selling these assets to outside investors, or was concerned about the risks they held to preferred investors in its private equity funds, it could foist them off on the unwitting insurance customers of Athene.

Athene could be to Apollo what Executive Life had been to Drexel Burnham Lambert—a constant buyer of Apollo merchandise as Executive Life had been a ready receptacle for Drexel's junk.

In October 2019, Black said as much when he described the relationship between Apollo and Athene as "special and symbiotic." Black's characterization was reminiscent of how Bill Rider, the federal savings and loan investigator, had described the ties between First Executive and Drexel—so close as to be almost inseparable.

What does "special and symbiotic" mean in practice for Athene policyholders? Regulatory filings tell the tale. In 2020, Athene Annuity & Life, the main insurer in Athene Holding's universe, had $54 billion in assets. Among those assets were $4.1 billion in stocks, bonds, and mortgage loans issued by related entities—its "parent, subsidiaries, and affiliates." By contrast, Athene competitor Prudential Annuities Life Assurance Corp. had $54 billion in assets but held only $231 million in investments in parent, subsidiaries, and affiliates in 2020.

In the spring of 2020, as the stock and bond markets were plummeting on COVID fears, one of Athene's "affiliated" holdings slammed the insurer with a huge loss. Athene reported that its 7 percent ownership stake in Apollo stock had generated a $300 million loss, almost one-third of the $1.1 billion loss reported by the insurer. Although the stock rebounded after the Federal Reserve launched its extravagant COVID response, that terrifying moment provided a glimpse into what Athene's "special and symbiotic" ties to Apollo might mean for policyholders in future fraught times.

Athene held other similarities to Executive Life. For example, Athene was aggressive with the reinsurers it used to "back" its policyholder obligations, just as Executive Life had been. Athene's reinsurers, remember, are there to step in and backstop Athene and its obligations if it gets into a fix. And unlike other, more conservative insurers, Athene's backstops come from *its own* affiliates. Such ties between affiliates defeat the purpose of reinsurance, which is supposed to spread risk among unrelated and financially solid entities.

In 2020, 95 percent of Athene Annuity & Life's reinsurance and coinsurance deals were struck with company affiliates—$54 billion out of $57 billion. For a comparison, New York Life Insurance Company, which carries the highest ratings from Moody's and Standard & Poor's (higher than Athene's), had zero reinsurance or coinsurance deals with affiliates.

Then there's the matter of where Athene's reinsurers are located—offshore and away from prying eyes. In this, Athene is going further than Executive Life did. At least Fred Carr's reinsurers were domestic.

Athene Holding, the parent company, and its reinsurers are all headquartered in Bermuda. Their dealings are off-limits to domestic regulators and cloaked in secrecy because Bermuda does not require its insurers to make extensive public disclosures. Athene's annual Bermuda filings consist of five pages and few details, versus the thousand-plus-page state filing for Athene's Iowa subsidiary.

Because offshore insurers are hard to tap for funds in an insurance company failure, Athene's policyholders would find it difficult to recover money from an offshore reinsurance company if things went awry. Indeed, a lawsuit filed on behalf of Athene shareholders against Apollo by a pension fund that contended Athene was paying Apollo "extravagant and expensive" fees was dismissed by a judge who said the Bermuda location made Athene unreachable for the plaintiffs.

Finally, just as Executive Life did, Athene has had its share of run-ins with the occasional aggressive insurance regulator. More on that later.

Another interesting Executive Life twist to the Athene setup involved the executive Apollo chose to build Athene: James Belardi, a former executive at Sun Life America, Eli Broad's Los Angeles–based life insurer. Broad, you'll recall, had warned insurance commissioner Garamendi about selling Executive Life's bond portfolio to Leon Black; the sale was too cheap, Broad had said. He then was allowed to take a significant stake in Aurora, the successor insurer to Executive Life.

Certainly, there was a lot for Apollo to like about having a captive insurance company in its financial services firmament. For policyholders, well, that was another story. Athene's policyholders, like those of Executive Life, would almost certainly be left holding the bag if something went wrong.

"When you look at the business model these guys use, where they're substantially increasing the risk in the bond portfolio, sooner or later, in my opinion, that has to come home to roost," a money manager named Patrick Dodd told *Bloomberg News* in 2012, three years after Athene started up. "All the upside would go to Athene if it worked out. And the downside would go to the annuity holders if it didn't."

Dodd knew what he was talking about. Until April 2011, he'd overseen investments at Liberty Life Insurance Co. in Greenville, South Carolina, focusing on what he called a "squeaky clean" portfolio—bonds issued by state governments and large, financially sound corporations. Liberty had sold $2.8 billion in annuities to customers interested in supplementing their Social Security payments in retirement, Bloomberg reported.

Then in 2011, Athene acquired Liberty; almost immediately, Liberty's holdings changed dramatically, Dodd said. Now they included securities backed by subprime mortgages, time-share vacation homes, and a railroad in Kazakhstan.

It made Fred Carr's investment style look positively prudent.

Athene grew furiously after its founding in 2009. By 2013, it had bought out three other large insurers with $6.1 billion in annuities outstanding. Four years later, in 2017, Athene began buying corporate pension obligations, exposing hundreds of thousands of retirees to risks they had not faced before.

This spectacular growth enriched Apollo, and Black and his fellow privateers took notice. Within ten years of Athene's creation,

Blackstone, Carlyle, and KKR had all bought insurance operations. Now it would be policyholders' turn in the pirate's barrel.

The effects on insurers' investment holdings was evident quickly. Research from AM Best, a top insurance rating firm, said that insurers acquired by private equity firms saw their investment portfolios' yields rise by 0.33 percent on average during the first year after the acquisition, increases that reflected higher-risk investments. Best also noted that during the first year of a private equity company's ownership, most reported larger risk-based capital owing to "the corresponding increase in investment portfolio risk."

State regulators were also watching Apollo's rise in the insurance industry, and some began to raise concerns. In 2013, the National Association of Insurance Commissioners formed a working group to analyze the risks posed by private equity's involvement in insurance.

The U.S. Treasury registered its own worries, noting in 2014 that the annuity business, with its long-term liabilities, required exceptional risk management capabilities, skills that the short-term private equity crowd might not have. Even the normally somnambulant Federal Reserve Board rang alarm bells about privateers' buyouts of insurers.

"Some believe these attributes could be inconsistent with the business model of private equity firms," Treasury officials wrote in a classic understatement, "thereby creating risks which regulators should monitor and/or mitigate when private equity firms acquire annuity writers."

In December 2016, Athene issued shares to the public for the first time. At last, investors could catch a glimpse inside Apollo's cash-generating machine. If you were counting on Athene being a safe investment, that glimpse might have been unnerving. As a report in *Pensions & Investments* noted at the time, Athene's profits were fueled by returns from its $72 billion investment portfolio "that includes an unusual amount of junk-rated debt" and other complex securities.

"This is characteristic of many private equity firms pushing limits, here into incestuous financial relationships, with the general goal of increasing aggregate fees to the firm," Lawrence Cunningham, a professor at George Washington University, told *Pensions & Investments*.

Joseph M. Belth is professor emeritus of insurance at Indiana University and a longtime industry analyst. Belth identified risks in Executive Life's operation back in the 1980s, well ahead of others. In Belth's view, private equity firms like Apollo are not well suited to the insurance industry. "I think private equity firms are in it for the quick buck and that is what troubles me," Belth said. "Their interest is in short-run profit and the insurance companies are not—that's a recipe for trouble."

As for Athene in particular? "Policyholders are pawns in the hands of people like Black," Belth said.

For decades, the privateers had taken over companies and even industries, laying waste to jobs, tax receipts, and prosperity. Now they were grabbing control of retirees' savings. An unhappy ending was almost certain, but still, no one moved to stop the juggernaut—not a financial regulator, not Congress, not an attorney general. All left the door wide open for predators to take control of retirees' savings and do what they'd done all along their ruinous way.

It was surely only a matter of time before another Executive Life debacle emerged.

• • • •

By mid-2022, almost four hundred ten thousand corporate retirees were trusting Athene to provide them with a prosperous retirement. They'd been given no choice in the matter—their former companies had sold their pensions to Athene without giving them the right to object. The benefits these companies reaped from the transactions were clear: a short-term monetary gain paid to them by Athene and the long-term benefit of not having to cover the payments they'd promised their retirees. Transferring their pension obligations to Athene meant corporations like Alcoa, Bristol Myers, General Electric, and Lockheed Martin were off the hook to their former workers.

That left the retirees very much at risk for problems that might arise from the Athene purchase—there would be no government agency to bail them out, for example, as they'd had in their corporate-sponsored pensions. That federal entity, called the Pension Benefit Guaranty Corporation, stepped in to shore up a troubled fund and guaranteed some future payments for its pensioners. The PBGC was to corporate retirees what the Federal Deposit Insurance Corporation is for bank depositors; it was the agency that had come to the rescue of the Noranda pensioners after Apollo was done savaging that company.

Of course, the pensioners forced into the Athene transfers were assured everything would be fine. "Participants covered by this transaction can be confident they will receive the same pension benefit, on the same schedule, as what they currently receive," Lockheed Martin said.

These pension deals had a telling name, however. They were called "pension risk transfers," and therein was their problem. The companies selling their *pension* obligations were *transferring* to another entity the *risks* associated with making these payments for years to come. A good thing for the companies, of course, but beneficial to the pensioners? Not so fast.

And with the PBGC backing gone, that meant retirees were at the mercy of whichever insurance company had bought the obligations. If that company failed, they'd be out of luck.

As these retirees' companies sold off their pensions to Athene, little did they know whom they were now banking on. They did not know that the safety and soundness of their retirement income were in the hands of the very entity that had plundered thousands of Executive Life policyholders thirty years earlier.

In the late 1980s, Executive Life had also helped corporations replace their pensions with annuities. A 1998 lawsuit filed on behalf of fifteen hundred beneficiaries of an RJR Nabisco pension involved in the Executive Life failure provides a cautionary tale about the risks associated with transferring pensions to insurers with risky practices.

Corporate pensions had been dying since the early 1980s, when companies began to recognize how costly these long-term obligations were. Finding ways to get rid of onerous pension promises became a rewarding pursuit for companies, even if it meant taking themselves into bankruptcy to jettison the obligations.

In the fall of 1986, Nabisco's board of directors voted to terminate some of its subsidiaries' pension plans. One of these plans, belonging to retirees of a unit called Aminoil, was overfunded. That meant it had more in assets than in liabilities it was obligated to pay out. Nabisco decided to buy an annuity equal to the amount it owed beneficiaries and keep the overfunded amount leftover for itself.

The company set about determining which annuity company it would sell its obligations to. To analyze the market it hired a consultant, who then sponsored a beauty contest of five different insurers. All had the highest safety ratings, the capacity to service the annuity, and "competence" in the annuity business, a lawsuit said. Executive Life was one of the contestants alongside more established companies Aetna and Prudential.

As the consultant continued its analysis, it became clear that Executive Life would win the assignment. It had offered the best bid for the business and it met all Nabisco's other criteria.

In 1987, Executive Life took over the $54 million annuity. You know what happened a few years later. Some of the Nabisco beneficiaries wound up receiving an average of 57 percent of what they were owed when John Garamendi sold Executive Life's bond portfolio to Leon Black and Apollo.

Shocked by the harm they'd suffered, the beneficiaries of the Nabisco pension sued their former employer, arguing that it had breached its duty to them by selecting Executive Life as the annuity provider. They also alleged negligence, recklessness, and "acting with disregard for the safety of the members of the Aminoil Retirement Plan." They wanted Nabisco to cover the losses they'd experienced as a result of the Executive Life mess.

Unfortunately, they lost. The judge hearing the case in the Southern District Court of Texas concluded that Nabisco had done its duty to its pension beneficiaries. Even though Executive Life had taken an "aggressive" stance on its investments, the insurer "would have recovered from the market losses that prompted the California Insurance Commissioner to seize the company within one year of the seizure," the judge ruled.

"The bonds held by Executive were not in default," she continued. "The specific borrowers had not failed to pay. When fears of default in the market generally had caused lenders to reduce the prices they were willing to pay other lenders to acquire this type of bond, California intruded itself; the drop in the market as a whole lowered the value of Executive's portfolio to a level that was less than its obligations. Unlike the conservator," she said, referring to Garamendi, "not every bondholder dumped its portfolio in an overreaction to a market decline. If the conservator had followed Executive's initial strategy, everyone would have been paid in full years ago.

"The nice man from the government of California [Garamendi, in other words] converted a temporary problem into a permanent disaster," the judge concluded. Nabisco's losing pensioners had also lost their case.

In March 2021, Apollo and Athene merged in an $11 billion deal. One immediate benefit to the combination—the company's stock could now gain membership in a stock index, an elite position that meant mutual funds aiming to mimic the performance of the Standard & Poor's 500 index, say, would have to buy it. Previously, Apollo had not met the requirements of index inclusion, but now the merged companies' stock did. If index fund managers had to buy Athene stock, those purchases could propel its share price.

When the deal was announced, nobody seemed to mind that Athene's Annuity and Life Co. had just signed a consent order with the Texas State insurance department for mishandling the conversion of annuity contracts it had bought from another insurer. It had sent inaccurate information to contract holders, failed to send annual statements and process loan payments on time, and had delayed annuity distributions. Athene paid $400,000 in penalties, the sort of penny-ante toll Athene was only too happy to pay; it did not admit to a violation of the Texas Insurance Code.

A year earlier, New York's Department of Financial Services had settled a case with Athene following a year-long investigation into its pension risk transfer business. The regulator had identified a brazen violation of state law: the Athene subsidiary conducting the pension activities had not bothered to become licensed in New York, but it had nonetheless conducted business with thousands of New York–based policyholders. Athene agreed to pay $45 million in penalties.

Apollo's spokeswoman declined to comment about Athene.

Finally, in September 2021, concerns about what the privateers might be doing to pensioners' investments began rising among state treasurers. Officials in Colorado, Illinois, and Wisconsin wrote to the Department of Labor "advocating for policies and practices that ensure the safekeeping of retirement assets in an orderly, transparent, and fiduciarily responsible manner." In their letter, the treasurers noted the growing clout of private equity–backed insurers in the pension market and the risks their exotic investments posed to beneficiaries. Citing a study from the Treasury Department's Federal Insurance Office, the letter also remarked that "private equity–backed insurers have become significant investors in illiquid and macroeconomic sensitive assets such as CMLs [commercial mortgage loans] and private placements, which are loans made to mostly private middle-market domestic and foreign companies."

In a market downturn, these types of investment could be decimated, the letter writers noted.

Just as 2021 was drawing to a close, the NAIC announced it was forming a task force to take "a deeper look" at the increasing number of insurers controlled by private equity companies. A report on the development in the *National Law Review* said: "It appears that regulators are most concerned with life and annuity insurers."

Once again, though, the regulators would stand down. By the

following summer, the NAIC working group had compiled recommendations for state insurance regulators to follow to assess
and monitor the risks in private equity–backed insurers' practices.
One area of concern was the lack of information about possible conflicts of interest in the investments made by insurers that
were related to the private equity firm. But the recommendations
were unlikely to stop the wave of private equity involvement in
insurance. In a note to its clients, the esteemed law firm of Willkie
Farr & Gallagher said: "Regulators are not averse to PE firms entering the market, and indeed, believe the growth of PE firms may
even be a net positive." It was another win for the plunderers.

CHAPTER SEVENTEEN

"No Evidence of Wrongdoing"

Leon Black Makes His Exit

Donald Trump swept into the White House amid shock and horror. How he had garnered enough votes to propel himself into the Oval Office would be the topic of consternation for years.

The financiers, however, felt differently—they knew Donald Trump had their backs. As Tony James, Blackstone's president, told reporters on an earnings call in early 2017, "the slate of policies that Trump has articulated and that Paul Ryan has articulated, if they came to pass in that form, would be beneficial for our portfolio companies. There is a sense of relieving some of the regulations that were choking many businesses."

Stephen Schwarzman, James's partner, became one of Trump's key economic advisors, seated beside the president at photo ops related to business discussions. Between July 19, 2020, and March 2021, Schwarzman gave almost $6 million to Trump and PACs promoting the president and the Republican Party. After Trump lost the 2020 election, in a November 6 call with other business leaders reported by the *Financial Times*, Schwarzman said Trump was within his rights to challenge the election results. It took the billionaire two weeks to acknowledge that Trump was the loser in 2020.

"People are allowed to support presidents," Schwarzman was quoted as saying in a December 2020 report in *Insider*.

It was easy to see why Schwarzman wanted Trump to stay in office. During his one-term presidency, Trump had gone much further than just benefitting the privateers by relaxing regulations on their companies. He also made sure that individual investors—sometimes referred to by Wall Streeters as the "dumb money"—would be allowed to pour their hard-won retirement money into private equity deals. The fact was, the titans wanted fresh "marks" and individual investors were the obvious next choice.

Companies sponsoring individual investors' retirement accounts are only permitted to offer prudent, relatively safe investments and must abide by rules written and enforced by the United States Department of Labor. This is the agency that enforces ERISA, the Employee Retirement Income Security Act of 1974, set up to protect investors from losing money to retirement savings scams.

For decades, companies handling investors' 401(k) and other retirement accounts under ERISA could not offer private equity investments or hedge funds. These investments' risks, high costs, opacity, and illiquidity—the inability to cash out quickly—made them inappropriate for retirement savers under the law.

But this changed under Donald Trump's Department of Labor, which in mid-2020 published a so-called information letter that the industry took as permission for private equity firms to prey on investors and their 401(k)s. As journalist David Sirota wrote at the time, the "letter could help Trump's private equity donors fleece 100 million workers," and it followed a $3 million donation from Schwarzman to Trump's reelection bid. The DOL was responding to Trump's request that government agencies "remove barriers to the greatest engine of economic prosperity the world has ever known: the innovation, initiative, and drive of the American people."

In publishing its information letter, DOL said it would "help Americans saving for retirement gain access to alternative investments that often provide strong returns" and would "ensure that ordinary people investing for retirement have the opportunities they need for a secure retirement." Never mind that academic research had shown that the returns on private equity had fallen to a level roughly matching those of low-cost stock index funds. Never mind that the investments were teeming with fees and impossible to sell. Never mind that the average individual investor is not savvy enough to analyze these deals. And no matter that the firms peddling these investments had helped to manufacture the enormous wealth gap that cleaved America in two. It was time to give the money-spinners a path to new riches: access to the $7 trillion sitting in individual retirement savings accounts.

Jay Clayton, Trump's chairman of the SEC, had long supported the DOL's change and said it would give Main Street investors wonderful new opportunities. "We want to make sure retail is not left behind," Clayton said in an interview, referencing a colloquial term for individual investors.

Not surprisingly, in March 2021, after leaving the SEC amid Trump's loss, Clayton joined Apollo's board as its lead independent director. His compensation was not disclosed, but other directors at Apollo earn as much as $290,000 a year. As lead independent director, Clayton could receive more.

Clayton's ascension to the Apollo board occurred as Leon Black stepped down under the Jeffrey Epstein cloud. In a public memo, Black allowed that the investigation into his Epstein relationship had been "deeply trying for me and my family, too." Even though the internal report had concluded "no evidence of wrongdoing on my part," he said, the pressures had "taken a toll on my health and have caused me to wish to take some time away from the public spotlight that comes with my family involvement with this great public company. It will be good for my family and me to step back and become more private for a period of time."

Apollo, Black concluded, would "soar to new heights" as a result of the firm's leadership change. The moment was bittersweet—his creation of Apollo, Black said, had been "the greatest achievement of my professional life."

Even as the Department of Labor opened the door to further ravaging of Main Street by the financial titans, some headwinds began blowing their way. By 2022, it seemed that finally, after decades of predation, private equity's dominance, swagger, and sway might be in doubt.

A first and powerful salvo came in a legal ruling in December 2020 from a respected federal judge, Jed Rakoff, in the Southern District of New York. Rakoff had been presiding over a dispute stemming from the bankruptcy of the shoe manufacturer Nine West, which, naturally, had been owned by a private equity firm just before it failed. The bankruptcy had been contentious, with some creditors accusing the company's private equity owner of stripping out and absconding with the company's most valuable brands, leaving lesser units to shoulder an unmanageable debt load resulting from the takeover. In other words, a typical plunderer play.

The case sprang from a $2 billion buyout of Nine West in 2014 by Sycamore Partners, a firm specializing in takeovers of consumer and retail companies. The business went bankrupt four years later. Sycamore has $10 billion in assets, was started in 2011, and is headquartered in New York City. As part of the transaction, Nine West sold two of its top brands, Stuart Weitzman and Kurt Geiger, to a Sycamore affiliate in a side deal.

After Nine West filed for bankruptcy, its creditors argued that the two brands had been sold to the Sycamore affiliate too cheaply and left the remaining Nine West operation unable to carry the excessive LBO debt. Investment bankers told the Nine West board that the company could only sustain a debt level that was five times its cash flow, but the debt in the Sycamore deal had totaled almost eight times the company's cash flow. When it approved the takeover, the board had not expressed a view on the side deal to sell off the Stuart Weitzman and Kurt Geiger brands and the heavy debt financing. It had simply agreed to the buyout based on the price offered by Sycamore to Nine West shareholders.

Which was not enough, Rakoff said. The directors should have analyzed the financial structure of the takeover to see if it was sound and feasible going forward. Nine West's debt had indeed been too onerous and had forced its crash to earth.

The crux of Rakoff's ruling was a shocker to all those who had approved takeovers based on their rich prices and moved on, pockets bulging. He held that when selling Nine West to Sycamore Partners, Nine West's directors should be held liable because the takeover's debt-heavy financial structure resulted in failure.

Rakoff said the board had been "reckless" in not investigating whether the company would be able to survive under its new financial construct. And he added that the directors could not "take cover behind the business judgment rule," which generally lets directors escape liability for their actions years later.

The Rakoff ruling was a game changer for the private equity world, lawyers said. Directors of a company selling out to a takeover firm could be sued if they did not analyze the financial aspects of the acquisition to ensure that it was rational and workable. No longer would directors skate free of any liabilities if they approved a merger that wound up in failure a few years later because of a massive debt load.

Rakoff's ruling involved just one case, but it set the stage for an entirely new reckoning on the impacts that takeovers have had on creditors, workers, pensioners, and taxpayers. In saying that the directors could be held liable for failing to analyze whether the company would thrive under its new owners, Rakoff was throwing out a bedrock concept among company boards. That concept: the only obligation a director had to a company's shareholders was to secure the best possible price in a sale. Now, thanks to Rakoff, other stakeholders and the future of the company itself had to be considered.

The verdict was reminiscent of the 1989 law Indiana had implemented to rein in that first takeover wave all those years ago. Deal lawyers warned that Rakoff's ruling could have a chilling effect on leveraged buyouts—as if that would be a bad thing.

As Rakoff's decree on directors' responsibilities in a takeover sank in, a further chink in the financiers' armor emerged in academic studies showing that the ballyhooed returns claimed by the private equity firms were no longer accurate. Stakes in low-cost stock market index funds, it turned out, were producing the same gains that costly and damaging private equity had since 2006, one study said. While the early years of the industry had produced outsized returns, those gains had now dissipated.

This falloff in performance was just coming into focus as Trump's Department of Labor began allowing private equity vehicles into retirement accounts. Perfect timing for another Wall Street rip-off of Main Street.

Some workers victimized by the pirates began to act as well.

Labor organizers found fertile ground among private equity–backed companies whose workers had grown tired of their abusive practices. In 2021, emergency department physicians, including Dr. Lin, who'd worked at TeamHealth, joined together to try to claw back their operations from the pirates. Setting up a group called Take Medicine Back, they worked to highlight how private equity firms imperiled patients by putting profits first. Later that year, an associated physicians' group filed the lawsuit against Envision Healthcare, the KKR-owned emergency department staffing company, alleging that Envision's control of emergency departments in the state violated its laws barring the corporate practice of medicine. Because California is among the more aggressive states on healthcare issues, the plaintiffs hoped their case would encourage the state's attorney general to file his own suit on the corporate practice of medicine.

Regulators also started to stir from their stupors. Under President Biden's appointee Lina M. Khan, the Federal Trade Commission began oiling its rusty anti-trust machinery, threatening to take her agency back to its early twentieth-century roots, when it was aggressive and wielded an anti-trust club to reduce unemployment and economic disparities. One area of early interest to the FTC was consolidation in healthcare, especially among small physician practices such as those in the dermatology and anesthesiology arenas. Bringing scrutiny to this arena would be revolutionary.

With Jay Clayton gone to Apollo, the new SEC chairman, Gary Gensler, launched regulatory reform aimed squarely at the privateers. In September 2021, he testified before Congress about ratcheting up transparency and disclosure requirements for private equity firms, especially regarding their fees and personal enrichment schemes.

Among the changes Gensler discussed was a heightened transparency around how the privateers' funds perform. He suggested requiring them to provide investors with the same comparison figures that buyers of mutual funds receive. He also warned that the SEC would crack down on conflicts of interest between the plunderers and their investors and advocated for greater regulatory scrutiny on practices used by these funds that might pose risks to the overall financial system as reckless home loan companies had done in the lead-up to the 2008 mortgage crisis.

The SEC also floated new rules that would ban "accelerated monitoring fees," those money-for-nothing charges that had generated millions of dollars for the pirates. These were the fees the SEC said Apollo had kept secret from its investors and led to the 2016 enforcement case.

Of course, all this talk of regulatory reform brought out the firms' lobbying arsenal. In 2021 alone, Blackstone Group spent almost $5.5 million lobbying, according to the Center for Responsive Politics, up from $3.7 million in 2019 when their pal Trump was in office. Of Blackstone's companies, TeamHealth spent the most on lobbying in 2021, a total of $1.3 million. Apria Healthcare, the Blackstone-owned company that submitted all those false claims to federal health programs in 2020, paid its lobbyists $100,000 in 2021.

KKR spent $4.5 million in lobbying in 2021, and Envision, its emergency medical staffing company, paid $1.13 million, the Center for Responsive Politics said.

But Apollo Global Management beat them all on the lobbying spree, spending $7.1 million in 2021, up from $4.7 million a year earlier. LifePoint, Apollo's hospital unit, paid almost $800,000 to lobbyists in 2021, the records show. Among the issues its lobbyists worked on were matters surrounding Medicare and Medicaid administration and legislation. Apollo lobbyists were also aggressively battling any legislation that aimed to forgive student loans dispensed by Apollo's for-profit diploma mill, the University of Phoenix.

Finally, in 2021, politicians on both sides of the aisle started to raise questions about the harm the privateers were doing to consumers in an array of industries. Their purchases of single-family homes to rent came under attack for raising tenant costs and hurting lower- and middle-class families.

Private equity's consolidation of hospitals became another flash point for both Democrats and Republicans. Richard Blumenthal, the Connecticut Democrat, and Josh Hawley, the Missouri Republican who fist-pumped the insurrection of the Capitol on January 6, 2021, and then scurried away in fear, are both on the Senate Antitrust Subcommittee; in a hearing in April 2021, they spoke out about problems associated with private equity ownership of healthcare companies. "The incentives and self-interest of the private equity funds drive the finances rather than respect and care for the patients who are there or the professional staff who ensure quality care," Blumenthal said.

It is too soon to say whether the devastation will be stopped. But these developments are a start.

There are other indications pirate capitalists might be feeling increased pressure. The fact that private equity firms are models of white male dominance, for example, doesn't play well nowadays. As public corporations have strived to increase diversity among their staff and executive ranks, these operations remained in the Stone Age. Their firms have fewer programs in place to promote diversity, according to a June 2021 analysis by consulting firm BCG that surveyed more than 4,000 workers at private-equity shops. The number who said they'd witnessed discrimination in their workplace was 13 percentage points higher than at public companies; meanwhile, fewer employees at private-equity-owned firms felt comfortable reporting the incidents they saw, the report said.

"PE-owned companies are behind their publicly traded counterparts in taking action," the report concluded. "This needs to change."

Gender diversity is another problem, a March 2021 report by Preqin found. Females made up only 20 percent of private equity employees and just 12 percent of those firms' senior roles were held by women. Corporate America, not exactly a paragon of gender equality, does far better: in 2021, women made up 24 percent of those in C-suite positions. Among manager ranks, women made up 40 percent.

Perhaps recognizing that extracting wealth from companies and their workers may not be an enduring business model, one of the big firms—KKR—has begun to award shares of company stock to lower-level workers at some of its entities. In 2015, for example, KKR bought C.H.I. Overhead Doors, a maker of residential and commercial garage doors. Anyone among C.H.I.'s 800 employees making less than $100,000 a year received stock in the company, an offer C.H.I. and KKR said was not in exchange for benefits, wages, or wage increases. When KKR sold C.H.I. in May 2022, hourly workers and truck drivers stood to receive an average $175,000 payout on their shares, in addition to $9,000 in dividends earned on their stock while KKR owned the company.

Between 2011 and mid-2022, KKR said it has awarded "billions" of total equity value in such arrangements "to over 45,000 non-senior employees across over twenty-five companies." Given that KKR has invested in almost 250 companies over that period, its website showed, the companies awarding stock to workers totals roughly 10 percent. The practice is undeniably admirable, but it doesn't begin to make up for decades of damage by pirate equity.

As we researched this book, the American Investment Council, the big industry lobbying group, suggested that we read a recent academic study showing that company workplaces that are backed by private equity have better safety records. The report, published in October 2021 in the *Review of Financial Studies*, analyzed data on workplace safety at 560 companies with at least $10 million in assets between 1995 and 2007. It found that annual injuries per employee fell by an average of between 0.74 and 1 percentage points from the four years before a company was acquired by a private equity firm to four years after.

This would certainly be good news, and we dug further into the study. We learned that there were some caveats. The decline in injury rates was smaller after more highly leveraged buyouts, the authors found, and they said: "one possible explanation for the decline in workplace injury rates after buyouts is the systematic automation or offshoring of dangerous jobs." The study also concluded that more dangerous establishments experienced smaller decreases in injury rates after buyouts.

Jonathan Cohn, the study's lead author, is the academic director at the Hicks, Muse, Tate and Furst Center for Private Equity Finance at the University of Texas, Austin. The Center says it provides students with "Private Equity Strength Training" to ensure they are "fully conditioned for careers with a deep understanding of the private equity market."

Another example that these firms recognize they have a public relations problem may be the foundations some of them have recently created to benefit those who are less fortunate. These methods of sanitizing questionable activities are as old as time itself, but among the financiers, they seem to be cropping up more frequently as scrutiny over their activities rises.

In February 2022, for example, Apollo launched the Apollo

Opportunity Foundation. Its goal? To "advance economic prosperity and expand opportunity." The firm said it planned to invest $100 million over ten years "in non-profit organizations working to expand opportunity for underrepresented individuals."

The foundation's website groans with platitudes. But this one may be best for its unadulterated hypocrisy: "We recognize our responsibility to drive positive change in society, and we are leveraging the entire Apollo ecosystem to create long-lasting value."

What the website didn't say is that with the new foundation, Apollo would get praise—and a welcome tax break—for donating a minuscule fraction of what it had extracted over the years.

While $100 million might sound like a lot, to Apollo it is infinitesimal. For example, that amount is considerably less than the $126 million in monitoring fees Apollo stood to collect in just one year—2013—from six companies it had already sold and was therefore no longer monitoring.

That $100 million was one-quarter of the dividends Apollo extracted from Noranda, the aluminum company it propelled to bankruptcy in 2016. The amount is also roughly equal to the annual transaction expenses and monitoring and legal fees Apollo siphoned from Taminco, the chemical company it owned for a spell.

Finally, here's another comparison point for the $100 million earmarked for the new Apollo foundation: the amount was far less than the $158 million Leon Black had paid to Jeffrey Epstein over the years for his unparalleled tax advice.

More than thirty years ago, treasury secretary Nicholas Brady predicted that "the market" would correct the excesses in the leveraged buyout arena. The fad that was so devastating to workers, pensions, and even taxpayers would end quickly, Brady said, because the economics would no longer work.

Brady was obviously wrong in his prediction. Or perhaps he was just three decades early.

What began as a small renegade world of Drexel Burnham Lambert–funded corporate raiders has morphed into an industry managing 12 million workers and generating 6.5 percent of gross domestic output. The assets under its control are essential to the well-being of our society, and the industry's winner-take-all model endangers our future.

But the industry has changed in other ways as well. Early on, profitable deals were there for the taking, because their targets were undervalued in the public market. Now, the trades are crowded with copycats, and the potential returns are riskier because the amount of leverage or borrowed money they need to deploy in the deals is rising.

This is key—leverage adds risk, and when it takes larger amounts of borrowed money at higher interest rates to generate the same returns, the perils in the transactions grow. This increase in risk-taking also signals that the economics of the transactions have become dubious or that there is too much money chasing the same deals.

When too much money crowds into identical trades, the outcome is always the same: severe losses. Think the mortgage mania of 2008, think the internet bubble of 2000.

In the late 1970s and 1980s, the raiders took over companies that were distressed or trading at discounts to the values assigned to their peers. Then, the buyout kings dressed the companies up for an IPO that would capture the improvement in valuation.

Over time these early, easy deals became scarce, and the profiteers had to look harder to find target companies. When they did, they had to resort to more active management of the firms they purchased. They'd slash costs, eliminate higher-paid union workers, and reduce employee benefits; shut down less profitable divisions; or acquire competitors to bolster the pricing power of the company they owned. As they ran out of opportunities, they began to buy polluting assets, such as coal operations, that were too toxic for other companies to hold.

Continuing their search for lush profits, the financiers also pursued industries, such as healthcare and education, that had long been understood to serve a social function. These industries are expected to have inefficiencies and generate lower profits because they must stand ready to serve society. To provide this service, they require excess capacity or backup inventory, both of which cost money.

The privateers' "streamlining" of these industries promoted for-profit schools that gouged students and did not educate them. The efficiencies they brought to healthcare eliminated "excess" hospital beds, nurses, and ventilators, as well as undermining personal relationships with the family physician.

Today, we seem to be nearing a new stage in the pirates' life cycle, one in which the body begins to eat itself as it runs out of external food sources. The shift was accelerated by the global pandemic and its impact on economic activity, high company valuations, and tighter monetary policy.

The founders of some of these storied firms are stepping down, making way for a new generation of looters. In the fall of 2021, Henry Kravis and George Roberts announced their retirements as co-CEOs at KKR. At the time, a KKR representative told the *New York Post* that the men would remain actively involved in the operation.

In the United States, there are now more than five thousand private equity firms, double the number a decade ago. That is far too many prospective buyers for the few available acquisition targets. Even celebrity Kim Kardashian has gotten in on the act, announcing in summer 2022 the launch of her own private equity firm with a former Carlyle partner; she plans to invest in media properties, consumer products, and e-commerce.

The busy competitive landscape in the industry has led to a sharp increase in prices the privateers pay for their takeovers. In 2009, the typical deal was done at eight times a company's earnings; this multiple now stands at fourteen. Twenty years ago, a typical buyout fund invested in ten to twelve companies. Nowadays, six to eight are the norm.

Sebastien Canderle is a private capital advisor who lectures at business schools. He is also the author of *The Good, the Bad and the Ugly of Private Equity* and writes periodic blog posts on a forum sponsored by the CFA Institute, a global association of finance professionals. In a February 2022 post called "Market Saturation Spawns Runaway Dealmaking," he argued that the current state of plunderdom "is simply transactional activity that is so completely unnecessary or pernicious that even deal doers cannot justify its occurrence."

For example, Canderle noted, far more buyouts are occurring among the privateers themselves, not with strategic buyers, such as corporations, or in initial public offerings of shares to new investors. These deals, in which one plunderer sells a company to another, are called secondary buyouts, or SBOs. Back in 2001 for example, less than 5 percent of buyouts were these kinds of secondaries. Now they account for at least 40 percent of private equity sales worldwide.

Moreover, the merry-go-round of secondary buyouts has begun to spin so dizzyingly that many of the privateers are only able to sell the companies they own *to other funds they run*. They conduct these transactions by selling a company out of one of their funds and into another, all in the same family. This is a quintessential example of self-dealing, but in Plunderland, anything goes. Besides, the benefits to the players are manifold.

This became a more common approach during and immediately after the COVID crisis, when the economic world all but stopped. Suddenly, the private equity firms could not sell these companies off—they had to hold them in their funds. And that resulted in a lower rate of return they expected to show investors. Rather than accept this reality, they arranged to sell the companies from one of their funds to another.

These transactions are lucrative. First, the players can charge transaction fees when they transfer a company between funds. And because the company being bought and sold in such a trade is typically valued at a higher price than it had been marked previously, the trades generate rich performance fees to the titans. Whether that higher price was fair or accurate was unclear.

In 2021, such self-dealing buyouts totaled $42 billion globally, up 55 percent from the prior year and 180 percent more than in 2019. These transactions also allow the privateers to continue reaping annual management commissions through the "continuation" funds as they are also called, fees they would not be earning if they'd sold the company to a third party.

Most troubling about this tactic, though, is the fact that neither investors in the selling fund nor those in the buying fund can tell whether the trades are being done at a fair price, Canderle pointed out. Because they are not conducted on what's known as an arm's-length basis, the price paid is suspicious. Of course, the dealmakers have a ready answer for this—they say the transactions have been vetted by "independent" lawyers and auditors. Never mind that the fees charged by those lawyers and auditors to make those opinions are paid for by the firms doing the deals.

In 2021, Apollo conducted just such a sale when its giant hospital company, LifePoint Health, was sold out of one Apollo fund and into another. Apollo had paid just under $1 billion for LifePoint when it bought the company, which became part of Apollo's Fund VIII, created in 2013. But when Apollo sold LifePoint into its Fund IX in 2021, it valued the transaction at $2.6 billion. Of course, those investors in Apollo VIII were thrilled with the sale, given that it generated a gigantic gain. But how did the investors in Apollo IX know that $2.6 billion was an appropriate price for LifePoint?

We asked that question of the folks at CalPERS, the huge public pension fund. As an investor in both of the Apollo funds, CalPERS gained in the LifePoint sale from Fund VIII but may have paid too much as an investor in Fund IX. Unfortunately, CalPERS declined to answer our question.

The fact remains that insider trades like these are fraught with conflicts. But Apollo has never shied away from conflicts of interest—in fact, the firm embraces them. We know that from its very first trade—Executive Life's junk bond portfolio.

Asked about the potential for conflicts in the LifePoint trade, Apollo's spokeswoman told *Bloomberg News*: "We worked with fund investors, independent advisers and multiple new co-investors to reach a fair and attractive transaction for both funds."

In other words: trust us.

A Scotsman and business writer named Bertie Charles Forbes founded *Forbes* magazine in 1917 and was famous for epigrams on the business of life. Sayings like "To be well thought of, think of others" or "Diamonds are chunks of coal that stuck to their job" were examples of Forbes epigrams. Forbes was decidedly pro-business, but he also recognized the pernicious aspects of predation in industry.

Forbes died in 1954, long before the current batch of plunderers had begun amassing their fortunes and depleting the treasure of others. But he knew their kind when he said: "The man who has won millions at the cost of his conscience is a failure."

When Leon Black resigned from Apollo, the firm he founded, he did not leave on a high note. But neither did he acknowledge any moral lapses or personal culpability. In fact, Black noted that the internal review of his relationship with Epstein had found no evidence of wrongdoing on his part.

As is often the case with executives who are forced to retire early, on his exit Black said he was planning to spend more time with his wife and family. He also wound up spending more time with his lawyers. In July 2021, he decided to countersue his former mistress who had accused him of rape and sexual abuse in their years-long affair. Black said she had libeled and extorted him and engaged in racketeering. The suit said his former mistress had demanded $100 million from him; Black also sued her law firm.

In January 2022, the case got only more sordid. Black filed new legal papers accusing Josh Harris, his longtime colleague and one of three founding Apollo partners, of financing the mistress's lawsuit. Harris had left the firm after being passed over for Apollo's top job when Black departed, and Black alleged he had become so irate at the slight that he'd acted "to assassinate" Black's character. In a literary flourish, Black's filing said: "Like Shakespeare's Iago, enraged by being passed over for promotion, he turned his wrath on his mentor and leader."

Harris responded by calling the allegations "desperate and

completely false." He had never met or spoken with the mistress or her representatives, Harris added, and had no involvement in the filing of her suit. In June 2022, the judge overseeing the conspiracy suit threw it out, saying Black's claims were "glaringly deficient." No matter; Black vowed to continue the legal fight.

New York's gossip columns had a field day with the developments. To outsiders, Black's accusations against his former partner of thirty years made him seem unhinged and small. Revenge is the weak pleasure of a little and narrow mind, said the Roman poet Juvenal.

Sue Watson had a slightly different take on Black's departure from Apollo and his salacious legal woes. "There is a special place in hell for these thieves," she said. "And that's what they are!"

Conclusion

Who Will Stop the Bleeding?

In mid-2022, as COVID receded and the world tried to return to normal, a handful of obscure legal filings inched quietly through Delaware Chancery Court. Most large American companies are incorporated in the state, so disputes involving these behemoths often land in its courtrooms.

The cases involved recent transactions among top executives at Apollo and Carlyle and had been filed by pension fund beneficiaries—firefighters, cops, and other union workers—who own shares in the companies. The plaintiffs in the suit against Carlyle said they'd been fleeced by a series of complex deals benefitting the firm's top executives, including billionaire founder David Rubenstein, and they said they had the company documents to prove it.

According to the filings, both Apollo and Carlyle had quietly changed the terms of their executives' contracts so the wealthy financiers could reap new and astounding payoffs at the expense of their shareholders.

The details outlined in the filings allege a novel and audacious enrichment tactic by Apollo's Black, Marc Rowan, and others, and Carlyle's former co-CEO Glenn Youngkin, who won the governorship of Virginia in 2021. The transactions not only paid these men millions of dollars in cash—Black received $283 million and Rubenstein $70.5 million—they magically transformed the former executives' massive company stockholdings into tax-free shares, meaning the men would never have to pay federal taxes on them when they were sold. The deals also meant their companies—and shareholders—were losing out on a financial benefit worth hundreds of millions of dollars related to the executives' missing tax obligations.

It was bad enough that this shift to tax-free status meant the federal government would receive no taxes on future stock sales. Even wilder, the deals would allow Black and his peers to receive generous tax deductions if they donated their shares to charity. Taxpayers, therefore, would lose twice on the transactions as the pillagers won two ways.

Few had noticed these deals, in part because they involved arcane tax laws. But they also flew under the radar because the privateers' firms had not been especially clear in describing them to their shareholders. In fact, the lawyers for the pension funds had spotted the transactions only because they were experts on the rules governing them and knew what documents to request to confirm their suspicions. Lawyers for the pension fund beneficiaries suing Carlyle said in their suit that the firm's top executives acted with an impunity that was both shocking and unacceptable. The pension fund beneficiaries "depend on the integrity of the financial markets to provide for their retirement," their lawyers said.

Asked about the allegations, representatives for the firms and the founders said they were meritless and that they would fight them in court. A spokesman for Youngkin said in a statement that the deal benefitted Carlyle shareholders and that an independent special committee of the company's board "retained independent experts and advisors to consider and approve" the transaction.

The outcome of these cases will not be known for a while. But they highlight a dispiriting fact about Plunderland: private litigants have been far superior in trying to hold these powerful people to account than regulators and other government officials. Even though plaintiffs don't wield the big sticks that securities regulators, anti-trust officials, or federal prosecutors do, they have done more to shed light on the industry's dark corners.

Both labor unions and academics have also contributed mightily to understanding the effects these firms have on their workers, customers, and pensioners. The study showing that nursing homes run by private equity–backed companies recorded 10 percent more deaths than their peers was shocking and revelatory. The continuing research on these predators' effects on other healthcare companies is also illuminating.

But almost every other entity intersecting with private equity is an enabler. Public pension funds and university endowments are a prime example—the billions of dollars flowing from these funds to the firms each year is their oxygen. If these investors cut off the flow, they would vastly diminish the damage these operators do in the future. It has long been a mystery why public pensions—whose workers are hurt most by the industry's predation—are in such thrall to them. And given the reduced returns these funds generate now—essentially identical to an S&P 500 index fund—jettisoning private equity should not be that controversial a decision.

State attorneys general could also do a better job enforcing existing rules, such as anti-trust laws or those that bar the corporate practice of medicine. And when they do bring cases, they should extract fines that are significant enough to get these wealthy firms' attention. State medical boards could also discipline physicians who enable the corporate practice of medicine.

Some in Congress have tried to curtail the money-spinners' power and might, with no success. In 2009, Jack Reed, the Rhode Island Democrat in the Senate, proposed a bill that would have increased disclosures and other transparency surrounding these firms. The legislation would have repealed the exemption enjoyed by some private investment advisors from registering with the SEC and would have authorized the agency to require investment advisors to submit records for federal supervision of systemic risk. It went nowhere.

In 2021, legislators in both the United States Senate and the House of Representatives introduced bills aimed at private equity abuses. Entitled the "Stop Wall Street Looting Act," the legislation would have increased the potential for legal liability for the funds, given worker compensation a higher priority in bankruptcies, and prohibited the payment of dividends to the funds and firms within two years of a buyout (think Noranda). The legislation would also have closed the carried interest tax loophole and would have levied ordinary income taxes on the money the firms and their executives receive that is currently taxed at lower capital gains rates.

These bills also died under immense lobbying pressure. The American Investment Council, the lobbying entity for private equity, warned that the bill threatened the economy, innovation, and jobs, and would "discourage investment." The business-friendly U.S. Chamber of Commerce issued its own "Economic Impact Analysis" of the bill, saying its "restrictions and taxes would be so impactful that, if enacted, even in a modest-case scenario, the country's workforce would be reduced by approximately 6 million jobs, and combined federal, state, and local tax revenues would drop by approximately $109 billion per year in the long run."

Were these figures accurate? It didn't matter. Once stated, "analysis" is treated as fact in D.C.

Several former staffers we spoke with, who helped draft the "Stop Wall Street Looting Act," or consulted on it, told us that as they began to write the legislation to increase regulation of the take-over titans, it became clear they were involved in a game like Jenga, where each move affects more than just the piece in play. They found that closing tax loopholes and eliminating "limited liability" status for private equity would also hurt small businesses and other entities that had nothing to do with the industry. The legislation's potential impacts on blameless businesses allowed the looters' lobbyists to contend that the bill was bad for Main Street America.

In fact, whenever elected officials or regulators try to rein in the plunderers, whether closing tax loopholes, increasing public disclosures, or preventing them from contributing to campaigns of public officials they do business with, it becomes clear how politically potent these firms are. Other financial companies—mutual funds, venture capital firms, and hedge funds—have strategies and interests that are diverse enough that they don't often come together to battle against Washington, but this elite group of strip-miners is different. Their standard approach to wealth extraction requires a coordinated, rapid-action lobbying effort each time their tactics come under threat.

In recent years, as the pernicious effects of the dealmakers have become more obvious, left-leaning groups and legislators have been the industry's loudest critics. But these people are gaining unlikely partners on the right in what appear to be growing denunciations. Although it is almost impossible to conceive of Elizabeth Warren and Tucker Carlson agreeing on anything, let alone financial regulation, at the end of 2019 Carlson, too, was attacking "vulture" capitalism, a business model that worships "ruthless economic efficiency" at the expense of "some obligation to the country around them." A younger group of conservatives are taking up the issue and seem bent on moving the Republican Party away from culture wars back to more populist efforts focused on families, workers, and economic security. Where private equity firms and their lobbyists and trade associations had it easy in their historic ability to dismiss the populist left as anti-business or radical socialists, now they may have to confront ideological opposition from the populist right.

Among the unlikely Republican voices warning about the ills of private equity is a veteran of one of the industry's biggest firms—Bain & Company. Oren Cass spent a decade at Bain and then became Mitt Romney's domestic policy director in his 2012 presidential run. In 2020, Cass founded American Compass, a conservative think tank with the mission of "reorienting political focus from growth for its own sake to widely shared economic development" that benefits families and communities. Its proposed solutions to private equity predation align with those of progressive Democrats and include legislation to require that these firms have a financial obligation to workers in a bankruptcy, elimination of the carried interest tax loophole, significant increases in fund disclosures, a ban on share buybacks, and a financial transactions tax.

Writing in the *American Prospect*, David Dayen, executive editor and a critic of private equity, suggests repealing a crucial section of the 1996 National Securities Markets Improvement Act, the law allowing investment managers to peddle funds to hundreds of investors as long as the buyers are "qualified," or sophisticated. As Dayen notes, repealing that section of the law would reduce the amount of capital available to the financiers.

While any legislation that explicitly takes on private equity appears doomed, it's possible that over time those on the left and right could compete to promote a "pro-worker" and "pro-family" agenda. In the meantime, regulators are the ones we need to rely on to effect change.

In October 2021, Allison Herren Lee, a Trump-appointed SEC commissioner and former acting chair of the agency, gave an arresting speech. In it, she highlighted the need to reconsider disclosure standards of private companies under the SEC's 1934 Exchange Act and increase transparency surrounding their operations.

The regulation Lee referred to establishes thresholds that govern when a company must register securities with the SEC; such registrations would result in much greater disclosures about the operations of the entities issuing the securities. Lee was pushing for a significant overhaul of disclosure standards that would result in new information to protect workers, investors, pensioners, and ultimately, taxpayers.

She called her speech "Going Dark: The Growth of Private Markets and the Impact on Investors and the Economy," and in it she noted how the current lack of transparency in the financial markets mirrored that of the 1920s, an era of such egregious financial manipulation that it resulted in the framework of securities laws in use today. A growing portion of the U.S. economy was operating in the shadows, she said, "a dynamic the Commission has fostered—both by action and inaction."

Lee was no partisan ideologue; she had served under a Democratic SEC commissioner before being appointed by President Trump and had been unanimously confirmed by the Senate. She had also served as a special assistant U.S. attorney and senior counsel in the complex financial instruments unit of the SEC's division of enforcement.

A call for more transparency from private companies meant a private equity firm might have to disclose every physician practice company, hospital, or nursing home it owned. Instead of being able to hide these investments behind a web of subsidiaries and holding companies, the ownership would be there for the public to see and, as important, for the Federal Trade Commission to review.

Following the speech, in February 2022, the SEC proposed a new rule governing private funds that would ban some of their more pernicious activities. They included barring the money-for-nothing monitoring fees charged to portfolio companies, preventing fund managers from being able to evade legal liability for acts of gross negligence, and prohibiting an advisor from borrowing money from a client. As is its custom, the SEC asked for comments on the rule.

One letter submitted to the SEC in favor of the rule counted twenty thousand signatures. Its message was clear: "Misleading information about costs and inflated returns allows private equity funds to siphon hundreds of billions of hard-earned dollars from retirees and use them to undermine the livelihood and well-being of workers and their communities. Put simply, Wall Street has figured out how to use money saved by current and future retirees to supercharge a business model that makes executives rich but destroys once thriving companies. Thank you for your recent proposal."

But the proposal soon ran into heated opposition from the powerful firms, even though most of the changes it suggested seemed fairly uncontroversial. Before the rule was finalized, though, the conservative United States Supreme Court published a bombshell decision that put the SEC on notice about any rule it issued. The decision involved the Environmental Protection Agency but signaled that any U.S. regulator's authority to issue rules could be eviscerated by a legal challenge.

The case was *West Virginia et al. v. Environmental Protection Agency et al.* and involved a 2015 EPA clean power plan rule limiting the amount of carbon dioxide emissions existing coal- and natural gas–fired power plants, like those owned by KKR, could spew into the atmosphere. And the Supreme Court said on June 30, 2022, that only Congress can decide the amount of pollution a plant can emit and that unless Congress had delegated specific authority to a regulator over such "major questions," then the regulator has no power to make rules of such economic consequence.

The American Investment Council used this ruling to send another letter to the SEC criticizing its proposed disclosure rule for private funds. "If Congress really intended to empower the Commission to 'fundamentally and dramatically alter the regulatory regime' for this massively important industry, while socking it with billions of dollars in added regulatory costs, Congress would have provided 'clear congressional authorization' to that effect," the council's president fumed. "This is a 'telling indication' that the current Proposal 'extends beyond the agency's legitimate reach.'"

Not surprisingly, the Supreme Court ruling has the SEC rethinking its every move. One SEC source tells us that everything it does is viewed through the lens of litigation risk, especially if a case is chosen by an activist Supreme Court to create a precedent.

But even if the SEC aggressively sought to use all of its legitimate authorities to promulgate meaningful rules over private equity fees, disclosures, and conflicts of interest, a larger unresolved problem remains—enforcement of those rules. If the past is any indication, the SEC's enforcement teeth are a lot less sharp than people think.

Stated simply, the SEC commissioners don't appear to be running the show. It turns out that these officials, appointed by an elected president and confirmed by the Senate, may not make most of the everyday decisions at the SEC. To streamline the five commissioners' workloads, Congress allowed the agency to delegate almost any of its authorities to career staff members. Once these authorities have been delegated, they are rarely pulled back. As a result, the senior career officials in all of the SEC's divisions—including investment management, enforcement, markets and trading—have gained broad power to decide standards, when to enforce or waive rules, and when to prosecute or not prosecute violations and violators.

When a significant issue comes up on which authority has previously been delegated to the staff, even if years earlier, it is generally brought to the specific division's director or that division's legal counsel. The division director in turn informs counsel what they intend to decide on the matter. If the staff has decided on the issue before, the division counsel will usually send a memo to commissioners informing them of the action the staff intends to take under what's called "delegated authority." This memo can take one of two forms; one is a so-called "action" memo, essentially stating, "Hey, we have to make a decision and given the following issues presented we don't want to make a decision without your input." Alternatively, staff could issue an "advice" memo, essentially letting commissioners know of a coming decision on an issue and asking that they raise any objections within a few weeks. As one former counsel to a commissioner told us, "In the years I was at the SEC, I only saw one 'action' memo." More common were advice memos, this person went on to say, and were typically written in a "nothing to see here" tone, justifying the decision the staff intends to make and limiting the likelihood that questions will be raised.

This process essentially means that, even if these memos pass their own staff to reach their desks, commissioners rarely object to the decisions made by career staff on waiving SEC rules. Of course, the commissioners could stop this spread of staff-led judgment calls if they wanted to. For example, commissioners could request their staff to show them every delegated authority memo on a certain topic—such as waivers on the SEC's pay-to-play rule. Then, the commissioners could force the full commission to vote on each related decision. Commissioners could also inform the SEC chair that they no longer want to see advice memos and instead want every pay-to-play ruling to go to a full commission vote.

Given the growing scope and might of the private equity industry, financial regulators should also consider adding the larger firms, especially those with captive insurance operations and that manage pension and individual retirement assets, to the list of institutions whose operations require closer monitoring because they could imperil the entire financial system. Such entities are known as systemically important financial institutions (SIFI), a category that arose out of the 2008 mortgage crisis when it became clear how dangerously interconnected our nation's financial system was. Monitoring SIFIs is the task of the Financial Stability Board, an international body that watches over the global financial system and makes recommendations about its safe operations.

Increased actions by anti-trust regulators would also help to stop the bleeding, and Lina Khan, chairwoman of the Federal Trade Commission, has discussed ramping up scrutiny on private equity deals. In a fall 2021 memo to her staff about priorities for the agency, Khan wrote: "The growing role of private equity and other investment vehicles invites us to examine how these business models may distort ordinary incentives in ways that strip productive capacity and may facilitate unfair methods of competition and consumer protection violations."

In June 2022, the FTC announced a landmark action addressing the problem of small acquisitions that may represent anticompetitive activities even though they fall under the threshold for examination. Private equity firm JAB Consumer Partners and its subsidiary National Veterinary Associates Inc. reached a consent agreement with the FTC requiring the firm to divest veterinary clinics it owned in Texas and California and also receive prior approval on future acquisitions of specialty and emergency veterinary clinics. "Private equity firms increasingly engage in roll up strategies that allow them to accrue market power off the commission's radar," said Holly Vedova, director of the FTC's Bureau of Competition. "The prior notice and approval provisions will ensure the Commission has full visibility into future consolidation and the ability to address it."

The Justice Department may also be stirring from its private equity stupor, some whistleblower lawyers say. In 2018, DOJ brought a rare case against a private equity firm for Medicare fraud committed by one of its portfolio companies—a singular example of prosecutors going up the corporate ladder to include financiers for punishment. The firm was small and relatively unknown—Riordan, Lewis & Haden of Los Angeles—and had nowhere near the clout of an Apollo or Blackstone. Nevertheless, prosecutors alleged it had participated in a kickback scheme to defraud the federal program providing health insurance for members of the military, veterans, and their families. The firm and its portfolio company agreed to pay $21 million to settle the charges; the firm "knew of and agreed to the plan" and "financed the kickback payments," prosecutors alleged. But, they added, "there has been no determination of liability."

In July 2021, DOJ sued Alliance Family of Companies LLC, a private equity–owned national electroencephalography (EEG) testing company, alleging it had made kickbacks and submitted false claims to Medicare. Ancor Capital, the firm holding a minority stake in the company, had learned about the misconduct when it did its due diligence before it invested, prosecutors said. But Ancor not only did nothing to stop the practices, the government said, it perpetuated the problematic behavior through its ongoing management agreement with Alliance. Ancor and Alliance settled the matter, paying $15 million; neither company admitted the allegations.

Jeb White, of the nonprofit Taxpayers Against Fraud, says he believes the Justice Department is finally ramping up its scrutiny on private equity–backed healthcare fraud. "There's a change recently at DOJ," White told us in mid-2022. "They are interested in reaching up the organizational charts at these companies to reach private equity firms that are driving illegal practices." But, he added, the cases take years to develop.

Anti-trust investigators at the Justice Department are also increasing their scrutiny on board members installed at companies by the private equity firms that own them. A late October 2022 report from Bloomberg stated that Apollo, Blackstone, and KKR were facing a Justice Department investigation into how these firms place directors at companies in the same sector that are supposed to compete against each other. "Board directors with seats on rivals in the same sector could influence those companies to act in ways that maximize gains for all—instead of competing vigorously to provide the best services or lowest prices to consumers," Bloomberg reported. The firms declined to comment, the report said.

It only takes one or two cases to get the looters' attention. And so, we wait and hope.

Afterword

After decades of smooth sailing and bounteous booty for the plunderers, the waters become choppier in 2023. Soon it became an all-out gale as higher interest rates added costs to private equity's business model and the public started to catch on about these shadow operators' antics.

In February, the Department of Labor announced one of its biggest child labor cases in history with details that were beyond horrific. Packers Sanitation Services Inc., a Wisconsin company hired to clean slaughterhouses throughout the midwestern United States in the overnight hours, had been employing children as young as thirteen to do its hellish and dangerous work. More than 100 kids, most of whom were migrants, had been exploited in this illegal, Dickensian setup, the Labor Department reported, and at least three minors had been injured working for the company.

Packers, known as PSSI, is owned by the Blackstone Group, the most prestigious private equity firm in America. But rather than escape scrutiny in this shocking story—when a company gets into trouble, its private equity owners typically remain offstage—Blackstone itself became a focus of the narrative.

As the sickening news of the child labor violations spread, Blackstone's executives had to respond to questions about the case. Why, reporters wanted to know, did a Blackstone-owned company hire children? Why had they been required to use hazardous chemicals and clean equipment including back saws, brisket saws, and head splitters? Perhaps employing these mostly migrant children was one of the "efficiencies" that private equity boast about bringing to the companies they purchase.

When the horrors surfaced, Blackstone had already owned PSSI for five years, having purchased the company from another private equity firm for more than $1 billion in 2018. In keeping with industry custom, Blackstone kept a close eye on PSSI operations, installing two of its own executives on the company's board of directors. Amid public scrutiny, it emerged that two workers had died on the job at PSSI, including one who was decapitated in a chicken chiller. And four other workers experienced accidents that resulted in amputations, according to records from the Occupational Health and Safety Administration. While meatpacking is a dangerous occupation, PSSI's safety record was dismal.

Blackstone did not respond to a question about the four amputations, but about the two deaths, the firm said PSSI safety protocols were not followed—a classic "mistakes were made" response assuming no blame. The firm was said it had been unaware that Packers had hired children, issuing a statement that it "has a zero-tolerance policy against employing anyone under the age of 18, and fully shares the DOL's objective of ensuring full compliance at all locations." PSSI said the same.

But the Labor Department told a different story. "Our investigation found Packers Sanitation Services' systems flagged some young workers as minors, but the company ignored the flags. When the Wage and Hour Division arrived with warrants, the adults—who had recruited, hired and supervised these children—tried to derail our efforts to investigate their employment practices," Mark Lazzeri, wage and hour regional administrator in Chicago, said in a statement.

PSSI paid a $1.5 million penalty and implemented an "18-point remediation plan" to employ only adults. Hoping perhaps that money might make the problem go away, PSSI also said it would create a $10 million fund to "enhance the well-being of children in the communities we serve and helping reduce the prevalence of the rising problem of underage workers." The fund will also aid the communities it operates in with "legal aid, education, poverty reduction, and health services," the company said.

It didn't work. Two of PSSI's larger customers cancelled their contracts with the company in April 2023 and by September, the company's quarterly earnings had fallen by half. The market price of a $1.2 billion loan to PSSI plummeted to fifty-two cents on the dollar, a sign of severe company distress and a possible restructuring or bankruptcy ahead. It was a rare case of comeuppance for PSSI's private equity owners.

In addition to being an embarrassing and tawdry moment for Blackstone, the PSSI revelations brought bothersome questions from several public pension funds that invest with the firm. The New York State Common Retirement Fund and California's two biggest public pensions, CalPERS and CalSTRS, took Blackstone to task amid the PSSI mess. But this turned out to be posturing; the funds did not curtail their future investments with Blackstone because of the child labor violations, the only punishment that would have had any meaningful impact on the firm. When we called CalPERS to ask if it was rethinking its investments with Blackstone after learning of the appalling practices at PSSI, a spokeswoman at the fund declined to comment. Nothing to see here, move along.

Blackstone hardly enjoyed being in the harsh glare of the PSSI spotlight. But it could take solace in this: since acquiring the company, the firm had extracted $400 million in cash from its operations.

. . .

A muscular Department of Labor was not the only peril the plunderers faced as 2023 bore on. Higher interest rates, ratcheted up by the nation's central bank in the hopes of curbing a nasty bout of inflation in the U.S., were an even bigger problem. Because large amounts of debt are required to conduct private equity's big buyouts, and because that debt typically carries interest costs that rise and fall alongside prevailing rates, the expenses associated with private equity's business model exploded. Not surprisingly, these higher costs pushed the companies paying them to the brink. Corporate bankruptcies among private equity–backed companies started to grow.

Woes among healthcare companies owned by private equity firms were especially notable. In December 2022, Moody's Investors Service published an in-depth report about looming defaults among these entities. "As rates rise and performance lags," Moody's said, many companies' financial positions will become unsustainable.

One company on the precipice, Moody's said, was Envision Healthcare, the hospital staffing company owned by KKR. A big provider of hospital emergency department staffing, an Envision predecessor company called EmCare had fired Dr. Ray Brovont for speaking out about code blue practices at his HCA hospital in Missouri. Those practices put patients throughout the facility at risk.

Envision and EmCare were also responsible for surprise medical bills, siphoning off enormous revenues from patients who had gone to their local hospitals thinking their treatments would be covered by their insurance. Envision had made sure the physicians serving in the hospitals' emergency departments were not covered by the insurance contracts set up with the hospital, meaning patients receiving care there would face outsized bills because the

ERs were considered "out-of-network." Patients had no way of knowing this beforehand.

Outrage over these practices forced action from an otherwise inert, dysfunctional Congress. The No Surprises Act, effective January 2022, diminished Envision's ability to collect on these surprise charges; combined with its heavy debt load, the law put the company's business model under intense pressure. Envision soon collapsed, filing for bankruptcy in May 2023, saying it was not generating enough revenue to cover its expenses and debt. Not a surprise, given the plunderers' modus operandi.

Private equity firms often boast about the "secret sauce" or managment expertise they provide companies to help them prosper. Envision's version, said Eileen Appelbaum, codirector of the Center for Economic and Policy Research, a think tank in Washington, D.C., was surprise medical bills. Once they were forced to abandon this practice, the company unraveled, the definition of an unsustainable business model.

Envision emerged from bankruptcy in November. As is typical, the process allowed it to jettison much of the debt KKR had heaved onto the company. Buyers of that debt were the losers, but so were patients who'd been forced to pay sky-high healthcare bills so Envision could profit, albeit temporarily.

Apollo came under the microscope, too. In December 2023, the U.S. Senate launched a bipartisan investigation into the role private equity has played in hollowing out rural hospitals across the country. Senators Sheldon Whitehouse, a Rhode Island Democrat and chairman of the Senate Budget Committee, and Chuck Grassley, the Iowa Republican who is its ranking member, announced the investigation that focused on Apollo's ownership of LifePoint hospitals, saying they were concerned about the impact private equity has had on the nation's healthcare system.

The investigation began after a male nurse assaulted at least nine sedated patients in 2021 and 2022 at Ottumwa Regional Health Center, a LifePoint facility in southeast Iowa. The nurse subsequently died from a drug overdose at the facility.

"Private equity buys out a hospital, saddles it with debt, and then reduces operating costs by cutting services and staff—all while investors pocket millions," Whitehouse said in a statement. "From facility closures to compromised care, it's now a familiar story."

As the Federal Reserve raised interest rates in 2023, placing more private equity–backed operations in a debt vise, the plunderers found it harder to sell companies they'd bought years earlier. The dollar value of these sales, known in the industry as "exits," fell 65 percent in the first half of 2023, to $131 billion. Meanwhile, public pensions, endowments, and other investors in private equity funds who were hoping to get their money back from these sales started getting nervous about the longer wait times to payouts.

As these investors waited for their returns, their appetite for new private equity fund investments waned. The amount of money raised by the industry fell to $517 billion in the first half of 2023, down 35 percent from the same period in 2022.

Carlyle, for example, closed its newest private equity fund in August 2023 at around $15 billion, well short of the $22 billion goal the firm had announced. Even raising that substandard amount had been a challenge—Carlyle had extended the deadline on the fund's closing and had even offered to let investors exchange their stakes in a previous fund for the new one.

Fewer deals by private equity titans also meant lower earnings for their firms. In the third quarter of 2023, Carlyle's earnings plummeted 71 percent from the same period a year earlier, and the amounts distributed to its shareholders fell by 43 percent. Assets under management fell 1 percent.

Carlyle's executives started talking about layoffs. Finally, a private equity firm tasting some of its own medicine.

Some private equity executives found ways to profit from the problems their illiquid deals had created. In November 2023, a former Apollo executive left the firm to create a company aiming to exploit a new market: It would acquire private equity–related assets that pension funds and other institutions couldn't offload because there was no after-market available where they might find interested buyers for their holdings. Just as Apollo's founders had profited from the Executive Life failure their junk bonds had helped to create decades earlier, this new fund would scoop up depressed holdings Apollo and other private equity firms had sold to pensions in better days.

And, just as Apollo did in the Executive Life failure, this new firm will no doubt buy assets at deeply discounted prices.

Faced with rising debt loads and lower cash generation, private equity–backed companies did what they could to avoid debt defaults. Their owners dug deep into their bag of tricks: instead of paying cash to meet interest costs on loan payments, the firms began using even more debt to meet those obligations. Called "payment-in-kind," these sorts of debt payments are risky, adding leverage to already heavily indebted enterprises. The tactic is a short-term fix, used by operators hoping interest rates would soon fall and bail them out of their binds.

· · ·

After decades of standing by as private equity amassed thousands of physician practices across American healthcare, in the fall of 2023, one government agency finally awakened to the threat these buyouts pose to patients.

In October, the Federal Trade Commission sued U.S. Anesthesia Partners, a private equity–backed anesthesia staffing company, contending that its serial acquisitions of anesthesiology practices in Texas had given it illegal monopoly power and raised customer costs. At the time of the suit, U.S.A.P. had 4,500 clinicians serving 2 million patients in nine states, including Colorado, Florida, Kansas, and Tennessee. Another indication of the power U.S.A.P. wielded in Texas was that one of its executives was the president of the Texas Medical Board, charged with protecting patients across the state.

U.S.A.P.'s conduct "resulted in egregious price increases for patients and their employers, on the order of tens of millions of dollars or more each year," the commission said when it filed the suit.

But the FTC did not stop there. In an unprecedented move, the commission sued the private equity firm backing U.S.A.P.—the venerable firm Welsh, Carson, Stowe & Anderson. The FTC accused Welsh, Carson of scheming with U.S.A.P. to harm patients by controlling the anesthesia market in the region.

The government hadn't often gone up the ladder to sue the private equity firm behind the company it decided to sue, and this new tactic was ominous for the plunderers. It signaled a heightened interest in expanding accountability to include the money men (often the source of these malicious practices), and not just the companies they financed.

That the FTC launched its first salvo against an anesthesiology staffing firm was not a surprise. Purchases of anesthesiology practices accounted for almost 20 percent of recent private–equity buyouts of physician practices, a February 2020 study in the *Journal of the American Medical Association Forum* found—the highest percentage involving a single specialty. Of course, anesthesia costs rose significantly after a private equity takeover, a February 2022 study published by *JAMA Internal Medicine* concluded. Analyzing more than 2 million anesthesia claims from 2012 through 2017, the study reported that patient costs rose 26 percent after anesthesiology practices were acquired by a plunderer. That outcome was confirmed by the FTC's case against U.S.A.P.

In response to the suit, a U.S.A.P. spokesman said: "The FTC's intended outcome threatens to disrupt and restrict patients' equitable access to quality anesthesia care in Texas and will negatively impact the Texas hospitals and health systems that provide care in underserved communities." Both it and Welsh, Carson said they would fight the suit and expected to prevail.

But the potential for similar antitrust lawsuits looms large across the healthcare field. According to the American Hospital Association, 65 percent of the physician practices acquired over the past five years were bought out by private equity firms. That figure dwarfs the percentage of acquisitions by health insurers, for example, which stood at 11 percent.

Another sign that the FTC was taking a more aggressive stance on private equity: the commission typically focuses on buyouts that meet a high-dollar threshold of over $100 million. Companies purchased by private equity firms often fall under that threshold, escaping scrutiny.

Until now. The FTC's suit indicates the government believes even smaller buyouts, such as roll-ups of physician practices, can give companies monopoly power, allowing them to raise prices for goods and services without fear of competitors' undercutting them. This case represents a genuine threat to the private equity strategy of amassing physician practices that had been small enough to fly under the anti-trust radar.

For decades, the private equity industry has claimed that it generates outsized returns compared with other asset types, like the stock or bond markets. That claim collapsed in 2023 when the returns for the prior year came in, losing 1.2 percent on average on their private equity holdings in 2022, according to Pitchbook.

At the same time, respected investors also spoke out about private equity's flaws. The famous duo running Berkshire Hathaway—Warren Buffett and his longtime partner Charlie Munger, who died in late 2023—discussed private equity at a public forum in January 2023. "The returns are not calculated in a manner I would regard as honest," Buffett said.

Encountering these head winds, the plunderers began to search for other wealth extraction opportunities. A promising one took them back in time to the insurance business, where Apollo made its first gargantuan trade.

In the 1980s, remember, Executive Life loaded up on risky junk bonds that led to its failure. Hundreds of thousands of policyholders, relying on the insurer to fund their retirements or other obligations—like paying for Katie Watson's care—got the shaft. But Leon Black and his partners at Apollo gained $3 billion from the insurer's demise, money that should have gone to policyholders.

History doesn't usually repeat itself in precisely the same way, but after enough time has passed and memories fade, similar circumstances have a habit of resurfacing.

Such a reprise is happening now. Thousands of policyholders are relying on Apollo and other risk-taking private equity giants to fund their retirements. The same firms that have done so much damage to other American industries—healthcare, retailing, consumer goods—are now increasingly in control of your financial future.

Today, these firms manage hundreds of billions in retirees' and other policyholders' assets. Apollo is at the forefront of this move through Athene, its insurance unit. Athene managed $236 billion of annuities and other securities in 2022 and has become the largest private equity player in the business. Its success has led competitors Carlyle and KKR to buy insurers or take over customer business from them. These firms now control 9 percent of the life insurance industry, up from only 1 percent in 2012 according to the *New York Times*.

The perils to policy holders in this shift are significant. Let's begin with investment risk. In decades past, pension managers overseeing retirees' money purchased highly rated bonds or a diverse mix of high quality and easily tradeable stocks so they could be sure to meet their obligations. But with private equity in the game, policyholders are taking much bigger chances because their managers are buying far riskier assets. Retirees may not even find out about these risks until it's too late.

"Within days of a P.E. acquisition of an insurance company, they tilt their bond portfolios to riskier assets," said Natasha Sarin, a professor at Yale Law School who compares the investments made by private equity and insurance companies. Gone are the top-notch corporate and government bonds that insurers historically held. Instead, they invest large portions of retiree funds in lower-grade securities, pools of commercial loans bundled together and sliced up, like the mortgage securities that amplified the mortgage crisis of 2008.

A key reason these commercial loan pools are so attractive to private equity insurers is the higher returns they generate—just as the junk bonds did for Executive Life, at least in the beginning. But there's another factor at work, thanks to a loophole regulators failed to close after the mortgage mess, around protection to policyholders if these securities go bad. Even though these loan pools are risky, insurers do not need to set aside more of a cushion in case of a failure. And this encourages them to load up on the riskier securities.

At the end of 2022, the National Association of Insurance Commissioners (NAIC) was considering an increase to the capital an insurer must set aside against these risky loan pools. Not surprisingly, the most aggressive of these insurers screamed, arguing that the securities are safe and sound. Athene released a slide deck, "Understanding Structured Credit," in which they argued in their inimitable Wall Street speak: "Structured credit products now provide investors better diversification, credit enhancement, and structural protections. As banks have pulled back from lending to U.S. businesses and consumers, these new, safer forms of securitization have provided the necessary financing for credit cards, cars, homes, commercial real estate, consumer loans, and small and medium sized businesses." Boring old corporate bonds, Athene said, are riskier than the newfangled products.

The NAIC backed off under the pressure. Meanwhile, Athene did what powerful investment firms usually do when faced with heightened regulatory attention—it hired the former chief executive of the NAIC to become head of U.S. government and regulatory relations.

The perils that these players' retirement account takeovers will bring extend well beyond the ratings of the investments they hold. Among them is risk posed by regulatory incompetence. As pensions shift from contracts protected under federal law into those overseen by state regulators, it is wise to recall how John Garamendi, the California insurance commissioner, gifted the $3 billion gain to Leon Black in the Executive Life failure.

Key retiree advocates including the Consumer Federation of America and the Pension Rights Center have voiced concerns to the Department of Labor. They cite the loss of spousal rights to benefits under these pension transfers and the possibility that creditors could go after retirees' benefits.

Some workers are recognizing the hazards. In May 2023, the US-Canadian union of hospitality workers, representing 300,000 members, sent a letter to actuaries and pension administrators warning that pension obligations should not be used "as a cheap funding source for private equity asset managers." Neither should these firms be allowed to use policyholders as a dumping ground for risky assets their affiliates have originated and cannot peddle elsewhere. To protect themselves, these groups and others are pressing the Department of Labor to require state protections on pension transfers to private equity firms similar to those offered under federal law.

The Department of Labor, as directed by Congress's 2022 Secure Act, is also considering changes to a rule requiring anyone selecting an annuity provider for pensioners to adhere to a so-called fiduciary standard that puts retirees first. On October 31, 2023, the White House issued a press release highlighting the need for greater consumer protection at the federal level.

The NAIC quickly shot back, arguing that the White House's contention that state insurance regulators provide inadequate protections "suggests either ignorance of, or willful disregard for, the hard work of the 43 states." Nevertheless, experts see a narrow chance that the enhanced duties proposed by the White House will be implemented in part because state regulators will go to extreme lengths to protect their regulatory turf.

Athene, too, complained about the White House proposal. "Even small changes" to the fiduciary duty rule could have unintended consequences, the insurer warned. Besides, it insisted, its products are safe for retirees.

But a look at the fine print in Athene's securities filings reveals a more nuanced description. Under law, these filings must represent reality, not hype, but they are rarely read by individual investors. Athene warns that management's assumptions and estimates may not come to pass and that "market and credit risks" could diminish the value of the company's investments, causing losses.

Even worse, insurers like Athene, whose business is monitored only by state regulators, commonly transfer some of their obligations to opaque offshore insurers, adding more risk to policyholders. The lack of strong regulatory oversight creates the same sorts of perils that contributed to the great financial crisis of 2008. Not to mention that trying to get your money out of a failed offshore insurer would be difficult.

But if a worker recognized these flaws and tried to opt out of a pension transfer, she would be out of luck. When a corporation decides to offload its pension to Athene or another insurer, its workers have no say in the matter. They're in the same situation that the workers at the RJR Nabisco unit were when Executive Life folded. Their pension payments, taken over by the insurer, went up in smoke and they could do nothing about it.

As private equity insurers entrench themselves more deeply into our financial system and economy, they become too big to fail. If

Congress and federal regulators don't eliminate private equity's risky conduct, it's not a question of if private equity will be at the center of a financial crisis, it is a question of when.

And that poses another grave threat, one that will affect all U.S. taxpayers, who will likely have to pony up for a bailout.

There is no doubt that if one of these private equity–backed insurers failed, putting the financial futures of tens of millions of Americans at stake, bailout demands would surface quickly. Recall the 2008 rescue of insurance giant American International Group, a backdoor bailout that was really designed to save Goldman Sachs, which faced a $5 billion hole if the insurer had collapsed.

Rescuing private equity–backed insurers helmed by billionaire elites might seem wrong. But as these firms tighten their tentacle grip on our financial system, such a bailout becomes ever more likely.

Once again—it's heads they win, tails you lose.

Acknowledgments

Journalism is not only a contact sport, it's very much a group effort. We are beyond grateful to the experts and market participants who helped us understand who wins and who loses in private equity. Thanks to Eileen Appelbaum and Rosemary Batt for their pathbreaking work on the ills caused by the industry and to the many other academics—Laura Olson, Brian Ayash, Ludovic Phalippou, Sabrina Howell, Richard Scheffler, to name a few—whose research has educated us and the rest of the world on this industry's impacts on humanity.

On the subject of group efforts, the team at Simon & Schuster is simply the best there is. We are so grateful to our editor, Stephanie Frerich, for recognizing the value in this book, for her editorial brilliance, enthusiasm, and guidance. She knows how to make complex material accessible to nonfinanciers and we love her outrage and her occasional "Oofs!" in the margins.

The entire crew at Simon & Schuster deserves an ovation. Brittany Adames, Emily Simonson, Priscilla Painton, and Jonathan Karp in editorial; Stephen Bedford in marketing; Brianna Scharfenberg and Julia Prosser in publicity; Phil Metcalf, production editor; managing editorial pros Amanda Mulholland, Maxwell Smith, and Lauren Gomez; Paul Dippolito in design and Alison Forner, art director; Meryll Preposi of desktop, Rick Willet, copy editor, Zoe Kaplan in production; Mikaela Bielawski in ebooks, Lyndsay

Brueggemann and Winona Lukito in demand planning; and Marie Florio and Mabel Taveras in subrights.

Thanks to our literary agents extraordinaire at Writers Representatives, for their advocacy, acuity, and support over the years. Kudos to Jeff Miller at Miller Korzenik Sommers Rayman LLP in New York for his expert legal advice and guidance on the manuscript.

We are grateful to our unnamed sources—you know who you are. Thank you for your views and your trust.

G.M. Acknowledgments

My immense respect and gratitude to Maureen Marr for trying to right the wrongs visited on Executive Life policyholders in the 1990s and for maintaining the amazing document trove relating to the insurer's seizure. She says she's no financial expert, but she sure knows a story when she sees one.

Thank you to the Watson family for cherishing your daughter Katie and fighting for her, no matter the cost, until the end of her life. I salute your outrage over the Executive Life debacle all these years later.

I'm indebted to Richard Greenberg, Robert Dembo, Mark Schone, and Rich Schapiro at NBC News Investigations for believing that reporting on private equity's impact on America is important. Thank you to Steve Thode, senior director of NBC News standards, for reading and commenting on the manuscript.

No one had a more significant role in my career than Jim Michaels, editor of *Forbes*, who taught me how to commit uncompromising financial journalism. Michaels recognized the contours of the Executive Life–Leon Black tale in real time and far earlier than anyone else. When he dispatched me to interview Fred Carr in 1990 as Executive Life neared the precipice, I had no idea I'd return to that story more than thirty years later in a book. Michaels probably knew, though, because, well, he was a genius. Thanks, also, to Steve Forbes for believing in my reporting.

Deepest admiration to Tim O'Brien and Winnie O'Kelley, my superlative former editors at the *New York Times* and decades-long friends. I'm also grateful for the backing my work received over twenty years at the *Times* from top editors Joe Lelyveld, Bill Keller, Jill Abramson, and Dean Baquet and investigative editor Matt Purdy. Business Day and Sunday Business editors—Glenn Kramon, Alison Cowan, Judy Dobrzynski, Jim Schachter, Tom Redburn, Jim Impoco, Larry Ingrassia, Dean Murphy, Jeff Sommer—were instrumental to my success as a reporter.

David McCraw gets a singular shoutout—and his own paragraph—for being the greatest First Amendment lawyer alive.

Dr. Robert McNamara at Temple University and Dr. Mitch Li at Take Medicine Back have educated me on the dangers of corporations practicing medicine and have done amazing work trying to save healthcare from for-profit predators. I bow to Dr. Ray Brovont, Dr. Ming Lin, Christine Ribik, and the many physicians and healthcare professionals who have not—and will not—compromise their integrity when the private equity bosses require them to.

J.R. Acknowledgments

Thank you to the late Stanley Sporkin, who, more than twenty years ago, freely offered himself in support of my efforts to provide independent research. The world is a bit less bright without

ACKNOWLEDGMENTS

his brilliance, commitment to transparency, and integrity and without the strength of his convictions.

Thank you to the many dedicated honest stewards of the public trust that I have gotten to know over the past decades. Whether on Capitol Hill or in federal agencies, you have earned that trust. Thank you for supporting this work with your knowledge and insights.

To Damon Silvers for his encyclopedic knowledge of financial history and his ability to offer unbiased perspectives.

To Tyler Gellasch for his friendship, guidance, and insights.

To the many colleagues and current and former clients who have always had my back and supported me in trying to do the right thing.

Notes

INTRODUCTION

1 *"Leveraged Buyouts and the Pot of Gold," the Congressional Research Service's report was called:* Leveraged Buyouts and the Pot of Gold (Economics Division of the Congressional Research Service, December 1987).

3 *Buyout dealmakers had lobbied heavily against:* David E. Rosenbaum, "Legislation On Buyouts Is Unlikely," *New York Times*, November 6, 1989.

4 *Nicholas Brady, the treasury secretary:* Ibid.

4 *Residents of nursing homes owned by private equity firms:* Atul Gupta, Sabrina T. Howell, Constantine Yannelis, and Abhinav Gupta, "How Patients Fare When Private Equity Funds Acquire Nursing Homes," NBER .org

4 *Another study tied:* Amy Stulick, "Private Equity Ownership Linked to Higher Medicare Costs, Increased Hospitalization," *Skilled Nursing News*, November 21, 2021.

4 *Beyond healthcare, a major and devastating focus:* Brian Ayash and Mahdi Rastad, *Leveraged Buyouts and Financial Distress* (Social Science Research Network, July 20, 2019), papers.ssrn.com.

5 *Stanley Sporkin, an aggressive prosecutor:* Sam Roberts, "Stanley Sporkin, Bane of Corporate Corruption, Dies at 88," *New York Times*, March 24, 2020.

6 *She said the hospital suspended her:* Andrew Wolfson, *Louisville Courier-Journal*, April 6, 2020.

6 *A few months later, in Lewiston, Idaho:* Brady Frederick, KLEW-TV, July 28, 2020.

6 *An investigation into the sixty-bed:* Jesse M. L. Mensik Kennedy, report by the Oregon Nurses Association, March 2021.

7 *When hard-driving financiers:* Joseph D. Bruch, Suhas Gondi, Zirui Song, "Changes in Hospital Income, Use, and Quality Associated with Private Equity Acquisition," *JAMA Internal Medicine*, August 2020.

7 *Even as it received this funding:* Eileen O'Grady, "Apollo Global Management Completes Merger of Kindred Healthcare and LifePoint Health, Shifts Some Hospitals to New Company," Private Equity Stakeholder Project, January 31, 2022.

7 *In 2021, the Apollo partnership:* Sabrina Wilmer, "Private Equity Powerhouse Books $1.6 Billion Profit Selling Hospital Chain—to Itself," *Bloomberg News*, July 29, 2021.

7 *In autumn 2020:* "Record Acquisitions and High Evictions by Corporate Landlords Draw Scrutiny from Congress," Private Equity Stakeholder Project, January 31, 2022, https://pestakeholder.org/news/record-acquisitions-and-high-evictions-by-corporate-landlords-in-2021-draw-scrutiny-from-congress-2/.

7 *A throng of large and prosperous landlords:* "A Report on Abuses by Four Corporate Landlords During the Coronavirus Crisis," Staff Report, House Select Subcommittee on the Coronavirus Crisis, July 28, 2022, https://coronavirus.house.gov/sites/democrats.coronavirus.house.gov/files/2022.07.28%20SSCC%20Staff%20Report%20Examining%20Pandemic%20Evictions.pdf.

8 *Announcing the tie-up with Pretium:* "Pretium and Ares Management Announce $2.4-Billion Take-Private Transaction with Front Yard Residential," Pretium press release, October 19, 2020, https://pretium.com/pretium-and-ares-management-announce-2-4-billion-take-private-transaction-with-front-yard-residential/.

8 *Cristina Velez and her daughter:* Gretchen Morgenson, "Large Corporate Landlords have Filed 10,000 Eviction Actions in Five States Since September," NBC News, October 26, 2020.

9 *"Hospitals like this used to be run by nuns":* Author interview (Morgenson).

10 *That year:* Dawn Lim, "Blackstone's Schwarzman Collects $1.1 Billion in Dividends, Pay," *Bloomberg News*, February 25, 2022.

11 *The number of multibillionaires:* Ludovic Phalippou, "An Inconvenient Fact: Private Equity Returns & the Billionaire Factory," June 10, 2020, https://papers.ssrn.com/sol3/papers.cfm?abstract_id=3623820.

11 *For example, a 2019 study:* "Report on the Economic Well-Being of U.S. Households in 2018," Board of Governors of the Federal Reserve, May 2019.

12 *by Aaron James, a philosophy professor:* Aaron James, *Assholes: A Theory* (Doubleday, 2012), https://catalog.libraries.psu.edu/catalog/9022369.

13 *A 2019 California Polytechnic State University study:* Ayash and Rastad, *Leveraged Buyouts and Financial Distress.*

14 *Between 2003 and February 2020:* Americans for Financial Reform, United For Respect Report, "Double Exposure Retail Workers Hammered by Private Equity," https://ourfinancialsecurity.org/wp-content/uploads/2020/12/double-exposure-PE-retail-jobs-12-2020-1.pdf.

14 *fast-food companies owned by a private equity firm:* Government Accountability Office, "Federal Social Safety Net Programs: Millions of Full-Time Workers Rely on Federal Health Care and Food Assistance Programs" October 19, 2020, https://www.gao.gov/products/gao-21-45.

15 *During the eviction moratorium:* Laura Strickler, "Four Corporate Landlords Engaged in 15,000 Evictions Despite CDC Moratorium, House Report Says," NBC News, July 28, 2022, https://www.nbcnews.com/politics/congress/four-corporate-landlords-engaged-15000-evictions-cdc-moratorium-house-rcna40360.

15 *Between 1990 and 2018:* Juliane Begenau and Emil Siriwardane, "How Do Private Equity Fees Vary Across Public Pensions?," March 15, 2022, https://papers.ssrn.com/sol3/papers.cfm?abstract_id=3526469.

16 *That translates to $1,067:* Annual Report, STRS Ohio, https://www.strsoh.org/employer/publications/annual-reports.html.

16 *And yet, the $143 million:* Gretchen Morgenson, "Private Equity and Hedge Funds Invested Cash for Retired Ohio Teachers," NBC News, June 9, 2021, https://www.nbcnews.com/business/personal-finance/private-equity-hedge-fund-firms-invested-pension-cash-retired-ohio-n1269885.

16 *At the same time:* Chibuike Oguh, "Blackstone CEO Schwarzman Took Home $610.5 Million in 2020," Reuters, March 1, 2021, https://www.reuters.com/article/us-blackstone-group-ceo-compensation-idUSKBN2AT2V7.

16 *For 2020 alone:* Securities and Exchange Commission filings.

17 *These companies generated:* Gretchen Morgenson, "Working for Companies Owned by Well-Heeled Private Equity Firms Can Mean Lower Wages for Employees," NBC News, October 9, 2021, https://www.nbcnews.com/business/personal-finance/working-companies-owned-well-heeled-private-equity-firms-can-mean-n1281146.

18 *Beginning in 2005, these money-spinners:* Bain & Co., "Global Healthcare Private Equity and Corporate M&A Report 2020," https://www.bain.com/globalassets/noindex/2020/bain_report_global_healthcare_private_equity_and_corporate_ma_report_2020.pdf.

18 *Higher prices and dubious practices:* Yale School of Public Health, "Yale Study Sheds Light on 'Surprise' ER Billing,'" November 17, 2016, https://ysph.yale.edu/news-article/yale-study-sheds-light-on-surprise-er -billing/.

18 *Putting profits ahead of patient care:* "Understanding the Corporate Practice of Medicine Doctrine," Nelson Hardiman Healthcare Lawyers, June 25, 2022, https://www.nelsonhardiman.com/hc-law-news/understanding -the-corporate-practice-of-medicine-doctrine-and-the-role-of-the -management-services-organization/.

18 *As a judge opining on such a case:* State v. Bailey Dental Co., 211 Iowa 781, 785 (Iowa 1931).

19 *In fact, by 2022, private equity had become:* See three members of the Maryland Board of Physicians, https://www.mbp.state.md.us/, and the president of Texas State Medical Board, https://www.tmb.state.tx.us/.

20 *And in the spring of 2020, that market received an unprecedented $750 billion:* Federal Reserve press release, "Federal Reserve announces extensive new measures to support the economy," March 23, 2020, https://www .federalreserve.gov/newsevents/pressreleases/monetary20200323b.htm.

21 *The government did provide:* Gretchen Morgenson, "Some Firms Thrived During Covid and Then Got Their PPP Covid Relief Loans Forgiven," NBC News, November 18, 2021, https://www.nbcnews.com/news/firms -thrived-covid-got-ppp-covid-relief-loans-forgiven-rcna5697.

21 *In 2020, Apollo was one of the first:* Ken Dilanian and Stephanie Ruhle, "Seeking Coronavirus Relief, Investment Firm with Ties to Kushner Emails Kushner, Trump Administration," NBC News, April 4, 2020, https://www .nbcnews.com/politics/white-house/seeking-coronavirus-relief-investment -firm-ties-kushner-emails-kushner-trump-n1176686.

22 *Making sure the message resonated:* OpenSecrets lobbying database, accessed September 20, 2022, https://www.opensecrets.org/federal-lobbying /clients/summary?cycle=2015&id=D000021845.

22 *The company got this money:* Alan Rappeport, "Trump Officials Awarded $700 Million Pandemic Loan Despite Objections," *New York Times,* April 27, 2020, https://www.nytimes.com/2022/04/27/us/politics/trump -pandemic-loan-yrc.html.

23 *In March 2022, YRC paid:* "Freight Carriers Agree to Pay $6.85 Million to Resolve Allegations of Knowingly Presenting False Claims to the Department of Defense," Press release, Department of Justice, March 14, 2022, https://www.justice.gov/opa/pr/freight-carriers-agree-pay-685-million -resolve-allegations-knowingly-presenting-false-claims.

23 *Between 1993 and 2018:* Subsidy Tracker at website Good Jobs First, https://subsidytracker.goodjobsfirst.org/parent/apollo-global-management.

CHAPTER ONE: "PIZZA THE HUT"

32 *Katie Watson was a brown-eyed toddler:* Author interview (Morgenson).

33 *A 2008 audit:* Department of Insurance, "Former Executive Life Insurance Company Policyholders Have Incurred Significant Economic Losses, and Distributions of Funds Have Been Inconsistently Monitored and Reported," California State Auditor, January 2008, https://www.bsa.ca.gov/pdfs/reports/2005-115.2.pdf.

34 *Some called it "the deal of the century":* Barry Rehfeld, "Profile/Leon Black; Dealmaker in the 1980's, Empire Builder in the 1990's," *New York Times*, February 2, 1993, https://www.nytimes.com/1993/02/21/business/profileleon-black-dealmaker-in-the-1980s-empire-builder-in-the.html.

34 *In 2021, a California court:* Author interview with Cynthia Larson, Orrick lawyer representing California Insurance Department (Morgenson).

36 *More than a decade after the deal occurred:* "Second Year Report to the President, Corporate Fraud Task Force," July 20, 2004, https://www.justice.gov/archive/dag/cftf/2nd_yr_fraud_report.pdf.

36 *Although the United States Justice Department:* Myron Levin, "California Amends Credit Lyonnais Suit," *Los Angeles Times*, February 1, 2002, https://www.latimes.com/archives/la-xpm-2002-feb-01-fi-black1-story.html.

37 *One of the most iconic images:* WSJ Staff, "Leon Black, The Man Who Bought 'The Scream,'" July 11, 2012, https://www.wsj.com/articles/BL-SEB-70776.

37 *He and his wife Debra:* Robin Pogrebin, "Collectors Leon and Debra Black Give $40 Million to MOMA," *New York Times*, November 19, 2018, https://www.nytimes.com/2018/11/19/arts/design/collectors-leon-and-debra-black-museum-of-modern-art.html.

37 *But tragedy struck:* Peter Kihss, "44-Story Plunge Kills Head of United Brands," *New York Times*, February 4, 1975, https://www.nytimes.com/1975/02/04/archives/44story-plunge-kills-head-of-united-brands-united-brands-head.html.

37 *Weeks after the executive:* Alan Riding, "Honduran Army Ousts Leader Named in Bribery Case in U.S.," *New York Times*, April 23, 1975, https://www.nytimes.com/1975/04/23/archives/honduran-army-ousts-leader-named-in-bribery-case-in-us-honduran.html.

38 *But despite obtaining his MBA:* Caleb Melby and Heather Perlberg, "Nobody Makes Money Like Apollo's Ruthless Founder Leon Black," *Bloomberg News*, January 16, 2020, https://www.bloomberg.com/news /features/2020-01-16/nobody-makes-money-like-apollo-s-ruthless-founder -leon-black?sref=lnrir5K3.

38 *Black went instead:* Ibid.

38 *There he earned the nickname:* Bob Ivry, "Leon Black in Winter," *Town & Country*, June 3, 2021, https://www.townandcountrymag.com/society /money-and-power/a36492766/leon-black-epstein-scandal.

38 *His credentials were nonexistent:* Gregory Zuckerman and Khadeeja Safdar, "Epstein Flourished as He Forged Bond with Retail Billionaire," *Wall Street Journal*, July 12, 2019, https://www.wsj.com/articles/epstein -flourished-as-he-forged-bond-with-retail-billionaire-11562975711.

38 *Two years after that:* Preeti Singh, "Apollo LPs Raise Concerns over Leon Black's Relationship with Jeffrey Epstein," *Private Debt Investor*, July 30, 2019, https://www.privatedebtinvestor.com/apollo-lps-raise-concerns-over -leon-blacks-relationship-with-jeffrey-epstein.

38 *In 2011, an Epstein investment unit:* Matthew Goldstein, Steve Eder, and David Enrich, "The Billionaire Who Stood by Jeffrey Epstein," *New York Times*, October 12, 2020, https://www.nytimes.com/2020/10/12/business /leon-black-jeffrey-epstein.html.

39 *And when Apollo offered shares:* "Investigation of Epstein/Black Relation-ship and Any Relationship Between Epstein and Apollo Global Manage-ment, Inc.," Dechert Inc., January 22, 2021, https://www.sec.gov/Archives /edgar/data/1411494/000119312521016405/d118102dex991.htm.

39 *This time, Black was careful:* Rebecca Davis O'Brien and Jenny Strasburg, "Jeffrey Epstein Used Opaque Charity Account at Deutsche Bank for Own Benefit," *Wall Street Journal*, September 12, 2019, https://www.wsj.com /articles/jeffrey-epstein-used-opaque-charity-account-at-deutsche-bank -for-own-benefit-11568286004.

39 *Over a period of five years, Black paid Epstein:* "Investigation of Epstein/ Black Relationship."

39 *Black said he was retiring:* Matthew Goldstein, "Leon Black Leaves Apollo Sooner Than Expected," *New York Times*, March 22, 2021, https://www .nytimes.com/2021/03/22/business/leon-black-apollo.html.

39 *If that weren't enough:* Jonathan Stempel: "Russian Model Suing Leon Black Alleges Billionaire's Ties to Jeffrey Epstein," Reuters, August 10, 2021, https://news.yahoo.com/russian-model-suing-leon-black-143425969 .html.

40 *To Sue Watson:* Author interview (Morgenson).

41 *Each man has been characterized:* Peter T. Kilborn, "Suicide of Big Executive: Stress of Corporate Life," *New York Times*, February 14, 1975, https://www.nytimes.com/1975/02/14/archives/suicide-of-big-executive -stress-of-corporate-life-suicide-of-a-top.html. See also Ivry, "Leon Black in Winter."

41 *Decades after his father's suicide:* Melby and Perlberg, "Nobody Makes Money Like."

42 *United Fruit supplied:* Thomas P. McCann and Henry Scammell, *An American Company: The Tragedy of United Fruit* (Crown Publishers, 1976).

42 *In 1968, United Fruit was facing:* Ibid.

42 *Investors believed Black would breathe:* Peter Chapman, *Bananas: How the United Fruit Company Shaped the World* (Canongate U.S., 2009).

43 *"Eli could not run the company":* McCann and Scammell, *An American Company.*

43 *His elbows were sharp:* Kilborn, "Suicide of Big Executive."

43 *Keen to reduce the company's crippling banana taxes:* Robert J. Cole, "Direct Bribe Bid Is Laid to Black," *New York Times,* May 17, 1975, https:// www.nytimes.com/1975/05/17/archives/direct-bribe-bid-is-laid-to-black -honduran-says-expresident.html.

44 *Papers from his attaché:* Chapman, *Bananas.*

44 *Initial news accounts:* See Kilborn, "Suicide of a Big Executive."

44 *At Black's funeral in Manhattan:* "Eli Black's Rites Attended by 500," *New York Times*, February 6, 1975.

45 *The effects of the revelation:* See Cole, "Direct Bribe Bid."

45 *Three years later:* Arnold H. Lubasch, "Guilty Plea in Foreign Bribe Case," *New York Times*, July 20, 1978.

45 *Congress convened hearings:* "The Activities of American Multinational Corporations Abroad," Hearings before the Subcommittee of International Economic Policy, the Committee on International Relations, U.S. House of Representatives, July and September 1975, https://babel.hathitrust.org/cgi /pt?id=pur1.32754077072001&view=1up&seq=34&skin=2021.

45 *Finally, lawmakers passed:* G. C. Hufbauer and J. G. Taylor, "Taxing Boycotts and Bribes," *Denver Journal of International Law & Policy,* January 1977, https://digitalcommons.du.edu/cgi/viewcontent.cgi?article=2106& context=djilp.

45 *In his book published a year earlier:* McCann and Scammell, *An American Company.*

47 *In September 1989, Drexel pleaded guilty:* Stephen Labaton, "Drexel, As Expected, Pleads Guilty to 6 Counts of Fraud," *New York Times*, September 12, 1989.

47 *Michael Milken, the head of:* Scott Paltrow, "Sobbing Milken Pleads Guilty to Six Felonies," *Los Angeles Times*, April 25, 1990, https://www.latimes.com/archives/la-xpm-1990-04-25-mn-322-story.html.

48 *Securities regulators interviewed Black:* Leon David Black, Biographical affidavit, Form 11, National Association of Insurance Commissioners, January 5, 2018.

49 *A tantalizing possibility presented itself:* All references to the early days of Black's new partnership and his creation of Apollo (pages 50 to 53) come from court documents related to the Executive Life seizure and sale, from the California Insurance Regulator Conservatorship and Liquidation Office website, https://www.caclo.org/perl/index.pl?document_id=6b1a89cbf49a48717fffe54fdea89577#start, testimony in the California state attorney general's lawsuit, investigator interviews conducted with participants after the takeover, and author interviews (Morgenson).

50 *Just six days after:* Letter dated April 30, 1990, setting forth "the general guidelines we have agreed upon pursuant to which Mr. Leon BLACK and Mr. John HANNAN" propose "to organize a limited partnership investment fund," produced in lawsuits involving the Executive Life transaction.

52 *One, however, was Western Union:* Confidential interview.

52 *In 1996, LeBow and Black would travel to Moscow:* "Russian Active Measures Campaigns and Interference in the 2016 U.S. Election Volume 5: Counterintelligence Threats and Vulnerabilities," Senate Committee on Intelligence, August 18, 2020.

52 *But the name had another:* Confidential interview.

54 *"Greed is all right, by the way":* Boesky commencement address at the UC Berkeley's School of Business Administration, May 18, 1986.

56 *In 1970, for example, figures from:* Walter W. Kolodrubetz, "Two Decades of Employee-Benefit Plans, 1950-70: A Review," *Social Security Bulletin* 1972, www.ssa.gov/policy/docs/ssb/v35n4/v35n4p10.pdf.

56 *With 401(k)s, individuals, who knew little about investing:* https://www.morningstar.com/articles/1000743/100-must-know-statistics-about-401k-plans%2056.

57 *That same year, the U.S. government:* Nancy L. Ross, "Eased Pension Fiduciary Rules Urged," *Washington Post*, April 25, 1978, www.washingtonpost

.com/archive/business/1978/04/25/eased-pension-fiduciary-rules-urged
/e6734ee8-9a90-43c4-82ca-041b208bbffc/.

58 *In 1987, at the height of merger mania:* https://www.ftc.gov/sites/default
/files/documents/reports_annual/10th-report-fy-1987-86/10annrpt1986-87
_0.pdf.

58 *Such requests—a first step in a process:* https://www.ftc.gov/sites/default
/files/documents/reports_annual/12th-report-fy-1989/12annrpt1989_0.pdf.

58 *But in 2021:* "FTC Adjusts Its Merger Review Process to Deal with Increase in Merger Filings," FTC press release, August 3, 2021, www.ftc.gov
/news-events/news/press-releases/2021/08/ftc-adjusts-its-merger-review
-process-deal-increase-merger-filings.

58 *In 1981, Reagan nominated John Shad:* "Regulating the Regulators: The
Executive Branch and the SEC, 1981-2008," Securities and Exchange
Commission Historical Society, https://www.sechistorical.org/museum
/galleries/rtr/rtr03b_shad_commission.php.

59 *In 1984, KKR's $1.1 billion buyout:* Sydney Shaw, "FCC Approves $1 billion Wometco Buyout," UPI, April 13, 1984, https://www.upi.com/Archives
/1984/04/13/FCC-approves-1-billion-Wometco-buyout/5642450680400/.

59 *That year also saw a hostile:* Al Delugach, "Disney, Raider to Pay Investors
for 'Greenmail': $45-Million Settlement Seen as First of Its Kind," *Los
Angeles Times*, July 13, 1989.

59 *And in 1986, a tax overhaul essentially incentivized the use of debt:* "The
Role of the Interest Deduction in the Corporate Tax Code," Mercatus Center, March 15, 2018, https://www.mercatus.org/publications/government
-spending/role-interest-deduction-corporate-tax-code.

60 *The debt-fueled buying spree resulted in almost $1.5 trillion:* Andrei
Shleifer and Robert W. Vishny, "The Takeover Wave of the 1980s," *Science*,
New Series 249, no. 4970 (August 17, 1990).

60 *So Black decided to bluff:* Ivry, "Leon Black in Winter."

61 *In 1984, Milken's salary and bonus:* Federal Deposit Insurance Corporation v. Milken et al., January 18, 1991, U.S. District Court, Southern District of New York, p. 72.

61 *By 1989, Jerome Kohlberg, Henry Kravis, and George Roberts:* Josh Kosman, *The Buyout of America* (Portfolio, 2009).

61 *In 1985, a report presented at the University of Michigan:* Gabriel Zuc-
man, "Rising Wealth Inequality: Causes, Consequences and Potential Responses" (Research Publications, Poverty Solutions at The University of
Michigan, 2015).

61 *By 2016, wealth held by the bottom 90 percent:* Ibid.

62 *A second measure, recorded by the Federal Reserve:* Alexandre Tanzi and Mike Dorning, "Top 1% of U.S. Earners Now Hold More Wealth Than All of the Middle Class," *Bloomberg News,* October 8, 2021, https://www.bloomberg.com/news/articles/2021-10-08/top-1-earners-hold-more-wealth-than-the-u-s-middle-class?sref=lnrir5K3.

62 *As G. Chris Andersen, head of investment banking at Drexel:* Portia Crowe, " 'Every Night, We Were in the Polo Lounge, Drinking Cristal' and Other Amazing Quotes About the Reign of the Junk Bond King," *Business Insider,* April 1, 2015.

63 *In early 1987, Congress convened hearings:* "Examination of the Need for Reform of the Procedures and Practices of Insider Trading, Financing of Hostile Takeovers, and Their Effects on the Economy and International Competitiveness, January 28, March 4, and April 8, 1987," Senate Committee on Banking, Housing and Urban Affairs.

63 *Brian Ayash, a finance professor:* Ayash and Rostad, *Leveraged Buyouts and Financial Distress.*

63 *In 1988, the biggest, brashest corporate brawl:* Bryan Burrough and John Helyar, *Barbarians at the Gate: The Fall of RJR Nabisco* (Harper & Row, 1989).

64 *Charles Tate, a founder of buyout firm Hicks, Muse, Tate & Furst:* "The Deal Decade: Verdict on the '80s," *Fortune,* August 26, 1991.

64 *During the 1970s, before the debt-fueled takeover mania:* "Defaults and Returns on High-Yield Bonds Through the First Half of 1991," Edward Altman, *Financial Analysts Journal* 47, no. 6 (November-December 1991): 67-77.

64 *At least one state didn't wait:* Stuart Taylor, Jr., "High Court Backs State on Curbing Hostile Takeover," *New York Times,* April 22, 1987.

64 *David Ruder, the new chairman of the SEC:* Ruder nomination hearing, United States Senate Committee on Banking, Housing and Urban Affairs, July 22, 1987, https://www.sechistorical.org/collection/papers/1980/1987_0722_RuderHearing.pdf.

64 *After the stock market crash of 1987:* Gary Klott, "Tax Bill Revision Seen on Takeovers," *New York Times,* October 31, 1987.

64 *Academic research subsequently showed:* S. Jarrell, "The Post-Merger Performance of Corporate Takeovers," *Semantic Scholar,* July 1, 1996, https://www.semanticscholar.org/paper/The-Post-Merger-Performance-of-Corporate-Takeovers-Jarrell/dd0610f49f96c6de08432443a014400b07672caf.

65 *John Shad, Reagan's SEC chairman:* Letter to James A. Baker III, Chief

of Staff, The White House, from John Shad, June 14, 1984, https://www
.sechistorical.org/collection/papers/1980/1984_0614_BakerShad
Leveraging.pdf.

65 *Two years later, the bomb dropped:* John M. Doyle, "SEC Files Insider
Trading Charges Against Drexel, Milken," *AP News*, September 7, 1988,
https://apnews.com/article/25a91d986437b80a5d401f7683c0e2ea.

CHAPTER THREE: "PROJECT SAVIOR"

67 *Led by an aggressive money manager named Fred Carr:* Carol Loomis,
"What Fred Carr's Fall Means to You," *Fortune*, May 6, 1991, https://
money.cnn.com/magazines/fortune/fortune_archive/1991/05/06/74977
/index.htm.

67 *Executive Life's high-paying products had lured:* California Insurance Office filings.

67 *Like most industries:* Annual financial report of Northwestern Mutual
Life Insurance Co., https://www.northwesternmutual.com/assets/pdf
/financial-reports/results/nm-annual-statement.pdf.

67 *By the time Drexel failed, junk bonds made up:* Executive Life Insurance
Company in Conservation, Attachment to Consolidated Proofs of Claim
of the Resolution Trust Corporation, Affidavit of Bill Rider, Senior Analyst, June 2, 1992, Los Angeles, CA.

67 *The two entities were joined at the hip:* Ibid.

68 *Black knew Carr, having encountered the insurance executive:* Confidential interview.

68 *By 1990, Black had already identified:* Ibid.

69 *In August 1990, the Black partnership:* Confidential interview.

69 *Acquiring a large portfolio in one fell swoop:* Confidential interview.

70 *The insiders' name for the Executive Life deal:* Confidential interview.

70 *Meanwhile Executive Life groaned:* First Executive Life Annual Statement
to California Regulators, 1990.

70 *So did the California insurance department:* Author interview with Roxani
Gillespi (Morgenson).

71 *As the California insurance department plumbed:* Confidential Memorandum to All Insurance Commissioners, from the Non-Investment Grade
Bond Working Group, State of Illinois Insurance Department, December
27, 1990.

72 *He had already voiced his views on Executive Life:* John Garamendi speech in Monterrey to Independent Insurance and Brokers of California, October 16, 1990.

73 *A graduate of UC Berkeley with a degree in business:* Garamendi court testimony, Garamendi v. Altus SA, et al., Consolidated with Sierra National Insurance Holdings, Inc., et al. v. Credit Lyonnais, SA, et al., March, 2, 2005.

73 *He ran as a consumer advocate:* Author interview with Roxani Gillespi (Morgenson).

73 *In 1988, he'd championed legislation:* Tom Furlong, "Garamendi Will Back Bill to Help Bass Acquire S&L," *Los Angeles Times*, August 5, 1988.

73 *From almost the first day he sat:* Garamendi court testimony, Garamendi v. Altus SA, et al.

73 *Baum's background was in real estate development:* Redwood Trust press release, September 24, 2012, https://ir.redwoodtrust.com/news/news -details/2012/Redwood-Trust-Announces-Departure-of-its-Chairman -George-Bull-and-Election-of-Richard-Baum-as-Chairman-and-Douglas -Hansen-as-Vice-Chairman-of-the-Board-of-Directors/default.aspx.

74 *In early March 1991, Marc Rowan:* Letter from Rowan to Henin, March 5, 1991.

74 *In his early months as commissioner:* Garamendi court testimony, Garamendi v. Altus SA, et al.

74 *Carr told the commissioner and his team:* Ibid.

75 *On April 4, 1991, in a major blow:* Harry DeAngelo, Linda DeAngelo, Stuart C. Gilson, "Perceptions and Politics of Finance," *Journal of Financial Economics* 41 (1996), http://marshallinside.usc.edu/ldeangel/Publications /FirstCapital.pdf.

75 *Six days later, Carr:* Letter to John Garamendi from Fred Carr, April 10, 1991.

75 *In a press release on April 11, Garamendi said:* "Statement by Insurance Commissioner John Garamendi regarding Executive Life Insurance Company," California Department of Insurance, news release, April 11, 1991.

76 *Even as the deal was being struck:* Edward I. Altman, "Defaults and Returns on High Yield Bonds Through the First Half of 1991," *Financial Analysts Journal*, November-December 1991.

CHAPTER FOUR: "I REALLY NEED TO UNDERSTAND WHAT YOU DO"

77 *The team was "completely busy with the First Executive deal":* Minutes, Management Committee Meeting of April 15, 1991, 245 Park Avenue; present P. Souviron, L. Black, J, Hannan.

77 *From the start, the insurance commissioner:* Garamendi court testimony, Garamendi v. Altus SA, et al.

78 *Later, it would emerge that:* "Credit Lyonnais and Others to Plead Guilty and Pay $771 Million in Executive Life Affair," FBI press release, December 18, 2003, https://archives.fbi.gov/archives/news/pressrel/press-releases /credit-lyonnais-and-others-to-plead-guilty.

78 *The Federal Reserve was dragging its feet:* Meeting Minutes, April 15, 1991.

79 *"Drexel worked through proxies":* Author interview (Morgenson).

80 *It consisted of a database:* Confidential interview.

80 *Black had dispatched Cogut:* Confidential interview.

80 *In addition to being Lowell and Mike Milken's lawyer:* Mary Zey, *Banking on Fraud: Drexel Junk Bonds and Buyouts* (Routledge, 2017).

81 *That year, the United Savings Association of:* Texas Federal Deposit Insurance Corporation, as Manager of the FSLIC Resolution Fund; Plaintiff-Appellant V. Maxxam, Inc v. Charles E. Hurwitz et al, No. 05-20808, United States Court of Appeals for the Fifth Circuit, www.ca5.uscourts .gov/opinions/pub/05/05-20808-CV0.wpd.pdf; Hart Holding Co. v. Drexel Burnham Lambert Inc., No. 11,514, Court of Chancery of the State of Delaware, New Castle, May 28, 1992, *Delaware Journal of Corporate Law*, Unreported Cases, Vol. 18, 1993.

81 *(Later he would testify that key information):* Scott Paltrow, "A Drexel Lawyer Accuses Milken's Brother of Deceit," *Los Angeles Times*, October 23, 1990.

82 *Black was a general partner of several of these partnerships:* Federal Deposit Insurance Corporation v. Milken et al, January 18, 1991, U.S. District Court, Southern District of New York.

82 *For example, Milken and his brother:* U.S. v. Milken, No. SS 89 Cr. 41 (KMW), United States District Court, S.D. New York, December 13, 1990. Note 5, https://law.justia.com/cases/federal/district-courts/FSupp/759/109 /1473275/.

82 *On April 16, 1991, from Apollo's Los Angeles headquarters:* Confidential Memorandum to Jean-François Hénin from Eric Siegel and Craig Cogut, April 16, 1991.

84 *Maureen Marr was worried:* Author interview with Maureen Marr (Morgenson).

86 *Hundreds attended; one was Vince Watson:* Author interview with Vince Watson (Morgenson).

86 *Garamendi attended the meeting:* Author interview with Maureen Marr (Morgenson).

89 *The lawyer had spent eight and a half years: SEC News Digest,* May 1991, www.sec.gov/news/digest/1981/dig052181.pdf, and *Bloomberg News* bio of Hartigan, https://www.bloomberg.com/profile/person/14013054?sref=lnrir-5K3.

90 *In a classic revolving door move:* Interview with Hartigan, *Los Angeles Business Journal,* Monday, September 15, 1997.

90 *She would later learn:* Confidential interview.

CHAPTER FIVE: "THE FIRE SALE APPROACH"

91 *Garamendi outlined:* Memo from Garamendi, May 21, 1991, to "Parties Interested in Financial Participation in Executive Life Insurance Rehabilitation Plan, General Statement of Objectives and Terms."

91 *The insurer held more than seven hundred different:* Amended and Restated Agreement of Purchase and Sale in Connection with the Rehabilitation of Executive Life Insurance Company, January 29, 1992.

92 *"We did not price the portfolio when it was sold":* Court testimony, Garamendi v. Altus SA, et al.

93 *Years later, Norris Clark, the insurance department's financial surveillance chief:* Confidential interview.

93 *Another regulatory blunder:* Howell E. Jackson and Edward L. Symons, Jr., *Regulation of Financial Institutions* (West Group, 1999).

95 *Among its findings:* "Executive Life Insurance Company Analysis of ELIC in Conservation and Aurora Under the MAAF/Altus Proposal," Salomon Brothers, November 1991.

96 *As one person involved in analyzing:* Author interview (Morgenson).

97 *Another sign that attracting more bidders:* Garamendi court testimony, Garamendi v. Altus SA, et al.

97 *In any case, the advantage given:* Harry DeAngelo et al, "The Collapse of Executive Life Insurance Co. and Its Impact on Policyholders," *Journal of Financial Economics,* December 1994.

98 *"FDIC must be a major brake":* Meeting minutes July 9, 1991.

98 *But this much is known:* Federal Deposit Insurance Corporation v. Milken et al.

98 *Threats to the deal from competing buyers:* Meeting minutes July 9, 1991.

98 *"A handshake should occur this week":* Ibid.

98 *The festivities took place at Chasen's:* Garamendi court testimony, Garamendi v. Altus SA, et al.

99 *The headline figure everyone was waiting for:* Eric N. Berg, "A Deal Raising Complex Questions," *New York Times*, August 8, 1991.

99 *A little-known fact about:* Confidential interview.

99 *A September 26, 1991, memo written by Karl Rubinstein:* "To: Richard Baum, FM: Karl L. Rubenstein, RE: ELIC Liquidation Value, 26 September, 1991."

100 *In September, the National Organization of Life and Health Insurance Guaranty Associations:* Richard Stevenson, "Junk Bonds Crucial in Executive Life Bids," *New York Times*, October 14, 1991.

101 *"Since May, there has been the greatest":* Letter to Garamendi from Eli Broad, Chairman and Chief Executive of Broad Inc., October 23, 1991.

102 *Before announcing this shift:* Author interview with Maureen Marr (Morgenson).

102 *Then Apollo began negotiating directly:* Ibid.

102 *In addition, the Aurora rehabilitation:* "Revised Executive Life Agreement Backed," UPI, December 12, 1991.

103 *"I am happy to announce":* Kathy Kristof, "French Group's Executive Life Bid Endorsed," *Los Angeles Times*, November 15, 1991.

103 *Under the Apollo/Altus deal, partnership documents show:* Letter to Jean-François Hénin from John Hannan, Lion Advisors, March 3, 1992.

104 *Neither was it publicized:* Confidential interview.

105 *In late December, he asked:* Garamendi court testimony, Garamendi v. Altus SA, et al.

106 *Phil Warden was a lawyer representing:* Author interview with Phil Warden (Morgenson).

107 *Other advisors had told Garamendi:* Author interview (Morgenson).

107 *"What's most remarkable about the Executive Life saga":* Amy Barrett, "In California, a Botched Buyout?" *Bloomberg News*, June 28, 1993.

CHAPTER SIX: "NO BOY SCOUT"

109 *Gillett Holdings:* Securities and Exchange Commission filings, Form 10-K, July 31, 2006, Note 13, https://www.sec.gov/Archives/edgar/data/812011 /000081201107000036/form10ka.htm.

109 *In 1994,* Forbes *magazine estimated:* Matthew Schifrin and Riva Atlas, "Hocus Pocus," *Forbes,* March 14, 1994.

110 *From 1991 through 2004, for example, Katie Watson:* Letter from Aurora Life Insurance Co. regarding Katie Watson's account value, March 7, 2006.

111 *By 1995, the third fund had collected $1.5 billion:* Phillip L. Zweig, "Leon Black: Wall Street's Dr. No the Ex-Drexelite Is Waiting for the Stock Market to Tank," *Bloomberg News,* July 29, 1996.

111 *One of those early investors was:* Ibid.

111 *As CalPERS considered Apollo's investment pitch:* Author interview (Morgenson).

112 *As it turned out, the new Apollo fund was just an average:* Arlene Jacobius, "The Sun Doesn't Shine on Apollo," *Pensions and Investments,* December 14, 2009.

113 *Out of the Executive Life portfolio:* Executive Life securities list.

113 *Suddenly, a new investor was acquiring:* Henin court testimony, Garamendi v. Altus SA, et al., Consolidated with Sierra National Insurance Holdings, Inc., et al. v. Credit Lyonnais, SA, et al.

114 *By Hénin's recollection:* Ibid.

114 *"The negotiations took place directly between":* Ibid.

114 *Well aware that the bonds sold so hurriedly:* Author interview with Maureen Marr (Morgenson).

114 *The solution, Cogut would later testify:* Cogut testimony, Garamendi v. Altus SA, et al., Consolidated with Sierra National Insurance Holdings, Inc., et al. v. Credit Lyonnais, SA, et al.

115 *Explaining the situation years later:* Ibid.

115 *But because California barred policyholders:* Court decision dismissing Attorney General Lockyer's case.

115 *One hidden connection involved Western Union:* Confidential interview.

116 *In restructuring New Valley, the Apollo partnership:* Stephanie Strom, "New Valley, Old Management," *New York Times,* October 9, 1994.

117 *over two decades later, in 2016, New York gossip columns:* Emily Smith, "This Is How an 80-Year-Old Billionaire Celebrates His Birthday," *New York Post,* February 3, 2016,

118 *One existing stake Apollo held was Gillett Holdings:* Confidential interview.

118 *In August 1990, it defaulted on $170 million in loans:* "Gillett Holdings to File for Chapter 11," *Los Angeles Times*, June 26, 1991.

119 *Black knew the Gillett situation well:* Phyllis Berman and Jean Sherman Chatzky, "Warming up for the Big Ones," *Forbes*, March 2, 1992.

119 *Later, Black's group would contribute $40 million:* Ibid.

119 *In 2003, Apollo entities held:* Securities and Exchange Commission filings and AP via *Deseret News*, "Apollo Dissolves Vail Resorts Stake," October 1, 2004.

120 *Finally, in at least one case, involving Farley:* Confidential interview.

120 *Keeping policyholders in the dark:* California State Bureau of Audit Report on ELIC, 2008, https://www.bsa.ca.gov/pdfs/reports/2005-115.2.pdf.

121 *Neither is there a detailed record:* California Insurance Department, Conservation and Liquidation Office website, https://www.caclo.org/perl/index.pl?document_id=f70aa978d186574c773826c8d368a676#start.

121 *even a Malibu ranch:* Kanter v. Kanter, Court of Appeal of the State of California Second Appellate, Dec. 20, 2011, https://www.casemine.com/judgement/us/5914f199add7b0493497c008.

121 *Garamendi was one of the trustees:* Conservation and Liquidation Office website.

122 *After the trust closed out in December 1996:* Executive Life Insurance Company Trust, Executive Life Insurance Company Real Estate Trust, Base Assets Trust, Combined Annual Report to Beneficiaries, December 31, 1996.

122 *A March 2006 letter to a policyholder:* Letter from Lisa Elder, Senior Manager, Aurora National Life Assurance Co., March 7, 2006, regarding a policyholder's account value increments.

122 *In the early 2000s, Fred Carr:* Confidential interview.

CHAPTER SEVEN: "THE REAL PLAYERS"

123 *By the summer of 1993, Marr:* Author interview (Morgenson).

126 *Five years later, a whistleblower would come:* "French Whistleblower Quizzed over Executive Life," *Expatica*, December 3, 2004, https://www.expatica.com/fr/general/french-whistleblower-quizzed-over-executive-life-118761/.

127 Bloomberg News *reported:* Barrett, "In California, A Botched Bailout?"

127   *When Garamendi ran for governor in 1994, Burkle and his wife had loaned his campaign $100,000:* Dan Morain, "Garamendi's Campaign Running on Lean Funding," *Los Angeles Times*, April 10, 1994.

127   *Burkle hired Garamendi to open: Los Angeles Business Journal*, June 1, 1998, http://labusinessjournal.www.clients.ellingtoncms.com/news/1998/jun/01/wsw/.

128   *At $49 a share, the takeover:* Paul Merrion, "Cha-Ching! Dominick's Money Machine," *Crain's Chicago Business*, October 17, 1998.

128   *"He's real smart and he's real hungry":* Ibid.

128   *Then, in December 2001, a bombshell:* John Carreyrou, "Credit Lyonnais's Defense in Lawsuit Takes Blow After U.S. Financier Agrees to Testify," *Wall Street Journal*, December 3, 2001.

129   *In January 2002, Wallace Albertson:* Letter to Attorney General Lockyer from Wallace Albertson, Los Angeles, CA, January 15, 2002.

129   *Lockyer obliged a few months later, adding Black:* "Attorney General Lockyer Expands Lawsuit Alleging Conspiracy to Raid Executive Life," Attorney General press release, January 30, 2002, https://oag.ca.gov/news/press-releases/attorney-general-lockyer-expands-lawsuit-alleging-conspiracy-raid-executive-life.

129   *Three years later, his suit was dismissed:* Deborah Vrana, "Lockyer's Executive Life Lawsuit Is Tossed Out," *Los Angeles Times*, August 16, 2005.

130   *In 2003, more than a decade after the Executive Life deal:* "Credit Lyonnais and Others to Plead Guilty."

130   *That 2008 audit by the state of California:* California State Bureau of Audit Report on ELIC, 2008.

130   *During that campaign, Garamendi was dogged:* "Mendoza Criticizes Garamendi's Failure to Testify at Executive Life Hearing," *Insurance Journal*, October 15, 2002.

131   *"The sale of the assets was at best negligent":* Ibid.

131   *One of those advisors, George Bull, received $110,000:* Kathy Kristof, "Adviser on Executive Life Said to Lack Experience: Securities Regulators Are Paying One Consultant $110,000 a Month to Evaluate a Junk Bond Portfolio Pivotal to the Sale," *Los Angeles Times*, October 23, 1991.

131   *From 1991 through 2020, records show:* Annual reports, Conservation and Liquidation Office website; California State Bureau of Audit report on ELIC, 2008.

131   *Even worse, some policyholders:* Documents provided to policyholders reviewed by author (Morgenson).

132   *In 1999, it concluded that the notice:* Gerenson v. Pennsylvania Life and

Health Insurance Guaranty Association, Supreme Court of Pennsylvania, April 7, 1999, https://www.anylaw.com/case/gersenson-v-pennsylvania-life-and-health-insurance-guaranty-association/supreme-court-of-pennsylvania/04-08-1999/8sZgX2YBTlTomsSBw7iQ.

132 *"Not only did they refuse":* Author interview with Marr (Morgenson).

133 *Testifying before a congressional hearing:* "The Collapse of Executive Life Insurance Co and Its Impact on Policyholders," House of Representatives Committee on Government Reform, October 10, 2002.

134 *With so many unanswered questions:* Morgenson letter to Judge Ruth A. Kwan, Superior Court of California, County of Los Angeles, Central District, November 4, 2021.

135 *"It was not protocol to destroy documents":* Author interview with Gillespie (Morgenson).

135 *"Maureen fought for us":* Author interview with Sue Watson (Morgenson).

136 *In a 2010 congressional hearing, Garamendi was still:* May 5, 2010, U.S. House of Representatives, https://www.c-span.org/video/?293330-1/house-session, at 7:46:29.

136 *As for Marr, she understands:* Author interview with Marr (Morgenson).

137 *"They were thieves in the night":* Author interview with Watson (Morgenson).

CHAPTER EIGHT: "STRONG ENOUGH TO STAND ON"

139 *And a 2019 study published by the government's own National Bureau of Economic Research:* Steven J. Davis et al., "The (Heterogenous) Economic Effects of Private Equity Buyouts," NBER, October 2019.

139 *Mark Cannon worked as a sales representative:* Author interview (Morgenson).

140 *"An exceptional criminogenic environment":* Author interview (Morgenson).

140 *In 1995, bank regulators referred 1,837 cases:* Gretchen Morgenson and Louise Story, "In Financial Crisis, No Prosecutions of Top Figures," *New York Times*, April 14, 2011.

141 *As financial prosecutions declined, so did:* "White Collar Crime Prosecutions for 2021 Continue Long Term Decline," TRAC Reports, August 9, 2021, https://trac.syr.edu/tracreports/crim/655/.

142 *In 1996, for example, Congress passed:* David Dayen, "Cut Off Private Equity's Money Spigot," *American Prospect*, July 28, 2022.

142 *the new law, largely the result of deregulatory fervor among the*

Republican-controlled House and Senate: G. Philip Rutledge, "NSMIA . . . One Year Later: The States' Response," February 1998, https://www .americanbar.org/groups/business_law/publications/the_business_lawyer /find_by_subject/buslaw_tbl_mci_nsmia/.

142 *In 1996, buyout firms raised $20 billion in fresh money:* Brad Meikle, "Through the Years with the Buyouts Newsletter," *Buyouts Insider*, June 10, 2002.

143 *The Taxpayer Relief Act of 1997:* Discussion of law's changes at Find law.com, https://www.findlaw.com/tax/federal-taxes/taxpayer-relief-act-of -1997.html.

143 *It had been accepted practice for years, but in 1993:* IRS Rev. Proc 93-27, www.irs.gov/pub/irs-drop/rp-01-43.pdf.

143 *But this element disappeared after then-Democratic Senator Kyrsten Sinema:* Brian Schwartz, "How Wall Street Wooed Sen. Kyrsten Sinema and Preserved Its Multi-Billion Dollar Carried Interest Tax Break," CNBC .com, August 9, 2022.

144 *Congress's barring of tax deductions on corporate salaries:* "The Executive Pay Cap That Backfired," *ProPublica*, February 12, 2016.

144 *These moves ballooned their total compensation:* Gretchen Morgenson, "Why Are CEOs of US Firms Paid 320 Times as Much as Their Workers?" NBCNews.com, April 7, 2021.

144 *As wages languished:* Thomas A. Durkin, "Credit Cards: Use and Consumer Attitudes," *Federal Reserve Bulletin*, September 2000, pp. 623–634.

144 *In 1989, one year's tuition at a private college:* "Here's the Average Cost of College Tuition Every Year Since 1971," *USA Today*, May 18, 2019.

145 *And in 2020, private equity finally got:* U.S. Department of Labor Information Letter on Private Equity, June 3, 2020. Release Number 20-1160-NAT.

145 *In their 2014 book:* Joseph R. Blasi, Richard D. Freeman, and Douglas L. Kruse, *The Citizen's Share: Reducing Inequality in the 21st Century* (Yale University Press, 2014).

146 *Author Blasi, a professor at Rutgers:* Author interview (Morgenson).

146 *The beginnings of Samsonite go back: Journey of Discovery, The History of Samsonite* (Samsonite, 2017); also Al Lewis, "Beatrice Felled Once Mighty Samsonite," *Denver Post*, June 2, 2006.

148 *In 1985, leveraged buyout kingpin KKR:* David Vise, "Beatrice Agrees to $6 Billion Buyout Offer," *Washington Post*, November 15, 1985.

148 *The company took the lackluster name E-II Holdings:* "In 1988, Mr. Riklis Bought Control of E-II Holdings," *AP News*, January 24, 1995.

148 *By 1990, loaded with Drexel debt:* Stephanie Strom, "E-II Holdings Wins Fight for Restructuring Plan," *New York Times,* May 26, 1993.

148 *Alongside Apollo as an investor:* James Kanter, "Court Clears Pinault, But His Firm Is Guilty," *New York Times,* May 12, 2005, also Marc Lifsher, "Artemis to Pay in Executive Life Case," *Los Angeles Times,* November 23, 2005.

149 *In 1993, Astrum bought Samsonite's primary competitor:* "Samsonite's Parent to Buy American Tourister," Associated Press, August 4, 1993.

149 *In 1994, before it issued public shares:* Samsonite 10-K for the year ended 1997, Securities and Exchange Commission filing, item 6, page 16.

149 *Then came the inevitable job cuts:* "Samsonite Plans to Cut 450 Jobs," *AP News,* November 1, 1996.

150 *In 1998, the firm announced talks to sell half:* "Samsonite Discusses Selling 50 Percent Stake to Pay Dividend," *New York Times,* March 24, 1998.

150 *Investors didn't like this deal either:* Justin Pettit, "Is a Share Buyback Right for Your Company?," *Harvard Business Review,* April 2001.

150 *More bad news arrived:* "Beatie and Osborn LLP commences class action," PR Newswire, September 18, 1998.

151 *Samsonite settled this:* "Business Briefs," *Pueblo Chieftain,* July 27, 2000.

151 *Samsonite was in a downward spiral:* "Moody's Downgrades Samsonite," March 25, 1999, https://www.moodys.com/research/MOODYS -DOWNGRADES-SAMSONITE-CORPS-SR-SUB-NOTES-TO-Caa1 -SECURED—PR_26913.

151 *In early 2001, Samsonite announced:* Michael Lauzon, "Samsonite Bags Denver," *Plastics News,* March 5, 2001.

151 *Bob Knapp was one of those laid off in the move:* Megan Verlee, "International Trade Good or Bad for Colorado?" Colorado Public Radio, April 20, 2016.

151 *Other Samsonite workers had difficulties:* Diane Ziebarth LinkedIn page, https://www.linkedin.com/in/diane-ziebarth-6426335a/.

151 *By January 2003, the company's net worth:* Samsonite Form 10-K, fiscal 2004, April 26, 2004, page F-4.

152 *Samsonite was in a liquidity crisis:* "Private Equity Firm to Buy Samsonite," *Los Angeles Times,* July 6, 2007.

152 *"The first of many successes":* Apollo Global Management website, "Our History, 1995," https://www.apollo.com/about-apollo/our-history.

153 *Telemundo filed for bankruptcy in July 1993:* "Telemundo Files for Chapter 11," Reuters, July 31, 1993.

153 *Apollo had a controlling stake:* John Lippman, "Apollo Brings in Investors to Purchase Telemundo," *Wall Street Journal*, November 25, 1997.

153 *By 1997, Apollo and another investment firm:* "AP Financial News at 11:10 a.m. EST Tuesday, Nov. 25, 1997," *Associated Press Online*.

153 *By 1996, the* Times of London *reported:* Garth Alexander, "Vulture Awaits Rich Pickings in the Crash," *Sunday Times* (London), August 11, 1996.

154 *In 1998, the firm raised $3.6 billion:* Palico.com, https://www.palico.com/funds/apollo-investment-fund-iv/41d62bdb349549f68ee25824575cdd1b.

154 *The $1.8 billion merger created:* "GranCare, Living Centers Plan Merger," *Bloomberg News*, May 9, 1997.

155 *An investigation ensued:* Mike Allen, "Ex-Treasurer in Connecticut Pleads Guilty," *New York Times*, September 24, 1999.

155 *During the trial it came out:* "Silvester Raised Rowland Money," *Hartford Courant*, September 30, 1999.

155 *Flipping companies among themselves:* Mergr M&A Deal Summary, "Ontario Teachers Pension Plan and Ares Private Equity Group Acquires Samsonite International," January 1, 2003, https://mergr.com/ontario-teachers-pension-plan-acquires-samsonite-international-sa.

155 *Then, in 2007, another spin:* "CVC to Acquire Samsonite for $1.7 Billion," Reuters, July 5, 2007.

156 *Samsonite International shares:* "Samsonite Shares Tumble in Hong Kong Debut," Associated Press, June 6, 2011.

156 *In December 2021, the company reported:* "Samsonite Announces Final Results for the Year Ended 2021," press release, March 16, 2022, https://www.prnewswire.com/news-releases/samsonite-international-sa-announces-final-results-for-the-year-ended-december-31-2021-301503988.html.

156 *Cannon, the former Samsonite employee:* Author interview (Morgenson).

CHAPTER NINE: "WE HAVE 2,500 FAMILIES THAT DEPEND ON US GETTING IT RIGHT"

157 *New Madrid, Missouri, is a town of three thousand:* "U.S. Census Bureau QuickFacts: New Madrid County, Missouri," https://www.census.gov/quickfacts/newmadridcountymissouri.

157 *It produces 263,000 metric tons of primary aluminum annually:* "Large Explosion Rocks Southeast Missouri Aluminum Plant," *AP News*, August 4, 2015, https://apnews.com/article/66836feaad0245398523c341fcfbc085.

158   *Apollo bought the smelter, Noranda Aluminum, in May 2007:* "Mine Company Sells U.S. Unit," *New York Times*, April 12, 2007.

158   *The company was not only the biggest employer:* "NMC R-1 to Seek Tax Hike to Balance Budget," *Sikeston Standard Democrat*, August 15, 2016.

158   *The remaining $1 billion necessary:* "Noranda Aluminum Holding Corporation Reports Second Quarter 2007 Results," press release via *Business Wire*, September 19, 2007.

158   *"We have 2,500 families":* "Noranda Aluminum Holding Corp.," *Manufacturing Today*, August 31, 2012.

158   *Bleeding the company dry:* Steve Gelsi, "Noranda, Which Earned Apollo a 3X Return, Gets Downgraded on Low Aluminum Prices," *Buyouts Insider*, August 26, 2015.

160   *Those were the stunning allegations in a 2007 lawsuit:* "Unsealed Lawsuit Claims Private Equity 'Collusion' at Blackstone, KKR, Bain Capital," *Chief Investment Officer,* October 11, 2012.

161   *Listen, for example, to:* Kaitlyn Kiernan, "4 Lessons From Carlyle's 7-Year Collusion Case," *Law 360*, September 2, 2014.

161   *And in a takeover of HCA:* Dahl v. Bain Capital Partners, LLC, et al., CIVIL ACTION NO.: 07-12388-EFH, U.S. District Court District of Massachusetts, March 12, 2013.

161   *Finally, in 2014 with the trial drawing near:* Dan Primack, "Private Equity's Giant Collusion Case Is Over, as Carlyle Folds," *Fortune*, August 29, 2014.

162   *Swarming the industry:* Ben Unglesbee, "The 'Explosion': When Private Equity Money Came for Retail," *Retail Dive,* November 8, 2018.

163   *Private equity "tends to drop retailers off a cliff":* Ben Unglesbee, "Retail's Largest Private Equity Buyouts and How They've Panned Out," *Retail Dive*, November 8, 2018.

163   *Seven major grocery chains backed by private equity:* Eileen Appelbaum and Rosemary Batt, "Private Equity Pillage: Grocery Stores and Workers at Risk," *American Prospect*, October 26, 2018.

163   *A 2019 analysis by the Private Equity Stakeholder Project:* "PE's Highly Leveraged Bet on Retail Puts a Million Jobs at Risk During the COVID-19 Crisis," Private Equity Stakeholder Project, July 10, 2020.

163   *Toys "R" Us paid $2.7 million in taxes:* Philip DeVencentis, "Toys R Us Bankruptcy May Hurt Wayne's Credit Rating, Moody's Says," NorthJersey.com, April 25, 2018.

164   *Another winner for the firm:* Rick Stouffer, "Investors Acquire GNC for $1.65B Cash," TribLIVE.com, February 10, 2007.

164 *The GNC trade generated more than:* Ibid.

164 *Just before the GNC score:* "Apollo Global Management Acquires Linens 'N' Things," Mergr M&A Deal Summary, February 1, 2006.

164 *Two years later, it was bankrupt:* "Linens 'n Things Files for Bankruptcy," Reuters, May 2, 2008.

164 *Apollo bought Claire's Stores:* "Apollo to Buy Claire's Stores for $3.1 Billion in Cash," CNBC.com, March 20, 2007.

164 *it, too, filed for bankruptcy:* Rebecca Shapiro, "Claire's Is Entering a New Chapter in Life: Bankruptcy," *HuffPost*, March 19, 2018.

164 *In April 2001, it launched its fifth investment fund:* Palico.com.

164 *Apollo also developed two new affiliates:* Palico.com and "Apollo Investment Corporation Announces Transformative Changes to Reinforce Position as a Pure Play Senior Secured Middle Market BDC," press release, August 2, 2022.

165 *Apollo had received a massive boost:* Jennifer Harris, "CalPERS Buys $600m Stake in Apollo," PERE News, January 22, 2013.

165 *All in, CalPERS invested:* "Private Equity Program Fund Performance Review," CalPERS website.

165 *But by 2009, CalPERS's $600 million:* Jacobius, "The Sun Doesn't Shine on Apollo."

165 *In April 2008, Apollo filed to sell:* Peter Lattman and Heidi Moore, "IPO for Apollo Management," *Wall Street Journal*, April 9, 2008.

166 *In its regulatory filing:* Michael de la Merced, "Apollo Struggles to Keep Debt From Sinking Linens 'n Things," *New York Times*, April 14, 2008.

166 *Back in the Show-Me State of Missouri:* Thomas Bradtke et al., "What Caused the Aluminum Industry's Crisis?," BCG Global, August 20, 2020.

167 *Most of its customers were nearby:* "Noranda Aluminum Holding Corp."

167 *Apollo cited the electricity contract:* Form S-1/A Noranda Aluminum Holding Corp., Securities and & Exchange Commission, January 15, 2010.

167 *"It's really all about making Noranda":* "Noranda Aluminum Holding Corp."

167 *On June 7, Noranda issued $220 million:* "New Issue—Noranda Aluminum Sells $220 mln 7.5-yr Toggle Notes," Reuters, June 5, 2007.

168 *During 2007, the year Apollo recouped:* Jonathan Hemingway, "2021 Wrap: Issuance Records Fall in Leveraged Finance as Q4 Caps Stunning Year," S&P Global Market Intelligence, December 18, 2021.

168 *Apollo was especially aggressive at this game:* "Leveraged Finance—US:

Tracking the Largest Private Equity Sponsors; LBO Credit Quality Is Weak, Bodes Ill for Next Downturn," Sector In-Depth, Moody's Investor Service, October 18, 2018.

168 *Earnings for the year ending December 31, 2008:* Form S-1/A Noranda Aluminum Holding Corp., Securities and & Exchange Commission, January 15, 2010.

169 *"Noranda is the crown jewel":* Testimony of Robert Mayer, August 28, 2008, before the Missouri Public Service Commission, Utility Division.

169 *After the firm submitted:* Roger Schwall, Securities & Exchange Commission, Noranda Aluminum Holding Corporation Registration Statement on Form S-1 Filed May 8, 2008, June 6, 2008.

169 *In April 2009, the Standard & Poor's ratings agency:* "S&P Cuts Noranda Aluminum Holding Facility," Reuters, May 7, 2009.

170 *The company took what it could get:* Geert de Lombaerde, "Noranda Slashes IPO Size," *Nashville Post*, September 27, 2022.

170 *A month later, the company sold:* "Apollo Will Sell 10M Shares of Noranda Aluminum," *AP News*, March 14, 2012.

170 *The company estimated:* "Noranda Aluminum Cuts 7 Percent of Workforce," *Tennessean*, December 18, 2013.

171 *It got an earful:* Public comments, Ameren Missouri-Investor (Electric), Noranda, No. ER-2014-0258 (n.d.).

171 *As the commission weighed Noranda's rate request:* Jeffrey Tomich, "In MO, Deep Divide Over Aluminum Maker's Plea for Rate Relief," *E&E News*, April 29, 2015.

171 *If it got the $25 million electricity reduction:* "Noranda to Lay Off 200 in Six Months," *Heartland News*, September 2, 2014.

172 *"It's a direct transfer of wealth":* Tomich, "In MO, Deep Divide."

172 *Another noteworthy stipulation:* Ibid.

172 *Noranda itself reaped no money:* Jacob Barker, "After Ameren Rate Cut, Noranda's Biggest Shareholder Sells Its Stake," *St. Louis Post-Dispatch*, May 13, 2015.

172 *Bankruptcy followed in February 2016:* "Noranda Aluminum Files for Bankruptcy," Reuters, February 8, 2016.

172 *"Plans had already been made":* Barker, "After Ameren Rate Cut."

172 *Because of the shortfall:* Jasmine Dell, "New Madrid R-1 School District Makes Up for Loss of Local Revenue," KFSV-12, August 16, 2016.

173 *"Yeah, that's about the best paying job around":* Barker, "After Ameren Rate Cut."

173 *After the Noranda smelter closed:* Brian Hauswirth, "Greitens: 'The

People of Southeast Missouri Are Ready to Work,'" missourinet.com, March 9, 2018.

173 *"But they are all so poor":* Karen Libby, "MO Gov Greitens Calls Special Session on SEMO Jobs," *Ozarks First,* May 18, 2017.

173 *Noranda's pensions, with 4,260 participants:* Objection by the Pension Benefit Guaranty Corporation, In Re Noranda Aluminum, IN THE UNITED STATES BANKRUPTCY COURT FOR THE EASTERN DIS-TRICT OF MISSOURI SOUTHEASTERN DIVISION, March 21, 2016.

173 *Gränges, a Swedish company:* "Gränges Acquires Noranda Aluminum's US Rolling Business," *Recycling Today,* August 25, 2016.

173 *The New Madrid smelter:* Geert De Lombaerde, "Noranda Has Deal to Sell Big Missouri Smelter," *Nashville Post,* October 3, 2016.

173 *Dallas Snider had headed the local steelworkers union:* Barker, "After Ameren Rate Cut."

CHAPTER TEN: "CAPITALISM ON STEROIDS"

175 *And with $2.16 trillion in expenditures:* Robert Pear, "Health Spending Exceeded Record $2 Trillion in 2006," *New York Times,* January 8, 2008.

175 *In 1970, for example, healthcare spending:* Bradley Sawyer, "Total Health Expenditures as Percent of GDP 1970-2017," Peterson KFF Health System Tracker, December 11, 2018, https://www.healthsystemtracker.org/chart /total-health-expenditures-as-percent-of-gdp-1970-2017-2/.

176 *The industry's business model:* Eileen Appelbaum and Rosemary Batt, "Private Equity Buyouts in Healthcare: Who Wins, Who Loses," Institute for New Economic Thinking, Working Paper No. 118, March 15, 2020.

176 *Some of the tactics were summarized:* "June 2021 Report to the Congress: Medicare and the Health Care Delivery System," MEDPAC, https://www .medpac.gov/document/june-2021-report-to-the-congress-medicare-and -the-health-care-delivery-system/.

177 *By 2021, some 11 percent:* Victoria Knight, "Congress, Feds Look Into Nursing Homes Owned by Private Equity," *Kaiser Health News,* April 22, 2022.

177 *As owners of these facilities:* Author interview with Laura Olson (Mor-genson).

177 *In 2011, for example:* "Private Investment Homes Sometimes Differed from Others in Deficiencies, Staffing, and Financial Performance," Government Accountability Office, July 2011.

178 *A 2017 academic study:* Aline Bos and Charlene Harrington, "What Happens to a Nursing Home Chain When Private Equity Takes Over? A Longitudinal Case Study," *The Journal of Healthcare Organization, Provision and Financing*, November 2017.

178 *Tony Chicotel, staff attorney:* Author interview with Tony Chicotel (Morgenson).

178 *In 2015, a trio of company insiders:* United States of America, ex rel. Christine Ribik, v. HCR ManorCare, Inc., Manor Care Inc., HCR Manor-Care Services, LLC, Heartland Employment Services, LLC, United States District Court for the Eastern District of Virginia, April 10, 2015.

179 *an investigation by the* Washington Post*:* Peter Whoriskey and Dan Keating, "Overdoses, Bedsores, Broken Bones: What Happened When a Private-Equity Firm Sought to Care for Society's Most Vulnerable," *Washington Post*, November 25, 2018.

179 *A year before, in a radio interview:* Ibid.

179 *Among the luminaries:* Oliver Burkeman and Julian Borger, "The Ex-President's Club," *Guardian*, October 31, 2001.

179 *Jay Powell is another example:* Christopher Leonard, "Jerome Powell's Fed Policies Have Boosted a System That Made Him Rich," *Fortune*, November 22, 2021.

180 *Carlyle has also been tarred by involvement in a high-profile pension scandal:* Danny Hakim, "Carlyle Settles with New York in Pension Case," *New York Times*, May 15, 2009.

181 *The July 2007 purchase appealed to Carlyle:* ManorCare, Form 10-K, Fiscal 2006.

181 *In response, Carlyle sent a "patients first" pledge:* "The Carlyle Group Issues 'Patients First' Pledge as Purchase of Nursing Home Company Manor Care Nears Completion," Carlyle Group press release, October 21, 2007.

181 *In 2008, as the financial crisis:* "Equity Firm Carlyle Calls 2008 a 'Humbling Experience,'" Reuters, May 29, 2009.

181 *In a deal generating $6.1 billion:* Megan Davies, "HCP and Carlyle's ManorCare in $6 Billion Asset Deal," Reuters, December 14, 2010.

182 *Now the company had to pay:* Eileen Appelbaum and Rosemary Batt, "The Role of Public REITs in Financialization and Industry Restructuring," Institute for New Economic Thinking, Working Paper 189, July 9, 2022.

182 *One of its earliest decisions:* "ManorCare to Lay Off Hundreds," *Toledo Blade*, September 10, 2011.

182 *Helping residents at the three ManorCare nursing facilities:* United States of America, ex rel. Christine Ribik, v. HCR ManorCare, Inc.

183 *"It was so easy to figure out the fraud":* Author interview Christine Ribik (Morgenson).

183 *ManorCare's abusive therapy sessions:* Ibid.

184 *This wasn't because ManorCare's patients had changed:* "Government Sues Skilled Nursing Chain HCR ManorCare for Allegedly Providing Medically Unnecessary Therapy," Department of Justice press release, April 21, 2015.

185 *In January 2010, for example:* Ibid.

185 *The allegations from Ribik:* Ibid .

186 *The 2018 investigation in the* Washington Post: ibid, Peter Whoriskey and Dan Keating, "Overdoses, Bedsores, Broken Bones: What Happened When a Private-Equity Firm Sought to Care for Society's Most Vulnerable," *Washington Post,* November 25, 2018.

186 *Responding to the* Post *investigation:* Ibid.

186 *By the time the DOJ took up:* United States of America, ex rel. Christine Ribik, v. HCR ManorCare, Inc.

187 *"We will not relent":* Ibid., "Government Sues Skilled Nursing Chain."

187 *But relent the DOJ did, just two years later:* Author interview, Jeffrey T. Downey (Morgenson).

188 *After all that she had done:* Author interview Christine Ribik (Morgenson).

188 *"Today, we are vindicated":* Alex Spanko, "DOJ Drops False Claims Act Case Against HCR ManorCare," *Skilled Nursing News,* November 9, 2017.

188 *Four months later:* Tracy Rucinski, "HCR ManorCare Files for Bankruptcy with $7.1 Billion in Debt," Reuters, March 5, 2018.

188 *It was purchased by ProMedica Senior Care:* Maggie Flynn, "Promedica CEO, ManorCare President Reveal Details of $70 Million Capital Plan," *Skilled Nursing News,* May 8, 2019.

189 *what ManorCare was accused of doing:* Gupta, Howell, Yannelis, and Gupta, "How Patients Fare When Private Equity Funds Buy Nursing Homes."

189 *Sabrina Howell, assistant professor of finance:* Author interview Sabrina Howell (Morgenson).

CHAPTER ELEVEN: CALL TO ACTION WENT UNHEEDED

191 *The healthcare gold rush began:* "Global Healthcare Private Equity and Corporate M&A Report 2020," Bain & Co.

191 *As the buyout mania spread:* "A Potential Influenza Pandemic: An Update on Possible Macroeconomic Effects and Policy Issues," Congressional Budget Office, May 22, 2006.

193 *In 2006, just a few months after:* "HCA Completes Merger with Private Investor Group," HCA press release, November 17, 2006.

194 *In 2010, just four years later:* David Whelan, "$2 Billion Dividend Means HCA Is Not Going Public This Year," *Forbes*, November 9, 2010.

194 *In August 2020, COVID-weary HCA nurses:* Cheryl Clark, "HCA Hospitals Accused of Requiring COVID-Infected Nurses to Work," *MedPage Today*, August 31, 2020.

194 *Jamelle Brown was an emergency department technician:* Gretchen Morgenson, "CEOs of Public U.S. Firms Earn 320 Times as Much as Workers," NBC News, April 7, 2021.

196 *By the time COVID arrived in 2020:* Gretchen Morgenson and Emmanuelle Saliba, "Private Equity Firms Now Control Many Hospitals, ERs and Nursing Homes. Is It Good for Health Care?," NBC News, May 13, 2020.

196 *On the books for decades, these statutes:* "Understanding the Corporate Practice of Medicine Doctrine," Nelson Hardiman Healthcare Lawyers, June 25, 2022, https://www.nelsonhardiman.com/hc-law-news/understanding-the-corporate-practice-of-medicine-doctrine-and-the-role-of-the-management-services-organization/.

197 *Both Envision and TeamHealth use:* Mitch Li and Robert McNamara, "The Reclamation of Emergency Medicine," Take Medicine Back, July 12, 2021.

197 *Some of the doctors who agree:* Gretchen Morgenson, "Doctor Fired from ER Warns About Effects of For-Profit Firms on U.S. Healthcare," NBC News, March 28, 2022.

198 *Envision forwards "operational documents":* Ibid.

198 *In a 2009 securities filing issued:* "State Laws Regarding Prohibition of Corporate Practice of Medicine and Fee Splitting Arrangements," Team Health Holdings, Form S-1, p. 84.

199 *The Blackstone spokesman downplayed:* Email correspondence with Blackstone, September 2022.

199 *A most disturbing example:* Morgenson, "Doctor Fired From ER."

202 *The physician was "more oppositional than supportive":* Raymond Brovont, M.D. v. KS-1 Medical Services et al, appeal from the Circuit Court of Jackson County, Missouri, October 13, 2020, in the Missouri Court of Appeals, Western District.

203 *A spokeswoman for Envision:* Ibid., Gretchen Morgenson, "Doctor Fired

from ER Warns About Effects of For-Profit Firms on U.S. Healthcare," NBC News, March 28, 2022.

203 *"The crisis of corporatization has really reached":* Author interview, Robert McNamara, MD (Morgenson).

204 *A group he is affiliated with sued Envision:* Gretchen Morgenson, "Doctors Sue Envision Healthcare, Say Private Equity-backed Firm Shouldn't Run ERs in California," NBC News, December 21, 2021.

205 *Medicare abuse in circumstances like these:* "EmCare, Inc. to Pay $29.8 Million to Resolve False Claims Act Allegations," Department of Justice press release, December 19, 2017.

206 *In 2015, for example, later disgraced New York attorney general Eric Schneiderman:* "A.G. Schneiderman Announces Settlement with Aspen Dental Management That Bars Company from Making Decisions About Patient Care in New York Clinics," New York Attorney General press release, June 18, 2015.

208 *For example, Sherif Z. Zaafran, MD:* Morgenson, "Doctor Fired from ER."

208 *In 2017, researchers at Yale University:* "Yale Study Sheds Light on 'Surprise' ER billing," Yale School of Public Health press release, November 17, 2016.

209 *They quietly created a phony grassroots entity:* Margot Sanger-Katz, Julie Creswell, and Reed Abelson, "Mystery Solved: Private-Equity-Backed Firms Are Behind Ad Blitz on 'Surprise Billing'" *New York Times,* September 13, 2019.

211 *These included urgent care centers:* "No Surprises Act," National Association of Insurance Commissioners, Center for Insurance Policy and Research, March 18, 2022, https://content.naic.org/cipr-topics/no-surprises-act.

211 *Blackstone's spokesman contended to us:* Email correspondence with Blackstone September 2022.

211 *In the deals, Envision shifted:* Bek R. Sunuu and Steve H. Wilkinson, "Credit FAQ: Envision Healthcare Corp.'s Two Major Restructurings in 100 Days," S&P Global Ratings, September 2, 2022, https://www.spglobal.com/ratings/en/research/articles/220902-credit-faq-envision-healthcare-corp-s-two-major-restructurings-in-100-days-12474331.

211 *As the* Harvard Business Review *reported:* Lovisa Gustafsson, Shanoor Seervai, and David Blumenthal, "The Role of Private Equity in Driving Up Health Care Prices," *Harvard Business Review,* October 29, 2019.

CHAPTER TWELVE: "LIKE WHEN HITLER INVADED POLAND IN 1939"

213 *Jazz had some drugs in development:* Jazz Pharmaceuticals, S-1 filing, March 9, 2007, p. 6.

213 *Against the $15 billion KKR counted in assets:* Eric Mogelof, KKR & Co. Investor Presentation, September 2021, p. 15. KKR's website lists Jazz as a 2004 acquisition, https://irpages2.eqs.com/download/companies/kkrinc /Presentations/KKR%20September%202021%20Investor%20Presenta tion.pdf.

213 *By 2007, KKR had three board seats:* Jazz Pharmaceuticals, DEF14A filing, April 28, 2008, p. 41.

214 *And in April 2005, before KKR finalized the deal, Jazz announced:* Daniel S. Levine, "Jazz Pharmaceuticals to Buy Orphan Medical for $122.6 million," *San Francisco Business Times*, April 19, 2005.

214 *"Orphan" drugs, as they are known:* "Orphan Drugs," FDA/CEDR, Small Business Chronicles, July 13, 2012, https://www.fda.gov/media/83372/ download.

214 *Orphan's main product was Xyrem:* "Treatment for Narcolepsy with Cataplexy and Excessive Daytime Sleepiness," https://www.xyrem.com.

214 *Also known as sodium oxybate:* "Stringent Rules for GHB for Narcoleptics," UPI, June 7, 2001.

215 *Still, the FDA required a so-called black box warning:* FDA Drug Safety Communication, June 17, 2012, https://www.fda.gov/drugs/drug-safety -and-availability/fda-drug-safety-communication-warning-against-use -xyrem-sodium-oxybate-alcohol-or-drugs-causing.

216 *A year later, in April 2006, Jazz received:* Jazz Pharmaceuticals, S-1 filing, March 9, 2007, p.14.

216 *"Indistinguishable from a carnival snake-oil salesman":* Alex Berenson, "Indictment of Doctor Tests Drug Marketing Rules," *New York Times*, July 22, 2006.

216 *for 2006, Jazz reported $45 million in sales:* Jazz Pharmaceuticals, S-1 filing, March 9, 2007, p. 41.

216 *Nevertheless, on June 1, 2007:* "Jazz Lowers Offering Price," Reuters, June 1, 2007.

216 *at the last moment the company had:* Alex Berenson, "Maker of Risky Narcolepsy Drug Plans IPO," *New York Times*, May 30, 2007.

217 *Six weeks later, more bad news:* Alex Berenson, "Maker of Narcolepsy Drug Pleads Guilty in U.S. Case," *New York Times*, July 14, 2007.

217 *It laid off 24 percent:* "Jazz Pharmaceuticals Cuts Another 71 Jobs, CFO Leaving," *Silicon Valley Business Journal*, December 15, 2008.

217 *Jazz also warned investors:* Jazz Pharmaceuticals 10-K, March 26, 2009, p. 47.

217 *But the most notorious price-gouger:* "'Pharma Bro' Martin Shkreli Is Ordered to Return $64 Million, Barred from Drug Industry," Associated Press, January 14, 2022.

218 *By 2010, Xyrem patients were paying four times:* Jim Edwards, "How a Sleeping Drug Company Increased Prices 300% Without Anyone Noticing," CBS News, November 12, 2010.

218 *Soon Jazz was reporting record sales:* Jazz Pharmaceuticals, Form 10-K, February 28, 2012, p. 56.

218 *Under the controversial deal:* Ibid., p. 1.

218 *Jazz was among KKR's top three performers:* KKR, Form 10-K, February 22, 2013, p. 103.

219 *By August 2021, the FDA had logged 27,000:* Virginia Hughes, "FDA Approves GHB, a 'Date Rape Drug' for Rare Sleeping Disorder," *New York Times*, August 12, 2021.

219 *As for Gleason:* Ronald E. Cramer, "The Administrative State and the Death of Peter Gleason, MD: An Off-Label Case Report," *Journal of Clinical Sleep Medicine*, March 15, 2019.

219 *In August 2021, a civil anti-trust:* Blue Cross and Blue Shield v. Jazz Pharmaceutical, United States District Court, Northern District of California. 3:20-cv-04667.

220 *As the debacle unfolded:* Gretchen Morgenson and Joshua Rosner, *Reckless Endangerment* (Times Books, 2011).

221 *Among those travelling:* Jon Flanders, Peter Lavinia, "Class Struggle Trumps Hate," *Jacobin*, May 12, 2017, https://jacobin.com/2017/05/trump -momentive-strike-white-workers-cwa.

221 *Blackstone's Schwarzman drew scorn:* "Inside Stephen Schwarzman's Birthday Bash," *New York Times*, February 14, 2007.

221 *This didn't stop Blackstone from issuing:* "The Blackstone Group Prices $4.133 Billion Initial Public Offering," Blackstone Group press release, June 21, 2007.

221 *Its top executives were now firmly:* The Blackstone Group, Form 10-K, March 12, 2008, p. 135.

222 *Still,* Forbes *pegged:* "The Complete List of World's Billionaires 2008," https://stats.areppim.com/listes/list_billionairesx08xwor.htm.

222 *Researchers studying the titans' returns:* "The Historical Impact of Economic Downturns on Private Equity," Neuberger Berman Private Equity

Team, May 13, 2022, https://www.nb.com/en/global/insights/the-historical -impact-of-economic-downturns-on-private-equity.

222 *In the first decade of the 2000s, according to Federal Reserve data:* Michael Ahn et al., "Household Debt-to-Income Ratios in the Enhanced Financial Accounts," Federal Reserve Board, January 2018.

222 *The law made it tougher for consumers:* Staff Reports, "Insolvency After the 2005 Bankruptcy Reform," Federal Reserve Bank of New York, April 2015.

223 *The average credit card debt per household:* Bill Fay, "The U.S. Consumer Debt Crisis," Debt.org, May 13, 2021.

223 *The wealth gap in the U.S. was widening:* "Rising Wealth Inequality: Causes, Consequences and Potential Responses."

223 *"It's a huge windfall":* John Ydstie, "Senate Seeks to Close Hedge Fund Tax Loophole," *Morning Edition,* NPR, June 14, 2010.

223 *Moreover, closing the loophole would generate:* Dan Harsha, "Closing Loopholes and Raising Revenue, New Tax Reforms Will Be Crucial to the Success of the Inflation Reduction Act," Harvard Kennedy School, August 16, 2022.

223 *The driving force behind all attempts:* Alec McGillis, "The Tax Break for Patriotic Billionaires," *New Yorker,* March 6, 2016.

224 *And Schwarzman of Blackstone chimed in:* Courtney Comstock, "Steve Schwarzman on Tax Increases: 'It's Like When Hitler Invaded Poland,'" *Business Insider,* August 16, 2010.

225 *In 2010, after a series of fits and starts:* KKR, Form 10-K, March 7, 2010, p. 205.

225 *But other investors had given Apollo's offering:* "Apollo Global Management: Red Flags in the S-I," Seeking Alpha, March 28, 2011.

225 *In 2010, for example, Apollo was forced:* "TPG and Apollo Said to Over-value Harrah's Stake Before Failed Public Offering," *YogoNet Gaming News,* November 25, 2010.

226 *In September 2010, the SEC created:* "Political Contributions by Certain Investment Advisers," Securities and Exchange Commission, September 13, 2010.

226 *Its first case came in 2014:* "SEC Charges Private Equity Firm with Pay-to-Play Violations Involving Political Campaign Contributions in Pennsylvania," SEC press release, June 20, 2014.

227 *Three years later, the SEC brought:* "10 Firms Violated Pay-to-Play Rule by Accepting Pension Fund Fees Following Campaign Contributions," SEC press release, January 17, 2017.

227 *From 2013 through the first half of 2018:* Securities and Exchange Commission, Orders Under Section 206A of the Investment Advisers Act of 1940 And Rule 206(4)-5€ Thereunder Granting an Exemption from Rule 206(4)-5(A)(1) Thereunder.

227 *In April 2016, an Apollo executive:* Securities and Exchange Commission Investment Advisers Act Release No. 5068; 803-00244, Apollo Management, L.P., November 28, 2018.

228 *In early 2019, the SEC let Apollo off:* Securities and Exchange Commission Investment Advisers Act of 1940 Release No. 5102 / January 28, 2019, in the Matter of Apollo Management, L.P., 9 W 57th Street New York, NY 10019.

228 *In 2019, for example:* SEC Comment Letter, Vanessa Countryman, Investment Adviser Association, August 9, 2019.

229 *Beginning in 2010, Apollo and its lawyers started working:* "Registered Funds Alert—The Evolution of Co-Investment Exemptive Orders and Why They Should Become Extinct," Simpson Thacher, October 2018.

229 *"In the exhaustive study of the industry":* "Protecting Investors: A Half Century of Investment Company Regulation," Securities and Exchange Commission, Division of Investment Management, May 1992.

230 *This case was no different: lawyers for Apollo:* IBID, "Registered Funds Alert," Simpson Thacher.

230 *Finally, in March 2016:* Ibid.

CHAPTER THIRTEEN: "MONEY FOR NOTHING"

232 *Taminco makes something called alkylamines:* Industry ARC, Alkylamines Market—Forecast (2022-2027), https://www.industryarc.com/Research/Alkylamines-Market-Research-500133.

232 *Owned since 2014 by the Eastman Chemical:* "Taminco Corporation Announces Definitive Agreement to Be Acquired by Eastman Chemical Company," Taminco press release, September 11, 2014.

232 *Under one of its private equity masters:* Cam Simpson, "U.S. Chemical Companies Face Few Legal Risks, and the Cartels Bank On It," *Bloomberg News*, December 1, 2020.

233 *CVC Capital is a big private equity firm:* Mergr M&A Deal Summary, July 4, 2007. https://mergr.com/cvc-capital-partners-acquires-taminco

233 *Immediately after the purchase:* Simpson, "U.S. Chemical Companies Face Few Legal Risks."

233 *By the time prosecutors made their case:* "Allentown Company Agrees to Pay Fines and Penalties Totaling $1.3 Million for Violating Procedures Related to Chemical Shipments," Department of Justice press release, October 27, 2015.

233 *Taminco was then owned by Apollo:* Mergr M&A Deal Summary, December 16, 2011, https://mergr.com/apollo-global-management-acquires-taminco.

233 *Taminco had 820 employees:* Form S-1 Registration Statement, Taminco Acquisition Corp., December 3, 2012, p. 92.

233 *As such, by law Taminco had to confirm:* Simpson, "U.S. Chemical Companies Face Few Legal Risks."

233 *As prosecutors later learned:* "Allentown Company Sentenced for Violating Procedures Related to Chemical Shipments," Department of Justice press release, November 20, 2015.

234 *In August 2011, a few months before Apollo:* "Allentown Company Agrees to Pay Fines and Penalties."

234 *The firm installed five directors:* Form DEF 14A, April 23, 2014, p. 9.

234 *But Apollo made out well:* Simpson, "U.S. Chemical Companies Face Few Legal Risks."

234 *That offering was not as lucrative:* "Taminco Prices IPO at $15, Below $18-20 Range," Nasdaq.com, April 17, 2013.

234 *After selling 10 million shares:* Form DEF 14A, April 23, 2014, p. 7.

234 *Every year Apollo owned Taminco:* "Management Fee Agreement Among Taminco Global Chemical Corporation, Taminco Acquisition Corporation and Apollo Management VII, L.P.," February 15, 2012, p. 2; exhibit 10.6 to S-1A filing, February 8, 2013.

234 *Taminco also paid $14.6 million to Apollo Global Securities:* Taminco Global Chemical Corp., Form S-1A filing, February 8, 2013, p. F-52.

235 *Most egregious of all, though:* Taminco Corp., Form 10-K, February 28, 2014, p. F-32.

235 *Consider the monitoring fees racked up:* Eileen Appelbaum, "How Private Equity Firms Defraud Investors by Extracting 'Fees' from Their Portfolio Companies," *Forbes*, April 29, 2014.

236 *And the payments* exceeded *Taminco's net income:* Taminco Corp, Form 10-K, February 28, 2014, p. 31.

236 *In September 2014, Apollo flipped:* "Taminco Corporation Announces Definitive Agreement to Be Acquired by Eastman Chemical Company," Taminco Corp. press release, September 11, 2014.

236 *emerged just:* Simpson, "U.S. Chemical Companies Face Few Legal Risks."

236 *When the Justice Department filed:* "Allentown Company Agrees to Pay Fines and Penalties."

236 *Eastman wound up on the hook:* Ibid.

237 *In 2015, the SEC launched:* "SEC Issues Devastating Risk Alert on Private Equity Abuses; Effectively Admits Failure of Last 5+ Years of Enforcement," *Private Equity Insights*, June 26, 2020, https://pe-insights.com/news/2020/06/26/sec-issues-devastating-risk-alert-on-private-equity-abuses-effectively-admits-failure-of-last-5-years-of-enforcement/.

237 *In the crosshairs because of its monitoring fee practices:* "Blackstone Charged with Disclosure Failures," SEC press release, October 7, 2015.

237 *And Apollo had to pay:* "Apollo Charged with Disclosure and Supervisory Failures," SEC press release, August 23, 2016.

237 *After the SEC brought the cases:* Email correspondence with Blackstone spokesman, September 2022.

237 *The SEC said Apollo had not told its own investors:* Ibid.

237 *Apollo agreed to cease and desist:* Ibid.

238 *But the scrutiny provided a business opportunity:* "As Heavier SEC Scrutiny Looms, Private Equity Regulator Igor Rozenblit Launches Consultancy," *Private Funds* CFO, June 24, 2021.

238 *The Pennsylvania Public School Employees' Retirement System:* Joseph N. DiStefano, "Pa. Pension Board Hires Apollo, a Fund with a History," *Philadelphia Inquirer*, June 19, 2017.

238 *Not according to an analysis:* Ibid.

239 *Analyzing $500 billion of investments:* Christine Idzelis, "$45 Billion: That's What This Study Says Pensions Lost in Private Equity Gains," *Institutional Investor*, February 25, 2020.

239 *In fact, employees earning between $150,000 and $1 million:* Executive Summary, Fourteenth Annual Private Equity & Venture Capital Compensation Report, https://privateequitycompensation.com/executive-summary/.

240 *In the late 1980s, only 4 percent of public companies:* Ryan Niladri Banerjee and Boris Hofmann, "Corporate Zombies: Anatomy and Life Cycle," Bank for International Settlements Working Papers, No. 882, September 5, 2020.

CHAPTER FOURTEEN: "OPPRESSING INDIGENOUS PEOPLE"

241 *"My water bill is $900!!!!":* "Affordable Water for All Bayonne Residents," iPetitions, https://www.ipetitions.com/petition/affordable-water-bay1?loc=view-petition.

241 *With a median household income:* United States Census Bureau, Quick Facts, Bayonne, NJ, July 1, 2021, https://www.census.gov/quickfacts /bayonnecitynewjersey.

242 *The private equity colossus:* Andrew Vitelli, "KKR Makes Splash with U.S. Water PPP Exits," *Infrastructure Investor*, January 26, 2018.

242 *Like Apollo, which cited:* "KKR 2014 ESG and Citizenship Report, Bay-onne Water and Wastewater Concession, a Public-Private Partnership," https://kkresg.com/assets/uploads/pdfs/case-studies/2014/KKR_ESG _2014_CaseStudies_ALL_v3.pdf .

242 *The deal guaranteed 11 percent:* Daniel Israel, "Board of Education Trustee Jodi Casais Leads Effort to Investigate Bayonne's Water Contract," *Hudson Reporter*, January 31, 2022.

242 *Then, six years later:* Vitelli, "KKR Makes Splash."

242 *Still, KKR didn't leave the scene entirely:* Daniel Israel, "Come Hell or High Water," *Hudson Reporter*, May 19, 2021.

243 *Ratepayers had to make up the difference:* Ibid.

243 *Not surprisingly, between 2012 and 2021:* Daniel Israel, "Will Bayonne Drown in Rising Water Bills?" *Hudson Reporter*, July 1, 2021.

243 *A 2021 report by the Association of Environmental Authorities:* Peggy Gallos, Executive Director, "Why Ratepayers Protections Are Needed in the U.S. Water Utility Privatization Push," Association of Environmental Authorities, October 21, 2021.

244 *As public outcry over Bayonne's water debacle:* Israel, "Board of Educa-tion Trustee Jodi Casais."

244 *Now director of Homeland Security for the Hudson County Sheriff's Office:* John Heinis, "Letter: Bayonne's Deal with United Water/KKR Wasn't Done in a Backroom & Was Necessary," *Hudson County View*, February 1, 2022.

244 *To get out of it, Bayonne would have to pay:* Israel, "Board of Education Trustee Jodi Casais."

245 *"Please break this contract":* Ibid., "Affordable Water for all Bayonne Res-idents," iPetitions.

245 *Another highlight, believe it or not:* KKR 2012 ESG and Citizenship Re-port: Case Study, "Toys R Us: Building Tools to Build Careers," https:// kkresg.com/assets/uploads/pdfs/case-studies/2012/toys-r-us.pdf.

245 *KKR took Toys private in 2005:* Parija Bhatnagar, "Group to Buy Toys 'R' Us for $6.6B," CNN Money, March 17, 2005.

245 *"The company is proud to support":* Ibid., KKR 2012 ESG and Citizenship Report: Case Study, "Toys R Us: Building Tools to Build Careers," https:// kkresg.com/assets/uploads/pdfs/case-studies/2012/toys-r-us.pdf.

245 *Five years later, Toys "R" Us was in bankruptcy:* Lauren Hirsch, "Toys R Us Files for Bankruptcy Protection," CNBC.com, September 18, 2017.

246 *Only after the firms were shamed:* Ben Unglesbee, "Toys R Us Owners Announce $20M Employee Fund," *Retail Dive*, October 1, 2018.

246 *Asked about its role in the failure:* Matthew Heller, "PE Firms' Role in Toys 'R' Us Collapse Questioned," *CFO*, July 9, 2018.

246 *Brian Ayash, the finance professor:* Ibid., Ayash and Rostad, *Leveraged Buyouts and Financial Distress.*

246 *"Responsible investment is a way of doing business":* Elizabeth Seeger, "What Does Responsible Investment Mean to KKR?," LinkedIn, August 9, 2018, https://www.linkedin.com/pulse/what-does-responsible-investment -mean-kkr-elizabeth-seeger/.

247 *In 2019, when KKR took a controlling interest:* Gretchen Morgenson, "Some Say a Local Bitcoin Mining Operation Is Ruining One of the Finger Lakes. Here's How," NBC News, July 5, 2021.

247 *KKR invested in the $6 billion project:* Ibid.

247 *Unlike Native American tribes in the U.S.:* Author interview with Sleydo' (Morgenson).

247 *"By violating our ability to be a self-determining people":* Ibid.

248 *A report by the Yellowhead Institute:* Hayden King, Sheri Pasternak, and Riley Yesno, "Land Back," A Yellowhead Institute Red Paper, October 2019.

248 *In late 2021, the Coastal Gaslink conflict:* Author interview with Sleydo' (Morgenson).

248 *In the fall of 2020, the project failed to comply:* Morgenson, "Some Say a Local Bitcoin Mining Operation."

249 *This followed two diesel spills:* Amanda Follett Hosgood, "Coastal Gaslink Fined $72,500 for Environmental Infractions," *The Tyee*, February 25, 2022.

249 *Even as the firm claims to be an environmentally aware investor:* Morgenson, "Some Say a Local Bitcoin Mining Operation."

249 *Between 2010 and 2020, private equity firms committed almost $2 trillion:* Ibid.

249 *As of October 2021, ten of the top:* "Private Equity Climate Risks: Scorecard 2022," Private Equity Stakeholder Project, September 21, 2022.

250 *Because private equity firms are so secretive:* Author interview with Alyssa Giachino (Morgenson).

250 *The Coastal Gaslink project has generated:* Ibid., Morgenson, "Some Say a Local Bitcoin Mining Operation."

250 *Along with students at the four other Claremont Colleges:* Jenna

McMurtry, "Students Demonstrate Against CMC Trustees' Fossil Fuels Investments," *Student Life*, October 8, 2021.

250 *Malcolm McCann, a student at Pitzer:* Ibid.

250 *So said a 2019 report published:* Victoria Tauli, "Indigenous People Are Guardians of Global Biodiversity—But We Need Protection Too," Reuters Events, May 7, 2019, https://www.reutersevents.com/sustainability /indigenous-people-are-guardians-global-biodiversity-we-need-protection -too.

251 *KKR's spokeswoman said the firm:* Morgenson, "Some Say a Local Bitcoin Mining Operation."

251 *Peter Dien, a Claremont College student:* McMurtry, "Students Demonstrate Against CMC."

251 *As for the Coastal Gaslink project, KKR's spokeswoman said:* Email with Kristi Huller, KKR spokeswoman, October 28, 2022.

251 *It's important to note that:* Mark Armoa, "Canada Sides with Pipeline, Violating Wet'suet'en Laws—And Its Own," *Grist*, November 18, 2021. https://grist.org/indigenous/wetsuweten-land-defenders/.

252 *Its 2021 annual report said:* KKR, Form 10-K for year ending December 31, 2021, February 28, 2022, p. 12.

253 *Not all private equity firms are pillagers:* Author interview with Clark Williams-Derry (Morgenson).

253 *In 2016, for instance, the private equity firm ArcLight Capital Partners:* Morgenson, "Some Say a Local Bitcoin Mining Operation."

253 *In July 2021, the Justice Department filed a complaint:* "United States Files Complaint and Reaches Agreement on Stipulation with Limetree Bay Terminals LLC," Department of Justice press release, July 12, 2021.

253 *"Private equity thinks it can squeeze":* Author interview with Tyson Slocum (Morgenson).

254 *The soot from coal-fired power plants:* Sarah McQuate, "Emissions from Electricity Generation Lead to Disproportionate Number of Premature Deaths for Some Racial Groups," *University of Washington News*, November 20, 2019.

254 *In 2015, for example, KKR and three other investors:* "As Climate Change Requires Cuts to Coal, Private Equity Buys More," Private Equity Stakeholder Project, June 12, 2020.

254 *Seven years later, it would file for bankruptcy a second time:* Ibid.

254 *When it went bankrupt the first time:* "A Closer Look at the Longview Power Bankruptcy," Fox Rothchild LLC, Delaware Bankruptcy Update, September 8, 2013.

254 *"The plant liked to advertise itself"*: Author interview with Jim Kotcon (Morgenson).

254 *Mothballing the plant would eliminate:* Economic Value, Longview Power website, https://longviewpower.com/economic-value

255 *In August 2022, Moody's Investors Service:* "Longview Power, LLC—Moody's Upgrades Longview Power, LLC's Senior Secured Term Loan to B3 from Caa1; Outlook Is Stable," August 18, 2022.

255 *KKR went so deep into fossil fuels over the years:* PrivCap interview with Marc Lipschultz, KKR's head of energy and infrastructure, April 2013.

255 *KKR kicked off an immense undertaking in shale oil and fracking:* KKR Annual Report 2010, "The Power of Partnership," East Resources.

255 *Just a year later, KKR and Pegula sold:* Ibid.

255 *In June 2010, KKR put $400 million:* "KKR Forms Shale Partnership with Hilcorp," Reuters, June 13, 2010.

255 *KKR received $1.13 billion:* "KKR to Exit Investment in Eagle Ford Shale in Connection with Sale of HilCorp Resources to Marathon Oil," KKR press release, June 1, 2011.

255 *The biggest debacle for the firm was:* David Carey, "KKR Burnt by Collapse in Energy Prices," *Australian Financial Review*, August 19, 2015.

256 *Seven years later, Energy Future Holdings collapsed:* Ibid.

256 *KKR's third energy bankruptcy:* Ibid.

256 *Between Energy Future Holdings and Samson Resources:* Ibid.

256 *Samson Resources has been subject to fines:* Alyssa Giachino, "KKR Energy Investments Troubled by Racial Injustice and Financial Losses," Private Equity Stakeholder Project, April 2021.

257 *In 2020, the company spilled more than twenty-one hundred barrels:* Ibid.

CHAPTER FIFTEEN: "HIDING IN THE BACKGROUND, RARELY HELD TO ACCOUNT"

258 *According to the Centers for Medicare and Medicaid Services:* Briggs Net News, September 29, 2022, https://briggshealthcare.blog/2022/09/29/latest-cms-cdc-and-nhsn-nursing-home-covid-19-data-8/.

258 *Some 70 percent of the nation's nursing homes:* Centers for Disease Control and Prevention, National Center for Health Statistics, https://www.cdc.gov/nchs/fastats/nursing-home-care.htm.

259 *Tony Chicotel, staff attorney at California Advocates for Nursing Home Reform:* Author interview with Tony Chicotel (Morgenson).

259 *As soon as COVID struck, Deb Timms became concerned:* Author interview, Deb Tims (Morgenson).

260 *Gilroy is part of Covenant Care, a nursing home company:* Covenant Care website, https://www.covenantcare.com/about/.

260 *The death rate at the 134-bed Gilroy facility:* Centers for Medicare and Medicaid Services data, https://data.cms.gov/covid-19/covid-19-nursing-home-data/data.

260 *Government data shows a surge in September 2020:* Ibid.

260 *As of March 2022, Gilroy held a 3-star rating:* Medicare.gov, Nursing Home Comparison website, https://www.medicare.gov/care-compare/#search.

260 *During the spring of 2021, when Wanda Malik moved her mother:* Author interview with Wanda Malik (Morgenson).

261 *In 2021, COVID deaths totaled 19.6 percent:* Centers for Medicare and Medicaid Services data.

261 *Ten years earlier, for example, the Government Accountability Office:* "Private Investment Homes Sometimes Differed from Others."

262 *Another study, in 2017:* Bos and Harrington, "What Happens to a Nursing Home Chain."

262 *Increased emergency room visits:* Amy Stulick, "Private Equity Ownership Linked to Higher Medicare Costs, Increased Hospitalization," *Skilled Nursing News*, November 21, 2021.

262 *A 2020 analysis of New Jersey nursing homes:* "Report: The Deadly Combination of Private Equity and Nursing Homes During a Pandemic," Americans for Financial Reform, August 6, 2020.

262 *The Long Term Care Community Coalition:* Dara Valanejad, Richard J. Mollott, and Eric Goldwein, "Meaningful Safeguards, Promising Practices and Recommendations for Evaluating Nursing Home Owners," Long Term Care Community Coalition, March 9, 2020.

263 *Over 1.4 million Medicare beneficiaries:* "Nursing Homes," United States Department of Health and Human Services, Office of the Inspector General, September 19, 2022.

263 *Eddie Martinez found this out firsthand:* Author interview with Eddie Martinez (Morgenson).

264 *Helene Luna is one:* Author interview with Helene Luna (Morgenson).

265 *Another former worker at the facility:* Confidential interview.

266 *Her death at Pacific Coast Manor was one of fourteen total COVID-related fatalities:* Centers for Medicare and Medicaid Services data.

267 *The U.S. has six thousand hospitals currently:* Fast Facts on US Hospi-

tals, 2022, American Hospital Association website, https://www.aha.org
/statistics/fast-facts-us-hospitals.

267 *Alteon Health, a private equity–backed healthcare staffing company:* Lev
Facher, "Amid Coronavirus, Private Equity-Backed Company Slashes Benefits for Emergency Room Doctors," *Stat*, April 1, 2020.

268 *The buyer? US Acute Care Solutions:* "US Acute Care Solutions Acquires
Alteon Health," Acute Care Solutions press release, February 21, 2022.

268 *"Private equity–backed health care has been a disaster":* Author interview
with Mark Reiter (Morgenson).

268 *Consider what occurred on April 2, 2020:* Morgenson and Saleba, "Private
Equity Now Controls Many Hospitals, ERs, and Nursing Homes."

268 *It "completely took out an entire level of service":* Author interview with
Audra Sprague (Morgenson).

268 *Before a hospital can discontinue a service:* "Hospital Essential Service Closures," Massachusetts Division of Healthcare Facility Licensure and Cer-
tification, Mass.gov website, https://www.mass.gov/info-details/hospital
-essential-service-closures.

269 *A 2021 study by Tong Liu:* Tong Liu, "Bargaining with Private Equity: Im-
plications for Hospital Prices and Patient Welfare," the Wharton School,
November 2021.

270 *As COVID raged in 2020 and 2021, so too did the dealmakers:* Kaitlyn
Dunn, Josphe Laska, and John LeBlanc, "Spotlight on Private Equity for
FCA Enforcement in 2022," Manatt, Phelps & Phillips, LLC, https://www
.jdsupra.com/legalnews/spotlight-on-private-equity-for-fca-7787443.

270 *Academics at the University of California, Hastings College of Law:*
Katherine L. Gudiksen, Alexandra D. Montague, Jaime S. King, Amy Y.
Gu, Brent D. Fulton, and Thomas L. Greaney, "Preventing Anticompetitive Contracting Practices in Healthcare Markets," The Petris Center
and The Source on Healthcare Price and Competition, September 2020.
https://petris.org/the-source-publishes-report-preventing-anticompetitive
-contracting-practices-in-healthcare-markets/.

270 *Under federal rules, companies making acquisitions:* "FTC Announces
Annual Update of Size of Transaction Thresholds for Premerger Notifi-
cation Filings and Interlocking Directorates," Federal Trade Commission
press release, January 24, 2022.

271 *From 2011 to 2019, private equity ownership of hospices tripled:* Molly
Redden, "Private Equity Is Gobbling Up Hospice Chains and Getting Involved in the Business of Dying," *HuffPost*, December 21, 2021.

271 *Indeed, between 2013 and 2020:* "Money for Nothing: How Private Equity Has Defrauded Medicare, Medicaid, and Other Government Health Programs, and How That Might Change," Eileen O'Grady, Private Equity Stakeholder Project, February 2021.

271 *About 51 percent of all Medicare recipients:* MedPAC Report, "Hospice Services," March 15, 2021, https://www.medpac.gov/document/chapter-11 -hospice-services-march-2021-report/.

271 *Melissa Aldridge, vice-chair of research:* "Hospice Tax Status and Ownership Matters for Patients and Families," *JAMA Internal Medicine*, August 1, 2021.

272 *Acquired by the Blackstone Group in 2008:* "Blackstone Completes Acquisition of Apria Healthcare Group Inc.," Blackstone Group press release, October 28, 2008.

272 *By 2021, three Blackstone executives served:* Apria, Inc., Form S-1, January 15, 2021, pp. 124-125.

272 *First was an $18.7 million transaction fee:* Merger agreement between Blackstone Management Partners V LLC and Apria Healthcare Group, Section 1, June 18, 2008.

272 *Then came the management fees:* Ibid., Section 4.

273 *Going forward, Apria had to pay Blackstone annual management fees of either $7 million:* Ibid.

273 *In 2007, prior to its acquisition by Blackstone:* Apria Healthcare Group, Form 10-K/A, September 11, 2008, p. F-4.

273 *That performance continued:* Apria Healthcare Group, Form 10-K, March 11, 2013, p. 38.

273 *Apria's losses under Blackstone are germane:* United States of America et al., ex rel. Martinez, v. Apria Healthcare Group, Inc. and Apria Healthcare LLC, Complaint in Intervention of the United States, United States District Court for the Southern District of New York, December 21, 2020.

273 *These missed visits were "widely recognized within Apria":* Ibid.

273 *The Justice Department's allegations:* Ibid.

274 *In April 2014, after years under Blackstone's ownership:* Ibid.

274 *And so, in August of that year, senior executives:* Ibid.

274 *Salespeople who generated large numbers of new users:* Ibid.

275 *To maximize the number of non-invasive ventilator:* Ibid.

275 *Its personnel didn't conduct regular visits:* Ibid.

275 *Apria submitted thousands of false claims:* Ibid.

275 *In December 2020, amid the pandemic, Apria settled:* "Acting Manhattan

U.S. Attorney Announces $40.5 Million Settlement with Durable Medical Equipment Provider Apria Healthcare for Fraudulent Billing Practices," Department of Justice press release, December 21, 2020.

275 *Apria entered into a corporate integrity agreement:* Corporate Integrity Agreement Between the Office of Inspector General of the Department of Health and Human Services, Apria Healthcare Group, Inc., and Apria Healthcare LLC, December 14, 2020.

276 *The Apria matter was the second time prosecutors:* "Vanguard Health Systems, Inc. Agrees to Pay $2.9 Million to Settle False Claims Act Allegations," Department of Justice press release, June 15, 2015.

277 *"Private equity can do terrible, terrible things":* Author interview with Laura Olson (Morgenson).

277 *In February 2021, a few months after Apria's settlement:* "Apria Announces Pricing of Initial Public Offering," Apria Inc., press release, February 10, 2021.

277 *By November of that year, Blackstone had reaped:* Apria Inc., Form S-1, November 8, 2021, p. 29.

277 *Between 2017 and 2021, regulatory filings show:* Apria Inc., Form 10-K, March 1, 2022, and Apria Inc., Form S-1, January 15, 2021.

278 *In spite of the fraud allegations:* Email correspondence with Blackstone spokesman Matthew Anderson (Morgenson).

CHAPTER SIXTEEN: "SPECIAL AND SYMBIOTIC"

280 *Starting in 2009, Apollo had set out to create:* Juan Carlos Arancibia, "Athene Continues Rapid Climb from Its IPO," *Investors Business Daily*, December 30, 2016.

280 *Just as Executive Life had done, Athene would specialize:* Athene website landing page, https://www.athene.com/.

280 *The insurer would also buy up billions of dollars of pension obligations:* "Athene Announces $4.9 Billion Pension Risk Transfer Transaction with Lockheed Martin," Apollo press release, August 3, 2021; "Athene Completes Significant Pension Risk Transfer Transaction with JCPenney," Apollo Press Release, April 1, 2021.

280 *In 2019, for example, the investment management fees:* Gretchen Morgenson, "As Insurance Companies Take Over Pension Plans, Are Your Payments At Risk?" NBC News, June 14, 2020.

281 *In October 2019, Black said as much:* "Athene and Apollo Announce

Transaction to Strengthen Strategic Relationship and Eliminate Athene's Multi-Class Share Structure," Apollo press release, October 28, 2019.

281 *In 2020, Athene Annuity & Life, the main insurer in Athene Holding's universe:* Morgenson, "As Insurance Companies Take Over Pension Plans."

282 *By contrast, Athene competitor:* Ibid.

282 *Athene reported that its 7 percent ownership stake in Apollo:* Ibid.

282 *For example, Athene was aggressive with the reinsurers it used:* Ibid.

282 *And unlike other, more conservative insurers:* Ibid.

282 *In 2020, 95 percent of Athene Annuity & Life's reinsurance:* Ibid.

282 *For a comparison, New York Life Insurance Company:* Ibid.

283 *Athene Holding, the parent company, and its reinsurers:* Ibid.

283 *Athene's annual Bermuda filings:* Ibid.

283 *Indeed, a lawsuit filed on behalf:* Mark Vandevelde and Sujeet Indap, "Bermuda Court Orders Halt to US Lawsuit Against Apollo," *Financial Times,* July 15, 2019.

283 *James Belardi, a former executive at Sun Life America:* Jim Belardi, "Our People," Apollo biography, https://www.apollo.com/about-apollo/our -people/jim-belardi.

284 *"When you look at the business model these guys use":* Zachary Mider, "Apollo-to-Goldman Embracing Insurers Spurs State Concerns," *Bloomberg News,* April 22, 2013, https://www.bloomberg.com/news /articles/2013-04-22/apollo-to-goldman-embracing-insurers-spurs-state -concerns?sref=lnrir5K3.

284 *By 2013, it had bought out three other large insurers:* "Athene Holding Ltd. to Acquire Aviva's U.S. Annuity and Life Business," Athene press release, December 21, 2012; "Athene Holding Ltd. to Acquire Liberty Life Insurance Company," *PR Newswire,* October 22, 2010; "Athene Holding Ltd. Acquires Investors Insurance Corp., Will Target Retail Fixed Annuity Sales," *Business Wire,* July 19, 2011.

284 *Four years later, in 2017, Athene began buying:* Morgenson, "As Insurance Companies Take Over Pension Plans."

285 *Research from AM Best, a top insurance rating firm:* Jennifer Johnson and Jean-Baptiste Carelus, "Private Equity Owned U.S. Insurer Investments as of Year End 2020, Capital Markets Special Report," National Association of Insurance Commissioners, 2021.

285 *In 2013, the National Association of Insurance Commissioners:* Leah Campbell and Allison J. Tam, "NAIC to Consider Private Equity Investments in Life and Annuity Insurers," Client Memorandum, Willkie Farr & Gallagher, May 20, 2013.

285 *The U.S. Treasury registered its own worries:* "Annual Report on the Insurance Industry," Federal Insurance Office, U.S. Department of the Treasury, September 2014, https://home.treasury.gov/system/files/311/2014_Annual_Report.pdf.

285 *Even the normally somnambulant Federal Reserve Board:* Nathan Foley-Fisher, Nathan Heinrich, and Stephane Verani, "Are Life Insurers the New Shadow Banks?," SSRN, September 10, 2021, https://papers.ssrn.com/sol3/papers.cfm?abstract_id=3534847.

285 *As a report in* Pensions & Investments *noted at the time:* Sonali Basak and David Carey, "As Apollo's Cash Cow Plans IPO, Questions Linger on Ties," *Bloomberg News*, November 28, 2016, https://www.bloomberg.com/news/articles/2016-11-28/as-apollo-s-cash-cow-plans-ipo-questions-linger-on-close-ties?sref=lnrir5K3.

286 *Joseph M. Belth is professor emeritus:* Author interview with Joseph Belth (Morgenson).

287 *By mid-2022, almost four hundred ten thousand:* "Pension Group Annuities," Athene website, https://www.athene.com/pension-group-annuities.

287 *"Participants covered by this transaction can be confident":* "Athene Announces $4.9 Billion Pension Risk."

288 *A 1998 lawsuit filed on behalf of fifteen hundred beneficiaries of an RJR Nabisco pension:* Bussian v. RJR Nabisco Inc, 21 F. Supp. 2d 680 (S.D. Tex. 1998) No. CIV.A. H-91-1533, United States District Court, S.D. Texas, September 2, 1998, https://law.justia.com/cases/federal/district-courts/FSupp2/21/680/2577701/.

288 *In the fall of 1986, Nabisco's board of directors:* Ibid.

289 *Shocked by the harm they'd suffered:* Ibid.

289 *The judge hearing the case in the Southern District Court of Texas:* Ibid.

290 *In March 2021, Apollo and Athene merged:* "Apollo and Athene to Merge in All-Stock Transaction," Apollo press release, March 8, 2021, https://www.apollo.com/media/press-releases/2021/03-08-2021-120032339.

290 *Athene's Annuity and Life Co. had just signed:* Official Order of the Texas Commissioner of Insurance, Athene Annuity and Life Company, 7700 Mills Civic Pkwy, West Des Moines, Iowa 50266-3862, Consent Order TDI Enforcement File No. 13589, February 1, 2021, https://www.tdi.texas.gov/commissioner/disciplinary-orders/documents/20216674.pdf.

290 *A year earlier, New York's Department of Financial Services had settled:* Annual Report 2020, New York State Department of Financial Services, p. 10, https://www.dfs.ny.gov/system/files/documents/2021/10/dfs_annual_rpt_2020.pdf .

291 *Finally, in September 2021, concerns about what the privateers:* Letter to Marty Walsh, Secretary, Department of Labor, September 16, 2021, from Michael W. Frerichs, Illinois State Treasurer; Sarah Godlewski, Wisconsin State Treasurer; and David L. Young, Colorado State Treasurer, https://www.apolloathenewatch.org/wp-content/uploads/20210916-Treasurer-Letter-to-DoL-Sec.-Walsh.pdf.

291 *By the following summer, the NAIC working group had compiled recommendations:* "Turning Up the Magnification: Regulators Have PeControlled Insurers Under the Microscope (Again)," *National Law Review* XII, no. 275 (October 2, 2022).

292 *In a note to its clients:* "NAIC Developments on Private Equity Ownership of Insurers," Client Alert, Willkie Farr & Gallagher, July 11, 2022, www.willkie.com/-/media/files/publications/2022/naicdevelopments onprivateequityownershipofinsurers.pdf.

CHAPTER SEVENTEEN: "NO EVIDENCE OF WRONGDOING"

293 *As Tony James, Blackstone's president, told reporters:* Transcript, Blackstone First Quarter 2017 Earnings Media Call, April 20, 2017, https://s23.q4cdn.com/714267708/files/doc_events/BLACKSTONE-Q1-2017-Media-Call-Transcript.pdf.

293 *Stephen Schwarzman, James's partner, became one of Trump's key economic advisors:* Israan Srivastava, "Stephen Schwarzman, '69, to Advise Trump," *Yale Daily News*, December 5, 2016.

293 *Between July 19, 2020, and March 2021, Schwarzman gave almost $6 million to Trump and PACs:* "Blackstone's Stephen Schwarzman Has Repeatedly Supported Donald Trump Despite His Growing Hate Speech, Calls for Violence, and Authoritarianism," Private Equity Stakeholder Project, January 13, 2021, https://pestakeholder.org/news/blackstones-stephen-schwarzman-has-repeatedly-supported-donald-trump-despite-his-growing-hate-speech-calls-for-violence-and-authoritarianism-2/.

293 *After Trump lost the 2020 election:* Andrew Edgecliffe-Johnson and Mark Vandeveld, "Stephen Schwarzman Defended Donald Trump at CEO Meeting on Election Results," *Financial Times*, November 14, 2020.

294 *"People are allowed to support presidents":* Daniel Gieger and Casey Sullivan, "Blackstone Billionaire Stephen Schwarzman Defended His Support for Trump," *Business Insider*, January 12, 2021.

294 *Companies sponsoring individual investors' retirement accounts:* "Pru-

dence and Loyalty in Selecting Plan Investments and Exercising Shareholder Rights," A Proposed Rule by the Employee Benefits Security Administration, Federal Register, October 14, 2021.

294 *But this changed under Donald Trump's Department of Labor:* "U.S. Department of Labor Issues Information Letter on Private Equity Investments," Labor Department press release, June 3, 2020, https://www.dol.gov/newsroom/releases/ebsa/ebsa20200603-0.

294 *As journalist David Sirota wrote:* David Sirota, "Trump Just Fulfilled His Billionaire Pal's Dream," BillMoyers.com, June 15, 2020.

294 *The DOL was responding to Trump's request:* "U.S. Department of Labor Issues Information Letter."

295 *In publishing its information letter, DOL said:* Ibid.

295 *Jay Clayton, Trump's chairman of the SEC:* Ibid.

295 *Not surprisingly, in March 2021, after leaving the SEC:* "Apollo Appoints Jay Clayton as Lead Independent Director," Apollo press release, February 18, 2021.

295 *In a public memo, Black allowed:* "Next Steps," Letter to Apollo Board of Directors from Leon Black, March 21, 2021.

296 *A first and powerful salvo came:* "Caveat Venditor: Sellers (and Their Directors) Beware, Nine West Has an Important Message for Boards Considering an Exit," Ropes & Gray Alert, December 10, 2020, https://www.ropesgray.com/en/newsroom/alerts/2020/12/Caveat-Venditor-Sellers-and-their-Directors-Beware-As-Nine-West-Has-an-Important-Message-for%E2%80%AF%E2%80%AF%E2%80%AF.

296 *The case sprang from a $2 billion buyout:* Ibid.

297 *Which was not enough, Rakoff said:* Ibid.

297 *Rakoff said the board had been "reckless":* Ibid.

298 *Stakes in low-cost stock market index funds:* "Public Versus Private Equity Returns: Is PE Losing Its Advantage?," Bain & Company, February 24, 2020.

299 *Setting up a group called Take Medicine Back:* Mitch Li and Robert McNamara, "The Reclamation of Emergency Medicine," Take Medicine Back White Paper, July 21, 2021.

299 *Later that year, an associated physicians' group filed a lawsuit against Envision Healthcare:* Gretchen Morgenson, "Doctors Sue Envision Healthcare," NBC News, December 21, 2021.

299 *Under President Biden's appointee Lina M. Khan:* Lina Khan, memo to staff on priorities, September 22, 2021, www.ftc.gov/system/files/documents/public_statements/1596664/agency_priorities_memo_from_chair_lina_m_khan_9-22-21.pdf.

299 *Meanwhile, Tim Wu, a law professor at Columbia Law School:* David McLaughlin, "Biden Adviser Tim Wu Bemoans Rise of Corporate Power Across Economy," *Bloomberg News*, September 30, 2021, https://www.bloomberg.com/news/articles/2021-09-30/biden-adviser-wu-bemoans-rise-of-corporate-power-across-economy?sref=lnrir5K3.

299 *With Jay Clayton gone to Apollo, the new SEC chairman, Gary Gensler:* Thomas Franck, "Gensler Says SEC Is Weighing New Rules, Greater Disclosure from Private Capital Funds," CNBC.com, January 10, 2022.

300 *The SEC also floated new rules that would ban "accelerated monitoring fees":* Chris Witkowski, "SEC Crosses the Rubicon, Proposes an Outright Ban on Certain PE Practices," Private Equity International, February 2022.

300 *In 2021 alone, Blackstone Group spent:* Open Secrets website, https://www.opensecrets.org/orgs/blackstone-group/summary?id=D000021873.

300 *Of Blackstone's companies, TeamHealth spent the most on lobbying:* Open Secrets website, https://www.opensecrets.org/federal-lobbying/clients/summary?cycle=2021&id=D000021873.

300 *Apria Healthcare, the Blackstone-owned company:* Ibid.

300 *KKR spent $4.5 million in lobbying in 2021:* Open Secrets website, https://www.opensecrets.org/orgs/kkr-co/lobbying?id=D000000358&lobbillscycle=2021; https://www.opensecrets.org/federal-lobbying/clients/summary?cycle=2021&id=D000000358.

300 *But Apollo Global Management beat them all on the lobbying spree:* Open Secrets website, https://www.opensecrets.org/orgs/apollo-global-management/lobbying?id=D000021845.

301 *Among the issues its lobbyists worked on:* Open Secrets website, https://www.opensecrets.org/federal-lobbying/bills/specific_issues?id=hr5376-117&client_id=D000021845&cycle=2022.

301 *Private equity's consolidation of hospitals:* Richard Blumenthal, "Treating the Problem: Addressing Anticompetitive Conduct and Consolidation in Health Care Markets," Statement Before the House Judiciary Committee Hearing, April 29, 2021.

301 *The fact that private equity firms are:* "How Private Equity Can Catch Up on Diversity," BCG Global, May 25, 2021, https://www.bcg.com/publications/2021/how-pe-owned-companies-can-catch-up-on-diversity.

301 *Their firms have fewer programs in place to promote diversity:* "How Private Equity Can Catch Up on Diversity," BCG Global, May 25, 2021, https://www.bcg.com/publications/2021/how-pe-owned-companies-can-catch-up-on-diversity.

302 *Gender diversity is another problem:* "Preqin Impact Report: Women in

Alternative Assets 2021," March 8, 2021, https://www.preqin.com/insights/research/reports/preqi-impact-report-women-in-alternative-assets-2021.

302 *Corporate America, not exactly a paragon:* "Women in the Workplace 2021," Leanin.org and McKinsey & Company, https://womenintheworkplace.com/.

302 *In 2015, for example, KKR bought:* Press release, "KKR to Acquire C.H.I. Overhead Doors From FFL," KKR website, June 23, 2015.

302 *Anyone among C.H.I.'s 800 employees:* Press release, "KKR and C.H.I. Employees Prove 'Ownership Works' With Sale of C.H.I. Overhead Doors to Nucor," Businesswire, May 16, 2022.

302 *When KKR sold C.H.I.:* ibid.

302 *Between 2011 and mid-2022, KKR said it has:* Ibid

303 *The report, published in October 2021: The Review of Financial Studies,* Vol. 34, No. 10, October 2021, Oxford University Press.

304 *In February 2022, for example, Apollo launched the Apollo Opportunity Foundation:* "Apollo Launches 'Apollo Opportunity Foundation' to Advance Economic Prosperity and Expand Opportunity," Apollo press release, February 22, 2022.

304 *The foundation's website groans with platitudes:* https://www.apollo.com/esg-corporate-social-responsibility/our-esg-initiatives/the-apollo-opportunity-foundation.

306 *In the fall of 2021, Henry Kravis and George Roberts:* Josh Kosman, "KKR Pioneered the Private Equity Business: Here Are Its Hits and Misses," *New York Post,* October 11, 2021.

307 *In the United States, there are now more than five thousand private equity firms:* Will Jackson-Moore and Vicki Kerrigan, "Can Private Equity Save the World Through ESG Investing?" PriceWaterhouseCoopers, January 18, 2021.

307 *Even celebrity Kim Kardashian:* Sophie Kiderlin, "Kim Kardashian Launches Private Equity Firm," CNBC.com, September 8, 2022.

307 *In 2009, the typical deal was done at eight times a company's earnings:* Sebastien Canderle, "Private Equity: Market Saturation Spawns Runaway Dealmaking," *CFA Institute Enterprising Investor,* February 9, 2022.

307 *Twenty years ago, a typical buyout fund:* Ibid.

307 *Sebastien Canderle is a private capital advisor:* Ibid.

308 *In 2021, such self-dealing buyouts totaled $42 billion:* Ibid.

308 *Of course, the dealmakers have a ready answer for this:* Author interview with Joanna Rose, Apollo spokeswoman (Morgenson).

309 *In 2021, Apollo conducted just such a sale:* Sabrina Willmer, "Private Eq-

uity Powerhouse Books $1.6 Billion Profit Selling Hospital Chain—to It-self," *Bloomberg News*, July 29, 2021.

309 *Apollo had paid just under $1 billion for LifePoint:* Ibid.

309 *Unfortunately, CalPERS did not want to talk:* Author email to CalPERS press department (Morgenson).

309 *Asked about the potential for conflicts:* Ibid., Sabrina Willmer, "Private Equity Powerhouse Books $1.6 Billion Profit Selling Hospital Chain—to Itself," *Bloomberg News*, July 29, 2021.

310 *In July 2021, he decided to countersue his former Russian mistress:* Josh Kosman, "Leon Black Slaps Back at Ex with Suit Denying Rape, Claiming Extortion," *New York Post*, July 19, 2021.

310 *Black filed new legal papers accusing Josh Harris:* Heather Perlberg, "Billionaire Leon Black Accuses Josh Harris of Trying to Destroy Him," *Bloomberg News*, January 24, 2022.

311 *Harris responded by calling the allegations:* Alan Gallindoss, "Leon Black–Josh Harris Feud Heats Up," *Jewish Business News*, January 26, 2022.

CONCLUSION

312 *In mid-2022, as COVID receded:* Gretchen Morgenson, "An Unusual Deal Gave Virginia Gov. Glenn Youngkin $8.5 million in Cash," NBC News, July 11, 2022.

312 *The details outlined in the filings:* Ibid.

313 *Lawyers for the pension fund beneficiaries suing Carlyle:* Ibid.

313 *A spokesman for Youngkin said:* Author email exchange (Morgenson).

315 *In 2009, Jack Reed, the Rhode Island Democrat in the Senate:* "Reed Introduces Bill to Regulate Hedge Funds," press release, Jack Reed, United States Senator from Rhode Island, June 16, 2009, https://www.reed.senate .gov/news/releases/reed-introduces-bill-to-regulate-hedge-funds.

315 *In 2021, legislators in both the United States Senate and the House of Representatives:* 117th Congress, Elizabeth Warren, Stop Wall Street Looting Act, October 21, 2021.

315 *The American Investment Council:* Nathan Williams, "Deep Dive: Ignoring Private Equity's Critics Is No Longer an Option," *New Private Markets*, March 9, 2020.

315 *The business-friendly U.S. Chamber of Commerce:* "Economic Impact Analysis of the Stop Wall Street Looting Act," Center for Capital Markets Competitiveness, Fall 2019.

316 *Several former staffers we spoke with:* Author interview (Rosner).

316 *Although it is almost impossible to conceive:* Jane Coaston, "Tucker Carlson on Why Conservatives Should Crack Down on 'Vulture Capitalism,'" *Vox*, December 10, 2019.

317 *Oren Cass spent a decade at Bain:* Oren Cass, https://orencass.com/.

317 *Writing in the* American Prospect*:* David Dayen, "Cut Off Private Equity's Money Spigot," *American Prospect*, July 28, 2022.

318 *In October 2021, Allison Herren Lee:* "Going Dark: The Growth of Private Markets and the Impact on Investors and the Economy," Allison Herren Lee speech, October 12, 2021.

319 *Following the speech, in February 2022, the SEC proposed:* Franck, "Gensler Says SEC Is Weighing New Rules."

319 *One letter submitted to the SEC:* https://www.sec.gov/comments/s7-03-22 /s70322-20127744-288929.pdf.

320 *The case was* West Virginia et al. v. Environmental Protection Agency*:* The United States Supreme Court, West Virginia et al. v. Environmental Protection Agency et al., October Term 2021, Argued February 28, 2022— Decided June 30, 2022, https://www.supremecourt.gov/opinions/21pdf/20 -1530_n758.pdf.

320 *The American Investment Council used this ruling:* Comment Letter, July 27, 2022, https://www.sec.gov/comments/s7-03-22/s70322-20134888 -306017.pdf.

320 *One SEC source tells us that everything it does:* Confidential interview.

321 *To streamline the five commissioners' workloads, Congress allowed the agency:* Ibid.

321 *When a significant issue comes up:* Ibid.

322 *In a fall 2021 memo to her staff:* Khan, memo to staff on priorities.

323 *In June 2022, the FTC announced a landmark action:* Press release, "FTC Acts to Protect Pet Owners from Private Equity Firm's Anticompetitive Acquisition of Veterinary Services Clinics," Federal Trade Commission, June 13, 2022.

323 *"Private equity firms increasingly engage in roll up strategies":* Ibid.

323 *In 2018, DOJ brought a rare case against a private equity firm:* "Compounding Pharmacy, Two of Its Executives, and Private Equity Firm Agree to Pay $21.36 Million to Resolve False Claims Act Allegations," Department of Justice press release, September 18, 2019.

323 *In July 2021, DOJ sued Alliance Family of Companies LLC:* "EEG Testing and Private Investment Companies Pay $15.3 Million to Resolve Kickback

and False Billing Allegations," Department of Justice press release, July 21, 2021.

324 *Jeb White, of the nonprofit Taxpayers Against Fraud:* Author interview with Jeb White (Morgenson).

324 *A late October 2022 report:* Leah Nylen and Dawn Lim, "Private Equity Firms Probed by U.S. on Overlapping Board Seats," *Bloomberg News*, October 28, 2022, https://www.bloomberg.com/news/articles/2022-10-28 /blackstone-among-pe-firms-under-doj-antitrust-probe-into-overlapping -board-seats?sref=lnrir5K3.

AFTERWORD

325 *In February, the Department of Labor announced:* Press release, "More Than 100 Children Illegally Employed in Hazardous Jobs; Food Sanitation Contractor Pays $1.5 Million in Penalties,," U.S. Department of Labor website, February 17, 2023, https://www.dol.gov/newsroom/releases/whd/ whd20230217-1.

326 *Blackstone had already owned PSSI for five years:* Dawn Lim, "New York Comptroller Presses Blackstone on Child Labor Use at Meat Plants," *Bloomberg News*, March 30, 2023, https://www.bloomberg.com/news/ articles/2023-03-30/blackstone-takes-heat-from-ny-after-portfolio-company -is-fined-for-child-labor?sref=lnrir5K3.

326 *Blackstone did not respond:* Amy Martyn, "Injuries at Meatpacking Company Are Too High," NBC News.com April 6, 2022, https://www.nbcnews .com/news/us-news/injuries-meatpacking-related-company-high-even -private-equities-profit-rcna16734.

326 *But the Labor Department told a different story:* Press release, "More Than 100 Children Illegally Employed in Hazardous Jobs, Federal Investigation Finds; Food Sanitation Contractor Pays $1.5 Million in Penalties."

326 *PSSI paid a $1.5 million penalty and implemented:* Laura Strickler, "PSSI, Slaughterhouse Cleaning firm fined for child labor, replaces CEO," NBCNews.com, April 5, 2023, https://www.nbcnews.com/business/busi ness-news/pssi-slaughterhouse-cleaning-firm-new-ceo-child-labor-fund -rcna78416.

327 *Two of PSSI's larger customers cancelled their contracts:* Reshmi Basu and Erin Hudson, "Child Labor Scandal Hits Blackstone-backed Slaughterhouse Cleaner," *Bloomberg News*, April 28, 2023, https://www.bloomberg

.com/news/articles/2023-04-28/slaughterhouse-scandal-sends-black stone-firm-s-debt-tumbling-44?sref=lnrir5K3.

327 *In addition to being an embarrassing:* Lim, "NY Comptroller Presses Blackstone on Child Labor Use at Meat Plants."

327 *When we called CalPERS:* Author email to CalPERS press department (Morgenson).

327 *But it could take solace:* "Blackstone Owned Sanitation Company Ordered to Stop Using Child Labor to Clean Slaughterhouses," Private Equity Stakeholder Project, November 26, 2022, https://pestakeholder .org/news/blackstone-owned-sanitation-company-ordered-to-stop-using -child-labor-to-clean-slaughterhouses/.

328 *Woes among healthcare companies:* "Credit Stress Is Rising, Setting the Stage for More Downgrades and Defaults," Moody's Investors Service, December 12, 2022, https://s3.documentcloud.org/documents/23452687/ moodys-healthcare-stress-report.pdf.

329 *Envision soon collapsed:* "KKR-backed Envision Healthcare Files for Bankruptcy," Reuters, May 15, 2023, https://www.reuters.com/markets /deals/kkr-backed-envision-healthcare-files-bankruptcy-2023-05-15/.

329 *Private equity firms often boast:* Michael Depeau-Wilson, "No Surprises Act Ruined 'Secret Sauce' of Envision, Expert Says," *Medpage Today*, June 16, 2023, https://www.medpagetoday.com/special-reports/exclusives /105068.

329 *Apollo came under the microscope, too:* Gretchen Morgenson, "Senators Launch Bipartisan Probe of Private Equity's Growing Role in U.S. Healthcare," NBCNews.com, December 8, 2023, https://www.nbcnews.com/ politics/congress/senators-grassley-whitehouse-probe-private-equity-us -health-care-rcna128070.

330 *The amount of money raised by the industry fell:* "Private Equity Outlook in 2023: Anatomy of a Slowdown," Bain & Company, February 27, 2023, https://www.bain.com/insights/private-equity-outlook-global-private -equity-report-2023/.

331 *In the third quarter of 2023, Carlyle's earnings plummeted:* Will Feuer, "Carlyle Group Posts Lower 3Q Revenue," *Wall Street Journal*, November 7, 2023, https://www.wsj.com/business/earnings/carlyle-group-posts -lower-3q-revenue-218fdfcf.

331 *In November 2023, a former Apollo executive left:* Rod James, "Morgan Stanley and Apollo Executives Launch Credit Secondary Firm," *Wall Street Journal*, November 8, 2023, https://www.wsj.com/articles/morgan-stanley -and-apollo-executives-launch-credit-secondary-firm-2dc04873.

331 *Their owners dug deep:* Lisa Lee, "Private Equity Makes Loan Payments with More Debt to Keep Cash," *Bloomberg News*, November 2, 2023, https://www.bloomberg.com/news/articles/2023-11-02/private-equity -pays-buyout-loans-with-more-debt-to-save-cash.

332 *In October, the Federal Trade Commission sued U.S. Anesthesia Partners:* Gretchen Morgenson, "FTC Sues Private-Equity Backed Anesthesia Staffing Firm," NBCNews.com, September 21, 2023, https://www.nbcnews.com/ health/health-care/ftc-sues-private-equity-anesthesia-firm-monopoly -drive-up-prices-rcna111472.

332 *Purchases of anesthesiology practices accounted for:* Gretchen Morgenson, "This Won't Hurt a Bit," NBCNews.com, October 10, 2022, https://www .nbcnews.com/health/health-care/anesthesiologist-putting-may-work -private-equity-firm-rcna51071.

333 *Of course, anesthesia costs rose significantly:* Yashaswini Singh, Ziriu Song, Daniel Polsky, et al., "Association of Private Equity Acquisition of Physician Practices with Changes in Healthcare Spending and Utilization," *JAMA Health Forum*, September 2, 2022, https://jamanetwork .com/journals/jama-health-forum/fullarticle/2795946.

333 *According to the American Hospital Association:* American Hospital Association, "Setting the Record Straight: Private Equity and Health Insurers Acquire More Physicians Than Hospitals," June 2023, https://www.aha .org/system/files/media/file/2023/06/Private-Equity-and-Health-Insurers -Acquire-More-Physicians-than-Hospitals-Infographic.pdf.

333 *The FTC's suit indicates the government believes:* Dylan Thomas and Annie Sabater, "US Antitrust Enforcers Set Sights on Private Equity Add-on Deals," *S&P Global Market Intelligence*, November 6, 2023, https://www.spglobal.com/marketintelligence/en/news-insights/latest -news-headlines/us-antitrust-enforcers-set-sights-on-private-equity-add -on-deals-78255450.

334 *For decades, the private equity industry has claimed:* Erin Arvedlund, "Private Equity Is Past Its Peak, Warns Pulitzer Prize–winning Author," *Pensions & Investments*, October 23, 2023, https://www.pionline .com/private-equity/private-equity-past-its-peak-warns-pulitzer-prize -winning.

334 *The returns are not calculated:* Video recording of Warren Buffett and Charlie Munger, January 8, 2023, https://www.youtube.com/watch?v=r3_41Wh vr1I.

335 *Apollo is at the forefront of this move through Athene:* Maureen Farrell, "A Shadow Lending Market in the U.S., Funded by Insurance Premiums,"

New York Times, October 4, 2023, https://www.nytimes.com/2023/10/04/business/private-equity-insurance.html.

335 *"Within days of a P.E. acquisition of an insurance company":* Ibid.

336 *At the end of 2022, the National Association of Insurance Commissioners:* Angela Best and Francisco Paez, "NAIC Treatment of Collateralized Loan Obligations," MetLife Investments website, https://investments.metlife.com/insights/public-fixed-income/naic-treatment-of-collateralized-loan-obligations/.

336 *Meanwhile, Athene did what:* "Former NAIC CEO Joins Athene as EVP," *Royal Gazette*, June 21, 2023, https://www.royalgazette.com/international-business/business/article/20230621/former-naic-ceo-joins-athene-as-evp/.

337 *In May 2023, the US-Canadian union of hospitality workers:* Michael Katz, "Union Warns Pension Funds to Be Wary of Private Equity–Backed PRT Insurers, *Chief Investment Officer*, May 24, 2023, https://www.ai-cio.com/news/union-warns-pension-funds-to-be-wary-of-private-equity-backed-prt-insurers/.

338 *Athene, too, complained:* Doug Niemann, "Understanding Structured Credit," Athene Presentation, November 4, 2022, https://irathene.q4cdn.com/886888837/files/doc_presentations/2022/Understanding-Structured-Credit_FINAL.pdf.

Additional Reading

. . . *and forgive them their debts: Lending, Foreclosure and Redemption from Bronze Age Finance to the Jubilee Year*, Michael Hudson (Islet, 2018).

Banking on Fraud: Drexel Junk Bonds and Buyouts, Mary Zey, (Routledge, 2017).

Barbarians at the Gate: The Fall of RJR Nabisco, Bryan Burrough and John Helyar (Harper & Row, 1989).

A Bubble That Broke the World, Garet Garrett (Little, Brown, 1932).

The Buyout of America, Josh Kosman (Portfolio/Penguin, 2009).

The Citizen's Share: Reducing Inequality in the 21st Century, Joseph R. Blasi, Richard D. Freeman, and Douglas L. Kruse (Yale University Press; 1st edition, June 24, 2014).

Debt: The First 5,000 Years, David Graeber (Melville House, 2011).

Den of Thieves, James B. Stewart (Simon & Schuster, 1992).

The Enchantments of Mammon: How Capitalism Became the Religion of Modernity, Eugene McCarraher (Belknap Press, 2019).

Ethically Challenged: Private Equity Storms U.S. Health Care, Laura Olson (Johns Hopkins University Press, 2022).

Private Equity at Work: When Wall Street Manages Main Street, Eileen Appelbaum and Rosemary Batt (New York, Russell Sage Foundation, 2014).

Unto This Last and Other Writings, John Ruskin (Penguin Classics, 1997).

Your Money and Your Life, a Manual for "the Middle Classes," Gilbert Seldes (Classic Reprint, 1938).

War and Peace and War, Peter Turchin (Plume, 2006).

About the Authors

Gretchen Morgenson is the senior financial reporter for the NBC News Investigations Unit. A former stockbroker, she won the Pulitzer Prize in 2002 for her "trenchant and incisive" reporting on Wall Street. Previously at the *New York Times* and the *Wall Street Journal*, she and coauthor Joshua Rosner wrote the *New York Times* bestseller *Reckless Endangerment: How Outsized Ambition, Greed, and Corruption Led to Economic Armageddon*, about the mortgage crisis. Prior to joining the *Times* in 1998, she worked as a broker at Dean Witter in the 1980s, and as a reporter at *Forbes*, *Worth*, and *Money* magazines. She lives with her husband and son in New York City.

Joshua Rosner is managing director at independent research consultancy Graham Fisher and Co. He was previously managing director at Medley Global Advisors, executive vice president at CIBC World Markets, and managing director at Oppenheimer. In 2001 Joshua was among the first analysts to identify the structural changes to housing and in 2006 published extensively on the coming collapse of the mortgage and structured finance markets. He has been interviewed on PBS, CBS, NBC, CNN, Bloomberg, CNBC, and Fox News, and featured in or written for the *New York Times*, the *Wall Street Journal*, Reuters, *Economist*, *Barron's*, and *HuffPost*. Joshua is the coauthor of the *New York Times* bestseller *Reckless Endangerment* with Gretchen Morgenson.